CONSTITUTIONAL QUESTIONS IN INDIA

Constitutional Questions in India

THE PRESIDENT, PARLIAMENT
AND THE STATES

A.G. NOORANI

OXFORD
UNIVERSITY PRESS

OXFORD
UNIVERSITY PRESS

Oxford University Press is a department of the University of Oxford.
It furthers the University's objective of excellence in research, scholarship,
and education by publishing worldwide. Oxford is a registered trademark of
Oxford University Press in the UK and in certain other countries

Published in India by
Oxford University Press
22 Workspace, 2nd Floor, 1/22 Asaf Ali Road, New Delhi 110002, India

First Edition published in 2000
Oxford India Paperbacks 2002
24th impression 2023
Digitally Printed in 2024

ISBN-13: 978-0-19-565877-4
ISBN-10: 0-19-565877-9
Printed at Manipal Technologies Limited, Manipal

To
My Family

Contents

SECTION III: THE STATE

Preface

This is a collection of some of my articles on constitutional issues in the last hectic decade, which witnessed the rise and fall of governments at the centre in the manner made familiar by the states. It contains references to enable further research in areas explored here. I am confident of better results than what I have accomplished; for, these articles were addressed to immediate crises, though the issues raised were of far reaching consequences. In the nature of things they are not definitive studies on the topic.

I am indebted to the editors of the journals in which they appeared. C.R. Irani, editor-in-chief of the *The Statesman* and Mr. N. Ram editor of *Frontline* deserve particular mention.

This year it will be thirty nine years since I began writing a column in *Indian Express*, then edited by that prince among men Mr. Frank Moraes. It has been a most rewarding experience.

Mumbai, 26 January 2000   A.G. Noorani

Introduction

Fifty years after the Constitution of India came into force, on 26 January 1950, there is a very large body of opinion in the country which holds that a review of its working has become necessary. Opinion is, however, divided on the scope of the review. One section believes that there is nothing fundamentally wrong with the Constitution and the review should be confined to the distortions that have crept in, during this half century, with a view to strengthening the safeguards against their recurrence in the future. Innovations can be made only if they can be engrafted on the existing system. Another holds that experience has shown that the Constitution is not suited to the genius of the people and a radical change is necessary. Most of those who share this view advocate the adoption of the presidential system. It is not fortuitous, but highly significant, that the first cries for an executive President were raised soon after the death of Jawaharlal Nehru on 27 May 1964. They were inspired by fears of instability. These fears have been renewed by nine changes of government at the centre in the last decade. By common consent, India has entered the age of coalitions. This experiment is, however, viewed with suspicion by many.

Unfortunately, for all the disquiet, neither school of opinion has cared to address itself to the problem in depth or to devise proposals after earnest research into practice and precedent in India and elsewhere. Such research alone can put forth with some degree of plausibility, an answer to the constitutional problem in its major dimensions.

It is undeniable that a real 'constitutional problem' exists. Not one of the major institutions and high offices established by the Constitution has worked satisfactorily; be it the President, Parliament, the Prime Minister, the Council of Ministers or the Supreme Court of India. Of these, the office of the President has acquired greater significance and authority in the last decade; especially since Dr. Shankar Dayal Sharma became President in 1992. Some of the decisions of his successor, Mr. K. R. Narayanan, aroused controversy—largely, but not always, uninformed and unjust—his integrity remaining unquestioned.

India's federalism has suffered grievously at the hands of successive governments at the centre, regardless of their political complexion and with uniform disdain for constitutional norms and values, or scruples for political morality. The office of the Governor of the State has been systematically abused for political ends by those in New Delhi who were conferred the patronage for that very reason. It is now, truly an office in great crisis. The office of the Chief Minister of states is also afflicted by the same abuse. Very many chief ministers owe their office not so much to the confidence of their Legislature Party as to the bounty of what is commonly called the Party's High Command. That the nomenclature is of Fascist provenance is lost on most.

There were some, however, who warned against the consequences of the practice even in its early years. Professor Reginald Coupland wrote in the early forties in his work *The Constitutional Problem in India,* a classic which has no equal in its field to this day, that 'the Congress's High Command' had shown (in the two years (1937–9) when Congress Ministries functioned in the Provinces) that, however loose the federal tie might be, however wide the autonomy of the Provinces in law, the intentions of the Constitution could in fact be contravened and a federal system converted, by unconstitutional but none the less effective means, into something like a unitary system'.[1]

Initiated during the days of the movement for India's freedom, the practice continued even after India attained independence and adopted a federal constitution, albeit with some unitary features. Nor was political abuse unknown then. The wise C. Rajagopalachari predicted it all. While in jail, he made the following entry, in his diary:

Elections and their corruptions (sic.), injustice and life power and tyranny of wealth, and inefficiency of administration will make a hell of life as

---

[1] I.R. Coupland, *The Constitutional Problem in India, Part II, Indian Politics 1936–1942,* Oxford University Press, 1942, p. 100.

soon as freedom is given to us. Men will look regretfully back to the old regime of comparative justice and efficient, peaceful, more or less honest administration.

The only thing gained will be that as a race we will be saved from dishonour and subordination. Hope lies only in universal education by which right conduct, fear of God and love will be developed among the citizens from childhood. It is only if we succeed in this that Swaraj will mean happiness. Otherwise it will mean grinding injustices and tyranny of wealth.

Contrary to common impression, all this and more was not absent from the minds of those who wrote the Constitution. Its prime architects were Jawaharlal Nehru, who presided over two major committees set up by the Constituent Assembly of India soon after its establishment in 1946; namely, the Union Constitution Committee and the Union Powers Committee. Vallabhbhai Patel presided over the Provincial Constitution Committee and the Advisory Committee on Fundamental Rights. The Indian National Congress, which was in an overwhelming majority in the Constituent Assembly, set up an Experts Committee with Nehru as its Chairman.

The Constituent Assembly elected Dr. Rajendra Prasad, one of the leaders of the Patna Bar, as its President. Though all the major policy decisions were taken in the councils of the Congress Party, its leaders showed themselves amenable to professional advice. The Assembly was served by a Constitutional Adviser, Sir B.N. Rau, and elected a Drafting Committee with Dr. Bhim Rao Ambedkar as its head. Its members were lawyers of eminence like Sir Alladi Krishnaswamy Ayyar and K.M. Munshi and men of wide experience in public affairs like Sir N. Gopalaswami Ayyangar, T.T. Krishnamachari, Sir Mohammed Saddulla of the Muslim League, and N. Madhava Rau.

They had all drunk at the fount of the British constitutional system and parliamentary practice; some more deeply and admiringly than others. Jawaharlal Nehru savoured a different and far headier brew. His *Autobiography* poured scorn on Indian liberals of old, constitutionalists *par excellence*, for seeing things 'through British spectacles of true-blue colour'. He was uncomfortable with the class composition of the Congress, no less.

Most of those who have shaped Congress policy during the last seventeen years have come from the middle classes. Liberal or Congressmen, they

have come from the same class and have grown up in the same environment
.... As the Congress became more and more representative of the rural
masses, the gulf that separated it from the Liberals widened, and it became
almost impossible for the Liberal to understand or appreciate the Congress
view-point. It is not easy for the upper-class drawing-room to understand
the humble cottage or the mud hut.[2]

That gulf widened over the years. In mid-1962 the late Professor
Myron Weiner wrote insightfully of 'India's Two Political Cultures';
one of them 'in the districts' while 'the second political culture
predominates in New Delhi'.[3] At the end of the millennium, India's
political culture presents a spectacle of baffling complexity. Some
aspects of which are disturbing, some others, revolting.

This has prompted a few writers and commentators to urge
replacement of the Constitution by one 'suited to the temper of the
people'. They ascribe the grossness in constitutional practice to
imperfections in the Constitution.

However, just as the Constituent Assembly was about to finish
its task, Dr. B. R. Ambedkar, Chairman of the Drafting Committee,
reminded it, in his reply to the debate on 25 November 1949, that

however good a Constitution may be, it is sure to turn out bad because
those who are called to work it happen to be a bad lot. However, bad a
Constitution may be, it may turn out to be good if those who are called
to work it happen to be a good lot. The working of a Constitution does
not depend wholly upon the nature of the Constitution. The Constitution
can provide only the organs of the State such as the Legislature, the
Executive and the Judiciary. The factors on which the working of these
organs of the state depend are the people and the political parties they
will set up as their instruments to carry out their wishes and their politics.
Who can say how the people of India and their parties will behave?

He added that it was 'futile to pass any judgement upon the
Constitution without reference to the part which the people and
their parties are likely to play'.[4]

The Chief Election Commissioner Mr. S.L. Shakhdher,
commented on the sad state of affairs at a meeting held under the

[2]Jawaharlal Nehru, *An Autobiography*, 1936, Fifth Impression 1987, pp. 416
and 420.
[3]Myron Weiner, *Political Change in South Asia*, Firma K.L. Mukhopadhyay,
1963, p. 114.
[4]*Constituent Assembly Debates* (hereafter CAD), vol. xl, p. 975.

auspices of the Citizens for Democracy and Voters' Council in New Delhi as far back as 26 September 1980. He said:

Political parties make strong demands for the conduct of free and fair elections to legislative bodies, but choose to ignore the application of the same principles when it comes to the functioning of their own party organs. It has been revealed before me in various cases, that I had occasion to hear, that parties do not follow their own constitutions. They hold no party elections. They function for years on an *ad hoc* basis. Sometimes there has been a tyranny of the minority over the majority because of undemocratic functioning and other practices. A few persons in a party occupying the vantage position in the apex body, quite often strangulate the democratic functioning and aspirations of the members of the party at the grass roots and keep the party under their strict control. The voice of the majority does not find expression in important decision making processes, thereby creating fissures in those organs and eventually leading to splits. I, therefore, suggest that there should be parliamentary legislation making it obligatory on the part of every political organisation to register their body and regulate their functioning by laying down broad outlines and norms.

Later in the year, he presented his Report on the General Elections of 1980 and repeated his criticism in this formal document which he presented to Parliament. He listed three major defects in that Report. One was that 'even the observance of the basic provisions of the Constitution of the party is absent', the second was the failure to hold organisational elections for years; the last was the lack of accountability 'to the highest organ consisting of the general body of members'.[5] These defects, so accurately and so authoritatively described, continue, still.

A democratic constitution cannot be worked by political parties which function undemocratically. Nor, if the sense of political morality is weak. As Pandit Hriday Nath Kunzru said in the Constituent Assembly on 16 June 1949: 'If we cannot expect common honesty from persons occupying the highest positions in the discharge of their duties, the foundation for responsible government is wanting, and the outlook for the future is indeed gloomy' (C.A.D., vol. viii, p. 920).

Ambedkar himself stressed that respect for constitutional morality is indispensable 'for the peaceful working of a democratic

---

[5]S.L. Shakhdher, *Electoral Reforms in India*, The Voters Council and Citizens for Democracy, 26 September 1980, p. 10.

Constitution'. In reply to the criticism, he said that the document was far too detailed that curbs had to be put on power because those who would wield it could not be trusted to play fair. 'Constitutional morality is not a natural sentiment. It has to be cultivated. We must realize that our people have yet to learn it. *Democracy in India is only a top dressing on an Indian soil which is essentially undemocratic*'.[6] (emphasis mine)

At the end of the Assembly's labours, Dr. Ambedkar warned that it was 'quite possible for this new born democracy to retain its form but give place to dictatorship in fact . . . . If we wish to maintain democracy not merely in form, but also in fact, what must we do? The first thing, in my judgement, we must do is to hold fast to constitutional methods of achieving our social and economic objectives . . . . It means that we must abandon the method of civil disobedience, non-cooperation and satyagraha . . . (They are) The Grammar of Anarchy and the sooner they are abandoned, the better for us'. The rest is so strikingly relevant to the situation today as to bear quotation *in extenso*:

The second thing we must do is to observe the caution which John Stuart Mill has given to all who are interested in the maintenance of democracy; namely, not 'to lay their liberties at the feet of even a great man, or to trust him with powers which enable him to subvert their institutions'. There is nothing wrong in being grateful to great men who have rendered life-long services to the country. But there are limits to gratefulness. As has been well said by the Irish Patriot, Daniel O'Connell, no man can be grateful at the cost of his honour, no woman can be grateful at the cost of her chastity and no nation can be grateful at the cost of its liberty. This caution is far more necessary in the case of India than in the case of any other country. For, in India, Bhakti or what may be called the path of devotion or hero-worship, plays a part in its politics unequalled in magnitude by the part it plays in the politics of any other country in the world. Bhakti in religion may be a road to the salvation of the soul. But in politics, Bhakti or hero-worship is a sure road to degradation and to eventual dictatorship.

The third thing we must do is not to be content with mere political democracy. We must make our political democracy a social democracy as well. Political democracy cannot last unless there lies at the base of it social democracy. What does social democracy mean? It means a way of life which recognizes liberty, equality and fraternity as the principles of life. These principles of liberty, equality and fraternity are not to be treated

[6]CAD, vol. vii, p. 38.

as separate items in a trinity. They form a union of trinity in the sense that to divorce one from the other is to defeat the very purpose of democracy. Liberty cannot be divorced from equality; equality cannot be divorced from liberty. Nor can liberty and equality be divorced from fraternity. Without equality, liberty would produce the supremacy of the few over the many. Equality without liberty would kill individual initiative. Without fraternity, liberty would produce the supremacy of the few over the many. Equality without liberty would kill individual initiative. Without fraternity, liberty and equality could not become a natural course of things. It would require a constable to enforce them. *We must begin by acknowledging the fact that there is complete absence of two things in Indian Society. One of these is equality. On the social plane, we have in India a society based on the principle of graded inequality which means elevation for some and degradation for others. On the economic plane, we have a society in which there are some who have immense wealth as against many who live in abject poverty.* On the 26th of January 1950, we are going to enter into a life of contradictions. *In politics we will have equality and in social and economic life we will have inequality.* In politics we will be recognizing the principle of one man, one vote and one vote, one value. In our social and economic life, we shall, by reason of our social and economic structure, continue to deny the principle of one man one value. *How long shall we continue to live this life of contradictions? How long shall we continue to deny equality in our social and economic life? If we continue to deny it for long, we will do so only by putting our political democracy in peril.* We must remove this contradiction at the earliest possible moment *or else those who suffer from inequality will blow up the structure of political democracy which this Assembly has so laboriously built up.* (emphasis mine)

The second thing we are wanting in is recognition of the principle of fraternity. What does fraternity mean? Fraternity means a sense of common brotherhood of all Indians—if Indian being one people. It is the principle which gives unity and solidarity to social life.[7]

He was, of course, confident that if the conditions he stressed were fulfilled, the Constitution would stand the test of time. In this, he was clearly right. For, if those conditions are not met, no other constitutional system will work, least of all the presidential system. Defectors who topple governments in the parliamentary system will bring a presidential government to a grinding halt if their demands are not met.

Ambedkar mentioned another consideration which is often overlooked. There is every danger that amendments of the kind being touted about, might be tailored to suit the exigencies of the

[7]CAD, vol. xi, pp. 978–9.

moment, if not, indeed, the needs of the majority of the day, and thus lose the support of an enduring national consensus. 'The Constituent Assembly in making a Constitution has no partisan motive ...The future Parliament, if it met as a Constituent Assembly, its members will be acting as partisans seeking to carry amendments to the Constitution to facilitate to (sic) the passing of party measures which they have failed to get through Parliament by reason of some Article of the Constitution which has acted as an obstacle in their way. Parliament will have an axe to grind while the Constituent Assembly has none,' pointed out Dr. B.R. Ambedkar, on 4 November 1948 while moving that the Draft Constitution, as settled by his Committee, be taken into consideration.

He concluded by asserting that '(I) feel that it (the Constitution) is workable, it is flexible and it is strong enough to hold the country together both in peace time and in war time. Indeed, if I may say so, if things go wrong under the new Constitution, the reason will not be that we had a bad Constitution. What we will have to say is that Man was Vile.'[8] Jawaharlal Nehru endorsed his view and said on 6 November 1948, 'A Constitution is something which should last a long time'.[9]

Dr. Ambedkar resigned from the Union Council of Ministers on 27 September 1951. He fought the first General Election in 1952 in opposition to the Congress and lost. Difference with the ruling party widened to the extent that he delivered an embittered and unflattering disavowal in the Rajya Sabha on 2 September 1953. 'People always keep on saying to me "Oh you are the maker of the Constitution". My answer is I was a hack. What I was asked to do, I did much against my will.' He added: 'I am quite prepared to say that I shall be the first person to burn it out. I do not want it. It does not suit anybody ...'[10]

Dr. Ambedkar's role in the framing of the Constitution has been either exaggerated or underestimated. The style and content of his performance in the Constituent Assembly as the prime mover of the Draft Constitution have been neglected completely. He was capable of a shocking factual error on a defining moment in Canada's Constitutional history, the Governor-General's refusal of a dissolution

---

[8]CAD, vol. vii, pp. 43–4.

[9]Ibid., p. 588.

[10]Dhananjay Keer, *Dr. Ambedkar: Life and Mission*, Popular Prakashan, 1962, p. 446.

to King Mackenzie in 1926.[11] He tended to be perfunctory, even testy and short, in his replies. On one occasion Mr. Mahavir Tyagi was provoked to express his 'fond wish that he (Dr. Ambedkar) and other members of the Drafting Committee had had the experience of detention in jails before they became members of the Drafting Committee'.[12] Evidently, the Doctor did not find preventive detention too distasteful when he was in power.

There was, doubtless, need for despatch. But one can only regret that the considerable treasure that lay in the *Constitutional Proposals of the Sapru Committee*, the Report of the Joint Committee on India Constitutional Reform, 1934 and the debates in the House of Commons on the Government of India Bill 1935[13]—on which Act our Constitution is modelled—were ignored. The Sapru Report's recommendations on a tribunal to try cases against delinquent judges of the superior courts is far more realistic than impeachment. Debates in the Constituent Assembly shed no light on the Inter-State Council envisaged by Article 263 of the Constitution. The Joint Parliamentary Committee (JPC) is eloquent on the subject.[14] Proceedings in the Committees set up by the Round Table Conference in London are most helpful; especially on President's rule. The Report of the Reforms Enquiry Committee (1924) headed by Sir Alexander P. Muddrinan is most instructive on a problem which plagues us still, seventy-five years later; namely immunity of legislators to charges of accepting bribes. Men like Mr. Mohammed Ali Jinnah and Sir Tej Bahadur Sapru were members of the Committee.

The authors of the Constitution opted for the British parliamentary system, as a matter of course, at the very outset of their deliberations at a joint meeting on 5 June 1947, of the Union Constitution Committee and the Initial Constitution Committee. Mr. Vallabhbhai Patel announced the decision in the Constituent Assembly on 15 July 1947: 'Both these Committees met and they came to the conclusion that it would suit the conditions of this country better to adopt the Parliamentary system of Constitution, the British type of Constitution with which we are familiar'.[15]

[11]CAD, vol. vii, p. 270.
[12]CAD, vol. ix, p. 1547.
[13]H.M.S.O. London, H.L. 6, 1 (Part 1), H.C. 5, 1 (Part 1).
[14]Ibid., p. 123
[15]CAD, vol. iv, p. 578.

The Parliamentary system rests largely on conventions. The draftsmen were careful to emphasize, time and again, in the Assembly that the President would have no more powers than the British Crown. They, however, used language which reflected the form, but not the reality, of the British Constitution. At least two Presidents found it a fertile source for aggrandizement of power—Dr. Rajendra Prasad in 1950 and Giani Zail Singh in 1987. Matters were made worse by dropping at the very last minute, on 11 October 1949, and for palpably wrong reasons, the Instruments of Instructions for the guidance of the President and the Governors.[16] They would have codified the conventions. The text of the Instructions to the President is reproduced in *The Framing of India's Constitution* by B. Shiva Rao.[17] Such a document was promised repeatedly from 17 July 1947 onwards.[18] A remarkable process of codification of conventions is now afoot in Australia.

It would, of course, be wrong to attribute the distortion and worse, in the working of our parliamentary system to the mere absence of a code of conventions.

The articles collected in this volume analyse some of the questions that arose in recent years on the powers and status of the President and the governors, as heads of state, at the centre and in the states, respectively, in a parliamentary system; the working of India's Parliament and its federation. They do not pretend to be definitive. It is hoped, however, that they will provide material enough for the interested reader to explore the subject further and form his own definite conclusions precisely on where and why the Constitution was badly mauled in its actual practice.

It is unnecessary to summarize them here. They are knit together by major premises which accord with the letter and the spirit of the Constitution. The President is neither a rubber-stamp nor overlord but a constitutional head of State endowed with significant, if limited, powers and functions. So is the Governor. Their discretion is particularly crucial when the electorate returns a hung legislature and when the Prime Minister or Chief Minister advises its dissolution. A number of articles in this volume discuss the abuses that became

[16]CAD, vol. x, pp. 114–16.
[17]Select Documents, vol. iv, pp. 67–8.
[18]M.M. Ismail, *The President and the Governors in the Indian Constitution*, Orient Longman, 1972.

the norm. The crises in Uttar Pradesh and Gujarat are discussed at some length as instructive case studies.

Source material is not hard to come by but there is a paucity of memories. *The Selected Works of Jawaharlal Nehru,* which have reached the year 1954 in Volume 24, Second Series, and *Sardar Patel's Correspondence* are most instructive, especially on issues of propriety.

The Constitution of India has not failed the nation. It is India's politicians who have tended to ignore or, worse, violate it for the ends of power and have sadly let down the country. Those who brand the supreme law of the land as a foreign implant would do well to reflect on the comments of one of India's staunch admirers Professor W.H. Morris-Jones, Constitutional Adviser to the Viceroy of India in 1947, and a scholar of high repute. Refuting Mr. Eldon Griffith's defence of the emergency, in a letter to *The Times* (London) on 25 June 1976, Professor Morris-Jones wrote:

Mr. Griffiths' jibe about 'exhibit A of the Westminster model abroad' misses the point that *it had become a specifically Indian achievement*; it only adds insult to the injury already suffered by Indian democrats. Such denigration has long been a sport in which high imperial Tory and revolutionary Marxist could find common enjoyment. Even your own leader (June 21) chose an odd time to point out the limitations of democracy under Congress; for an incomplete democracy is diminished further, not remedied, by illiberalism.

Nor can one easily detect any clear and consistent signs that the elite-mass gap which you deplore is being closed by the present regime of Mrs. Indira Gandhi? And just how may the change 'accord better with indigenous habits'? *Are habits never modified? Had not growing numbers of Indians begun to make the habits of liberal democracy indigenous?* Surely it is a 'massive' loss when damage is done to a way of political life *which in two decades had already converted into citizens so many who had been subjects beyond the political pale* . . . Moreover, the 'gains' are doubly suspect. In origin they are at best uncertainly attributable to Mrs. Gandhi's dose of autocracy. In their effects they appear too fragile to endure. *Unitedly, Indian democracy had freely mobilised demands and grievances; in its place is put none of the usual alternative.*[19] (emphasis mine)

The Constitution of India is very much an Indian achievement and Indian democracy, which it nurtures and protects, has struck roots in the Indian soil. These achievements were predicted by some British

[19] *The Times* (London), 14 July 1976.

statesmen even as some others tried to impede their fruition. Foremost among the former was Thomas Babington Macaulay. His infamous Minute on Indian Education, dated 2 February 1835, denigrating Indian learning and languages has been justly attacked.[20]

Less known is the peroration with which he concluded his speech in the House of Commons on 10 July 1833. 'It may be that the public mind of India may expand under our system till it has outgrown that system; that by good government we may educate our subjects into a capacity for better government; that, having become instructed in European knowledge, they may, in some future age, demand European In titutions. Whether such a day will ever come I know not. But never will I attempt to avert or to retard it. Whenever it comes, it will be the proudest day in English history. To have found a great people sunk in the lowest depths of slavery and superstition, to have so ruled them as to have made them desirous and capable of all the privileges of citizens, would indeed be a title to glory all our own. The sceptre may pass away from us. Unforeseen accidents may derange our most profound schemes of policy. Victory may be inconstant to our arms. But here are triumphs which are followed by no reverse. There is an empire exempt from all natural causes of decay. Those triumphs are the pacific triumphs of reason over barbarism; that empire is the imperishable empire of our arts and our morals, our literature and our laws.'[21]

India's awakening to its right to freedom found expression initially in demands for responsible government on the British model. The decision on 5 June 1947 was a logical culmination of that phase of India's history. The generation of politicians that is now at the helm of the nation's affairs comprises some who are familiar with and accept the British model. Many others reject it. Messrs. Devi Lal, Omprakash Chautala, Laloo Prasad Yadav and their predecessors like Biju Patnaik, Partap Singh Kairon and Bakshi Gulam Mohammed were not exactly avid readers of A.V. Dicey's *Introduction to the Study of the Law of the Constitution* or Erskine May's celebrated work *Parliamentary Practice*. A proprietor of a firm brought up in the ways of the master of a *pedhi* will not become a practitioner of corporate norms and culture merely

[20]For the text see, *Speeches by Lord Macaulay with his Minute on Indian Education*, Selected with an Introduction and Notes by G.M. Young, Oxford Univrsity Press, 1935; pp. 345–61.
[21]Ibid; p. 155.

because he chooses to make the family firm a limited company, on the tax consultants' advice. But if some politicians have little taste or aptitude for parliamentary democracy, as it functions in the United Kingdom, Australia and Canada, they have not shown a preference for any other system which would uphold democratic values. Their approach is simply nihilistic.

The cure lies in the renewal of India's political life and in the revival of the political culture which once produced men of stature and worth in our public life. It lies, above all, in a remoulding of the outlook and, with it, the quality of our public life. Arthur James Balfour's introduction to the second edition of Walter Bagehot's classic *The English Constitution* delivered a caution we cannot afford to ignore: 'constitutions are easily copied, temperaments are not; and if it should happen that the borrowed constitution and the native temperament fail to correspond, the misfit may have serious results. It matters little what other gifts a people may possess if they are wanting in those which, from this point of view, are of most importance. If, for example, they have no capacity for grading their loyalties as well as for being moved by them; if they have no natural inclination to liberty and no natural respect for law; if they lack good humour and tolerate foul play; if they know not how to compromise or when; if they have not that distrust of extreme conclusions which is some-times misdescribed as want of logic; if corruption does not repel them; and if their divisions tend to be either too numerous or too profound . . .'[22]

The Constitution of India very much accords with the Indian political genius. It is another and lamentable fact that India's politics are in a pathetic shape today.

---

[22]Walter Bagehot, *The English Constitution*, Oxford University Press, 1928; p. xxii.

I

THE PRESIDENT

1

The Options When a
Government Loses its Majority[1]

A crop of constitutional questions began to face the Indian nation in the aftermath of the Bharatiya Janata Party (BJP)'s withdrawal of support to the National Front on 23 October 1990. They will continue to nag us till the Lok Sabha meets on 7 November and for few days thereafter. There were four distinct issues:

First, was Prime Minister V.P. Singh bound to resign from office soon after the BJP withdrew its support, or was he entitled to secure a verdict on his stewardship from the Lok Sabha?

Second, if his motion of confidence is defeated in the Lok Sabha on 7 November, is he entitled to dissolve the Lok Sabha in favour of a verdict of the people? What are the powers and duties of the president in such a situation?

Third, is the president bound, in that event, to ask the single largest party in the Lok Sabha, the Congress(I), to form a government?

Last, if the Congress(I), on being so asked, fails to drum up a majority and asks for the Lok Sabha's dissolution, is the president bound to grant it?

The first query: One of the greatest living authorities on constitutional law and practice, Professor Geoffrey Marshall of Oxford, said in a letter to *The Times* (London) of 20 September 1985 that 'if parliament is truly hung there will be no obligation on

---

[1] The context of this article was the fall of V.P. Singh's government in October 1990. This article appeared in *Sunday Mail*, 4 Nov. 1990.

the present government to resign until defeated in the House'. Another authority, Professor E.C.S.Wade, expressed a similar view.[2]

The Committee of Governors set up by the president endorsed this view in its report submitted in 1971. It dealt with the question of when a ministry is to be considered to no longer enjoy the confidence of the house due to loss of majority support when the house is *not* in session. In the light of Indian experience, it considered three contingencies: a single party ministry losing its majority because of a split or defections, a coalition falling apart, and *a majority government* being 'subsequently denied' support by one of the supporting parties, as in the present case.[3]

The report said that its answer to the third situation would be the same as its answer to the first. What was that answer? 'Ask the chief minister to face the assembly and prove his majority within the shortest possible time.' This is precisely what the president, R. Venkataraman, did on 24 October. He 'advised the prime minister to prove his majority' in the Lok Sabha. The prime minister agreed. It follows that his continuance in office after the BJP withdrew its support was perfectly justified.

The second query, regarding dissolution. No prime minister is *entitled* to dissolution as of right, as Churchill told the House of Commons on 29 March 1944: 'The utmost he can do is to consider advice to the crown.' But if the ministry commands a majority, the head of state has little discretion.

The correct constitutional practice was excellently summed up in a letter to *The Times* on 2 May 1950 by 'SENEX' (it was later revealed that this was none other than Sir Alan Lascelles, the king's private secretary). It bears quotation *in extenso:*

It is surely indisputable (and common sense) that a prime minister may ask—not demand—that his sovereign will grant him a dissolution of parliament, and that the sovereign, if he so chooses, may refuse to grant this request ... no wise sovereign—that is, one who has at heart the true interests of the country, the Constitution, and the monarchy—would deny a dissolution to his prime minister unless he were satisfied that: (1) the existing parliament was still vital, viable, and capable of doing its job;

---

[2]E.C.S. Wade and A.W. Bradley, *Constitutional and Administrative Law*, 10th edn, ed. A.W. Bradley. (London: Longman ELBS, 1985), p. 21.

[3]*The Role of Governors, Report of the Committee of Governors*, (New Delhi: President's Secretariat, Rashtrapati Bhavan, 1971), pp. 43–45.

(2) a general election would be detrimental to the national economy; (3) he could rely on finding another prime minister who could carry on his government, for a reasonable period, with a working majority in the House of Commons.

This statement of principles governing dissolution defies improvement.

The third query. If the government is defeated on the floor of the Lok Sabha, is the president *bound* to invite the largest single party, the Congress(I), to form a majority despite the fact that it has no support from the National Front, the BJP, or the Left parties? The report of the Committee of Governors says that the leader of the largest single party in the house has no such right: 'no absolute right as leader of the largest single party or group to claim that he should be entrusted with the task of forming a government to the exclusion of all others. The relevant test is not the size of a party but its ability to command the support of the majority of the legislature.'[4] If the National Front ceases to command the confidence of the Lok Sabha, the Congress(I) can hardly claim to have 'a working majority'. Its object in making this claim would of course be to demand a dissolution shortly after it assumes power.

The fourth and last query. Can the Congress(I) ask for a dissolution in such circumstances? The greatest authority on the subject is Professor Eugene A. Forsey. His work, *The Royal Power of Dissolution of Parliament in the British Commonwealth,* is recognized as a classic. He is emphatically of the view that if an alternative government assumed office and asked for an immediate dissolution or was at once defeated on a critical division, it would be the duty of the crown *'to recall the former Government and grant it dissolution'.*[5]

In his letter mentioned above, Professor Geoffrey Marshall also argued that if 'the leader of the largest alternative party ... could not find a majority to support his programme, he would not be entitled to dissolve.' To grant him dissolution would be grossly unfair to the prime minister he replaced. As Mr Roy Jenkins pointed out in a letter to *The Times* on 26 April 1950, 'the crown would be placed in the intolerable and dangerous position' of granting to an obvious minority prime minister what it had earlier refused to a prime minister who commanded majority support but lost it later.

If, therefore, the National Front government were defeated in

[4]Ibid., p. 29.
[5]Oxford University Press, London, 1943, p. 263.

the Lok Sabha on 7 November, its leader would have been justified in asking for dissolution of the house. The president would then be justified in asking the Congress(I)'s leader, as a formality, if he could form a government. He would not be justified in accepting its claim to be able to do so, given the state of things; least of all to grant it dissolution. The proper course would be to accept the existing government's advice to dissolve the Lok Sabha.[6]

---

[6]As it happened, defeated in the Lok Sabha on a motion of confidence on 7 November 1990, V.P. Singh resigned as prime minister without, however, advising dissolution (R. Venkataraman, *My Presidential Years,* Harper Collins, Delhi 1990, p. 440). On 10 November Chandra Shekhar was sworn in as prime minister with Rajiv Gandhi's (i.e. the Congress(I) President's) support, and that of some small groups (ibid., p. 442).

2

When Can a Budget be Deferred and When Should Parliament be Dissolved?[1]

The president, Mr R. Venkataraman, faces grave but clear choices in the days ahead. Recent events have totally belied the assumptions on the basis of which he invited Mr Chandra Shekhar to form a government. Mr Rajiv Gandhi's assurances to the president on 8 November 1990 that he would support the government have proved to be insincere, and the entire experiment has proved a failure, as was widely expected. The present Lok Sabha has been denuded of usefulness and viability, ceasing to serve as a source of democratic legitimacy or political stability for any government. It does not sustain the Janata Dal nor can it support a Congress(I) regime without violence to constitutional principles and political morality. The government's inability to present a budget to parliament is an acknowledgement of its lack of parliamentary support, itself a ground for its resignation. In each of the previous seven cases when a vote-on-account was sought the government's majority in the house was not in doubt at all. Mr Chandra Shekhar's assurance on 23 February 1991 that a regular budget would indeed be presented at the end of May or early June is unworthy of credence, as will be pointed out.

Dr B.R. Ambedkar's authoritative exposition in the Constituent Assembly on the pertinent provisions of the Constitution shows precisely in what circumstances a budget can be deferred. Briefly,

[1] *The Indian Express* 5 March 1991. Mr. Chandra Shekhar resigned as Prime Minister on 6 March 1991.

Article 112 of the Constitution enjoins the president ('shall') to lay before parliament the 'annual financial statement' showing the estimated receipts and expenditure of the government. Article 113(2) mandates the Lok Sabha's sanction for expenditure other than that charged upon the Consolidated Fund of India. After the budget grants are thus sanctioned, an Appropriation Bill (Article 114) must be passed. Article 115 provides for supplementary grants.

Article 116, on votes on account, is an exception to this scheme ('Notwithstanding anything in the foregoing provisions ...'). It enables the Lok Sabha: (a) to make grants in advance in respect of the estimated expenditur : 'pending the completion of the procedure prescribed in Article 113' for the voting to budget grants or, (b) to meet 'an unexpected demand upon the resources', or (c) to make 'an exceptional grant'.

The seven precedents for votes on account genuinely related to problems in the 'completion of the procedure' for the preparation and presentation of the budget. In the present case, the finance minister, Mr Yashwant Sinha, was ready to present his budget but was asked not to do so for political reasons alone. Article 116 does not apply and the omission to present a budget under Article 112 is a clear violation of the Constitution.

On 8 June 1949 Dr Ambedkar explained the *raison d'etre* of the vote on account. It is the time factor, not expediency. 'The budget is an enormous thing' involving many details, 'and if you also have the provision that the budget must be passed before the end of the official year is over, then you must have a very limited time fixed for the discussion of the budget.' He added: 'The vote on account procedure which we propose to introduce by an amendment provides for parliament allowing a lump sum grant to the executive to be spent upon the services of the year for say about two months or so, so that the two months will be available to parliament to discuss in (sic) a much greater length—I don't say fully—the budget provisions. ...' The vote on account is thus intended not to postpone a budget but to facilitate detailed discussion of it.

This was also made amply clear: 'If the house, therefore, desires that it should have more time to discuss the details of the budget, some provision has to be made in the Constitution whereby it will be open to the house to allow the executive a lump sum out of the Consolidated Fund, covering an expenditure of two months if the house wants two months for discussion'. Not two months for postponing a discussion, as now.[2]

This is the clear legal position. The record proves its perversion. The opening salvo was Mr Rajiv Gandhi's famous threat, so odd from a supporter:'In case the budget affects poorer section of society, the Congress will be disturbed and we do not know what we will do then.'The convenor of the economic cell of the AICC(I), Mr Pranab Mukherji, was despatched to talk to Mr Yashwant Sinha. Mr Mukherjee gave the game away on 18 February by saying that there was nothing wrong with a vote on account now, with the preparation of a full-fledged budget left for the next government. He 'darkly hinted', a correspondent reported, that 'his party's full support might not be available to the government to defend its budget proposals'. He said significantly, 'if the government slips on any little thing, it will collapse.'

On 19 February 1991 the Congress (I) spokesman, Mr V. N. Gadgil, said: 'We will judge the government on the merit of each issue.'The following day Mr Chandra Shekhar confirmed the deferral of the budget but ascribed it to the 'peculiar situation' created by the poll in Tamil Nadu. Encouraged by this, the Congress(I) advised the Andhra Pradesh government too to go for a vote on account by invoking Article 206, the replica of Article 116. This is a fraud on the Constitution.

While the leader of the Congress (I) in the Rajya Sabha, P. Shiv Shankar, demanded on 22 February 'an apology to the nation' from the government he professes to support, the party president, Mr Rajiv Gandhi, flatly denied (23 February) that he had assured the president that he would support the government for at least a year.[3] His game plan is clear. Designed initially to topple the government before the budget, it aims now to withdraw support after the vote on account, form a government thereafter, and advise dissolution of the Lok Sabha when, with the official machinery at his command during the polls, the prospects of electoral victory would be brighter?

It is unthinkable that the president would have accepted Mr Rajiv Gandhi's assurances had he suspected them to have been so transient and frail. Constitutional precedents, however, afford him

[2] *Constituent Assembly Debates* (CAD), vol. viii, p. 726.
[3] For an assertion to the contrary, see R. Venkataraman, *My Presidential Years* (Harper Collins, 94), p. 438

ground enough to reject Mr Gandhi's pleas. Unfortunately, in his concern to avert a general election in the charged atmosphere last year, the president accepted a Congress (I)–Janata Dal (S) arrangement which had none of the features essential for the installation of a minority or a coalition government. There was not even a claim to accord on the bare minimum of an agreed programme. Moreover, as an authority points out, such an 'agreement should be made public'. This has not been done to this day. The honourable course for Mr Chandra Shekhar is to resign and advise the president to dissolve the Lok Sabha. The president cannot reject the advice and ask Mr Rajiv Gandhi to form a ministry in view of his lack of solid majority support, not to forget his refusal to form a government earlier. There is a clear risk in rejecting such advice from 'the minority prime minister'.

As an authority, S.A. de Smith points out a propos the queen: 'She might be mistaken in her belief that a stable alternative government could be formed without an election, in which case she would be obliged to grant the new prime minister what she had refused to his predecessors, thus conveying in some quarters an impression of partisanship.'[4] The embarrassment is greater still when the new PM is defeated at the polls. On this the authorities are unanimous. Wade and Bradley mention another consideration: 'It might be particularly difficult for the sovereign to be reasonably certain that another prime minister could command a working majority in the house.'[5] In Mr Gandhi's case it is certain that he cannot, except through sordid deals and defections.

Nothing less than what Dr Rodney Brazier picturesquely calls a 'published copper-bottomed party pact on an alternative government' can avoid any embarrassment of having to grant dissolution to one head of government having refused it to his predecessors'. The leaders of these parties must be 'prepared to take over the government without a dissolution'. Dr Brazier shows how the mess can be avoided in an uncertain situation. 'It would be less controversial for the queen to accept a request to dissolve parliament than to seek an alternative.'[6]

Defeat in the house does not disqualify the prime minister from advising dissolution either. 'If the government is defeated in the

[4]S.A. de Smith, *Constitutional and Administrative Law,* 5th edn ed. Harry Street and Rodney Brazier (Harmondsworth: Penguin Books 1985), p. 130.

[5]Wade and Bradley, op. cit.

[6]Rodney Brazier, *Constitutional Practice*, 2nd edn (Oxford University Press, 1994), pp. 38–9.

House of Commons on a motion of confidence or of no confidence, the prime minister must either ask for a dissolution or tender the resignation of himself and his ministerial colleagues', says a standard work on constitutional law.[7] Dissolution is never an easy choice but the guidelines are clear. They were stated with such clarity and precision by Sir Alan Lascelles, private secretary to the king, in a letter to *The Times* (London) published on 2 May 1950, that many quote it as an authoritative statement of the law. He wrote:

In so far as this matter can be publicly discussed, it can be properly assumed that no wise sovereign, that is, one who has at heart the true interest of the country, the constitution, and the monarchy—would deny a dissolution to this prime minister unless he were satisfied that: (1) the existing parliament was still vital, viable and capable of doing its job; (2) a general election would be detrimental to the national economy; (3) he could rely on finding another prime minister who could carry on his government, for a reasonable period, with a working majority in the House Commons.

A poll will undoubtedly be expensive, but the existing parliament is not at all 'capable of doing its job'. No alternative government with an assured 'working majority' is in sight. Besides, the political situation has changed radically since 1989. The election manifestos of almost all the parties have been torn up.

As Churchill wisely said in the House of Commons on 2 June 1931: 'No Government which is in a large minority in the country, even though it possesses a working majority in the House of Commons, can have the necessary power to cope with real problems.' This is all the more true of the present government, or the one Mr Rajiv Gandhi hopes to form.

If the PM persistently refuses to advise dissolution, it is open to the president to insist that he tender such advice. Nor are the people helpless. 'A dissolution is in its essence an appeal from the legal to the political sovereign.'[8] Jayaprakash Narayan was fond of quoting this dictum of Dicey's during his agitation for the dissolution of the Bihar assembly. It is not an unworthy precedent but it shold be invoked sparingly, and as the last resort.

[7]Quoted in 'the Report of the Hansard Society Commission on Electoral Reform', June 1976, p. 12.

[8]A.V. Dicey, *An Introduction to the Study of the Law of the Constitution*, 10th edn, (London: Macmillan ELBS, 1959), p. 433.

3

Dissolution of the Lok Sabha and Adoption of the Budget[1]

The press communiqué issued by the Rashtrapati Bhawan 13 March 1991 is the longest ever to emanate from there. It not only announces the president's order, under Article 85(2)(b) of the Constitution, to dissolve the Lok Sabha, but states at a some length the reasons for it and, tacitly, for the delay in its announcement. Inasmuch as it reveals a certain sense of accountability to the people by their elected president, never too evident in the past, this step deserves appreciation. When the soundness of a conclusion is accepted, one is generally tempted to ignore the premise on which it is based, but a president's reasoning is of consequence. Besides, so grave were some of the issues raised since Mr Chandra Shekhar resigned as prime minister on 6 March, that a calm constitutional retrospect is not amiss.

At the outset, the spuriousness of the two issues raised by some in the Congress (I) deserves to be exposed. One concerns the prime minister's oath of office and the other his government's competence to sponsor legislation in parliament after he had resigned from office. Mr Harsharan Verma is responsible for getting the first brushed aside by the Supreme Court on 19 November 1984[2]. He had earlier doggedly challenged the legality of two chief ministers of UP, Messrs C.B. Gupta and T.N. Singh, continuing in office. In 1979 he trained his gun on Prime Minister Charan Singh. One of the grounds was that Chaudhury Charan Singh had failed to take a fresh oath of

[1] *The Indian Express* 21 March 1991.
[2] *Harsharan Verma v Charan Singh & Ors.* (1985), 1 Supreme Court Cases (SCC) 162.

office when he continued as caretaker prime minister after his resignation. The Supreme Court gave short shrift to the argument in a single page order of refreshing brevity.

Equally untenable is the argument that the government could not sponsor legislation. The president's letter to the prime minister on 6 March explicitly asked him 'to continue in office till the new government is formed'. The government, accordingly, continued in office 'during the pleasure of the President', as Article 75(2) requires. Moreover, received the full support of the Lok Sabha in the passage of the vote-on-account on 11 March.

There is, however, a rather disturbing statement in the communiqué—after consulting eminent lawyers and also party leaders, the president 'reached the conclusion that it would be safer to have the financial provisions passed by parliament'. This is an allusion to the suggestion by some lawyers that the Appropriation Bill can be enacted by the president by promulgating an ordinance under Article 123. That the ambit of the president's ordinance-making power is coextensive with parliament's legislative competence has been repeatedly declared by the Supreme Court.

There are however two snags in regard to the budget or a vote-on-account. The ordinance would set at naught the elaborate scheme advisedly framed by the architects of the Constitution. It would be subversive of the fundamentals of democratic government and set a dangerous precedent. Now is the time to consider the matter closely, before another such crisis arises.

The Appropriation Bill (Article 114) and the vote on grants (Article 113[2]) are inextricable parts of an entire scheme whose principal element is parliamentary control over the public purse. First, the president is enjoined by Article 112 ('Shall') to lay before parliament the 'annual financial statement' showing the estimated receipts and expenditure of the government for the year. Article 113(1) next provides that expenditure which is charged on the Consolidated Fund of India 'shall not be submitted to the vote' of parliament but this will not prevent 'the discussion' of the estimates in either house of parliament.

As regards estimates relating to expenditure other than that charged on the Consolidated Fund, Article 113 (2) says that they 'shall be submitted in the form of grants to the Lok Sabha and the Lok Sabha shall have power to assent, or to refuse to assent, to any demand, or to assent to any demand subject to a reduction of the amount specified therein'.

This elaborately devised check is set at naught if the demands are deemed to have been passed by an ordinance and parliament is asked to ratify it subsequently, after the money has been spent by the president's council of ministers which had advised him to issue the ordinance. Note that the power to pass the grants falls exclusively under the purview of the Lok Sabha, the house of directly elected representatives of the nation. The power to ratify a presidential ordinance is however vested by Article 123 (2) equally in both houses of parliament. Recourse to an ordinance would, therefore, subvert the Lok Sabha's exclusive legislative competence in regard to money Bills. Significantly, Article 110 (3) vests in the speaker of the Lok Sabha the power to determine whether a Bill is a money Bill or not and his decision is 'final'. Moreover, Article 113 (3) provides that 'no demand for a grant shall be made except on the recommendation of the president'. It would surely be incongruous for the president to enact his own 'recommendation' by an ordinance bypassing the Lok Sabha, and then seek its ratification by both houses of parliament.

The final step, the Appropriation Bill, is linked to the passage of grants. Article 114(1) makes the linkage clear. 'As soon as may be after the grants under Article 113 have been made by the Lok Sabha, there shall be introduced a Bill to provide for the appropriation out of the Consolidated Fund of India of all money required ...'

Article 116 provides for votes on account to be passed exclusively by the Lok Sabha. Its *raison d'etre* has been discussed earlier. Finally, Article 114(3) lays down peremptorily that 'subject to the provisions of Articles 115 and 116, no money shall be withdrawn from the Consolidated Fund of India except under appropriation made by law passed in accordance with the provisions of this article.' No ordinance can set this constitutional provision at naught. It embodies the time-honoured principle of control over public money by the directly elected lower house of parliament in democracies.

A great American judge wisely said 'It is a *Constitution* we are expounding.[3] No one can go through the debates in the constituent assembly on 8 June 1949 on these provisions without being struck

[3]Chief Justice John Marshall in *McCulloch v Maryland*, 4 Wheaton 316 (1919).

by the concern for parliamentary control expressed by Dr B. R. Ambedkar. Let it be remembered that Articles 202 to 206 contain an identical scheme for the States. Mr Mulayam Singh Yadav's manoeuvres in the assembly on 12 March on the Appropriation Bill are a fair warning.

In 1968 a similar crisis had arisen in Punjab. The speaker adjourned the Assembly for two months on 6 March before it could pass the budget. The governor prorogued the House and enacted the Punjab Legislature (Regulation of Procedure in Relation to Financial Business) Ordinance. It barred the assembly from adjourning without its own consent until the financial business was completed. The assembly's authority was upheld, not undermined. The Supreme Court upheld the validity of the ordinance on 30 July 1968.[4]

On 6 March 1991 the president, while accepting the PM's resignation, declared that 'on the dissolution of the Lok Sabha, a decision will be taken separately.' Mr Chandra Shekhar told newsmen outside Rashtrapati Bhavan that 'the president has assured me that he will take a decision on dissolution within 24 hours'. The press communique of 13 March is altogether unconvincing on why this deadline so sensibly laid down, was extended.

There then existed a clear majority in the Lok Sabha in favour of the passage of the vote-on-account. The National Front, the Left parties, the BJP and, of course, the Janata Dal(S) were all in favour of it. This was evident in the debate in the house before the prime minister went to Rashtrapati Bhavan. All that they insisted on was dissolution. There was no real danger of a constitutional crisis arising by the house not passing the vote.

The communique tells us that 'Questions whether the president could resort to issue of an ordinance in case parliament failed to pass budgetary measures to cover expenditure during 1991–92 also cropped up'. One wonders why. In view of the clear majority in support of the vote, the question of promulgating an ordinance on the advice of a government lacking a majority in the Lok Sabha was worse than academic.

Nor is the explanation that 'as necessary, budgetary and other legislative measures have since been passed by both the houses of parliament' convincing. There was every prospect of their passage

[4]*State of Punjab v Sat Pal Dang* AIR 1969 SC 903.

on 6 or 7 March. What prevented that was the uncertainty over the dissolution. Sir Ivor Jenning's classic *Cabinet Government* cites one clear instance of Queen Victoria giving an assurance of dissolution in advance of the act to Lord Derby as far back as 1858. In 1991 those who sought such an assurance from an elected president, a propos a hung Lok Sabha torn by sordid deals, did not act improperly.[5]

In the event, the president's unfortunate extension of the deadline which he had himself set for 6 March, by a whole week, enabled those very deals to be discussed with greater ardour and with greater damage to public morality. The communiqué's assertion that 'no political party has staked a claim to form an alternate government' is less than accurate, in that it records the reality that finally emerged after all the attempts at deals had failed during the extended period. The truth is that in November 1990 the Lok Sabha had demonstrated its incapacity to support any viable government.

An understandable eagerness to avoid a poll in the charged atmosphere led the president to accept Mr Rajiv Gandhi's assurances of support to Mr Chandra Shekhar which fell far short of the 'copper-bottomed' assurances that should have been demanded. While the Congress(I) publicizes Mr Gandhi's phone call to the president, his letter to the latter embodying his assurance remains unpublished. Once he reneged on them, there was no warrant for contemplation of any other course than dissolution.

Mr Chandra Shekhar now presides over a 'caretaker government'. No one should be surprised if he or any of his colleagues argue that the concept finds no place in the text of the Constitution. A full bench of seven judges of the Madras high court however recognized the concept in a judgement of great erudition delivered on 10 October 1979 on a petition by the redoubtable Mr Cho Ramaswami against Mr Charan Singh.

The court said, 'Though the Constitution itself does not refer to a caretaker Government or define as to what a caretaker government is, yet it is possible to understand the expression, 'care-taker government' as the government in power after dissolution of the Lok Sabha and before its reconstitution.' A

[5]Ivor Jennings, *Cabinet Government*, 3rd edn (Cambridge: Cambridge University Press, 1969), p. 422.

caretaker prime minister, according to Dr Rodney Brazier, presides 'over routine matters of government' President Venkataraman must ensure that the norms of a caretaker regime are observed by this government.

4

A President's Moves for Constitutional Amendment[1]

The first thing that strikes one about President R. Venkataraman's deservedly unsuccessful moves for a national government is the depth of his concern that the general elections will throw up yet another hung Lok Sabha and his earnestness of purpose. Neither is in question, and neither affects the citizen's undoubted right to subject the president's action to careful scrutiny. This is all the more so in the case in point because he has raised some far-reaching issues affecting the polity at this critical hour and, thus, invited scrutiny. It is his judgment that is in question. Piecing together the credible reports by responsible correspondents of national dailies, based on the revelations by the politicians who had met the president, one is astonished that he should have gone as far as he did.

His proposals were in two parts. One envisaged the establishment of a national government to conduct the polls that remain to be held. The Vice-President of the BJP, Mr K.R. Malkani's statement to the press on 23 May 1991 is most informative in the specific details he revealed which, incidentally, also find ample corroboration in other reports.[2] He said that the President felt that the national government, to be formed now, could function for three weeks until the elections were over. In the event that no party won a majority, the government could continue in office even after the

---

[1]The context of this article was president R. Venkataraman's moves for the establishment of a national government following Mr. Rajiv Gandhi's assassination in 1991. The *Indian Express*, 2 June 1991.

[2]*Hindustan Times*, 24 May 1991.

polls. The leadership question could be settled by the parties after consultation among themselves.

This proposal was dismissed for reasons that are obvious and sound. It was neither necessary nor feasible and was, in any event, premature. Mr Rajiv Gandhi's tragic assassination should, indeed, prompt some serious reflection on the need for the politics of consensus in a democratic system; some effort to bridge the gaps in a society riven with dissension it could well do without; some soul searching is essential by all to whom the nation's well-being matters.

However, as Mr Malkani so aptly put it with exquisite brevity, what confronts us today 'is a tragic situation, not a crisis situation'. Three prime ministers died in office and in the wake of grave crises. Panic is no response to the foul crime that snatched away from our midst the young leader of the largest political party in the country; nor is stability promoted by resorting in desperation to ill-considered and extreme measures.

It must be recognized, however, that the constitutional head of state is perfectly entitled, and in certain situations bound in duty, to press the political parties to form a national government. King George V did so on 24 August 1931 when he asked the Labour prime minister, Mr Ramsay MacDonald, not to press his resignation but, instead, form a national government. On the king's appeal the Conservatives and the Liberals agreed to serve under Mr MacDonald in a national government. However unsound the proposal was, its propriety is not in doubt.

One is not equally confident about the president's second proposal which envisaged convening a constituent assembly to amend or even to rewrite the Constitution and, possibly, the cancellation of the elections. This proposal was first mooted on 22 May when the president met leading political figures on the morrow of Mr Rajiv Gandhi's assassination, and was reported in the press the following day.

Mr Malkani spelt out the details quite precisely on 23 May. The president 'gave the impression that if the parties were willing, the current elections may be cancelled and a constituent assembly may be constituted at some future date'. Mr Atal Behari Vajpayee, on his part, tried to pour cold water over this proposal by calling it a 'passing reference'. That he, nonetheless, characterized it as an action that would 'disrupt the current election process and open a Pandora's box' suggests that he did not regard the president's exercise in loud thinking to be innocuous.

In any event, it is not normal for heads of state to indulge in thinking aloud in times of crisis before top-ranking leaders of the nation's political parties unless they really mean to make serious proposals for the leaders to pursue. Moreover, the content of what some call 'loud thinking' was strikingly similar, addressed though it was to several interlocutors separately.

That the president mooted a constituent assembly to those he met on 22 May is a fact as established as it is shocking. The assembly would be an extra-constitutional body which parliament has not the power to convene. At the very least, neither the president nor those who advised him to make this proposal could have been unaware of the murky background of the idea of a constituent assembly.

It was first mooted in the unfortunate majority ruling of the Supreme Court in February 1967 in the celebrated Golakh Nath case.[3] A narrow majority of six to five ruled that parliament was not competent to abridge or take away the fundamental rights even by amending the Constitution. One of the finest constitutional lawyers the country has known, whose integrity was beyond reproach, Mr M.C. Setalvad, had no hesitation in expressing the view that 'the majority decision clearly appears to be a political decision, not based on the true interpretation of the Constitution'.[4]

Unable to convincingly meet the obvious objection that the ruling would render a part of the Constitution eternal or permanent, the two judges who delivered the majority ruling suggested, in sheer desperation, recourse to a constituent assembly. Neither of them, Justices K. Subba Rao and M. Hidayatullah, was however able to convincingly indicate the legal sanction. Justice Subba Rao suggested that the assembly could be set up by parliament in exercise of its residuary powers of legislation in the Union list. (Entry 97 List I). This is however a power to legislate *under* the Constitution, not to rewrite it. Mr Justice Hidayatullah suggested that parliament 'must amend Article 368 [which enables it to amend the Constitution] to convoke another constituent assembly, pass a law under item 97 ... to call a constituent assembly' which

---

[3] *I.C. Golak Nath v State of Punjab*, AIR 1967 SC 1643.
[4] M.C. Setalvad, *My Life* (Bombay : N.M. Tripathi, 1970), p. 587.

would be free 'to abridge or take away the fundamental rights if desired'.

Mr H.M. Seervai's refutation of both is unanswerable:

'If a law made by parliament to amend Part III [embodying the fundamental rights] in the exercise of its residuary power and in compliance with Article 368, is void ... a law passed by the same parliament convening a constituent assembly and authorizing it to do that very thing must be equally void, for what parliament cannot do itself, it cannot authorize another body to do ...

Again, such a law would not attract Article 368, for under that Article, on a Bill being passed and receiving assent as there provided [the] Constitution stands amended; and it would be futile to amend the Constitution to enable a constituent assembly to abridge fundamental rights ... *On principle it is difficult to understand how, if a freely elected Parliament cannot be trusted to amend Part III as provided by Article 368, another body, set up by the same parliament, can acquire higher authority. Therefore, a constituent assembly is either legally impossible or wholly unnecessary.*'[5]

At any rate, in the Keshavananda Bharati case in 1973, 13 judges of the Supreme Court overruled Golakh Nath's case.[6] The idea was revived during the Emergency on 15 November 1975 by Mr Uma Shankar Dixit, a member of the Union cabinet close to Mrs Indira Gandhi. Around the same time a mysterious paper was circulated proposing the establishment of a presidential system.

According to an informed correspondent, President Venkataraman would like the constituent assembly 'to work on amendments which would have answers for a hung Parliament. Whether it should be a Presidential form of government or some other form providing for an all-party or a national or coalition government would be for the Constituent Assembly to decide.'

It bears recalling that shortly after Mr Nehru's death, Mr R. Venkataraman had, in a letter to the All India Congress Committee (AICC) on 27 May 1965, forwarded a draft resolution proposing the establishment of a Presidential system, The letter is very interesting.[7] Among the reasons it cited for the change were 'the

[5]H M. Seervai, *Constitutional Law of India* 1st edn (Bombay: N.M. Tripathi, 1967), p. 1109.

[6]*Kesavananda Bharati v State of Kerala*, AIR 1973 SC 1461.

[7]For text, see A.G. Noorani, *The Presidential System: The Indian Debate* (New Delhi : Sage, 1989), pp. 29–32.

defeat of the Congress ministry in Kerala by the defection of the Congressmen themselves, the resignation of a group of Congressmen from Mysore, the growth of 'dissidentism' in a large number of political parties.' These indicated to him that the 'internal stability of our country is weakening'. Another reason was the 'multiplicity of parties.'

The merits of this proposal apart, it is sad to see a president sworn to 'preserve' the Constitution suggesting its replacement in an hour like this in order to tide over a momentary 'crisis'. There is surely no national consensus in support of this idea. It can only divide the nation. Nor are the rules of the parliamentary system in regard to a hung parliament as uncertain as the president evidently imagines.

Dr Rodney Brazier's work, *Constitutional Texts*, published in 1990 devotes 60 pages to texts of documents on the topic while his study *Constitutional Practice* contains sound advice in such situations.[8] Indeed, the Sarkaria Commission propounded a set of rules for governors to follow if the electorate returns a hung State assembly. So did the Report of the Committee of Governors. Mr David Butler's study, *Governing Without a Majority*, throws much light on the issue.[9]

Great Britain had two general elections in 1910. It had hung parliaments in 1923, 1929 and 1974. As B.N. Rau remarked, 'minority governments are more common than is commonly supposed'.[10] The farce enacted from November 1990 to March 1991 should not drive us to wrong conclusions. The Chandra Shekhar ministry was based on a tenth of the Lok Sabha and Mr Rajiv Gandhi's letter of support did not contain the pledge to support it for a year; it was given orally.

The president failed also to insist on the other conditions so well summed up by Dr Brazier: 'a copper-bottomed agreement on majority coalition, its leadership, proposed disposition of ministerial offices, and agreed queen's speech, together with an equally sound guarantee that coalition government would not seek a dissolution within a reasonable time'.[11]

[8]Rodney Brazier, *Constitutional Texts* (Oxford: Oxford University Press, 1990), pp. 64–120.

[9]David Butler, *Governing Without a Majority*, (London: Macmillan, 1983).

[10]B.N. Rau, *India's Constitution in the Making* (New Delhi: Orient Longman), p. 207.

[11]Brazier, *Constitutional Practice*, pp. 38–9.

The queen should stipulate 'that the ultimate agreement [among the parties] should be made public'. Her object should be to ensure that she 'should not be embarrassed by an early demise of that coalition or by an early request for another general election'. Had the president followed this counsel he would not have suffered the embarrassment he later did. The fears that nag the president today are unreal. They have arisen not because the rules of the parliamentary system are uncertain, but because he did not follow them last year.

5
The President and the Governors[1]

'The position of the Governor is exactly the same as the position of the president', Dr B.R. Ambedkar, Chairman of the drafting committee, authoritatively declared in the Constituent Assembly on 30 December 1948.[2] The Kumudben Joshis in non-Congress(I) States and their mentors in New Delhi do not appear to realise that in harassing State governments run by opposition parties they are playing with fire.

Dr Ambedkar's statement was in reply to a pointed interruption by a member, Mr Mohammed Tahir, when defining the discretionary powers of the president. Mr Tahir asked: 'How will it explain the position of the governors and the ministers of the States where discretionary powers have been allowed to be used by the governors?' Dr Ambedkar's categorical reply followed, dispelling the impression that as constitutional head of state the governor enjoys greater powers vis-à-vis the State government than the president does vis-à-vis the council of ministers at the Centre. The Supreme Court has upheld Dr Ambedkar's exposition.

It is time that this fundamental principle is asserted every time a Congress(I) politician, kicked upstairs as governor, misbehaves with the State government in order to win back a position at the Centre. Does the government of India concede the same powers of obstruction to the president?

A lot was heard in 1987 on the president's power to dismiss a

[1] *The Indian Express*, December 1988.
[2] CAD., vol. vii, p. 1186.

government without a vote of censure by the Lok Sabha. On 21 August 1984 however a spokesman of the Government of India had no qualms in asserting in the Rajya Sabha, in justification of NTR's dismissal by Governor Ram Lal, that 'it is the pleasure [sic] of the governor to decide whether any particular leader has lost the majority'. Surely what applies to the goose in the State capitals applies also to the gander in New Delhi.

Nobody in his senses suggests that the partisan conduct of Congress(I) governors, acting at the behest of the Congress(I) regime at the Centre, should be regarded as a precedent in sound constitutional practice. That, however, is no reason why each time a grave lapse occurs its implications at the Centre should not be pointed out. The rules of the parliamentary system are identical in both cases. Wilful delay in according assent to Bills, ordinances, nominations to the upper house and to statutory offices is as improper on the part of a governor as it would be on the part of the president.

The governor of Karnataka, Mr P. Venkatasubbiah, took more than three months to accept the State government's recommendations for five nominations to the legislative council. He accepted three after a long delay and the rest only on 25 November 1988. His conduct was indefensible. Even the tepid Sarkaria report states categorically that the pertinent provision of the Constitution, Article 171, 'does not provide for the exercise of discretion by the governor'. Governor Ram Dulari Sinha has sat long on the draft ordinance submitted for her assent by the Kerala government on the vice-chancellorship of Calicut University. She returned, unapproved, its list of nominees to the senate of Kerala university.

Overshadowing both governors is the towering personality of Ms Kumudben Joshi whose place in the annals of gubernatorial impropriety is now beyond challenge. Soon after the Constitution came into force, the attorney-general, Mr M.C. Setalvad, was asked to give an opinion on the Governor's powers. He expressed the view that in the new setup it would be inappropriate for a governor to have direct contacts with secretaries and heads of department.[3] Practice conformed to this sound opinion. Ms Joshi began flouting

[3]Valmiki Choudhary ed., *Dr Rajendra Prasad: Correspondence and Select Documents*, (Delhi : Allied Publishers, 1991), vol. 14, pp. 104–10 and 280–91, *See* p. 72 for Prasad's views on imposition of president's rule in Punjab in 1951. *See* also K.M. Munshi (ed), *Indian Constitutional Documents* (Bombay: Bharatiya Vidya Bhavan, 1967), vol. 1, p. 574, para 23.

it systematically not long after she assumed office as governor of Andhra Pradesh in November 1985.

Immediately preceding the crisis over the nomination of Justice R.N. Agarwal to the office of Lok Ayukta of the State was Governor Joshi's wilful delay in according assent to the Andhra Pradesh Rashtra Karshaka Parishad and Allied Bodies Bill, 1988. It was sent to her on 2 September 1988; she gave her assent on 24 November. Irrespective of the final result in the controversy over Justice Agarwal's appointment, her conduct must prompt a quest for remedies against such abuse of the governor's office. Is our constitutional system, indeed, powerless in the face of such mis-demeanour?

The facts are gross. Section 3 of the Andhra Pradesh Lok Ayukta and Upa Lok Ayukta Act, 1983, enjoins ('shall') the governor to appoint a Lok Ayukta provided two conditions are fulfilled. The person shall be a judge or a retired chief justice of a high court and the chief justice of the high court must be consulted. Justice Agarwal retired as chief justice of the Delhi High Court. The chief minister, Mr N.T. Rama Rao, had consulted the chief justice of the Andhra Pradesh High Court, Justice Yogeshwar Dayal, before recommending Justice Agarwal's name to the governor on 13 November. A writ petition challenging the recommendation was rejected by the high court on 22 November.

Ms Joshi had returned the file twice on 14 and 19 November and, for good measure, summoned the chief secretary, not the law minister, on 16 November to seek clarification. The high court's order of 22 November notwithstanding, she returned the file for the third time that night with another set of queries. Apparently, Mr N.T. Rama Rao's letter to President R. Venkataraman was written on 22 November before this aggravating fact. The motion tabled in the Lok Sabha on 24 November censuring her conduct, and the Opposition MPs' deputation to the president the following day demonstrate the intensity of resentment she aroused.

The episode should prompt a firm restatement of the correct constitutional position and a search for correctives against such actions. First and foremost, the fundamental principle must be affirmed that as constitutional head of state in a parliamentary system, the governor's powers are no greater than those of the president. Dr Ambedkar had effectively refuted the notion that greater 'discretionary powers' are invested in governors. Still in some quarters the contrary impression evidently continues to persist and deserves to be dispelled.

Article 163 (I) provides that 'there shall be a council of ministers with the chief minister at the head to aid and advise the governor in the exercise of his functions, except in so far as he is by or under this Constitution required to exercise his functions or any of them in his discretion'. If no such exception was carved out of Article 74 in relation to the council of ministers at the Centre, it implies not that the president has no discretionary powers at all. Of course, he has.

Dr Ambedkar mentioned two of them in the constituent assembly on 30 December, 1948 before Mr Mohammed Tahir interrupted him to ask his famous question. The two presidential 'prerogatives' are the appointment of the prime minister and the dissolution of the Lok Sabha.[4] Both are, of course, governed by the established conventions of the British constitution on which our parliamentary system is modelled, as Dr Ambedkar and other draftsmen of the Constitution repeatedly acknowledged and the Supreme Court has with equal emphasis affirmed.

Right to Question

In regard to these powers as constitutional head of state, 'the position of the governor is exactly the same as the position of the president'. This covers matters like assent to Bills, ordinances, nominations to the upper house and to statutory offices. Of course, neither the president nor the governor is a rubber-stamp. They have an undoubted right to question, to call to account, to ask for information, to advise, to encourage, and to warn.

What, then, is the scope of the exception carved out in the governor's favour by Article 163(I)? No more than what it states, 'except insofar as he is by or under this Constitution required to exercise his functions or any of them in his discretion'. There are four categories of such explicit exceptions. The governor is required by Article 200 of the Constitution to reserve a Bill for the president's consideration 'which in the opinion of the governor' would derogate from the powers of the high court if it became law. Next, comes the governor's report to the president under Article 356 recommending president's rule. The third category comprises the governor's special responsibility for a particular region. Initially it covered Assam alone

[4]CAD, vol. vii, p. 1186.

(Tenth Schedule). Later amendments (Article 371A, 371C, 371F, 371H) conferred special responsibilities on specified matters on the governors of Nagaland, Manipur, Sikkim, and Arunachal Pradesh. Article 371 empowers the president to confer special responsibilities on the governors of Maharashtra and Gujarat with regard to Vidarbha and Marathwada and, respectively, of Kutch and Saurashtra. Lastly, under Article 239, the president can ask a governor to act as administrator of an adjoining Union Territory.

As the Sarkaria commission put it, the discretionary power conferred by Article 163 on the governor is 'limited' by the clear language of the provision. 'Article 163 does not give the governor a general discretionary power to act against or without the advice of his council of ministers.'[5] Dr Ambedkar's expositions in the constitutional assembly were clear. The governor 'is required to follow the advice of his ministry in all matters' (31 May 1949). He has 'hardly any discretion at all'. He has to act on the advice of the chief minister and his ministers 'with respect to any particular executive or legislative action that he takes'.[6]

Landmark Cases

In both the landmark cases of Ram Jawaya Kapur (1955)[7] and Samsher Singh (1974),[8] the Supreme Court put the governor on a par with the president as 'constitutional head of the executive'. In Samsher Singh's case, Chief Justice Ray listed the exceptions and said 'in all other matters' the governor acts 'in harmony' with the council of ministers. So well established is the parity, bar the exceptions, that in his concurring opinion in Samsher Singh's case, Justice Krishna Iyer saw no incongruity in mentioning the chief minister in brackets while discussing the prime minister: 'prime minister (chief minister)'—vis-à-vis the president.

In Dr Raghukul Tilak's case (1979) the Supreme Court went further still. It ruled that the Governor's office is 'not subordinate or subservient to the government of India. He is not amenable to

---

[5]Commission on Centre–State Relations, Report, pts 1 and II. (General Manager, Govt. of India Press, 1988), Pt 1, p. 1171, para 4.3.08 (popularly known as Sarkaria report, after its chairman, Justice R.S. Sarkaria).

[6]CAD., vol. viii, pp. 467–69.

[7]AIR 1955 SC 549, *see* also *U.N. Rao v Indira Gandhi*, AIR 1971 SC 1002 and *K.N. Rajagopal v M. Karunanidhi*, AIR 1971 SC 1551.

[8]AIR 1974 SC 2191.

the directions of the government of India, nor is he accountable to them for the manner in which he carries out his functions and duties.'[9]

If this is the incontrovertible constitutional position; what we witness today is a blatant attempt to subvert it by questioning the president's legitimate powers, on the one hand, and on the other attributing to the governors powers to which they are not entitled. The result in each case is the aggrandizement of the government of India and its head, the prime minister.

The remedy is however the same in both cases. It is the assertion of legitimate presidential power as constitutional head, at the Centre, and over the governors. They are the president's appointees. On 26 November 1970, the president appointed a committee of five governors to study and formulate norms and coventions governing the role of governors under the constitution. Much has happened since they reported in 1971. One principle however no one can contest: the president has every right and power to pull up an erring governor. In grave cases he has a duty to do so; and not on the advice of the Government of India, for the Governor is not amenable to its instructions, nor on matters that fall in the governor's domain as constitutional head, but for transgressions of constitutional propriety where the governor has clearly misbehaved.

Tackling an Errant Governor[10]

For more than one reason the CPI(M)'s general secretary, Mr Harkishen Singh Surjeet, erred grievously in writing to Prime Minister Mr P.V. Narasimha Rao, on 3 and 5 September 1993 demanding the removal of Mr Romesh Bhandari from the office of governor of Tripura. He should instead have addressed his letters to the president of India, Dr Shankar Dayal Sharma. Under the Constitution, the governor is appointed by the president and holds office 'during the pleasure of the president' [Article 156(1)]; not the prime minister.

The objection is, however, not only on the ground of form. One is not oblivious of the fact that under the Constitution the prime minister's advice will as a rule govern the president's decision.

[9] *Hargovind Pant v Dr Raghukul Tilak*, AIR 1979 SC 709.
[10] *The Statesman*, 8 October 1993.

However, the Constitution itself, by establishing a parliamentary system, based on conventions recognized repeatedly by the Supreme Court, endows the head of state with a measure of discretionary power. It is too late in the day to question either its existence or its limits. The sole question is whether, on the facts of a particular case, the president owes a duty to intervene, if need be, without or even contrary to the advice of the prime minister.

The facts are incontrovertible. Sweeping denials and evasive statements, smoothly delivered, do not constitute a reply at all to charges based on facsimiles of documents and transcripts of telephonic conversations published in the press. Their genuineness has not been questioned at all; indeed, it has been tacitly accepted by all.

My Surjeet's letters refer to the disclosures in *The Statesman*, on 26 and 27 August and on 4 September 1993, and draw pointed attention to the knots into which Mr Bhandari has tied himself up in his replies, as the clever are wont to do. At the very least, the evidence established a prima facie case on two counts. First, 'Mr Bhandari's efforts at fabricating evidence to implicate senior leaders of the BJP and the Congress(I) by linking them to the pay-offs made by Harshad Mehta in the securities scandal'. Secondly, intriguing against the government of Tripura headed by Mr Dasarath Deb. Since then, further evidence has come to light that convincingly establishes a third count: a cover-up operation in relation to the first two.

The transcript of Mr Romesh Bhandari's telephone conversation with Mr Randhir Jain, published by *The Statesman* on 19 September shows that on the very day (27 August) that he blithely claimed that he was not the one to get involved in such devilish plots, Mr Bhandari was advising Mr Jain to frame a denial and, more damning still, to destroy the incriminating evidence and deny knowledge of it.'You better tear up whatever you have, my dear boy, and tear up every document you have got ....''You have to say you have no knowledge of the documents'.

It is, of course, a clear duty on the part of the prime minister to advise the president to sack a governor who has behaved in this manner. If however Mr P.V. Narasimha Rao faiis to discharge his duty, is Dr Shankar Dayal Sharma absolved of his duty to act? Or, are we to believe that under the Constitution the president of India is powerless in such a situation?

Fortunately, we have clear and authoritative dicta from none other than Dr B.R. Ambedkar, Chairman of the drafting committee of the constituent assembly, which establish that the president is amply endowed with the power to dismiss a governor who has behaved the way Mr Romesh Bhandari has. No one, not even the prime minister or a union minister, is outside the reach of the president's power of dismissal in cases of misconduct.

Dr Ambedkar explained to the constituent assembly on 31 December 1948, the significance of the expression used in the Constitution a propos both ministers and governors: namely, that they hold office 'during the pleasure of the president'. With regard to ministers, the expression is used in Article 75, which figured as Article 62 in the draft constitution. Dr Ambedkar said:

It would be perfectly open under that particular clause of Article 62 for the president to call for the removal of a particular minister on the ground that he is guilty of corruption or bribery or maladministration, although that particular minister probably is a person who enjoyed the confidence of the House. I think honourable members will realize that the tenure of a minister must be subject not merely to one condition but to two conditions and the two conditions are purity of administration and confidence of the house.[11]

Thus, the president can dismiss a prime minister or any other minister on these grounds, in the exercise of his own discretion, though he commands the confidence of the Lok Sabha. Is that reserve discretionary power, then, denied to the president in relation to a delinquent governor only because he enjoys the backing of the prime minister, and a prime minister who, thus, renders himself privy to the governor's wrongs?

To be sure, the degree of proof varies in both cases. No president can lawfully dismiss a prime minister who enjoys the confidence of the Lok Sabha except on the ground of incontrovertible proof of misconduct. Those who pressed President Zail Singh in mid-1987, on the basis of the evidence available till then, months before the publication of the Bofors documents, to dismiss Rajiv Gandhi from the office of prime minister acted with a singular lack of any sense of responsibility or scruple and for their own sordid ends. It was just as well that Giani Zail Singh rejected their motivated advice.

[11]CAD, vol. vii, p. 1186.

In contrast to the elected prime minister, the governor is appointed by the centre. That does not imply that he can be dismissed arbitrarily, but it does imply that a far lesser degree of proof is required in the case of a governor as against that of any union minister who enjoys the confidence of the Lok Sabha. The prime minister and the council of ministers are responsible to the Lok Sabha and can be thrown out of office by a vote of no-confidence. Not so the governor. Some members of the constituent assembly suggested that the grounds for his removal be spelt out in the Constitution itself.

Dr Ambedkar did not accept the suggestion. His exposition in the constituent assembly, on 31 May 1949, is very relevant:

What Professor Shah wants is that certain grounds should be stated in the Constitution itself for the removal of the governor. It seems to me that when you have given the general power, you also give the power to the president to remove a governor for corruption, for bribery, for violation of the Constitution or for any other reason which the president, no doubt, feels is legitimate ground for the removal of the governor. It seems, therefore, quite unnecessary to burden the Constitution with all these limitations stated in express terms when it is perfectly possible for the president to act upon the very same ground under the formula and the governor shall hold office during his pleasure.'[12]

Clearly, the president enjoys a far wider discretion in the dismissal of a governor than in the case of a union minister.

The responsibility for maintaining a vigil on the behaviour of governors thus cast on the president is all the graver for the fact that the governor is not only not subject to a vote of no-confidence by any legislature but is also free from the process of impeachment to which even the president and judges of the Supreme Court are subject. The governor's tenure of office depends on the 'pleasure' of the president alone.

In the past, presidents have not hesitated to pull up governors for breaches of duty. Ajit Prasad Jain resigned as governor of Kerala in January 1966 because he had actively canvassed for Indira Gandhi's election as leader of the Congress parliamentary party on Lal Bahadur Shastri's death in Tashkent. President Shankar Dayal Sharma has clearly indicated that his role model is President Rajendra Prasad. In his foreword to volume 19 of *Dr Rajendra Prasad: Correspondence and Select Documents*, edited by Mr Valmiki Choudhary, Dr Sharma

[12]CAD, vol. viii, p. 469.

described it as 'the corpus of standard reference material which many may consult hereafter'. The foreword is dated 23 May 1993.

There are four letters by Rajendra Prasad which establish the principle of presidential surveillance of governors. One is a letter dated 14 January 1959, to the governor of Bombay, Sri Prakasa, warning him of the danger of even being associated with a memorial fund to a dear friend, Rafi Ahmed Kidwai. Another, dated 10 February 1959, asks the governor of Andhra Pradesh, V.V. Giri, not to be absent from his post 'for any length of time'. Similar instruction was given to the governor of Madhya Pradesh, H.V. Pataskar.

Lastly, Rajendra Prasad pulled up the governor of Punjab, N.V. Gadgil, in his own gentle manner, for making political pronouncements. In a letter to Gadgil, dated 25 July 1959, the president wrote: 'It is best for persons like you and me not to talk in public about controversial matters, particularly when they relate to subjects with which we are not immediately concerned. It is best not to become a subject of press controversy and criticism.'[13]

That was a gentle reprimand for gubernatorial loquacity. Dr Shankar Dayal Sharma might ask himself how Dr Rajendra Prasad would have reacted to proven misconduct on the part a governor. He would have given him the order of the boot. That is precisely what Mr Romesh Bhandari deserves today. The sooner it is delivered, the better.

The President's Power to Dismiss Governors[14]

It is unthinkable that Ms Sheila Kaul would have taken so long to resign as governor of Himachal Pradesh were it not for the protection that the prime minister, P.V. Narasimha Rao, extended to her. She brought sheer disgrace to her office in the last days of her public life. Mr. Narasimha Rao's performance in the dying days of his regime has been no better.

On 17 April 1996 Justice Kuldip Singh and Faizan Uddin of the Supreme Court expressed a clear opinion that she ought to step down. 'In today's state of rampant corruption, if some persons go and occupy high constitutional positions, they cannot think they are safe. We have seen in the *hawala* case some persons are still

---

[13]Delhi Allied Publishers Ltd, 1993, pp. 73, 76, 93, and 136 respectively.
[14]*The Statesman*, 30 April 1996 and 1 May 1996.

cooling their heels in gubernatorial positions because of immunity', an allusion to P. Shiv Shankar and Motilal Vora, governors respectively of Kerala and UP.

The CBI has accused Sheila Kaul of allotting 43 shops in prime localities in New Delhi to close relations and friends in total violation of the government's policy she had formulated in December 1994 as union urban development minister. Two persons on her staff were arrested then, well before the hearing. The Judges' hint was explicit. 'Can't the president of India say that she should step down? This is a must keeping in view the dignity of the office.'

No president and no prime minister with any sense of values could or would have ignored so explicit an observation. President Shankar Dayal Sharma acted that very day and sought the prime ninister's advice. Mr Narasimha Rao deliberately stalled a decision even as late as 19 April when he met the president. His record on accountability has been consistently shoddy.

Santosh Mohan Deb continues as minister, Bailadila or no. Kalpnath Rai was shielded for a long time and ejected only after the electoral debacle in the south. Mrs Kaul's misconduct was public knowledge even while she was union minister. She was sworn in as governor of Himachal Pradesh on 17 November 1995 in order to provide her immunity from accountability. For the same reason, A.R. Antulay was appointed chairman of the Irrigation Development Corporation of Maharashtra Ltd, a subterfuge designed to shield him from criminal accountability, as Justice Kotwal of Bombay High Court noted.

The Press release from Rashtrapati Bhavan on 20 April 1996 was perfectly justified.[15] The president faced an unprecedented situation. There were the Supreme Court's explicit observations, on the one hand, and the prime minister's decision to stall, on the other. The president decided not to acquiesce in the prime minister's decision and decided also to take the people, the ultimate masters, into confidence. In doing so, Dr Sharma has rendered high service to the presidency and contributed handsomely to repairing the damage inflicted on it by some of his predecessors, including Mr R. Venkataraman.

The press release merits close analysis. It was issued 'with reference to reports that have appeared in a section of the press' and added that 'the president is yet to receive any advice of the union cabinet relating to the governor of Himachal Pradesh'. It set out the position

[15] *The Times of India*, 21 April 1996.

taken by the president on 19 April in his discussion with the prime minister, and what the latter 'subsequently conveyed to the president'. Apparently, true to form, Mr Narasimha Rao was noncommittal in the talks. The prime minister saw 'no constitutional bar to the CBI instituting a preliminary inquiry against Mrs Kaul', which presumably also included her own interrogation though this was not overly explicit. The prime minister however wished to wait till the Supreme Court had considered 'different aspects relating to the immunity enjoyed by a governor under Article 361 of the Constitution' on 23 April. 'Further action would be possible in the light of its interpretation, the prime minister had stated'.

Thus on 23 April the court would have been faced with the unacceptable situation of a President not sacking Mrs Kaul despite its remarks on 17 April. This would have exposed him to embarrassment. 'In this connection the president has again sought the advice of the prime minister', the press release added, and quoted the president's letter. A proper course, properly made public in a spirit of accountability.

There is a wholly erroneous impression that the president could not have dismissed the governor without the prime minister's advice. In truth, the Constitution empowers the president to dismiss both on the ground of corruption. However, the president can sack the prime minister only in exceptional circumstances when there is either proof beyond reasonable doubt or of so strong a probative value as to require an inquiry, which is possible only after his demission of office. There would be a lesser standard of proof in the case of any union minister other than the prime minister and a far lesser one still in the case of a governor who, as head of state, is expected to meet stricter tests.

The constitutional provision is identically worded in all these cases. Article 75(2) of the Constitution says that 'the ministers shall hold office during the pleasure of the president'. This includes their head, the prime minister. Article 156(1) says: 'The governor shall hold office during the pleasure of the president'. Explaining the import of Article 75(2), which was Article 62 in the draft to the constituent assembly on 31 December 1948, B. R. Ambedkar said:

It would be perfectly open, under that particular clause of Article 62, for the president to call for the removal of a particular minister on the ground that he is guilty of corruption or bribery or maladministration, although that particular Minister probably is a person who enjoyed the confidence of the house. I think honourable members will realize that the tenure of a minister must be subject not merely to one condition but to two conditions and the two conditions are purity of administration and confidence of the house. The Article makes provision for both.

On Article 156, Dr Ambedkar said on 31 May 1949:

This power of removal is given to the president in general terms ... It seems to me that when you have given the general power, you also give the power to the president to remove a governor for corruption, for bribery, for violation of the Constitution or for any other reason which the president no doubt feels is legitimate ground for the removal of the governor. It seems, therefore, quite unnecessary to burden the Constitution with all these limitations stated in express terms when it is perfectly possible for the president to act upon the very same ground under the formula that the governor shall hold office during his pleasure. I, therefore, think that it is unnecesary to categorize the conditions under which the President may *undertake* the removal of the governor.

The language makes it clear that he can act on the basis of his individual judgment ('feels') without the prime minister's advice. The expression 'during the pleasure' has the same meaning in Article 156 as it has in Article 75.

In one of his more famous dicta, Sir Ivor Jennings said: 'The most elementary qualification demanded of a minister is honesty and incorruptibility. It is, however, necessary not only that he should possess this qualification but also that he should appear to possess it.'[16] This qualification applies to the governor, as head of state, with greater rigour. Correspondingly, the president can act on evidence far weaker than in the case of a minister. Reasonable suspicion is ground enough for a governor's removal. In Mrs Kaul's case, he had the CBI's report.

The Issue of Immunity[17]

The issue of immunity under Article 361 no longer arises in Mrs Kaul's case after her resignation but nonetheless deserves consideration. It reads:

[16]Cabinet government; p.106.
[17]This is a continuation of the article on Ms Sheila Kaul's belated resignation as governor of Himachal Pradesh. An earlier version of it was published in *The Statesman*, 1 May 1996. CAD vol. viii p. 469.

(1) The president or the governor shall not be answerable to any court for the exercise and performance of the powers and duties of his office or for any act done or purporting to be done by him in the exercise and performance of those powers and duties.

Provided that the conduct of the president may be brought under review by any court, tribunal or body appointed or designated by either house of parliament for the investigation of a charge under Article 61;

Provided further that nothing in this clause shall be construed as restricting the right of any person to bring appropriate proceedings against the government of India or the government of a State.

(2) No criminal proceedings whatsoever shall be instituted or continued against the president, or the governor of a State, in any court during his term of office.

(3) No process for the arrest or imprisonment of the president, or the governor of a State, shall issue from any court during his term of office.

(4) No civil proceedings in which relief is claimed against the president, or the governor of a State, shall be instituted during his term of office in any court in respect of any act done or purporting to be done by him in his personal capacity, whether before or after he entered upon his office as president, or as governor of such State, until the expiration of two months next after notice in writing has been delivered to the president or the governor, as the case may be, or left at his office stating the nature of the proceedings, the cause of action therefore, the name, description and place of residence of the party by whom such proceedings are to be instituted and the relief which he claims.

[On 23 April the Court declined to consider its implications in view of the changed circumstances.]

Note, that while Clause (4) does permit recovery of money for a private civil wrong, Clause (2) bars all proceedings for any crime against society. Clause (1) is based on the rule of British constitutional law that the crown can do no wrong with its corollary that for every act of the crown the government is responsible. The second proviso to Clause (1) embodies that corollary.

Clause (2) was drafted in a mindless imitation of the British model. In Britain the courts are the crown's courts and the monarch cannot be punished in courts established by her or him. That is why Dicey was of the view that 'if (to give an absurd example) the queen were herself to shoot the premier through the head, no court in England could take cognizance of the act'. True, the bar, under Clause (2), is not perpetual but 'during his term in office'. It is, nonetheless, offensive to the very concept of a republican democracy.

In India, all—the president, governors, and the courts—are creatures of the Constitution and derive their authority from that very single source.

When the provision was very briefly discussed in the constituent assembly on 8 September 1949, Mr H.V. Kamath voiced his doubts and hoped that Dr Ambedkar or T.T. Krishnamachari would 'clarify the content of Clause (2)'. Neither cared to do that.[18]

The question he raised was whether the head of state 'has no liability for any criminal act committed by him during his term of office'. Relatedly, 'whether as soon as a prima facie case is made against him, the president should resign his office'.

On one point there can be no doubt. *If Clause (2) did not exist originally and was ought to be inserted by constitutional amendment, it would be struck down by the Supreme Court as violative of the basic structure of the Constitution.* Clause (4) of Article 329A, inserted by the 39th Amendment to nullify the Allahabad judgment and to oust the Supreme Court's jurisdiction to try India Gandhi's election case on the merits was struck down by the court as the rule of law and equality before the law are integral parts of the basic structure of the Constitution.

That is why Indira Gandhi dropped the 40th Amendment Bill, gazetted on 9 August 1975, to confer on the president, the prime minister, and governors complete immunity from criminal proceedings for 'any act done by him, whether before he entered upon his office or during his term of office'.

Mrs Kaul's case has served to establish that Clause (2) prevents prosecution, not interrogation. The president's permission is of course not necessary for that. However, if the investigations before, during, or after the interrogation establish a prima facie case of crime, the president would be perfectly justified in administering to the governor, or for that matter a union minister, the order of dismissal.

---

[18]CAD, vol. ix, p. 1121.

6

British Conventions and the Indian Constitution[1]

The fact that our Constitution, with its 395 articles and nine schedules, is one of the most elaborate in the world does not imply that it does not have in addition tacit provisions. It is based on the recognized conventions of a parliamentary form of government which it establishes both at the Centre and in the States.

For quite a long time some people, politicians and others, professed not to see anything but the written word, and rejected the conventions altogether. This was particularly done with regard to the president's powers which laid bare the political motivation underlying the arid intellectual exercise. It is however grossly improper to tinker with the Constitution and distort its meaning in order to achieve personal political objectives.

Fortunately, the Supreme Court has delivered a judgement, on 17 March 1971, which gives a quietus to these efforts by recognizing the force and relevance of the essential constitutional conventions concerning parliamentary government.[2]

A petition had been filed in the Madras high court for a writ of *quo warranto* against the prime minister, Mrs Indira Gandhi, and for a declaration that she had no constitutional authority to hold the office of prime minister of India. The reason was that Article 75 (3) of the Constitution laid down that 'the council of ministers shall be collectively responsible to the house of the people,' and how could it be so responsible after the house has been dissolved? The alternative

---

[1] *The Indian Express,* 4 May 1971.
[2] *U.N. Rao v Indira Gandhi,* AIR 1971 SC 1002.

was for the President to exercise executive power directly or through officers subordinate to him.

The Madras high court was not impressed by these arguments and rejected the petition. The petitioner appealed to the Supreme Court and lost again, but the Supreme Court has made some pertinent observations on constitutional interpretation and has very clearly given legal recognition to constitutional conventions concerning the parliamentary system of government.

Its observations are very clear:

It was said that we must interpret Article 75(3) according to its own terms regardless of the convention that prevail in the United Kingdom. If the words of an article are clear, notwithstanding any relevant convention, effect will no doubt be given to the words. But it must be remembered that we are interpreting a Constitution and not an Act of parliament, a Constitution which establishes a parliamentary system of government with a cabinet. In trying to understand one may well keep in mind the conventions prevalent at the time the Constitution was framed.

In plain words, the court recognized that the provisions of our Constitution are based on certain British conventions regarding the cabinet and that to ignore the latter would be to misinterpret the former.

As Mr Granville Austin has recalled in his work *The Indian Constitution*, early in the day the framers of the Constitution had to face this question: 'Should the well-known conventions of cabinet government, as practised in England be included in the Constitution in the form of written provisions, or could India rely on the honesty of her leaders and their grounding in the traditional behaviour demanded by the parliamentary system to protect the democratic working of her political institutions?'[3] The Constitution-framers chose the latter course and the Supreme Court has given effect to their intention. At one stage they had decided to codify some of the conventions in the form of an instrument of instructions but later changed their mind.

It may be mentioned that as early as 1955 the Supreme Court had held that:

Under Article 53(I) of our Constitution, the executive power of the union is vested in the president but under Article 75 there is to be a council of

---

[3]Granville Austin, *The Indian Constitution: Cornerstone of a Nation*, Delhi: Oxford University Press, 1966, p. 132.

ministers with the prime minister at the head to aid and advice the president in the exercise of his functions. The president has thus been made a formal or constitutional head of the executive and the real executive powers are vested in the ministers or the cabinet. The same provisions obtain in regard to the government of States; the governor or the *rajpramukh*, as the case may be, occupies the position of the head of the executive in the State but it is virtually the council of ministers in each State that carries on the executive government. In the Indian Constitution, therefore, we have the same system of parliamentary executive, as in England and the council of ministers consisting, as it does, of the members of the legislature is, like the British cabinet, 'a hyphen which joins a buckle which fastens the legislative part of a State to the executive part.[4]

The existence of a council of ministers to aid and advise the president is mandatory. The president cannot act except on its advice. Rejecting the appellant's contention that after the dissolution of the Lok Sabha the council of ministers should go and the president should govern directly, the Supreme Court said: 'The constituent assembly did not choose the presidential system of government. If we were to give effect to this contention of the appellant we would be changing the whole concept of the executive. It would mean that the president need not have a prime minister and ministers to aid and advise him in the exercise of his functions. As there would be no council of ministers, nobody would be responsible to the house of the people. With the aid of advisers he would be able to rule the country at least until he was impeached under Article 61.'

This is enough to demonstrate how nonsensical are the proposals for president's rule at the Centre which some people in the country made in 1970.

The judgment however opens up a new vista. Since the court takes cognizance of conventions of parliamentary government, will a judicial remedy be available after all in those areas where the governor has flouted them at the Centre's instance?

---

[4]*Ram Jawaya Kapur* v *The State of Punjab AIR* 1955 SC 549.

7

Codifying the Conventions[1]

Somewhere along the line in 1949, the framers of India's Constitution lost patience. They rashly rushed the proceedings. On one aspect crucial to the success of parliamentary democracy, they let the nation down; namely, a code of conventions to guide the president and the governors in the exercise of their constitutional powers. It was contemplated at every stage but was abandoned in the final moments. Governors have felt themselves free to act as the Centre directs them. Presidents have been capricious; witness Mr N. Sanjiva Reddy in 1979 and Mr R. Venkataraman in October 1990, and March 1991.

As early as 17 July 1947, Sardar Patel told the constituent assembly that 'a Schedule according [sic] to the traditions of responsible government will be framed and put in'. Members demanded that the Schedule be put in first before the Clause, conferring power on governors, was adopted. Patel angrily retorted: 'It has been suggested that there is no guarantee that the schedule will come. There is as much guarantee about it as a guarantee that the house will meet tomorrow'.[2]

Events justified their scepticism. Patel was unable to keep his promise despite his explicit assurance that 'the Schedule must contain the specific duties that he has to perform. Therefore, what the conventions are should be specified fully and in detail'. In short, the conventions of the parliamentary system would be fully codified because codification, admittedly, was both possible and desirable.

In October 1948 the assembly's drafting committee decided that

[1] *The Statesman*, 24 March 1994.
[2] CAD, vol. iv pp. 648–9.

'It would be desirable to append to the Constitution an Instrument of Instructions for the president just as there is one for the governors'[3] Accordingly, a draft Schedule III-A was prepared. As late as on 23 May 1949, its chairman, Dr B.R. Ambedkar, told the assembly in effect, in response to a query by its president, Dr Rajendra Prasad, that the instrument would be there.[4]

However, on 11 October 1949, a little over a month before the Constitution was adopted, another member of the drafting committee, Mr T.T. Krishnamachari, announced that the draft Schedule III-A was being dropped. 'It has now been felt that the matter should be left entirely to convention rather than be put into the body of the constitution.'[5]

This was begging the question. The issue was codification of conventions. T.T. Krishnamachari's arguments were spurious and time has exposed the falsity of his argument that codification was 'unnecessary and superfluous' and that the directions to the president and the governors 'really should arise out of conventions that grow up from time to time, and the president and the governors or their respective spheres will be guided by those conventions'. In plain words, conventions would be developed in the future. The results are there for all to see.

Contrast that sophistry with the sagacity of these words:

... It is in the public interest that there be a higher level of awareness about the Constitution, and this awareness would be enhanced if the Constitution provided a more accurate description of the way we are governed. Is it appropriate, in a democracy, for fundamental elements in that democracy to be left in an uncertain form understandable only (and then imperfectly) by those trained in law and political science? Leaving aside the educational argument, the best argument for codification is that *the powers of the head of state and the government of the day should be carefully defined in the interests of avoiding unnecessary uncertainty, if not chaos, in times of constitutional crisis, and to offer clear guidance to the head of state so that the office is not unfairly accused of political partiality.* [Emphasis Mine]

[3]B. Shiva Rao (ed), *The Framing of India's Constitution: Select Documents.* (New Delhi : Indian Institute of Public Administration, 1968) vol. iv, pp. 67–8.

[4]CAD, vol. viii, pp. 215–6, See Justice M.M. Ismail, *The President and the Governors in the Indian Constitution* (New Delhi : Orient Longman, 1972) an outstandingly able work.

[5]CAD, vol. x, pp. 114–6.

These words occur in the report of the Republic Advisory Committee set up by the Prime Minister of Australia, Mr Paul Keating, on 28 April 1993. Entitled 'An Australian Republic:The Options', the report contains a wealth of material and rich insights on the working of the parliamentary system that are of profound relevance to us.[6]

The committee was asked to propare 'an options paper which describes the minimum constitutional changes necessary to achieve a viable Federal Republic of Australia, maintaining the effect of our current conventions and principles of government'. Neither the structure of government nor the federal character was part of the remit. However, if the crown's representative, the governor-general, was to be replaced by an elected head of state, while 'maintaining the existing conventions, the question had to be faced whether it was not desirable to codify them.

Codification

Constitutional renewal has been afoot in Australia since 1973 when the first Australian convention met in Sydney.The governor-general's dismissal of the Labour Prime Minister, Mr Gough Whitlam, hastened the process. The convention met in Melbourne, (1975), Hobart (1976), Perth (1978), Adelaide (1983), and Brisbane (1985).

A Constitution commission was also set up. It submitted its final report in June 1988. Its advisory committees, especially the one on executive government, produced weighty reports. All in all, the reports of the conventions, the commission, and its advisory committees provide a feast for Indians concerned with constitutional renewal. Capping them is the report of the Republic Advisory Committee. It speaks for the work culture and work ethic there that the deadline of 1 September 1993 was extended only by a month.

Unlike our Sarkaria commission on Centre–State relations, representatives of the States were also appointed. It also speaks for the sincerity of the members that while the report is thorough and draws on constitutional learning, which it shares with the reader, its style of expression is lucid and free from the pompous verbosity and ostentatious quotation that mark legal pronouncements and debate in India. To Indians, what is of greatest relevance is the dis-

[6]An Australian Republic; The options; vol. I, The Report of the Republic Advisory Committee Commonwealth Government Press; Colombia; p. 98.

cussion on 'the reserve powers' of the head of state in a parliamentary system, especially in regard to three topics : the appointment of the prime minister, his dismissal, and the dissolution of the lower house of parliament. On all these there is ample material to enable codification to great advantage.

The report is scrupulously fair as an 'options paper' for public debate. 'It sets out both sides of the question but does not conceal its own preference. Dr Herbert Evatt, an eminent jurist and once Australia's foreign minister, favoured codifying the reserve powers in positive law as 'definite constitutional rules, enforceable, if necessary, by the ordinary courts of law'. He was not the only one to knock the myth of non-justiciability of conventions for a six. Sir Ivor Jennings had noted that 'the major principles are firmly fixed and can be stated with almost as much accuracy as the major principles of the common law. . . They are rules whose nature does not differ fundamentally from that of the positive law of England'.[7] In 1982 the Canadian Supreme Court has described them, sometimes commented upon them, and given them such precision as is derived from the written form of judgment'.[8]

The report sets out admirably worded draft texts to draw upon. One might differ on their content or on the formulations, but the exercise compels high praise. For instance, on the dismissal of the prime minister: 'If the head of state believes that the government of the Commonwealth is contravening a fundamental provision of this Constitution or is not complying with an order of a court ...'[9] The formulation in S.A. de Smith's classic on *Constitutional Law* is: 'purporting to subvert the democratic basis of the Constitution'.[10] The concept is identical. The existence of the power is not in doubt nor the desirability of its codification along with the other 'reserve powers' of the Constitution.

The time has come to rectify the grave error committed in 1949 with baleful consequences, for it is precisely on these discretionary 'reserve powers' that the polity is torn apart.

[7]Ivor Jennings, *The Law and the Constitution*, (London : University of London Press, (ELBS) 5th edn, 1973), p. 72.

[8]Re: Amendment of the Constitution of Canada, 125, D.L.R. (3d) 1 cited with approval in *SC Advocates-on-Record Association v Union of India* (1993), 4 SCC 441 at p. 646, para 352.

[9]Report, p. 104.

[10]De Smith, op. cit, p. 127.

8

The President and Ordinances[1]

O ne never put it beyond the Narasimha Rao government to seek the president's signature to two palpably politically motivated ordinances, namely, one for shortening the period of poll campaigns from three weeks to two and the other to extend reservations to Dalit Christians, now that parliament is no longer in session. One had however every reason to be confident that Dr Shankar Dayal Sharma would refuse to sign the ordinances opposed by every party in the Opposition and whose patent violation of the Constitution could have only invited a stern verdict from the Supreme Court. In a historic decision on 19 March 1996 the president did just that. This is a landmark decision for the rule of law and the authority of the president in a parliamentary democracy.

It must be realized that the president's and the governors' power to make laws is itself an anachronism. No such power is conferred by any other democratic Constitution, exposing the arguments of its defenders as spurious. If a tax is invalidated by the courts, the remedy is to summon parliament while declaring a clear intention to cure the defect in the tax law for all to know.

Countries of the territorial dimensions of Canada and Australia know of no such power. Dr B.R. Ambedkar was able to persuade the constituent assembly to accept the provision by claiming that a yet more drastic power that the governor-general enjoyed, of making ordinances *without* the requirement of legislative ratification, had been dropped, namely, Section 43 of the Government of India Act, 1935.

[1] *The Statesman* 21 March 1996.

Article 123 of the Constitution empowering the president to promulgate ordinances, and Article 213 which so empowers governors, are modelled on Section 42 of the Act of 1935. Like the provision of preventive detention (Article 22), we have to live with them until our democratic fibre becomes strong enough to prompt us to repeal them. While we are stuck with them, however, such safeguards as they provide must not be whittled down.

Article 123 (1) stipulates two principal conditions: 'If at any time, except when both houses of parliament are in session, the president is satisfied that circumstances exist which render it necessary for him to take immediate action he may promulgate such ordinances as the circumstances appear to him to require.' Recess of parliament is one condition. The other is as obvious. It is the honest belief on the part of the president, that is, the government of India, that circumstances had arisen *after* parliament went into recess, 'which render it necessary for him to take immediate action'.

No president who is asked to sign an ordinance can ignore this limitation, nor can a court of law. In the nearly half a century since the Constitution was drafted the doctrine of a subjective satisfaction immune to judicial review has been buried beyond recall in the law reports. Dicta of Dr Ambedkar and of the Supreme Court provide ample guidance and *warning* to the president. On 23 May 1949, Dr Ambedkar provided an authoritative exposition of the provision: 'It is not difficult to imagine cases where the powers conferred by the ordinary law at any particular moment may be deficient to deal with a situation which may *suddenly and immediately* arise.... The *emergency* must be dealt with ...' [emphasis mine, throughout).[2]

Twenty years later, in the banks nationalization case, the Supreme Court drew attention to the limitations. Justice J.C. Shah noted that 'exercise of the power is strictly conditioned' and pointedly remarked: 'Determination by the president of the existence of circumstances and the necessity to take immediate action on which the satisfaction depends, is not declared final'[3] The 38th Amendment to the Constitution, enacted during the Emergency, sought to do just that; namely, make the president's satisfaction 'final and conclusive'. It was repealed by the 44th Amendment in 1979.

In the bearer bonds case, in 1981, the Supreme Court referred

[2]CAD, vol. viii, p. 214.
[3]R.C. *Cooper v Union of India* (1970), 1 SCC 248 at p. 276.

to ordinances as 'emergent legislation' to deal with an 'emergent situation'. Justice P.N. Bhagwati said that the power is 'hedged in by limitations and conditions'[4] That very year, the Supreme Court, while pronouncing on the validity of the National Security ordinance, 1980, re-enacted as an Act of parliament, recalled Dr Ambedkar's exposition in the constituent assembly. Chief Justice Y.V. Chandrachud said: 'That power was to be used to meet *extraordinary* situations and not perverted to serve political ends. The constituent assembly held forth, as it were, an assurance to the people that an extraordinary power shall not be used in order to perpetuate [sic] a fraud on the Constitution ... That assurance must in all events be made good and the balance struck by the founding fathers between the powers of the government and the liberties of the people not disturbed or destroyed.'[5]

That assurance has been systematically violated largely because of the court's own hesitation in pronouncing upon the validity of an ordinance simply because it had been re-enacted by parliament, a logic the late H.M. Seervai sharply criticized. Also, since it could decide the case on other issues, it did not go into the validity of the ordinance.

What is termed judicial activism today is a recompense for judicial passivity in earlier days. We have, however, an equally authoritative exposition of constitutional practice from a former President, Mr N. Sanjiva Reddy. Chapter 7 of his memoirs *Without Fear or Favour*, records his refusal to sign an ordinance proposed by Charan Singh to provide 'financial help from the public exchequer to candidates seeking election' as also a proposal for 'reservation of jobs for backward classes', besides new judicial appointments and 'a long-term contract of a commercial nature with a foreign party'.[6]

The fact that the Lok Sabha had been dissolved is a formal distinction. In all but name, the present Lok Sabha has breathed its last to no one's regret. Dr Shankar Dayal Sharma had ample ground to resist Mr P.V. Narasimha Rao's ploys. One must hope that in future presidential scrutiny will extend to all ordinances, pre-poll or other.

---

[4]*R.K. Garg v Union of India* (1981), 4 SCC 675 at pp. 686–7, (The Bearer Bonds Case).
[5]*A.K. Roy v Union of India* (1982), 1 SCC 271 at p. 292.
[6]*Charan Singh and Caretaker Government*, Ch. 7, Allied, 1989, pp. 44–6.

9

The President's Powers and
the Hawala Case[1]

'C ommonwealth statesmen would do well to reflect that a republican form of government, in which the executive assumes independence of the trusteeship of the Crown, leads straight along the path to Tea Pot Dome, Watergate or Mulder and the Sanjay motor factory ...' Lord Hailsham was, of course, uttering sheer nonsense when he wrote this in 1979. A republic that adopts the parliamentary system can well endow its president with the reserve powers that belong to the crown in Britain. India has done precisely that.[2]

Two Conditions

Article 75(2) of the Constitution says: 'The ministers shall hold office during the pleasure of the president'. An authoritative exposition of its import was provided by Dr B.R. Ambedkar in his speech to the constituent assembly on 31 December 1948. (Article 75(2) of the Constitution was Article 62(2) in the draft Constitution). He said:

That means that a minister will be liable to removal on two grounds. One ground on which he would be liable to dismissal under the provisions contained in Clause (2) of Article 62 would be that he has lost the confidence of the house, and secondly, *that his administration is not pure, because* the word

[1] *The Statesman*, 11 and 12 March 1996.
[2] John Kerr, *Matters for Judgment*, Foreword by Lord Hailsham, Macmillan, 1979, p. xvii.

used here is pleasure. *It would be perfectly open, under that particular clause of Article 62, for the president to call for the removal of a particular minister on the ground that he is guilty of corruption or bribery or maladministration, although that particular minister probably is a person who enjoyed the confidence of the house.* I think [the] honourable member will realize that the tenure of a minister must be subject not merely to one condition but to two conditions and the two conditions are *purity of administration* and confidence of the house. The article makes provision for both. [Emphasis mine, throughout].[3]

Needless to add, the word 'ministers' in Article 75(2) embraces the prime minister. Of course, in a parliamentary democracy the undoubted power of the head of state to dismiss the prime minister or any other minister, recognized by all modern authorities on the British constitution, can be exercised only in exceptional circumstances carefully defined by the authorities. In 1987 some carpetbaggers and charlatans pressed President Zail Singh to sack Rajiv Gandhi from the office of the prime minister on evidence of culpability in the Bofors scandal, which then was far from possessing even strong probative force against him (it acquired that quality after mid-1988). There was of course reasonable suspicion; but no more than that in mid-1987.

The clue lies in the word 'guilty' which Dr Ambedkar used. It does not require conviction by court. It does imply, however, existence either of proof beyond reasonable doubt or, at the very least, of so strong a probative value as to require a credible and independent inquiry such as would be possible only after termination of his tenancy of office and official residential premises. No president will exercise that power unless there is a national, not partisan, clamour for removal. He must have national support, and not act on personal or partisan considerations.

The President is not however powerless in the circumstances. He has every right to know the full facts of a scandal that is rocking the nation and to demand pertinent information from the prime minister. Article 78 guarantees this right. It says that 'it shall be the duty of the prime minister... (b) to furnish *such information* relating to the administration of the affairs of the Union... *as the president may call for* ...' This clearly makes the president's demand mandatory. A 'duty' is cast on the prime minister; a corresponding right accrues to the president.

[3]CAD, vol. 7, pp. 1185–6.

In 1987, public discussion was concentrated on the possibility of Rajiv Gandhi's dismissal; a matter of legitimate anxiety. Unfortunately, another aspect, on which the president was absolutely right, was neglected. It concerned his right to know the facts of the Bofors and HDW scandals from the prime minister.

On 8 April 1987, the president and the prime minister decided to ask the cabinet secretary, Mr B.G. Deshmukh, and the secretary to the president, Mr S. Varadan, to discuss the constitutional issues. Exactly a week later, on 15 April the talks were scuttled when Mr P. Chidambaram, the minister of state for home, asserted a claim that no prime minister in any parliamentary democracy had ever made.

He said: 'The president calls for information, the prime minister gives the information. The president asks for advice, the prime minister gives him such advice. *The prime minister is also entitled to advise about the nature of information, about the consequences of information, about what information should be available at what time. It is subject to the advice of the prime minister*' [emphasis mine].

In short, if the prime minister advises the president that 'this is the information that is sufficient ... the president is bound by that advice'. Article 78 admits of no such qualification. Mr Chidambaram's assertion was wholly false and ruinous to our parliamentary system.

Every clause of Article 78 can be traced to the British model which the founding fathers adopted while constructing the structure of our parliamentary democracy. All authorities are agreed on the documents which the British crown is entitled to read: the cabinet papers, minutes, and decisions, foreign office despatches and telegrams, and 'other state papers'. As Jennings puts it, 'most papers, other than those relating to purely party matters, which go to the prime minister, go to her [the queen]'.

When on one occasion in 1912 the prime minister was remiss he received the following rebuke from the king: 'I quite appreciate all your difficulties and sympathize with you accordingly, but I do look to my prime minister for that confidence which will ensure his keeping me fully informed on all matters, especially those which affect questions of such grave importance to the state and indeed to the Constitution.' During the Second World War 'the king received all the important documents sent to the prime minister as minister of defence'.

The clearest statement of the rule comes from the magisterial authority of Sir Arthur Berriedale Keith, a great authority on constitutional law, a Sanskrit scholar, and a friend of India whom the founding fathers greatly respected. He wrote: 'The one clear rule is the sovereign is entitled to the fullest information in any sphere in which he has indicated desire to be kept informed and must be given it on any issue which comes before him. The rule does not help effectively so as to prevent disputes arising as to failure to inform, but it precludes refusal to supply when asked for'.[4]

What the prime minister initially sends to the president is, naturally, for him to decide. However, once the president asks for information under Article 78(b) the rule 'precludes refusal to supply when asked for'.

In Samsher Singh's case, Justice V.R. Krishna Iyer, while ruling that the president and the governor must act on the advice of their ministers, held: 'Article 78, wisely used, keeps the president in close touch with the prime minister on matters of national importance and policy significance and there is no doubt that the imprint of his personality may chasten and correct the political government ...' How can this be possible if the information he receives is determined by the very prime minister whom it is his function and duty to 'chasten and correct'? Indeed, how can the president exercise his vigil on what Dr Ambedkar called the 'purity of the administration' if the prime minister is permitted to withhold information on scams and scandals at will? Incidentally, Rajiv Gandhi himself cited this 'celebrated' case in his correspondence with the president.

Giani Zail Singh's last letter to the prime minister in the correspondence they had exchanged since March 1987 was published on 30 May. Rajiv Gandhi had recalled the legal opinion given to Jawaharlal Nehru by the attorney-general, Mr M.C. Setalvad, and Sir Alladi Krishnaswamy Aiyar on the contentions raised by President Rajendra Prasad. Unfortunately, the president had made certain claims to power which were wholly untenable. This prejudiced many even on his valid points. The Giani, however, quoted with telling effect a note on the President's powers, dated 6 October 1950, by Mr Setalvad in response to the President's note of 21 March 1950. Mr Setalvad said:

[4]A. Berriedale Keith, *The King and the Imperial Crown: The Powers and Duties of His Majesty*, London: Longmans, Green & Co., 1936, p. 249.

The president, it appears to me, would have no independent authority to deal with the comptroller and auditor-general. If the president has reasons to believe that 'there is something wrong in which the Ministry is concerned' or that 'the comptroller and auditor-general has been for some reason or the other unable or unwilling to keep a proper check and audit and that his inability, unwillingness or inactivity' suits the ministry, the president is *entitled*, acting under Article 78, to call upon the prime minister to furnish to him all necessary information in regard to these matters.'

He added

As to the question of the president having access to the secretaries of the various departments apart from the independently from the ministries. I do not think that the Constitution contemplates such a course. Article 78 in the case of the president and Article 167 in the case of the governors provide machinery by which the president and the governor have respectively to be furnished information as to the affairs of the Union or the State as the case may be. The Constitution seems to contemplate the prime minister as representing the council of ministers being the point of contact between the president on the one hand and the council of ministers on the other. This provision, in my view, necessarily results in the inference that it would not be open to the president to have direct access to the various departments under the control of each of the ministers. It may be that in order to ensure the efficient supply of information to the president as contemplated by the Constitution, the prime minister or the other ministers may arrange for information to be supplied to the president direct by the secretaries of the department and may also arrange for the president interviewing those secretaries from time to time as he may require.'[5]

Three points emerge clearly from Mr Setalvad's opinion. One is that Article 78 is absolute. The president's right to know is not dependent upon the prime minister's advice. Secondly, it was based on the tacit assumption that the prime minister himself was not so involved in the matter on which information was sought as to have a motive for its suppression or distortion. Lastly, there was nothing intrinsically wrong in civil servants meeting the president.

In the 45 years that have elapsed since Mr Setalvad set out his view, presidents and governors have freely summoned civil servants to provide information, as have chief election commissioners and

[5]K.M. Munshi, *Indian Constitutional Documents*, 1967, vol. 1, p. 574 (*see* ft 3 to I.5).

even army chiefs. Once, Dr Rajendra Prasad, alarmed at press reports about military preparations in Pakistan, summoned not only Defence Minister Baldev Singh but also 'Generals Kulwant Singh, Carriappa and Thorat ... I wanted to know what information the defence ministry had and what preparations were being made to meet the eventuality ... We talked for a long time ...'

Surely, far greater is the latitude which the president enjoys with regard to the Central Bureau of Investigation (CBI) which is a creature of a statute, and particularly since: (a) it is under the direct control of the very prime minister whose conduct it is supposed to investigate, and (b) the CBI has established a proven record of gross and persistent dereliction of duty in sensitive matters.

There is reason enough to believe that the prime minister has not been overly diligent in the discharge of his duties towards the president in the *hawala* scam. Mr P.V. Narasimha Rao met Dr Shankar Dayal Sharma a full two weeks after the matter emerged in the open in the Supreme Court.

There is another factor that fortifies the president's rights. It is now proved beyond a shadow of doubt that the Rao government survived the vote of no-confidence in the Lok Sabha on 28 July 1993 through sheer bribery and, further, that proof of this tends to corroborate the statement of Mr S.K. Jain to the police on 11 March 1995. The vote was 265 to 251. Eight votes less and the government would have fallen. (Interestingly on that day, 28 July 1993, our prime minister promised electoral reforms and the Lok Pal).

For over two years, this government has ruled without moral authority and continues still to do so. The president would be perfectly within his rights in summoning not only the CBI director but also the investigating officers to report to him continuously on the progress in the *hawala* as well as the Chandraswami cases. His interest will raise the morale of the officers and will also infuse some confidence in a nation that is disgusted at the sordid ways of some of our leading politicians, in and out of power.

10
Options in a Hung Lok Sabha

By all tests, Dr Shankar Dayal Sharma has performed commendably in the high office of president of India. His gravest test will however come only in the second week of May 1986, when a hung Lok Sabha emerges from the general election. Barring the leaders themselves, all are agreed that no single party is likely to win a majority in the house. What are the rules that the president should follow in such a situation?

Article 75 (I) of the Constitution says that 'the prime minister shall be appointed by the president ...' Clause (3) adds: 'The council of ministers shall be collectively responsible to the house of the people'. Ergo, the prime minister must command a majority in the house at the time of the vote of confidence. However, in an uncertain situation, how is the president to determine initially which of the party leaders will make good his claim to majority support?

Until they dropped it in the final stages of the proceedings of the constituent assembly, on 11 October 1949, the framers of the Constitution had proposed instruments of instructions to guide the president and the governors. Para 2 of the instructions to the president enjoined him 'to appoint a person who has been found by him most *likely* to command a stable majority in parliament as the prime minister'[1] (emphasis added). This is of little help except in that it explicitly permits the president to act, as he must, on probabilities.

A mistaken assessment will invite charges of partisanship. Moreover, the politician first commissioned to form a government is enabled to lure support.

---

[1] *See* B. Shiva Rao, *The Framing of India's Constitution*, vol. iv pp. 84–6 for the text of the draft Instrument of Instructions to the president. It can still be inserted in the Constitution with suitable changes.

Debates in the constituent assembly are instructive. On 30 December 1948, Dr B.R. Ambedkar said, 'Under a parliamentary system of government, there are only two prerogatives which the king or the head of the state may exercise. One is the appointment of the prime minister and the other is the dissolution of parliament. With regard to the prime minister it is not possible to avoid vesting the discretion in the president.'

Mohammed Tahir asked: 'On a point of order, how will it explain the position of the governors and the ministers of the State where discretionary powers have been allowed to be used by the governors?' Ambedkar replied: 'The position of the governor is exactly the same as the position of the president.'[2] Three propositions emerge clearly. The president enjoys discretion, as do the governors, and their position 'is exactly the same' as heads of state in a parliamentary system.

The rules of the parliamentary system apply to them *equally*. Those concerning the governor are no more an aspect of Centre–State relations than those that bind the president. To anticipate, the Sarkaria commission on Centre–State relations went presumptuously beyond its remit in laying down the rules for governors on this point (nor had any of its three members either the qualification or equipment to codify this complex topic of constitutional law, and had been appointed without any consultation with the Opposition and were ardent centrists).

Ambedkar was quite alive to the possibility of a multi-party system working our Constitution. When a member suggested that ministers must belong to the majority party, he said, on 31 December 1948, that 'it would be perfectly possible and natural that in an election, parliament may consist of various numbers of parties, none of which is in a majority. How is this principle to be invoked and put into operation in a situation of this sort where there are three parties, none of which has a majority?'[3] The impression that the Constitution envisaged a two-party system is false.

Its first test came in 1967 when the Congress lost a majority in several States. The question was raised in the Lok Sabha on 5 April 1967 a propos the Rajasthan ministry. The union home minister, Y.B. Chavan, promised to seek legal opinion. In a letter dated 17

[2]CAD, vol. vii, p. 1158.
[3]CAD, vol. vii, p. 1186.

May 1967 to three former chief justices of India, Justices M.C. Mahajan, A.K. Sarkar and P.B. Gajendragadkar, former attorney general M.C. Setalvad, and the then advocate-general of Maharashtra, H.M. Seervai, he posed these queries:

Three distinct views have been expressed on this matter. One view has been that the leader of the largest party in the legislature should be invited to form the government irrespective of the consideration whether or not such a party commands a stable majority.

Supporters of this view have also suggested that the governor should use his influence to secure advice to summon the newly elected legislature as early as may be possible so that the extent of the support to the ministry may be tested in an open constitutional forum.

The second view has been that if the party in power had failed to secure an absolute majority in the newly elected legislature, the leader of that party should not be invited to form the government even if it were the largest single party in the legislature and that, instead, the leader of the Opposition or the leader of the next largest party should be invited to form the government. The reasoning behind this view is that the electoral verdict should be regarded as, in effect, disqualifying the party in power for holding office for a further term.

The third view is that the governor should make the endeavours to appoint a person who has been found by him, as a result of his soundings, to be most likely to command a stable majority in the legislature.[4]

Only Setalvad and Seervai cited authorities. The others gave *ipse dixit* of little value.

Setalvad, Seervai, and Mahajan plumped for the second course. There was no endorsement of the first course and complete agreement on the third; an obvious counsel but of little practical value. It simply begs the question. Incidentally, Mahajan on 18 June 1967, gave the opinion that 'the powers of the governor ... in the appointment of the chief minister are the same as the president has in the appointment of the prime minister'.

The governor is 'not bound to invite the leader of the largest party or the leader of the Opposition'. Also, 'if a political party in power has failed to obtain an absolute majority, the governor should respect the manadate of the people and call upon the leader of the

---

[4] The Union Home Minister's letter and the opinions given by the five jurists have not been published in book form. I am indebted to a dear friend, the late T.C.A. Srinivasavaradan, then Joint Secretary, Union Ministry of Home Affairs, for furnishing me with copies of these documents in cyclostyled form.

Opposition to form the government, provided the Opposition or a coalition of the Opposition parties are in such numbers as to be able to form a stable government'.

A.K. Sarkar, then busy in the committee of inquiry on steel 'transactions', gave a scrappy opinion against both the first and the second courses mentioned by Chavan and ended with the safe counsel of the third. P.B. Gajendragadkar was no more illuminating. The third view was correct, he said, rejecting the first two.

By far the best opinion was penned by the former attorney-general, Setalvad, on 15 June 1967 (obviously, the stay at St. Patricks in Ooty, where the opinion was written, helped). It quoted copiously from recognized authorities. One in particular from Ivor Jennings[5] is very relevant.

It is expected that when a government is defeated either in parliament or at the polls, the queen should send for the leader of the Opposition. There may be two or more parties in Opposition. But the practice of the present century has created an 'official' Opposition whose leader is 'the leader of the Opposition'...The largest party in Opposition is the 'official' Opposition. The rule is that on the defeat and resignation of the government, the queen should first send for the leader of the Opposition. This rule is the result of long practice, though it has hardened into a rule comparatively recently. Its basis is the assumption of the impartiality of the crown. Democratic government involves competing policies and thus the rivalry of parties ...

The queen's task is only to secure a government, not to try to form a government which is likely to forward the policy of which she approves. To do so would be to engage in party politics. It is, moreover, essential to the belief in the monarch's impartiality not only that she should act impartially, but she should appear to act impartially. The only method by which this can be demonstrated normally is to send at once for the leader of the Opposition ...

Jennings proceeded to add that 'this rule has for its corollary the rule that before sending for the leader of the Opposition the monarch should consult no one. If he takes advice first, it can only be for the purpose of keeping out the Opposition or its recognized leader.[6]

Setalvad endorsed the rule completely as one 'based on the principle that the wishes of the electorate must be respected'. *The*

[5]Ivor Jennings *Cabinet Government*, p. 32
[6]op. cit., p. 40.

rule should be followed 'even when the largest single party in the newly elected house is still the party which was the governing party before the election though it has failed to obtain an absolute majority'.

There is an obvious proviso to the rule. If the former opposition party is simply not in a position to form a government, the head of state must turn to the erstwhile party in power. Setalvad said a coalition of parties may be formed after or even before the polls.

H.M. Seervai accepted Jennings' view. If independents hold the balance, they must be consulted individually. He was unrealistic in dismissing the advantage that accrues to the party first called upon to form a government. Setalvad's was by far the more erudite and weighty opinion than that of any of the others.

The Sarkaria commission's report ignored the jurists' opinions and propounded its own rules. The governor should sound the parties 'in the order of preference indicated below: 1. an alliance of parties that was formed prior to the elections; 2. the largest single party staking a claim to form the government with the support of others, including 'independent'; 3. a post–electoral coalition of parties, with all the partners in the coalition joining the government; 4. a post–electoral alliance of parties, with some of the parties in the alliance forming a government and the remaining parties, including 'independents', supporting the government from outside.'[7]

The subject was also discussed in the report of the Committee of Governors (1971) appointed by the president 'to study and formulate norms and conventions governing the role of governors'. It decisively rejected the rigid arithmetical test of the leader of the largest single party: 'He has, however, no absolute right as leader of the largest single party or group to claim that he should be entrusted with the task of forming a government to the exclusion of all others ... a numerically smaller party may command the support of a majority in the legislature'.[8] Nor did this report cite the jurists' opinions. They have, astonishingly, by and large been ignored.

All this exposes the utter absurdity of R. Venkataraman's 'objective' test of summoning the parties in the order of their numerical strength which he propounds in his memoirs as a great contribution to constitutional practice. When V.P. Singh met him and handed over letters of support by the Left Front and the BJP,

[7]Sarkaria Report, prt 1, p., para 41.10.53.
[8]Report of the Committee of Governors, p. 29.

President Venkataraman replied that '*as the largest single party had not staked its claim to form the government, I invite you* [V.P. Singh] *as the leader of the second largest party to form the government*', not as one who, with the Left and the BJP's support, commanded a majority nor as one whom the people had preferred to Rajiv Gandhi whom they had rejected. Venkataraman himself concedes that an invitation to the latter 'would have been resented by all the people'.[9] This proves the validity of the Jennings' thesis whose logic is obviously beyond Venkataraman's grasp, for, on his own showing, he would have merrily sworn in Rajiv Gandhi had he staked a claim to form a government, mocking the people's verdict on Bofors and much else.

British precedent and the dicta of eminent authorities do not support any such arithmetical test and shed much light on the rules that President S.D. Sharma should follow.

S.A. de Smith's authoritative work *Constitutional and Administrative Law* says that when 'no party has an overall majority in the house', the queen will have to decide who has 'a reasonable prospect' of maintaining himself in office. 'That person will normally, *but not invariably*, be the leader of the largest party in the House of Commons.'[10] Professor Rodney Brazier's work cites an example of a hung house: Labour 290, Conservatives 260, the Liberal Democrats 80, and others 20. Labour's claim could be defeated if the Conservatives and the Liberal Democrats combined. The precedents of 1923, 1929, and 1974 support Labour's claim, but 'those precedents are *not* prescriptive'[11]

Britain seen saw two general elections within a year, in January and December 1910, each returning a hung parliament. In the second, the Liberals and the Conservatives won an equal number of seats (272) but the Liberals were able to form a government with the support of Labour and the Irish Nationalists. The Liberals had been in power since 1905.

The three oft-cited precedents of 1923, 1929, and 1974 are instructive, but in each case the background must be borne in mind. The general election of 6 December 1923 yielded the following result: Conservatives 258, Labour 191, Liberals 151, others 3 in a house of 615 seats.

[9] *My Presidential Years,* Harper Collins, Delhi, 1994
[10] De Smith, p. 176. see also p. 173.
[11] Brazier, p. 37.

The Conservatives, led by Stanley Baldwin, were in power and had sought dissolution only a year after the previous election. None of the major parties favoured a coalition. Baldwin wanted to resign at once but was persuaded, not least by the king himself, to stay on till parliament met *five weeks later*. Meanwhile, the king's private secretary, Lord Stamfordham, was busy taking the soundings. The Liberals and Labour combined to defeat Baldwin on the king's address by 72 votes. On 22 January 1924, six weeks after the polls, the Labour leader, Ramsay MacDonald, was sworn in as prime minister.

Some writers cite this as a precedent for the rule that a prime minister defeated in the polls need not resign at once but can await his fate at the hand of the new house, but nobody has followed this precedent since 1924. There is the magisterial authority of Jennings against it.[12] Seervai referred to it in his opinion. It is necessary to stress this because Narasimha Rao is likely to try every gimmick to cling to power even after defeat.

Another authority well known in India for his studies on elections, David Butler, has drawn on Indian precedents to demonstrate that the course that Baldwin followed would be improper. In an article in Chandra Shekhar's magazine *Young India*[13] entitled 'Ten Constitutional Questions' he phrased Question 2 thus: 'If the government is defeated at the polls, does the prime minister have to resign at once?' The answer was: 'In Britain in 1970 and 1979 the prime minister went to the queen to give up office within minutes of the Opposition winning the seat that gave it a majority. In India in 1977 Mrs Gandhi resigned a day or so after the election result became plain and so did Mr Charan Singh in 1980. If victorious prime ministers feel obliged to resign, how much stronger is the requirement for one who has been worsted at the polls.' He recalled that in 1952, 1957, 1962, 1967, 1971, and 1984 the victorious prime minister had resigned. No Indian prime minister who loses a majority at the polls has therefore a right to stay in office and demand a trial of strength in the house. Baldwin's precedent is discredited in Britain and discarded in India.

The second case of a hung parliament arose from the results of the election on 30 May 1929: Conservatives 260, Labour 288, Liberal

[12]Cabinet Government, p. 491.
[13]December, 1999.

59, others 7 in a house of 615. Baldwin resigned immediately as prime minister and MacDonald returned to power.

The third case to a degree falls somewhere between the other two. The results of the elections of 28 February 1974 were: Labour 301, Conservatives 297, Liberals 14, Scottish National 7, Plaid Cymru 3, Ulster Unionists 11, SDLP 1, others 2 in a house of 635 seats. The Conservatives polled 37.8 per cent and Labour 37.1 per cent of the popular vote. Instead of resigning at once, Prime Minister Edward Heath began parleys with the Liberal leader, Jeremy Thorpe, for a coalition. The Liberals rejected the offer and Heath resigned on 4 March. Harold Wilson formed a minority Labour government without any outside support.

The question is however whether Wilson sought and obtained from the queen an assurance of dissolution? It is beyond question that, as a defeated prime minister, Heath could not have sought a *second* dissolution, and not merely because he had tried to drum up a majority and failed.

What, however, were Wilson's rights? There is Asquith's famous dictum that the crown is not bound by advice that exposes the people 'to the tumult and turmoil of a series of general elections so long as it can find other ministers who are prepared to give it a trial'.

Rodney Brazier holds that an incumbent government that loses an election has no right to a second dissolution.[14] A minority or coalition government formed by the former Opposition, after the elections, has a strong claim to a dissolution although 'the alternative course of the queen seeking another administration should not be ruled out'. The claim to dissolution by the prime minister appointed after the polls becomes stronger 'the longer the hung parliament were to last as that parliament would have done its job for a period'.

The crucial test is the existence of a credible alternative to the government which seeks early dissolution. If such a coalition exists, the minority government should be refused dissolution. In order to avoid the embarrassment of a coalition government collapsing soon and itself seeking a dissolution which was refused to its predecessor, the head of state would be justified in insisting on 'a copper-bottomed agreement on a majority coalition' in writing which should be made public. R. Venkataraman flouted the norms in swearing in

[14]Brazier, pp. 41–7 for a full discussion.

Chandra Shekhar as prime minister in 1990 on the basis of Rajiv Gandhi's oral assurances on which he soon reneged.

Consider, in this context, another case. In 1985, elections were held to the Ontario legislative assembly after Prime Minister William Davis sought dissolution. His party, the Progressive Conservatives, won 52 seats, the Liberals 48, and the New Democrats 25 in a house of 125. Davis decided to form a minority government while the other two formally agreed on a two-year programme of government. A motion of no-confidence was passed against Davis' government and the coalition took over. Davis could not have asked for dissolution and, indeed, did not.

Two points need to be noted. First, it is perfectly legitimate for the head of state to assist the parties to form a coalition if no alternative is in sight, *without of course being partisan*. Wade and Bradley's work, *Constitutional and Administrative Law*, holds that 'the Sovereign would have to initiate discussions with and between the parties to discover....Whether a coalition government could be formed'. George V did that.

The president would therefore be justified *in extreme cases* in convening an all-party conference in Rashtrapati Bhavan to prod the parties to produce a government without himself participating in its deliberations.

Secondly, the parties must have leaders elected by themselves not ones chosen by the head of state as Macmillan was in 1963. Vernon Bogdanor has proved, though, that Home rather than Butler enjoyed their party's support. In 1965, the Conservatives drew up leadership election rules (see *The Times* (London) of 20 April 1996, for Vernon Bogdanor's letter. He is the author of *Multi-Party Politics and the Constitution*). These are instances of potential coalition partners insisting on a change of leadership of another partner. Labour refused to serve under Neville Chamberlain, Jeremy Thorpe dropped a similar hint to Edward Heath. It is very likely that the Congress's allies might make a similar demand for the replacement of scam-scarred Narasimha Rao.

Precedents apart, the three possible scenarios drawn by David Butler, in his incisive study *Governing Without A Majority*, help in formulating the guidelines. One envisages three near equals in a three-way split; another, two dominants plus smaller groups and a variant of two strong parties and a weak one requiring *more than two* parties to secure a majority. 'It is not self-evident who would form the government in any of these situations.' *It is the background preceding the dissolution and the situation after the results come in that together will provide the clues.*

Summing up

If one may sum up the rules that emerge from precedents and dicta of authorities, it is submitted that:

1. An incumbent prime minister should not be invited to form a government once his party loses its majority in an election *even if it emerges as the single largest party.*

2. The president should, in such a case, invite the next single largest party to form a government.

3. Both rules are, however, subject to the overriding proviso that any coalition that commands a majority in the house is entitled to be invited to form a government.

4. The president ought to insist on clear agreement on the coalition's leader, besides a common minimum programme plus an accord to work in coalition, both of which should be in writing and made public. There must be a written undertaking not to seek dissolution for a specified, reasonable period of time in order to avert the kind of situation that the Rajiv Gandhi–R. Venkataraman deal created in 1991.

5. No party is entitled to demand any assurances from the president that he grant a dissolution in the event of its government's collapse. Such a demand would be improper. The established rules as to grant of dissolution should prevail in all cases.

6. In *extreme* cases the president can ask the parties to hold discussions among themselves under his auspices *but without his participation.*

7. At all times a government must be in place to tender advice to the president, if need be, as a caretaker government. The government must go on. Indian democracy brooks no interruption.

11

Appointment of a Prime Minister: President Shankar Dayal Sharma's Lapse[1]

It is a great pity that Dr Shankar Dayal Sharma should have sullied, at this hour, an exemplary record in the high office of president of India, one that outshone that of all his predecessors since Dr Zakir Hussain, who breathed his last in 1969. His appointment of the BJP leader Atal Behari Vajpayee as prime minister on 15 May was most certainly not inspired by partisan motives. Secular to the core, the president courageously denounced, in public, the demolition of the Babri mosque. The decision was the product of a grossly misinformed understanding of the relevant constitutional conventions of the parliamentary system. Worse, it was executed in a manner that suggested wilfulness and lack of candour. Neither respect for the man, nor, for that matter, the egregious ineptness of the Opposition, should be allowed to obscure the fact that he has inflicted serious damage on the polity and on the office at its apex.

In retrospect, one wished Rajiv Gandhi had not acted sensibly in 1989 so that R. Venkataraman could have tried out then his 'objective' test; namely that the single largest party should be invited to form a government. That would then have exposed its spuriousness. The record casts in darker hue the invitation to the BJP, both on facts and the law.

Let us first consider the rules of constitutional law applicable to the situation before turning to the record of the events from 10 to 15 May 1996. It is trite to say that the Constitution itself provides

[1]*Frontline*, 14 June 1996.

us guidance. Anyone who reads the debates in the constituent assembly will appreciate that it was based on the conventions of the unwritten British constitution as culled from recognized authorities. British, Canadian, and Australian lawyers find little difficulty in this exercise. It is the privilege of the Indian 'jurist' to ignore the texts and voice instant opinion. British authorities cannot be ignored, however.

In at least four major cases, ending with *Samsher Singh's* case (1974), the Supreme Court has ruled that the powers of the president and governor are similar to those of 'the crown under the British parliamentary system'.[2] British conventions have been judicially noted. They form part of Indian law.

How does the single largest party test fare in the light of the authorities? *Nowhere as an inflexible rule but only as rule of thumb in order to implement a fundamental principle* which is that the ministry should enjoy the confidence of the house. It should be able to secure acceptance of the address and passage of the budget and Bills. A political party that has 120 members in a house in which 240 others are prepared to tolerate it, has better claims than one which is 140-strong but is detested by all.

The Instrument of Instructions to Governors issued under the Government of India Act. 1935 required them to appoint as prime minister of the province one who 'is most likely to command a stable majority in the legislature' and in consultation with his ministers 'who will *best* be in a position collectively to command the confidence of the legislature' (emphasis added, throughout).[3] A contest between two imperfect claims is inherent in the situation.

The framers of the Constitution drafted instructions to the president that adopted the first part ('a stable majority') but dropped the document at the last moment, leaving conventions rather than the text to govern practice. However, Article 75 (3) makes the council of ministers 'collectively responsible' to the Lok Sabha. The report of the Committee of Governors appointed by the president (1971) said, 'The relevant test is not the size of a party but its *ability* to command the support of the majority in the legislature. It may be that a party, even though leading in relative strength in a legislature, *may not be able to obtain the support of other members. In*

[2] AIR 1974, SC 2192.
[3] B. Shiva Rao, vol. iv, p. 84.

contrast, a numerically smaller party may command majority support with the help of other parties or groups' (emphasis added). The Sarkaria report (1988) says that 'the party or combination of parties which commands the *widest* support in the legislative assembly should be called upon to form the government' (Para 411.03).

The phraseology differs. The concept remains the same. Three British works on constitutional and administrative law share the same view. S.A. de Smith speaks of a ministry 'with a reasonable prospect of maintaining itself in office.[4] Wade and Bradley opr for 'that person who is in the best position to receive the support of the majority'.[5] Hood Phillips' fo:mulation is 'a ministry that can hold a majority in the house'[6] *Ordinarily* the single largest party would fit the bill and should be invited. There have however been instances where, by reason of its policies or its leadership, such a party has been *shunned* by the rest, thus rebutting the presumption of its majority support. In such cases, either the leader had to go or the party had to forego power. In 1924, the Liberals refused to have any truck with the Conservatives, the largest party. In consequence, Labour formed the government. In 1940, Labour refused to enter into a coalition with Neville Chamberlain as its head. He had to make way for Churchill.

The situation in India in 1996 is far clearer in this respect. The BJP has for well over a decade prided itself on its uniqueness: its distinctive brand of 'secularism'. Such a party should morally accept power only on its own strength. Midway through the election campaign, Vajpayee said that his party would stake claim to power only if its strength was in the region of 220 in the new Lok Sabha[7]

The BJP secured no mandate to form a government. It won 161 seats in a House of 543 (of which only 537 went to the polls), garnering 20.7 per cent of the popular vote. Allies promised another 34 seats (the Shiv Sena 15; the Akali Dal 8; the Samata Party 8, and the Haryana Vikas Party 3). The total of 195 fell short of the magic figure of 269 by as many as 74. However impressive this phalanx may have appeared to some, it marked the outer limit of what was legitimately possible.

[4]De Smith, p. 176

[5]Wade and Bradley, pp. 236–7.

[6]O. Hood Phillips, *Constitutional and Administrative Law*, ed. O. Hood Phillips and Paul Jackson, ELBS, Sweet & Maxwell, 7th edn, 1987, p. 320.

[7]Vidya Subrahmaniam, 'Election 1996', *Times of India*, 14 May 1996

'A senior BJP functionary' gave the game away on 10 May.'Once we are called upon to form the government, the attitude of newly elected MPs towards the BJP might change and they may be willing to be 'partners', he told Anil Saxena of the *Times of India* (11 May). Also, none of them, he added, would be interested in another round of early elections.

That very day, 10 May, Vajpayee paid a 'courtesy call' to the president. The following day L.K. Advani and party colleagues formally staked a claim to form the government. The report of this meeting in the *Hindustan Times* (12 May) made curious reading. Dr Sharma 'asked the BJP leaders as to how much time they would require to 'prove their majority on the floor of the House', and at the same time Vajpayee told reporters '*I feel a heavy burden has been cast on me*'. Had the president hinted to his visitors that the BJP would be asked to form the government?

There followed a series of events to expose the BJP's utter isolation. On 12 May the Chief Minister of Andhra Pradesh, N. Chandrababu Naidu, declared his support for a 'secular and democratic Third Front government' and rejection of the BJP and the Congress. On 13 May, Tamil Nadu's Chief Minister, M. Karunanidhi, said the DMK would support neither the BJP nor the National Front.

The Congress spelt out its stand on 12 May in a resolution declaring its support to 'political parties which are totally committed to secular democracy', and this was formally communicated by P.V. Narasimha Rao to the president the following day. By then the Tamil Maanila Congress and the Asom Gana Parishad had publicly rejected the BJP's overtures. Narasimha Rao's letter also expressed opposition to the BJP's claim.

Having 'got its act together', to use the ungainly phrase in vogue, by electing the chief minister of Karnataka as leader on 14 May, the National Front–Left Front combine called on the president the same day.

There is fortunately a detailed account of the proceedings in the statement, issued on 15 May by over 30 leaders of the Third Front who had met the president the day earlier. Its clarity and precision are altogether rare in Indian political documents. The president has not contested their version[8].

[8]For the text, see *People's Democracy*, 19 May 1996.

The delegation presented to the president a list of 11 parties with the signatures of their respective leaders claiming a total strength of 171 fortified both by the Congress resolution of 12 May and Narasimha Rao's letter of 13 May. However, 'the president indicated that he would like to receive a positive letter of support to Mr Deve Gowda from the Congress (I).' According to one reliable report, he wanted it *by 2 p.m.*, the next day, 15 May.[9]

On 11 May the president had told the leaders that he would take a decision only after the formal constitution of the Lok Sabha. Reportedly, the three election commissioners' appointment with the president, for presentation of the list of members, was advanced from 6 p.m. to 1.35 p.m. on 15 May. At 11 a.m. that day Vajpayee was summoned to meet the president at 2 p.m., immediately after the election commissioners had left.

He was not asked to explore the possibility of forming a ministry. He was *appointed* prime minister. The press communiqué issued from Rashtrapati Bhavan said, 'The president has been pleased to appoint Shri Atal Behari Vajpayee as the Prime Minister ...' Unlike R.Vankataraman's communiques in 1989 and 1990 when V.P. Singh and Chandra Shekhar, respectively, were appointed prime ministers, no reasons were cited in support of the decision. The letter of appointment must have been written hours before the meeting.

The president did not wait for Narasimha Rao's letter which he knew could not be long in arriving. It reached him at 3.25 p.m. and read 'In lieu of the earlier letter, the CWC extends its support to H.D. Deve Gowda for forming a new government.' That Narasimha Rao deliberately delayed despatch of his letter does not exculpate the president. This was a case of government formation, not of lodging tenders for a contract by a deadline. The undisputed fact is that on 15 May Shankar Dayal Sharma knew that, (a) the BJP did not have a majority and also could not acquire one, given the declared stance of the various parties, and (b) the Third Front, for all its weaknesses, stood a far better chance of commanding a majority in the Lok Sabha *with Congress support* (318 in all). He chose to overlook its claims and did so in a manner that does him no credit. A large majority of the Lok Sabha is agreed on one point : the BJP must not run India's affairs.

All along, Narasimha Rao, hoped that, (a) the BJP would not

[9]Harish Gupta, *The Indian Express*, 16 May 1996.

be called upon to form a government, and (b) failing it, the Congress would be. AICC general secretary Janardhana Poojary said on 14 May that 'actually we are the second largest party if the BJP's attempt fails'. A former union minister said the same thing that day.[10]

None of this obscures one depressing fact: Sharma sought Narasimha Rao's letter on 14 May yet went ahead and appointed Vajpayee as prime minister without waiting for it knowing fully well it was on the way. In doing so he acted exactly as N. Sanjiva Reddy had done on 22 August 1979. He had led Chandra Shekhar and Jagjivan Ram to believe that they could send details of the support they enjoyed. Less than an hour later they heard that he had dissolved the Lok Sabha. Not an example for any president to follow.

[10]The *Times of India*, 15 May 1996

12

When A Prime Minister Resigns: Deve Gowda's Resignation[1]

In all the expressions of resentment at the Congress(I) President, Sitaram Kesri's withdrawal of support to the Deve Gowda government, one aspect has been sadly overlooked. It is his and his colleagues' breach of faith with the President, Dr Shankar Dayal Sharma. This has a great bearing on the course that the president should follow in the wake of the Deve Gowda government's defeat in the Lok Sabha on 11 April 1997. He has an opportunity to rectify a sad, but understandable, oversight on his part last year and by his predecessor, R. V. Venkataraman, in November 1990.

Both inducted into office a ministry that could command a majority in the Lok Sabha only with support pledged by parties that did not join it in a coalition. In neither case was the pledge as firm as was required in the circumstances. The president ought to ensure that history is not repeated for the second time as a farce far more ludicrous than before.

Article 75(3) makes the council of ministers 'collectively responsible' to the Lok Sabha. The report of the Committee of Governors appointed by the president (1971) said: 'The relevant test is not the size of a party but its ability to command the support of the majority in the legislature. It may be that a party, even though leading in relative strength in a legislature, may not be able to obtain the support of other members. In contrast, a numerically smaller party may

[1]An earlier version of this article was published in the *Statesman*, 20 April 1997.

command majority support with the help of other parties or groups'.[2] The Sarkaria report (1988) says that 'the party or combination of parties which commands the widest support in the legislative assembly should be called upon to form the government'.[3] In 1924, the Liberals refused to have any truck with the largest party, the Conservatives, and supported instead, Labour which formed the government.

One analogy is apposite. On Harold Macmillan's resignation as prime minister the chief whip of the Conservative party sounded the members on their choice of successor on the basis of three questions '1. Who would you like to see in office? 2. Do you want any runners up? 3. Is there anybody you would rather not see in office?' A party which has 40 members in a house of 100 but is rejected by the rest has less claim to be asked to form government than one with 30 which can command majority support.[4]

The absurdity of Venkataraman's view is exposed by his admission that had Rajiv Gandhi himself not declined to accept office after his electoral defeat in 1989, he would have felt himself bound as president to invite him to become prime minister because the Congress(I) had emerged as the single largest party.

The crucial question that faces the president now is how in future a minority ministry can be inducted into office, on the pledges of its supporting parties. In this context, the observations of the Committee of Governors are very relevant:

We witness an assortment of parties with widely divergent programmes and policies ... combining themselves to form what are now called Samyukta Vidhayak Dals, the only agreement among them being the agreement to get into government. The basic conditions which would ensure a stable government by such combinations are, first, that the different parties should enter into combination as a unit, and, that they should remain faithful to the combination.

It is no function of the head of state to ask, as K. Krishna Rao did as governor of Nagaland whether the claimants to power are ideologically united. All the authorities are however agreed that he is entitled to try to ensure that they are likely to have 'a stable majority': not ideology but the programme is what matters.

[2]p. 29.
[3]Para 411.03.
[4]For a breezy account, see Randolph S. Churchill, *The Fight for the Tory Leadership* Heinemann, 1964, Ch. ix

The best statement of the law is in Dr Rodney Brazier's book, *Constitutional Practice*.[5] It is a singular quality of his analyses that, unlike some lawyers, he reckons fully with political realities. He cites a hypothetical case of a general election returning 290 Labour MPs, 260 Conservatives, and a hundred divided among groups. Labour stakes a claim, but the Conservatives drum up a coalition. The course he counsels to the head of state is to ask for evidence 'of a copper-bottomed agreement on majority coalition, its leadership, proposed disposition of ministerial offices, and agreed queen's speech, together with an equally sound guarantee that coalition government would not seek a dissolution within a reasonable time'. The queen should stipulate 'that the ultimate agreement among the parties *should be made public*'. She should ensure that 'she would not be embarrassed by an early demise of that coalition or by an early request for another general election'. This course is strikingly appropriate to our situation.

R.Venkataraman felt genuine concern for the country's welfare when V P Singh was defeated in the Lok Sabha on 7 November 1990, L K Advani's *rath yatra* had aroused communal rancour and caused bloodshed. Two days earlier, however the Congress(I) spokesman had no answer to a newsperson's query 'what are the policies and programmes on the basis of which you will extend cooperation to Mr Chandra Shekhar?' who had defected from the Janata Dal with sufficient numbers to technically qualify for a 'split'.

Venkataraman records in his memoirs, *My Presidential Years* that he

probed the nature of the support and the minimum period it would last. Rajiv Gandhi told me that his support to Chandra Shekhar was neither temporary nor conditional ... I asked Rajiv Gandhi if this support would continue at least for one year. He replied: 'Why one year? It may extend to the life of parliament'. As I wanted to have something in writing, I handed to him a formal letter inquiring whether the Congress(I) was 'able' and 'willing' to provide a 'viable' government and ask him to send a formal reply before 5 p.m. that day [8 November]. The reply arrived promptly at 5 p.m. stating that the Congress(I) was not staking a claim for forming the government but offered 'unconditional support' to the group headed by Chandra Shekhar'.[6]

[5]Oxford University Press; Second Edition 1994.
[6]R.Venkataraman, *My Presidential Years*, Harper-Collins, Delhi, 1994 p. 438.

Barely 10 weeks later, Rajiv Gandhi felt himself free to withdraw his pledged support. H K L Bhagat was sent to the president. 'He indicated that groups led by Devi Lal and Arun Nehru were prepared to support Rajiv Gandhi to form a government. I was shocked beyond words. I wondered what had happened to the *written* guarantee of 'unconditional support' and *oral promise of backing for at least one year* to the Chandra Shekhar Government.'[7] Chandra Shekhar resigned in deserved humiliation on 6 March 1991.

Probably relying on this precedent, President Sharma also did not ask for more than what the Congress(I) offered in May 1996. True to form, P V Narasimha Rao wrote to him conveying a vaguely worded resolution of the Congress Working Committee (CWC) on 12 May declaring its support in 'the formation of a secular government'. On 15 May 1996, an hour after the BJP leader, Atal Behari Vajpayee, was invited by the president to form a government, he received another letter from Rao which said: 'In lieu of the earlier letter, the CWC extends its support to H D Deve Gowda for forming a new government.' It was support to an individual.

On 30 March 1997, his successor, Sitaram Kesri, wrote to the president reciting the resolutions of 12 May, and 4 November 1996, and 16 February 1997. The letter of 15 May 1996 was deliberately ignored. He notified: 'In view of the changed situation, the Congress party is compelled to withdraw its support from the United Front Government headed by Shri H.D. Deve Gowda with immediate effect. I take this opportunity of requesting you to take such steps as you consider necessary.' The following day he sent a CWC resolution staking a claim to form a government. On 14 April the CWC explained that the demand had only been made in order to avoid a 'political vacuum'. Withdrawal of the letter of 31 March was imperative if the UF was to be supported once again.

The situation, as of now, is that the BJP Government resigned on 28 May 1996 having failed to muster a majority as it said it would. So did the UF. The Congress, for obvious reasons, has no title to being asked to form a government either. Vajpayee rightly said at Lucknow on 14 April that the president would have to complete the entire circle, as he put it, and to think afresh whether a new combination of the same parties should be invited to form a government. There is as yet no reason to dissolve the Lok Sabha

[7]Ibid., p. 472

and every reason to avoid the drastic step, but nor is any of the parties *entitled*, as such, even to be invited to explore the formation of a government. The ball is in their court.

If a dissolution is to be averted, it is for a new combine to produce the kind of 'copper-bottomed' accord, based on a written guarantee of support for a defined term on the basis of a minimum common programme, which Rodney Brazier defined so well. *Such a pact must be made public before the leader is invited.* The Rashtrapati Bhavan communiqué that follows should mention it.

13

President S.D. Sharma's Conclave[1]

If King George V could invite the leaders of the Labour, Conservative, and Liberal Parties to a conference in the Indian Room of Buckingham Palace on 24 August 1931, in order to resolve a national crisis, the president of our republic, surely, wields no less authority in similar crises to summon party leaders to attend a conference at Rashtrapati Bhavan. A biographer records that 'in his best quarter deck manner, the King impressed on the three party leaders that before they left the Palace, there should be a communiqué to end speculation at home and abroad. Then he withdrew to his own rooms to let them get on with it'.[2]

This was understandable, for it was they who had to arrive at a political arrangement. It is, however, very significant that in all these long years spreading over a century, none of the British monarchs or the Canadian and Australian governors-general, not to forget the governors of their many provinces, ever felt the need to convene the kind of conference that President Shankar Dayal convened on 2 and 3 June 1997.

The questions he raised there were by no means novel. The Conference of Governors is as established an institution as the Conference of Chief Ministers. This year the President decided to alter its format. In a letter of invitation, dated 3 May 1997, to leaders of 10 political parties, he wrote:

[1] *The Statesman*, 24 and 25 June 1997.
[2] Kenneth Rose, *King George V*, Weidenfield & Nicolson, 1983, p. 376.

This year, it is proposed that the attention of the conference be focused mainly on the following theme:'The role of the constitutional head, when, following an election, no party or combination of parties appears to have secured a majority.' With a view to enabling fuller consideration of the subject, I am inviting leaders of political parties also to join the conference and express views on behalf of their respective political parties. A tentative programme of the conference is attached herewith.

The basic problem which he defined, has been discussed threadbare for decades. A whole corpus of practice and precedent exists. That among the ten invitees were Bal Thackeray, Sitaram Kesri, and 'Shri Lalu Prasad' shows that, contrary to the common impression, Shankar Dayal Sharma is a man with a slightly naughty sense of humour. It shows also that, contrary, again, to common impression, he has little compassion. Had it been otherwise, he would not have imposed the burden of resolving that problem on men with the slender intellectual resources of these three gentlemen, not to overlook the claims to similar considerations of a good many he appointed as governors. A word about the background.

In December 1995 Sharma had set up two committees. The one on minorities had three Muslims, a Christian, a Sikh, and two Hindus. None of the Muslims is known for espousing the cause of redressal of genuine Muslim grievances. The two Hindus were Romesh Bhandari of UP and Krishna Pal Singh, both of whom won undying fame for stellar performances in their respective States, UP and Gujarat, not long ago. Its terms of reference were: '(i) To record such observations and reflections as might be of use to the Central and State governments in better securing the well-being of the minorities towards fulfilling the ideal enshrined in the preamble to the Constitution; and (ii) To prepare a report thereon for being placed before the president.' The report has been sent to the central government. The people as well as the states have been kept out of it all. The committee on the Role of the Governor as Chancellor had a better cast, a sensible remit, and an equal disdain for the public.

A glance at the programme of the conference suffices to reveal the lack of serious thought and preparation behind the venture. The first session on 2 June was to last from 9.30 hrs to 13.00 hrs. 'Leaders of political parties will join for Session-I of the conference'. Ten politicians were thus invited to have their respective say on 'the theme' in these 210 minutes. At the second session of the day and two others the following day, of equal duration, the only participants were the president, the vice-president, the prime minister, ministers, governors, lieutenant governors, and officials. All, the first included, were held in camera. The object of the exercise, besides the airing of 'views', was not stated in the letter of invitation. It emerged in the president's inaugural address on 2 June.

He said: 'If our discussion in the conference promotes the identification of any principles, norms or procedures that appear to be useful to be kept in view by constitutional heads and by political parties, a major gain will have been secured.' Such formulation of the principles and procedures implies codification of the conventions of the parliamentary system, albeit limited to some topics.

Had the venture succeeded in this task, would the results have been of any value at all? What value has of a body of rules on constitutional law drawn up by politicians and political appointees at such a conclave? The Supreme Court has ruled that the governor is 'not amenable to the directions of the government of India ... His is an independent constitutional office'. How can he be bound by a communiqué of the Governors' Conference? Sharma himself quoted this ruling. He pleaded for 'acceptance of the need to build healthy conventions', but it is his governors who have violated well established conventions, apparently without any check and with utter impunity.

The president added: 'This conference may well render important service by having a key issue in Indian politics addressed by the constitutional authorities with the advantage of having the views of leaders of political parties. The record of the proceedings of the conference would then comprise reference material of permanent value.' Since that record has been kept under wraps, evidently at his instance, it is meant to guide governors 'with the advantage of hearing the views of politicians as well'. When questioned, they can well cite the secret record.

Not surprisingly, the president quoted from the conventions on the parliamentary system propounded by the commission on Centre–State relations headed by Justice R.S. Sarkaria (retd) and comprising a bureaucrat and an economist. Its remit was Centre–State relations, and no more. It had neither the authority nor, one adds with regret, the competence to formulate the conventions.

They are not an aspect of federalism at all but of the parliamentary system. B.R. Ambedkar authoritatively explained the correct position to the constituent assembly on 30 December 1948. Asked pointedly about 'the position of the governors and the ministers of the state where discretionary powers have been allowed to be used by the governors', he replied:'The position of the governor is exactly the same as the position of the president'. Will the Sarkaria report's rules apply also to the president?

Sharma referred to the report of the Committee of Governors (1971). Evidently, neither his advisers nor he himself had done their homework. He did not refer to all documents of direct relevance to his problem that first arose in a substantial way as long as 30 years ago when the Congress monolith cracked in some states, notably Rajasthan which witnessed the first parade of MLAs in Raj Bhavan. On 17 May 1967, the Union Home Minister, Y.B. Chavan, wrote to three former Chief Justices of India, M.C. Mahajan, A.K. Sarkar, and P.B. Gajendragadkar, and two constitutional lawyers who can truly be called jurists, M.C. Setalwad and H.M. Seervai. 'Three distinct views' on the course to follow, once the electorate returns a hung legislature, were clearly set out in the letter. One of them was the claim of 'the leader of the largest single party'. It is bad enough to ignore precedents in other parliamentary systems and pretend, each time that a crisis arises, that it presents a novel situation. It is far worse to ignore Indian precedents of direct relevance.

The president sprang on his unsuspecting and captive audience at the conference on 2 June a set of nine queries. They were not annexed to his letter of invitation. The politicians were not warned in advance. The headmaster propounded them in the class and expected answers in the 210 minutes allotted to his 10 political invitees in this viva voce examination. On their part, they behaved like good schoolboys. Each said his piece. They did not tell him, as they could and, indeed, should have, that they had not had any notice of queries such as these. Apparently the CPI(M) alone went with a prepared note. It was, naturally enough, a response to the letter, not the queries.

A glance at them reveals the inspiration: Sharma's recent experience with Narasimha Rao, A.B. Vajpayee, and Sitaram Kesri, difficult customers all. The very first query read:

Ought the leader of the government that has failed to secure a majority in a general election be obliged to tender his resignation and that of the members of his council of ministers, and if so, when? (i) immediately on the outcome of the election being apparent, or (ii) on the new house being notified as constituted, or (iii) only on an indication from the constitutional head?' [read: Sharma's proddings to a very reluctant Rao to resign in May 1996].

Incidentally, classics on British constitutional law discuss this topic in great detail. It is not a novel situation, as Sharma imagined.

There was the query about the president reading the address to parliament before the new government, inducted amidst controversy, that had won a vote of confidence—as the Vajpayee regime required him to do in its brief days of glory.

When a government is formed on the basis of support from more than one party, and support to the government is indicated to have been withdrawn by one or more of the parties, it being evident that the viability of the government may have been materially impaired, should the constitutional head: (a) take no immediate cognizance of the withdrawal of support, leaving it for the concerned party or parties to move a motion of no-confidence in due course, or (b) ask that the council of ministers seek a vote of confidence from the relevant house?' [the Kesri act of last March].

The answer surely is that it would depend on the facts of each case. All one can say is that if the government is manifestly, demonstrably reduced to a minority, the president (or governor) must ask it to secure a vote of confidence; not if there is room for doubt. The Opposition must hold itself in rein till the legislature meets. Even this is subject to a proviso: public disquiet. If it arises, a vote is imperative.

Some of the queries were detailed to the point of trivia; others were delightfully vague: 'What steps may be taken to safeguard and ensure that the institution of the constitutional head is enabled to function as an impartial and independent constitutional authority?' Answer in 20 minutes and answer to the point, please. One good answer would be: don't appoint as governor a man who is not a gentleman. The participants responded, each in his own way. Kesri surprised everyone by launching on a defence of his conduct. The BJP's S.S. Bhandari jumped on the largest single party bandwagon from which the CPI(M)'s Prakash Karat pulled him down with ease through a note by the veteran Harkishan Singh Surjeet, and a presentation of his own. Both have been published. The agnostic

CPI(M) was the only party to take the Bishops' Conclave seriously, even though some of its participants deserve to be unfrocked in public.

In his concluding remarks on 3 June, the president made two claims. One was that 'Public attention has been focused on the subject and on the wide range of views forthcoming on almost every aspect. This may stimulate discussion on the subject in various other fora, bodies and occasions.' The other was that 'there is a broad convergence in perception relative to some wholesome and positive approaches'. Both are highly questionable. *The Statesman* revealed on 4 June how the proceedings were 'kept tightly under wraps'. Only the president's remarks were released. Even the text of the prime minister's speech was withheld. Portions were publicized but the process was interrupted halfway. One is disturbed, incidentally, to find Inder Kumar Gujral saying that 'unless the states are involved, foreign policy would remain only a sort of monopoly of a few bureaucrats'. Involvement of the states is desirable; not so the slur on the professionals. Such a slur is best left to ambitious 'experts' who aspire to share power without either the equipment or the discipline of the professionals in service.

As for the claim of 'convergence', United News of India (UNI) referred on 4 June to 'seven broad guidelines evolved' at the conference. No communiqué recording them was issued. What one gathers from sources is a set of seven 'guidelines which did not warrant the exercise. Some of them are wrong in law.

Shankar Dayal Sharma was able to secure two rules dear to his heart that bore much anguish in 1996. One says: '(1) The head of a council of ministers that has failed in an election to secure a majority of the seats in the relevant legislature, should forthwith tender his resignation and that of members in his council of ministers.' The other reads: '7) The securing of a vote of confidence by a government when required to do so, should precede the address of a constitutional head spelling out the policies and programmes of that government.'

Experience however has not made him much wiser, one fears. Consider this:

(4) Where a combination of parties proposes to stake a claim to form government, it would be *desirable* [sic] that ahead of staking a claim: (i) the respective political parties/groups/others resolve to coordinate their legislature strengths with each other to form government; (ii) the members of the concerned legislature parties (and groups and others) meet and

elect a leader; and (iii) a modicum of commonality of approach in governance is spelt out—including arrangements for inter se coordination between the concerned parties.

No one should be surprised that this was all the conference could 'achieve'. Even this achievement is purely illusory. It rests on Sharma's *ipse dixit*, for we have neither the record of the proceedings nor a record of the 'convergence' accepted explicitly by the political parties as distinct from the conferees at the Governor's Conference. The guidelines have neither sanction nor authority nor worth. They are the ill-digested product of a misconceived venture. Neither the procedure nor content was satisfactory. The president of India had no right to convene such a conference: still less to conduct it the way he did.

It was an exercise in self-indulgence. He could have said whatever he wished a few weeks hence on relinquishing the presidency where, on the whole, he acquitted himself with dignity and much credit; indeed, far better than any president since Zakir Hussain.

The 'crises' he faced were not unique nor as grave as those faced before in India or elsewhere, In Australia a series of constitutional conventions was held following Governor-General John Kerr's dismissal of Gough Whitlam as prime minister in 1975. It is the Government of India which must organize such conferences in consultation with the states. A president can prod the prime minister, but no president has a right to take the initiative on his own; least of all to execute it in this manner. It was intrinsically fraught with danger. Mercifully, people took in their stride. A fundamentally misconceived venture, conducted without thought or preparation, ended in a miasma of tall claims leaving behind no result of worth; only traces of futility not unmixed with potential for public harm.

Ambedkar warned the constituent assembly on 4 November 1948 that, unlike it, 'the future parliament if it met as a constituent assembly, its members will be acting as partisans seeking to carry amendments to the Constitution to facilitate to [sic] the passing of party measures which they had failed to get through ... Parliament will have an axe to grind while the Constituent assembly has none'.[2]

The warning applies to all, regarding both the text and the conventions underlying the text of the Constitution. Restraint is an acute necessity.

[2]CAD, vol. vii, p. 43.

14

Appointing a Prime Minister[1]

President K.R. Narayanan's letter to the BJP leader, Atal Behari Vajpayee, on 10 March conforms to high standards of constitutional rectitude. Constitutional practice in the parliamentary system distinguishes between an invitation to explore the possibility of forming a ministry, thus implicitly recognizing, the prima facie claims of the invitee and actual appointment. Closer to the first is the 'commission' to form a ministry which combines virtual but not formal appointment with the tentativeness of exploration in an uncertain situation.

The president's letter notes that the BJP 'is the single largest party in the Lok Sabha and the largest pre-election alliance' and very correctly asks Vajpayee 'to let me know whether you are able and willing to form a stable government which can secure the confidence of the house'. As will be pointed out this is the proper test; as neither that of arithmetical majority nor of the single largest party can claim to be. Vajpayee met the president immediately on receipt of the letter and said he was indeed in a position to form such a government. Subsequently, a Rashtrapati Bhavan communiqué announced that 'the president asked Mr Vajpayee to furnish documents in support of his claim from concerned political parties and individuals. He has agreed to do so'. Had President Shankar Dayal Sharma followed this course on 15 May 1996 he would have spared himself much embarrassment. Instead, he ritually followed the single largest party test. The communiqué issued from Rashtrapati Bhavan that day simply said that 'the president has been pleased to appoint Shri Atal Behari Vajpayee as Prime Minister ...' No reasons were given unlike the communiqués of 1989 and 1990.

[1] *The Statesman,* 15 and 16 March 1998.

There are, however three reliable but neglected guides to assist the president in the appointment of the prime minister when the electorate returns a hung Lok Sabha. They hold good, no less, for appointments of chief ministers by governors in similar situations One is a rule enunciated by Ivor Jennings on the basis of established constitutional practice. Another is the Instrument of Instructions which the framers of the Constitution carefully drew up for the guidance of the president and the government when exercising their discretionary powers as heads of state in a parliamentary system. They dropped it at the eleventh hour for no reason at all. The last is a judgment of the Supreme Court of Sri Lanka which knocks for a six the doctrine of the head of state's unfettered discretion and establishes the availability of judicial review in cases of constitutionally improper appointment.

One vital aspect has been completely overlooked in recent discussions on post-election scenarios. The electorate, it is true, did not vote the BJP to power; only returned it as the largest single party. It however decisively rejected the incumbent United Front and, at one remove, its erstwhile supporter, the Congress. Jennings' dicta in his celebrated work *Cabinet Government*[2] apply:'It must not be thought, however, that the absence of a strict two-party system gives the queen a discretion to summon as prime minister whom she pleases. It is an accepted rule that when a government is defeated, either in parliament or at the polls, the queen should send for the leader of the Opposition'.

He emphasized that 'This rule is the result of long practice, although it has hardened into a rule comparatively recently', and added: 'Its basis is the assumption of the impartiality of the Crown ... It is, moreover, essential to the belief in the monarchy's impartiality not only that she should in fact act impartially, but that she should appear to act impartially. The only method by which this can be demonstrated clearly is to send at once for the leader of the Opposition.'

Avid though he was for power, Rajiv Gandhi recognized the force of this rule when, in 1989, he turned down President R. Venkataraman's invitation to form a government on the basis of a mindless application of the notion that the largest single party should always be invited to form a government. In doing so, Rajiv Gandhi showed more sense than Venkataraman did. A spate of

[2]Jennings, *Cabinet Government*, p. 32.

scandals had led to his rejection by the electorate. Retaining him in power by a decision at Rashtrapati Bhavan would have aroused deep public resentment Rajiv Gandhi would have been defeated in the very first session of the Lok Sabha and Venkataraman would have been stripped of any claim to respectability.

Those who tried to cobble together a majority in the Lok Sabha recently betrayed a similar lack of constitutional rectitude and political sense. In 1996 the Congress government was decisively defeated. The BJP emerged as the largest single party with 161 seats in a house of 543 of which only 537 went to the polls. It won 20.7 per cent of the popular vote. Its allies contributed another 34 seats. The total of 195 fell far short of the 269 seats it needed; by 74 in fact. As against this, there was the united opposition to its assumption of power by all the others. This was obvious the day the BJP leader, Atal Behari Vajpayee was sworn in as prime ninister on 15 May 1996.

The situation is significantly different in 1998. Divisions are the norm. The Congress and the UF were each split internally on a coalition and on their leadership, let alone the leadership of the coalition. The Left was also divided. So indeed, were the BJP and its many allies on the three issues of Ayodhya, Article 370, and a uniform civil code, but they did agree to exclude these issues, from their common agenda.

If politically it made no sense for the Congress and the UF to even contemplate another attempt at power, it was utterly improper constitutionally. The BJP won 178 seats and its allies 73 in a House of 543. It received singly 26 per cent of the popular vote and 37 per cent together with its allies. Three features stand out. This block of 251 was only 21 votes short of a majority. However, no alternative with a credible claim to a majority was anywhere in sight at any time. Differences within and between the Congress and the UF surfaced no sooner the counting of votes were over. Lastly, even had they united, the Congress and its allies were only 166 strong and the UF 96, yielding a total of 262 to parties that had fought one another in the elections. The electorate had rejected both; especially the UF, which was in power. Jennings' dicta applied.

It is true that even by 10 March all the strength that the BJP and allies could muster was 261 MPs; 11 short of a clear majority. This was not however a case of the largest single party waging a battle against the rest, whether the latter is divided or united. It is a case of a clear preponderance of strength, narrowly short of a majority, vis-a´-vis the rest who are in no position to provide an alternative. The electorate gave no mandate for power to the BJP but did deliver a strong hint that in the situation of 1998, the BJP should be in power on the basis of the alliances it had forged and the pledges it had publicly given to its allies. As one of them, George Fernandes, the Samata Party leader, reminded the BJP on 4 March. 'One-third of the members who [will] form the government belong to parties which, with the exception of the Shiv Sena, have no affinity with the BJP ideology in the sense that they have their own policies and programmes.'

The chairman of the drafting committee B.R. Ambedkar authoritatively explained the scope and the limits of the president's discretion in the constituent assembly on 30 December 1948: 'Under a parliamentary system of government, there are only two prerogatives which the king or head of the state may exercise. One is the appointment of the prime minister and the other is the dissolution of parliament.' Incidentally, he did mention the alternative, namely, 'to require that it is the house which shall in the first instance choose its leader, and then on the choice being made by a motion or resolution, the president should proceed to appoint the prime minister'. Since this alternative method was not adopted, it is clear that the 'composite vote' which the Supreme Court ordered in the UP case on 23 February 1998 was in direct violation of the intention of the framers of the Constitution as it was of the Constitution itself. Ambedkar added that if the president made a wrong choice, it was open to the Opposition to remove the prime minister by a vote of no confidence.

The president's discretion and that of the governors is not unfettered. It is governed by established conventions. In 1993 the Supreme Court of India, like the Supreme Court of Canada, exploded the myth that conventions are not judicially enforceable.

It is now established beyond challenge that courts can quash an order by a head of state appointing the chief executive just as they can order the dismissal of the holder of the office or of dissolution of the legislature on the ground, in each case, that it is violative of established conventions.

They can be ascertained from recognized authorities, but cannot be invented ad hoc and instantly by judges or constitutional 'experts' in off-the-cuff answers to questions from the media.

A landmark judgment of the Supreme Court of Sri Lanka, delivered on 16 August 1993, is particularly relevant. Elections to the provincial council (PC) were held on 17 May 1993. The court quashed orders of appointment of chief ministers by the governors of north-western and southern councils. Three recognized political parties were in the fray: the United National Party (UNP), the Democratic United National Front (DUNF), and its ally, People's Alliance (PA) led by Sirimavo Bandaranaike's Sri Lanka Freedom Party (SLFP). None of the parties gained an absolute majority. In the north-western provincial council, the UNP won 25, the PA 18, and the DUNF 9 seats. In the southern PC, the UNP won 27, the P A 22 and the DUNF 6. Though the PA–DUNF alliance was in majority in both provinces, in both the UNP was asked to form the government. The UNP, then in power at the Centre, followed the Indian example and got its own party installed in power no matter how improperly.

Article 140 F(4) of the Constitution of Sri Lanka reads:

The governor shall appoint as chief minister the member of the provincial council constituted for that Province, who, in his opinion, is best able to command the support of majority of the members of that council. Provided that where more than one half of the members selected to a provincial council are members of one political party, the governors shall appoint the leader of that political party in the council as chief minister.

Since none of the three political parties had won more than half of the seats, the proviso was inapplicable.

G.M. Premachandra (DUNF) and Amarasiri Dodangoda (PA) filed petitions in the Court of Appeal on 24 May, against the governors of NWP, Montague Jayawickrema, and of the SP, M.A. Bakeer Markar, challenging the appointment of the chief ministers. The Court of Appeal referred the issues of the law to the Supreme Court for its rulings.

The facts were clear. In both provinces, secretaries of the allied parties had submitted to the governors, on 19 May, declarations of agreement to work together backed by affidavits by all their councillors. As against this, both the UNP appointees submitted letters claiming majority support but did not explain how that was achieved nor did they identify the councillors whose additional support gave them a majority.

The Supreme Court heard and decided the two cases together.

Its judgment constituted a precedent of high persuasive value in our courts since the constitutional scheme is almost identical. The court said:

We have no doubt whatsoever as to the purpose for which Article 154 F(4) gave the governor a discretion. By the exercise of the franchise the people of each province elect their representatives for the purpose of administering their affairs. The governor is given a discretion in order to enable him to select as chief minister the representative best able to command the confidence of the council, and thereby to give effect to the wishes of the people of the province. The discretion is not given for any other purpose, personal or political.

The Court ruled that this was not a 'political question'. The governor's decision cannot be based on policy but on an objective verifiable criterion for 'assessment of support in the council'. It quoted extensively from rulings of our Supreme Court. Its observation that 'the Indian Article 163 [sic] does not specify any guideline' is true only in the literal sense. It presumably had in mind Article 164 which simply empowers the governor to appoint ministers. This is however based on and regulated by conventions of parliamentary democracy, debates in the constituent assembly and Supreme Courts rulings. The Supreme Court of Sri Lanka applied the principles of administrative law to the governor's exercise of his discretion.

The court further ruled:

The exercise of the powers vested in the governor of a province under Article 154 F(4), excluding the proviso, is not solely a matter for his subjective assessment and judgment; it is subject to judicial review by the Court of Appeal. In applications for quo warranto, certiorari and mandamus, the court of Appeal has power to review the appointment, *inter alia*, for unreasonableness, or if made in bad faith, or in disregard of the relevant evidence, or on irrelevant considerations, or without evidence … The governor's decision involves a constitutional power and duty of the governor, and a constitutional right of the petitioners (in common with the other Councillors) to the proper exercise of such power and duty; judicial review is not excluded.

The petitions were remitted back to the Court of Appeal for trial in the light of the Supreme Court's ruling. Its judgment on 8 October 1993 underlines the implications of the apex court's judgment.

It is thus plain to see that where the petitioners have adduced the best possible evidence in support of their claims the persons appointed as chief ministers have adduced no credible information of their claim of support by a majority of the members. The bald statements of support referred in the documents of the respondents cannot stand scrutiny in the light of solemn declarations made by the members of the two parties who constitute a majority that they support the respective petitioners for appointment as chief ministers. Any person would be acting grossly unreasonably if he decided to base his decision without taking into consideration the uncontradicted evidence adduced by the petitioners and upon the hearsay and unverifiable claims made by the persons appointed as chief ministers.

The scope of judicial review was to test the 'reasonableness' of the governor's decisions.

The governors have not considered the best evidence in regard to the matters which they are bound to consider. It also shows that governors have chosen to act on hearsay claims that are unverifiable ...

'It has to be borne in mind that the power of appointing a chief minister is vested in the governor by the Constitution being the supreme law of the land. [The] Constitution lays down the criteria on which such an appointment should be made. The discharge of its power is a matter of grave public concern. It cannot be shrouded in a veil of secrecy. We have to observe that the claim of each governor that he made the appointment on the basis of undisclosed confidential inquiries, tends to cast the basis of the respective decisions into secrecy.

The governors' orders were quashed as being 'unreasonable and illegal'. Writs of mandamus were issued to them 'to appoint a chief minister of the province according to law'. The net result is a caution to all concerned. First, the power of appointment of the chief executive, whether at the centre or in the provinces, is strictly regulated by conventions established over the years. Secondly, those conventions, ascertainable from recognized authorities, have the force of law. Lastly, the power of appointment is not exempt from judicial review.

15
Selecting a Prime Minister: 1969–1999

The President's Role[1]

L ike the fall of a tottering drunk, the BJP government's collapse on 17 April, was predictable though none could tell when and where, on which issue, it would happen. Inebriation with power and sustained recourse to sordid stratagem, in the manner perfected in Uttar Padesh in October 1997, disentitle it to sympathy or any claim to superior morality. Angry denunciations by ministers dreading life without power, such as Murli Manohar Joshi's wild attack on the president on 23 April inspired no doubt by his mentors, remind one of Junius's celebrated letter of 14 February 1770 on the resignation of the Duke of Grafton: 'The violence of their proceedings is a signal of despair. Like broken tenants, who have had warning to quit the premises, they curse their landlord, destroy the fixtures, throw everything into confusion, and care not what mischief they do to the estate.'

The spectacle, however, of a Sonia Gandhi baring in public her appetite for power, on the strength of credentials to national leadership that would shame a fledgling politician, is revolting. This is particularly so when one recalls that her ally is one of the most unprincipled politicians in the country who contributed to fouling the communal atmosphere in Tamil Nadu and fostered the personality cult with a gaucheness even Rajiv Gandhi would have found repulsive. J Jayalalitha will assuredly be called to account one

[1] *The Statesman*, 26–28 April 1999.

day. The worms that have since been crawling out of the woodwork on both sides of the fray are beneath contempt.

Ours has been a polity split down the middle in which even sensible people have been driven to one side or the other to escape the greater evil of their perception: the communal BJP, with its VHP and Bajrang Dal allies and an impressive record of persecution of minorities to its credit, or the Congress (I) with its *damnosa hereditas* of stinking corruption. In a perverse bid 'to evolve a consensus', the BJP government tried to beat the Congress record on corruption even as the Congress under Rajiv Gandhi and P.V. Narasimha Rao had appeased the Hindutva forces.

This is reflected in our murky politics to which successive presidents have been witness : fragile political alliances and ambiguous electoral verdicts; divided political parties and broken promises. More than one president has been treated to sheer deception. A Constitution erects only the skeleton of the body politic. Politics provides the flesh and blood and shapes constitutional conventions. As the Supreme Court has ruled in at least four major cases, the text of the Constitution must be interpreted in the light of the established conventions of the British parliamentary system. To them, we have added some of our own; some in amplification, others in perversion.

Now, between the fall of the BJP government and the swearing in of the next, is the best time to consider calmly some issues that keep raising their heads with disturbing frequency. They concern nothing less crucial or sensitive than the role of the president in crises such as these. This is by no means peculiar to India, as this passage in Jennings's *Cabinet Government* shows:

It is true, as Lord Balfour said, that 'no constitution can stand a diet of dissolutions'; but dieting would be demanded only because the Constitution failed to carry on its proper function of providing a government with a stable majority. If the electorate persists in returning a nicely-balanced house, it will impel a coalition or compel one party to support another without coalition. But political forces alone can produce such a result. The queen can suggest it but not compel it. If the Opposition coalesces, it is not unreasonable for a minority government to challenge the coalition in the country. If the government finds additional support, the question does not arise. If the major parties break up, the whole balance of the Constitution alters; and then, possibly, the queen's prerogative becomes important.[2]

[2]Jennings, p. 427.

However, if exigency impels the president to be umpire, expediency cannot be his sole guide. He must abide by the rules. There are four distinct questions to be answered. First, what is the proper test for inviting the leader of a party to form a government in a hung parliament? Second what is the nature of proof of fulfilling that test that the president is entitled to ask of him before swearing him in as prime minister? Third is the president entitled, then, also to stipulate that he secure a vote of confidence in the Lok Sabha within a specified period? Lastly, precisely what change of circumstance would warrant the president asking the incumbent prime minister to therefore seek such a vote, once again. An incontrovertible record of 20 years, set out below, exists to guide us, in providing the answers and distilling the rules, and to bind us as well; for, it is based on national consensus.

It is absurd to rely on the numbers that existed on 17 April when the BJP government was defeated. As Harold Wilson said in 1964, a week is a long time in politics. Both sides have suffered erosions. Signatures by leaders have little value. On 18 April the Telugu Desam Party leader N. Chandrababu Naidu said 'there will be no tie up with the BJP'.

It is the situation that exists at the present moment of decision that is relevant. Two rules brook no evasion. One, propounded by Jennings, has been accepted by jurists like M.C. Setalvad and H.M. Seervai: 'It is an accepted rule that when a government is defeated, either in parliament or at the polls, the queen should send for the leader of the Opposition ... Its basis is the impartiality of the crown ... The only method by which this can be demonstrated clearly is to send at once for the leader of the Opposition.' No lists are required. A vote in the house cannot be nullified by lists outside, no matter how long, procured later. If a solid group with a manifest majority has since emerged it can challenge the new government in the house. If it wins there it should be invited to form a government anew.

The second rule is that the president has neither a right to insist on actual majority support nor on proof beyond doubt. He must act on a balance of probabilities leaving it to the Lok Sabha to confirm or reject his choice within a short period.

No problem arose after the general elections of 1952, 1957, 1962, and 1967 since in each the Congress won a clear majority. In 1967, it won 283 seats in a house of 522. Its parliamentary party split in two on 13 November 1969.The winter session of parliament opened four days later. On 17 November, the Swatantra Party and the Jana Sangh moved an adjournment motion in the Lok Sabha on India's humiliation at the Rabat conference.The Congress (O) supported them. Indira Gandhi survived as prime minister (by 306 to 104 votes) with the support of the CPI, CPM, Socialists, DMK, Akalis and Independents, President V.V. Giri did not ask her to secure a vote of confidence on 13 November. She won a landslide victory in the 1971 general election.

In 1977 the Janata party won a comfortable majority only to split in 1979. *That is an episode which is instructive and relevant today.* On 15 July, Morarji Desai resigned as prime minister because the party had lost its majority in the Lok Sabha while it was debating Y.B. Chavan's motion of no-confidence. He however also claimed that no single party commanded a majority in the house and the Janata, as the largest single party, was in a position to form a government. He did not resign as party leader.The following day Charan Singh resigned as deputy prime minister and formed a new party, Janata (Secular). On 18 July President N Sanjiva Reddy, as was proper, invited the leader of the Opposition,Y.B. Chavan, to form a government. On 22 July Chavan reported failure but said 'there has emerged a combination of parties and groups which . . . would be able to provide a viable and stable government'.

Charan Singh claimed to be the leader of such a 'combination'. On 23 July, the president wrote to him and to Desai asking both 'to let me have the names of members of the Lok Sabha who are willing to lend their support to you as their leader in order to *satisfy myself* whether you have the necessary majority in the Lok Sabha' within two days. On 24 July the Congress (I) extended support to Charan Singh.

Two lists were submitted, both of doubtful integrity. Reddy found that 'Charan Singh's list showed a majority of 24'. On 26 July the president wrote to Charan Singh inviting him to form a government on these novel terms: 'I trust that in accordance with the highest democratic traditions and in the interest of *establishing* healthy conventions, you would seek a vote of confidence in the Lok Sabha at the earliest possible opportunity, say by the third week of August 1979. The word 'establishing' made clear his decision to set a new precedent anew.

Two factors made this necessary. One was President Reddy's

consciousness of his own lack of credibiliy which prompted him to issue as unusual press note on 21 July denying 'that he has political ambitions of his own'. The other was the inherently risky lists procedure. When Morarji resigned, Chavan was rightly invited. He declined but made a pact with Charan Singh. This combination should have been invited *without demur*, leaving Morarji free to challenge it in the house. This is the procedure approved by all authorities, Jennings included. The president had only to form the initial *prima facie* view on majority support in the Lok Sabha. Reddy chose instead to 'satisfy myself' about it with rival lists. A bad precedent was set with grave consequences.

Charan Singh was sworn in as prime minister on 28 July. The Lok Sabha met on 20 August after the Congress(I) withdrew its support. He advised dissolution. On 22 August the president dissolved the Lok Sabha in violation of the rule that a prime minister facing a motion of no-confidence has no right to advise dissolution of the House. The proper course was to proceed with the debate. On the prime miniser's defeat the leader of the Oppositon, Jagjivan Ram, should have been asked to form the government.

One pronouncement of the times bears recalling today. On 7 August 1979, George Fernandes alleged 'a well-organized and smartly orchestrated exercise mounted by the RSS-Jana Sangh forces for the total takeover of the Janata Party'. In an obvious reference to A.B. Vajpayee and L.K. Advani, he wrote: 'The carefully cultivated self-abnegation postures of some RSS-Jana Sangh leaders were but a flimsy facade for the power grabbing ...' A little over a decade later, he became their staunch ally.

Whether the vote of confidence was in vogue earlier in the states or not, Reddy's precedent was followed in the states thereafter and at the Centre a decade later. In the 1980 and 1984 general election to the Lok Sabha the Congress(I) was voted to power with a clear majority. The last decade has seen the 1979 precedent ripen into an established convention contested by no one. The 1989 election yielded a divided verdict—the Congress (184 seats), the National Front let by the Janata Dal (145), the BJP (82), and the Left Front 55.

President R. Venkataraman, nonetheless, invited Rajiv Gandhi to form a government. He had sense enough to decline. On 1 December 1989, the president announced: 'I have invited Shri V.P. Singh ... to form a government and take a vote of confidence in the Lok Sabha within 30 days of assuming office.' The president had received declarations of support to the National Front from the BJP and the Left.

On 23 October 1990, the BJP informed the president of its withdrawal of support to the NF government. Mentioning this and citing the respective strengths of the political parties in the House, a Rashtrapati Bhavan communique´ noted the government's loss of a majority and said: 'The President has, therefore, advised the Prime Minsiter to prove his majority in the house of the people. The prime minister has agreed to do so before 7 November.' This was the first instance when a government at the Centre was asked to seek such a vote because it was perceived to have lost majority support. The winter session of parliament was to commence in November, anyway.

On 9 November, the president issued a communique´ which revealed the course he later adopted. He had asked the Congress(I), once again, to form a government. It declined, offering 'unconditional support' to Chandra Shekhar. Thereafter, the president sounded the BJP and the Left Front. Both declined, Chandra Shekhar 'produced evidence of support to his group' of 50-odd defectors from the Dal and from other parties. 'The president is satisfied prima facie that the group ... has the strength to form a viable government'. Chandra Shekhar was invited to form the government 'and prove his majority in the house ... on or before 30 November 1990'.

True to form, Rajiv Gandhi reneged on his promise to the president ('Why one year? It (his support) may extend to the life of Parliament'). Chandra Shekhar resigned in ignominy on 6 March 1991 but, unlike VP Singh, advised dissolution. On Rajiv Gandhi's tragic assassination, P.V. Narasimha Rao was elected leader of the Congress (I) parliamentary party on 20 June 1991. The electorate had once again given an unclear verdict. The Congress won 225 seats in a house of 520; the BJP, 119; the Janata Dal 55, and the Left 47. Rao was straightaway appointed as prime minister on 20 June but asked 'to establish your majority in the Lok Sabha within four weeks'. Rao's motion of confidence was carried, by 241 votes to 111 on 15 July 1991. The National Front and the Left abstained since neither wanted fresh elections. Two years later, an 28 July 1993, Rao defeated a motion of no-confidence by 265 votes to 251—with support of the Jhankhand Mukti Morcha (JMM) members.

Rao lasted a whole five-year term. From 1996 we enter a phase of hung paliaments, recurrent political crises, and repeated presidential interventions. Both the Reddy stipulation of 1979 on the initial appointment and the Venkataraman directive of 1990 after loss of confidence were followed. There was no protest from any of the affected parties.

For once, President Shankar Dayal Sharma stumbled badly after the 1996 general election. The BJP won 161 seats in a house of 543 (of which only 537 went to the polls) and 20.7 per cent of the popular vote. Allies promised another 34 seats (the Shiv Sena 15; the Akali Dal 8; the Samata Party 8 and the Haryana Vikas party 3). The total of 195 fell short of the magic figure of 269 by as many as 74.

'A senior BJP functionary' gave the game away on 10 May: 'Once we are called upon to form the government, the attitude of newly-elected MPs, towards the BJP might change and they may be willing to be 'partners'.' Besides, none of them, he added, would be interested in another round of early elections. The BJP staked a claim to form a government on 11 May. Three days later the United Front (comprising the former National Front and the Left) presented to the President a list of 11 parties signed by their respective leaders claiming a total strength of 171 fortified by the Congress vague resolution of support to 'secular democracy' on 12 May and an explicit letter of support on 13 May. Sharma knew that this letter was on its way to him. It reached him at 3.25 p.m. on 15 May. At 2 p.m. he had already appointed Vajpayee as prime minister with full knowledge of the fact that he did not command a majority. With Congress support the UF was 318 strong. Vajpayee was sworn in on 16 May. He was 'advised' to 'secure a vote of confidence' by 31 May. Facing certain defeat in the Lok Sabha on 28 May, Vajpayee announced his decision to resign. He had forced the president to read his address to parliament on 24 May knowing full well that he lacked a majority. H.D. Deve Gowda was appointed prime minister on 1 June 1996 on the same terms and secured a vote of confidence in the Lok Sabha.

The crunch came on 30 March 1997. The Congress president, Sitaram Kesri, wrote to the president withdrawing support to the Gowda government. He also staked a claim to be appointed prime minister. Like Vajpayee in 1990, he wrote, not to the prime minister, but directly to the President. If the practice of signifying support to the prime minister by letters to the president is followed, the beneficiary cannot complain if its withdrawal is also delivered to the same office. Parliament was due to meet on 21 April. President Sharma declined to wait for three weeks. On 31 March he asked Gowda to secure a vote of confidence by 7 April but relented to extend the term by four days. On 11 April, Gowda lost by 158 votes to 292 with eight abstentions. On 14 April Sharma asked Gowda to take steps for 'disposal of important financial business'.

Kesri wrote to the president on 18 April, extending support to 'a new leader of the United Front other than Gowda. I.K. Gujral was appointed Prime Minister on 21 April with a direction to seek a vote of confidence a mere two days later. The Congress and the UF were also directed to inform the president of their accord on a coordination committee in order to dispel his doubts on the stability of the new set up. Nothing can work in the state of our politics. Not even Prof Rodney Brazier's prescription of a 'copper-bottomed agreement' on coalition.

The Jain Commission submitted its interim report on 28 August, 1997. Parliament had only to reassemble on 20 November for the Congress to demand the ouster of the DMK from the UF government. On 28 November 1997, Sitaram Kesri wrote to president K.R. Narayanan informing him of the Congress's withdrawal of support to the government and also 'staking its claim to form the government and we are sure, given a chance, we would be able to prove our majority on the floor of the House'. Unlike Deva Gowda, Inder Kumar Gujral resigned that very day but without advising dissolution of the Lok Sabha. Constituents of the UF informed the president that they would not support a Congress or a BJP government. On 3 December Advani publicly confessed: 'We needed 47 to split the Congress. We got around 40.' He of course, never practised horse trading. The 40 were a gift of providence. Dissolution was inevitable.

On 3 December the council of ministers met to advise dissolution the president acted on this advice the following day. As has been pointed out earlier, the dissolution, though inevitable, was utterly irregular. Jennings held that a cabinet that has resigned cannot advise dissolution.

After, or in anticipation of defeat, the council of ministers can either 'resign or dissolve'. True, in a situation where no alternative existed the president, who can act only on advice, had to seek the advice of the prime minister who had resigned. If an alternative had existed, the president should have asked its leader for advice after appointing him prime minister.

In the March 1998 elections the ruling UF was defeated. The BJP won 179 seats, and its allies 73 in a House of 543. It received singly 26 per cent of the popular vote and 37 together with the allies. Three features stand out. This block of 251 was only 21 votes short of a majority. No alternative with a credible claim to a majority was anywhere in sight at that time. Differences within and between the Congress and the UF surfaced no sooner than the counting of votes was over. Lastly, even had they united, the Congress and is allies were only 166 strong and the UF 96, yielding a total of 262 to parties that had fought each other in the elections. The electorate had rejected both.

The president rightly asked Vajpayee, on 10 March, 'to let me know whether you are able and willing to form a stable government which can secure the confidence of the house.'

The president did not however stop at that. After Vajpayee called on him claiming the support of 252 MPs, the president asked him 'to furnish documents in support of his claim from concerned political parties and individuals. He had agreed to do so'. Given the absence of any alternative in sight, this was a mechanical application of a rule applied in an ambiguous situation. He also held consultations with other parties. On 12 March Vajpayee submitted letters of support from 240 MPs. Jayalalitha sent her letter pledging 'total and unconditional support' to Vajpayee to the President on 14 March.

An elaborate communique issued by Rashtrapati Bhavan on 15 March said:

The number of MPs supporting the formation of a government by the BJP now comes to 264. This number—264—remains short of the halfway mark in the total house of 539. However, when seen in the context of the TDP's decision, as conveyed to the president by Shri Chandrababu Naidu, to remain netural, the number of 264 does cross that mark ... The president has also advised Shri Vajpayee to secure a vote of confidence on the floor of the house within ten days of his being sworn in.'

Sworn in as prime minister on 19 March, Vajpayee won a vote of confidence in the Lok Sabha on 28 March by 274 votes to 261; a precarious margin of 13.

Compare Narayanan's communique´ of 15 March 1999 with

Sanjiva Reddy's identical letters of 23 July 1979 to Morarji Desai and Charan Singh and the letter's enduring and baleful influence becomes glaringly apparent. The president of India asserts the right to 'satisfy myself whether you have the necessary majority in the Lok Sabha'. He has absolutely no right to do so. One grants that in our part of the world letters of support are accepted in practice, but only in special, ambiguous situations. In 1993 the Supreme Court of Sri Lanka, exercising judicial review over the appointment of chief ministers, noted that as against letters of support by one side the other had filed affidavits by a'l the legislators pledging to work together in a ministry.

Constitutionally, the decision on majority support belongs exclusively to the house. The president or governor is not called upon to decide that when inviting a claimant to form a government. Moreover the test is not actual majority at all.

The intention of the framers of the Constitution was reflected in the Instrumention of Instructions they had drafted for the president, (They dropped it for other reasons). It directed him 'to appoint a person who has been found by him to be most likely to command a stable majority in Parliament as the prime minister'. The word 'likely' was used to permit an element of rational conjecture. The report of the committee of governors noted that 'a numerically smaller party may command majority support with the help of other parties' which a larger party may not. If this be the test, the degree of support and nature of its proof must also change. Proof is not at all necessary in a situation like that in May 1996 and March 1998, when the ruling party had been defeated and a large conglomerate had come to the fore unmatched by any other.

The winner must be sworn in without much ado. For greater assurance, however the stipulation as to a confirmatory vote of confidence in the house must be retained. What of such a vote when the circumstances change? The Sarkaria report was wrong in speaking of governors receiving memoranda from MLAs expressing lack of confidence in the government 'during the period the assembly remains prorogued'. Neither the president nor a governor has any business to hang a letter box outside his mansion to receive such documents. The dissenters' only forum is the floor of the house.

If, however, a coalition rips apart or the ruling party splits so as to reduce the government manifestly and demonstrably to a minority regime, making its continuance for long a clear offence to democratic governance, the head of state can advise a vote of confidence. For that matter, if public opinion becomes utterly hostile to the government, he can, in some cases, even force a dissolution, as authorities recognize. Bihar in 1974 was a fit case for such a forced dissolution. It.all depends on the circumstances.

This is not a game of musical chairs. It is something far worse. The past master in the game, Harold Wilson, described it vivdly. It is the 'the practised performances of latter-day politicians in the game of musical daggers: never be left behind holding the dagger when the music stops'.

Postscript

The general elections to the 13th Lok Sabha, in September–October 1999, returned Atal Behari Vajpayee to power once again as head of the National Democratic Alliance, a coalition of 21 parties. He was invited to form a Government by President K.R. Narayanan on October 11, 1999 without being required to provide the President with prima facie proof of majority support in the House or on assurance that he would seek a vote of confidence. There within a stipulated time, as before. The NDA having won 296 seats in a House of 538, its ability to form a government was beyond dispute. The President's decision was implicitly accepted by all.

SECTION

II

PARLIAMENT

16
Dissolution of the Lok Sabha[1]

The President, Dr Shankar Dayal Sharma, faces a difficult question on whether to dissolve the Lok Sabha in the circumstances he faces. The discretion is entirely his, albeit governed by well-settled rules on dissolution of parliament. Authorities of highest eminence have defined these rules.

Dr B.R. Ambedkar told the constituent assembly in the clearest possible terms, on 30 December 1948, that 'under a parliamentary system of government there are only two prerogatives which the king or the head of state may exercise. One is the appointment of the prime minister and the other is the dissolution of parliament'.[2]

Five months later, on 18 May 1949, while rejecting Professor K.T. Shah's amendment making it obligatory for the prime minister to state in writing the reasons for advising the president to dissolve the Lok Sabha, Dr Ambedkar said: 'If the object of Prof. K.T. Shah [sic] is that the prime minister should not arbitrarily ask for dissolution, I think that object would be served if the convention was properly observed.' He mentioned at some length the British crown's right to reject advice for dissolution of the House of Commons and to find, instead, an alternative government and added: 'In the same way, the president of the Indian union will test the feelings of the house whether the house agrees that there should be dissolution or whether the house agrees that the affairs should be carried on with some other leaders without dissolution.' It was for the president 'to test the feeling of the house and to find out whether

[1] *The Statesman*, 13 April 1997.
[2] CAD, vol. vii, p. 1158.

the prime minister was asking for dissolution of the house for bona fide reasons or for purely party purposes.'[3]

The 42nd Amendment (1976) to the Constitution made no difference. As the then law minister, Mr H.R. Gokhale, assured the Lok Sabha on 29 October 1976, the amendment to Article 74(1) of the Constitution, which made the council of ministers' advice to the president binding, 'only reproduces the position which has always been there all along, and, therefore, I do not wish to go into the need for introducing this clause.'[4] Communiqués issued from Rashtrapati Bhavan on the dissolution of the Lok Sabha, in 1979 and 1991 in particular recorded clearly that the president had exercised his own discretion. The concurring judgment of Justices V.R. Krishna Iyer and I.N. Bhagwati in the famous case of Samsher Singh, decided by the Supreme Court in 1974, mentioned dissolution as one of the 'few well known exceptional situations' in which the president is free to exercise his discretion.[5]

The court decisively rejected the plea that the provisions of the Constitution should be interpreted 'according to its own terms regardless of the conventions that prevail in the United Kingdom'. The letter of the Constitution is based on the British Constitution. Every textbook on British constitutional law quotes as an accurate and authoritative statement of the law on dissolution a letter by 'Sensex' published by *The Times,* (London) on 2 May 1950. He was none other then Sir Alan Lascelles, private secretary to the king. It bears quotation in full:

It is surely indisputable (and common sense) that a prime minister may ask—not demand—that his sovereign will grant him a dissolution of parliament and that the sovereign, if he so chooses, may refuse to grant this request. The problem of such a choice is entirely personal to the sovereign, though he is, of course, free to seek informal advice from anybody who he thinks fit to consult.

In so far as this matter can be publicly discussed, it can be properly assumed that no wise sovereign—that is, one who has at heart the true interest of the country, the constitution, and the monarchy—would deny a dissolution to his prime minister unless he were satisfied that: (1) the existing parliament was still vital, viable, and capable of doing its job; (2) a general election would be detrimental to the national economy; (3) he

---

[3]CAD, vol. viii, pp. 106–7.
[4]*Lok Sabha Debates,* Eighteenth Session, Fifth Series, vol. lxv, no. 5, Col. 268.
[5]AIR 1974 S.C. 2192.

could rely on finding another prime minister who could carry on his government, for reasonable period, with a working majority in the House of Commons. When Sir Patrick Duncan refused a dissolution to his prime minister in South Africa in 1939, all these conditions were satisfied, when Lord Byng did the same in Canada in 1926, they appeared to be, but in the event the third proved illusory.[6]

In the present case these principles apply with yet greater force. What Mr Charan Singh's law minister, Mr S.N. Kacker, said on 10 August 1979 is particularly relevant. The president's 'transitory satisfaction that Mr Charan Singh had more support than Mr Morarji Desai needed to be ratified by the Lok Sabha through a vote of confidence'. Mr Charan Singh promised, on 5 and 15 August 1979 to demit office as prime minister if he was defeated on a vote of confidence. He reneged on the promise and advised dissolution; a piece of advice that President N Sanjiva Reddy accepted flouting all norms.

In 1996 Mr Atal Behari Vajpayee resigned because he could not muster a majority in the Lok Sabha. He properly refrained from advising the president to dissolve the Lok Sabha. As it happened, Mr H.D. Deve Gowda was able to muster a majority and to retain it till 30 March 1997.

In a pronouncement regarded as a classic on the subject the Liberal statesman, Mr H.H. Asquith, himself a barrister and a former prime minister, cautioned the King on 18 December, 1923 against the crown putting the electorate,

To the tumult and turmoil of a series of general elections so long as it can find other ministers who are prepared to give contrary advice. The notion that a ministry which can not command a majority in the House of Commons ... a ministry in a minority of 31 per cent ... in these circumstances is invested with the right to demand a dissolution is as subversive of constitutional usage, as it would, in my opinion, be pernicious to the general and permanent interest of the Nation at large.[7]

A great authority, Dr Eugene A Forsey, wrote in his great work on *Dissolution of Parliament*:

[6]For the text, *see* also Geoffrey Wilson, *Cases and Materials on Constitutional and Administrative Law*, Cambridge University Press, 2nd edn 1976, pp. 22–3 and Brazier, *Constitutional Texts*, (Oxford: Oxford University Press, 1990), pp. 113–14.

[7]Speech to the National Liberal Club quoted in Forsey, p. 89.

With a multi-party system it might be necessary [sic] for the crown to refuse dissolution and to consult the leaders of the various Opposition parties or even prominent private members or to call on such personages, successively, to form governments. If all possible alternative prime ministers declined the task, there would clearly be no course open but to retain the existing government in office (or, if the government to which dissolution had been refused had resigned forthwith, as Mr [McKenzie] King did in 1926 in Canada, recall it, and grant its request for dissolution). If, on the other hand, an alternative government assumed office and asked for an immediate dissolution, or was at once defeated on a critical division, it would be the duty of the crown to recall the former government and grant it dissolution.'[8]

[8]Forsey, p. 263.

17

Dissolution on Prime Minister's or Cabinet's Advice ?[1]

Were it not for the alertness of some, a grave crisis might have erupted in the aftermath of the Deve Gowda government's failure to secure a vote of confidence in the Lok Sabha on 11 April 1997. Deve Gowda, apparently, intended to advise the president to dissolve the Lok Sabha against the advice of his party, the Janata Dal, its allies in the United Front, and his cabinet colleagues. 'He was bent upon going to the polls as caretaker prime minister', the Dal's president, Laloo Prasad Yadav, charged in a press interview on 27 April 1997.

The charge does not, however, rest on the *ipse dixit* of a discredited politician. Three days earlier, a responsible person, Mr N. Chandra Babu Naidu, Chief Minister of Andhra Pradesh, had alleged at Hyderabad (24 April) that 'Deve Gowda not only had plans to dissolve the Lok Sabha but also made abortive attempts to get about 60 Congress MPs to defect in order to remain in power'. Apparently, when operation defection failed, contingency plans for dissolution were to be carried out but were foiled.

Hitherto, the entire debate on the dissolution of the Lok Sabha turned on the sole issue of the binding force of the prime minister's advice to the president to dissolve the Lok Sabha and the rules governing the president's discretion to accept or reject the advice. We have never considered in earnest whether it is the prime minister's sole prerogative to tender such advice or must be based on a decision by his council of ministers.

[1] *The Statesman*, 11 May 1997.

This issue is of academic significance now for two reasons. Deve Gowda has gone and nobody expects his successor, Inder Kumar Gujral, to resort to such tactics. The very academic nature of the issue enables calm and objective consideration. Coalition politics have come to stay. An issue of this nature arises only in a crisis situation when partisanship clouds judgment.

Article 74(1) of the Constitution says explicitly that 'there shall be a council of ministers with the prime minister at the head to aid and advise the president who shall, in the exercise of his functions, act in accordance with such advice.' It adds: 'Provided that the president may require the council of ministers to reconsider such advice, generally or otherwise, and the president shall act in accordance with the advice tendered after such reconsideration.'

The Supreme Court has ruled time and again that the letter of the Constitution must be read in the light of the established conventions of the British parliamentary system on which the framers of our Constitution avowedly modelled it. Article 74(1) does not rob the president of his discretion on dissolution. Successive presidents have recorded that implicitly in communiqués issued from the Rashtrapati Bhavan while ordering mid-term dissolutions (1979 and 1991). Article 74 clearly requires advice by the council of ministers. It is another matter that it is the prime minister who conveys the advice.

In contrast, Article 48(1) of Pakistan's constitution, as originally enacted in 1973 to serve Z.A. Bhutto's interests, read: 'In the performance of his functions, the president shall act on and in accordance with the advice of the prime minister and such advice shall be binding on him.' A separate provision, Article 58(1) says that 'the president shall dissolve the national assembly if so advised by the prime ministe. ...'

As amended by the Eighth Amendment, Article 48(1) enjoins the president to act on 'the advice of the cabinet or the prime minister'. Article 58(1) survives to make the prime minister's advice on dissolution. Such provisions do not disfigure our Constitution. (The recent 13th Amendment does not affect either of these provisions.) It repeats the English amendment on other points.

However, in all consistency, if the conventions of the parliamentary system apply to the president's discretion on dissolution, surely they do no less on the prime minister's power to tender advice on it as distinct from that of his cabinet. What, then, have the authorities on the British constitution to say on this neglected issue ?

To begin with, we find a thorough discussion in Ivor Jennings' magisterial work *Cabinet Government.* He held that 'The advice to dissolve was, at least until recently, submitted by the prime minister on the decision of the cabinet.' A resumé of dissolutions since 1841 ends with this conclusion: 'No dissolution since 1918 has been brought before the cabinet, and all prime ministers since Mr Lloyd George have assumed a right to give the advice.'[2]

If one were to stop at this exposition, as all so often happens in partisan debates conducted with selective quotations, one would form a wholly erroneous impression of the law. British prime ministers got away with it because in each case none of them seriously questioned the need for dissolution. When Churchill advised dissolution in 1945, while his coalition partners were away attending the Labour Party conference, it was because a general election was overdue at the end of the war and everyone wanted it.

However, earlier in the same work, while discussing the prime minister's position generally,[3] Jennings made this important qualification: 'There is only one check upon abuse of this peculiar consequence of the prime minister's position. The queen must not intervence in party politics. She must not, therefore, support a prime minister against his colleagues. Accordingly, it would be unconstitutional for the queen to agree with the prime minister for the dissolution of the government in order to allow the prime minister to override his colleagues.'

This takes care not only of dissolution but also of any constitutional coup to 'reconstitute the government'; for example, a sudden, even surreptitious, resignation by the prime minister and the surreptitious swearing in of a new cabinet which puts the old to pasture.

No prime minister, especially one who heads a coalition, but also one who heads a single party ministry, has the right to advise the termination of the life of the Lok Sabha on his own. No president should act on such advice without consulting the prime minister's colleagues in the cabinet if differences are suspected, not to forget the parties in opposition.

[2]Jennings, p. 419.
[3]ibid., p. 86.

In his work on constitutional law, Professor Stanley de Smith, who lent lustre to Cambridge, agreed with Jennings; 'Protests notwithstanding, a refusal would be justified and broadly acceptable if a prime minister, placed in a minority within his own cabinet and threatened with repudiation by his parliamentary party, suddenly asked for a dissolution in order to forestall the prospect of his imminent supersession.'[4]

Dr Geoffrey Marshall demonstrates in his work *Constitutional Conventions* that Jennings' statement on the record since 1918 ceased to be altogether accurate in more recent years. Consultations with cabinet colleagues became the norm even in the Thatcher era, however informally. He holds too that the prime minister's primacy loses weight if his cabinet is split.[5]

Lastly there is the bible on dissolutions, Dr Eugene A. Forsey's book *The Royal Power of Dissolution of Parliament in the British Commonwealth*, now sadly, out of print, states emphatically that 'to allow the Prime Minister alone to advise dissolution would certainly be contrary to the general trend of constitutional tradition, both in Britain and overseas; it would also be objectionable on grounds of public policy as tending to increase unduly the Prime Minister's personal power.'[6] At the end of the work he sums up, citing precedents and the dicta of Sir A. Berriedale Keith[7], Jennings, and Harold Laski, that the crown is not obliged to grant dissolution at the request of a minority of a cabinet.' With the authorities so weighted in that direction, it is pointless to sum up the obvious.

[4]De Smith, op.cit., pp. 130–1.

[5]Geoffrey Marchall; *Constitutional Conventions: The Rules and Forms of Political Accountability*; Delhi: Oxford Univrsity Press, 1986, pp. 51–53.

[6]Forsey, p. 254.

[7]A. Bekriedale Keith, *The King and the Imperial Crown, The Powers and Duties of His Majesty*, London: Longmans, Green, & Co, 1936, p. 176.

18

An Irregular Dissolution[1]

In issuing a detailed communiqué from Rashtrapati Bhavan setting out his reasons for dissolving the Lok Sabha on 4 December 1997, President K.R. Narayanan has demonstrated a high sense of presidential accountability to the nation. In contrast to the laconic communiqués of the past, this 20 paragraph document meticulously records the course of events during the week since 28 November when the Congress (I) withdrew its support to the UF government and staked its claim to form a government. It is what lawyers call a 'speaking order'. It convincingly explains why the president issued an order under Article 85(2) (b) of the Constitution of India dissolving a Lok Sabha that first met on 22 May 1996. The order has been widely approved as a realistic acceptance of the inevitable.

That is no reason why some of the constitutional issues which were aired during that fateful week or which the order itself raises should be neglected. The result was inevitable; but the process was irregular. For instance, is it open to a council of ministers that has resigned to advise the president to dissolve the Lok Sabha ? It would be most unfortunate if this utterly unprecedented and unconstitutional action is accepted as a sound precedent.

To begin with the fundamentals, the dicta of Dr B.R. Ambedkar in the constituent assembly and of Justice V.R. Krishna Iyer in Samsher Singh's case, decided by the Supreme Court in 1974, accord with the established principle of the British parliamentary system on which our Constitution is based, as the Supreme Court has recognized more than once, that the head of state enjoys a significant degree of discretion when the prime minister advises him to dissolve the directly elected lower house of parliament.

[1] *The Statesman*, 11 December 1997.

This does not however at all imply that the head of state can order a dissolution without advice. His discretion is governed by established rules and precedents. Not only can he reject advice to dissolve, thus entailing the dismissal of the government, but can also compel dissolution and insist on advice to that effect, which is known as 'forced dissolution'. Faced with a fraudulent Proclamation of Emergency President Fakhruddin Ali Ahmed could have dismissed Indira Gandhi from the office of prime minister and appointed an Opposition leader to the post on the understanding that he would advise dissolution and thus take the issue to the country.

As Jennings puts it, 'the king cannot exercise his prerogative of dissolution without 'advice'.[2] He regards 'a dissolution without the intervention of ministers' as being 'impossible'. Another authority holds that dissolution 'would be unconstitutional' if it is done 'without or against the advice of her [the Queen's] ministers' Ambedkar told the constituent assembly on 4 November 1948 that the president 'can do nothing contrary to their [the ministers'] advice nor can he do anything without their advice.'[3] On 30 December 1948, he mentioned dissolution as one of the prerogatives he will enjoy, the other being the appointment of the prime minister. On 18 May 1949, he said that the president 'will test the feelings of the house' on its dissolution. It must, however, be based on the prime minister's advice. It has become necessary to dilate on the obvious because all through the week the obvious and incontestable was questioned. Pranab Mukherjee confidently asserted in a TV interview, on 2 December 1997 that advice was not necessary.

Three other issues merit discussion: dissolution on the advice of a prime minister facing a censure motion; of one who heads a minority government; and of one who has resigned. The resolution passed by the union council of ministers, on 3 December makes much of the fact that, while communicating its resignation to the president on 28 November it decided not to recommend dissolution of the Eleventh Lok Sabha on account of its anxiety about a fresh poll within two years as also for the reason that the president may like to explore the possibility of formation of an alternative stable government.

Expression of such noble thoughts should not delude anyone

[2]Jennings, *Cabinet Government*, p. 416.
[3]CAD, vol. vii, p. 32.

into thinking that it had any choice in the matter. The Lok Sabha was seized of a motion of no-confidence in the council of ministers by Mamata Banerjee. It is an incontestable rule, as Eugene Forsey formulated it, that 'if a motion of censure or want of confidence is under debate but has not yet been voted on, and the Cabinet tries to forestall a probable or even possible defeat by asking for dissolution, then it is clearly the crown's duty to refuse'.[4] The report of The Governors' Committee (1971) held the same view: 'If there is a no-confidence motion against a ministry and the chief minister, instead of facing the assembly, advises the governor to dissolve the assembly, the governor need not accept such advice but should ask the chief minister to get the verdict of the assembly on the no-confidence motion.'[5] It is unnecessary to add that the norms of parliamentary practice are the same in the states and at the centre.

There is a mistaken notion that a minority government cannot advise dissolution. It can and its advice would be accepted if no alternative government is in sight. A government defeated on a motion of no-confidence is also within its rights in seeking the people's verdict. Circumstances alter cases. Was it a vote on a major issue of policy ? If the house is viable, recently elected, and the government, having lost its confidence, seeks to prevent an alternative government from assuming power by advising dissolution, such advice should be rejected.

Jennings states the rule thus: 'It is a further result of the fact that the strength of the government rests on the electorate that it can, if defeated in the House of Commons, appeal to the people by advising a dissolution of parliament. It is a question of tactics whether it will resign or dissolve. Its resignation almost invariably involves a dissolution. It depends on the political temper of the moment whether it is likely to gain or lose if it allows its opponents to dissolve.'[6]

The choice is starkly clean: 'resign or dissolve'. It resigns and lets the Opposition advise dissolution or stays put and itself advises dissolution. It was left to the UF government to resign on 28 November and advise dissolution on 3 December. This is unheard of and clearly unconstitutional. The Prime Minister Inder Kumar

[4]Forsey, op. cit., p. 263
[5]Report of the Governors' Committee, p. 56.
[6]Jennings, *Cabinet Government*, p. 492.

Gujral's letter to the president on 28 November was unambiguous. The Rashtrapati Bhavan communiqué of 4 December records that 'The president accepted Shri Gujral's resignation and requested him and his colleagues to continue in office till alternative arrangements are made.' Once its resignation was accepted, the government lost any right whatever to tender any advice on any matter of consequence bar the rituals of its departure.

Jennings is quite explicit that it is 'not customary for the cabinet to meet after a resignation except for the determination of questions consequent upon their resignation'[7]. An illustration he proceeds to cite is telling. A Whig government headed by Lord Melbourne came to power after the 1835 elections. It resigned in 1839 owing to an 'inadequate majority'. Peel accepted the commission to form a government but differences arose with the queen. He writes: 'The most notable exception occurred in 1839. Queen Victoria and Sir Robert Peel could not agree as to the positions of the ladies of the bedchamber. Lord Melbourne's cabinet met again and formally advised the queen to refuse Peel's demands. Greville said that this action was unconstitutional and for once Greville was right.' The jibe at the clerk of the council is due to his doubtful credibility. *For fifty years he listened at the door/And heard some secrets and invented more.*

Jennings' option is all the more weighty because eventually Peel did not form a government. Melbourne accepted responsibility for the queen's refusal to change her ladies and continued in office, without an effective majority, until 1841 when his government was defeated on a motion of no-confidence. Even so, Jennings holds that the Melbourne government had no right to tender any advice between the time it resigned and its resumption of office, when Peel declined the queen's commission. There is no precedent of a government that has resigned advising dissolution. The proper course for the UF government was to face the motion of no-confidence and, on its defeat, advise dissolution. With the Congress(I), it wished to avoid a debate on the Jain Commission report which would have affected their options in the elections. Neither the BJP nor the Congress was eligible to be asked to form a government and not only because neither had a majority. The BJP was given an opportunity in 1996 and could not deliver. The Congress(I) twice declined to form a government; in May 1996 and in April 1997.

[7]Ibid, p. 89.

The UF Government's belated advice on dissolution, though unconstitutional, was one in which all concurred. The BJP told the president on 3 December that 'they would not have any objection'. The Congress(I) reported on 2 December that it had 'no breakthrough to report to the president' on its parleys with the UF. The president could hardly have asked either of them to form a government and, on their failure, grant a dissolution to them rather than to the UF. Those two in effect joined in the UF's advice on dissolution. In the circumstances, a correct, indeed, the only possible, course was taken by the president. The UF's political calculations led it to avoid the democratic procedure of parliamentary defeat. It secured a dissolution on 4 December 1997 unconstitutionally which it could not have on 28 November. Given the situation, it is a moot question whether the president should or could have insisted that the government face the Lok Sabha.

19

The Prime Minister in the Rajya Sabha[1]

Wе have made it a rule that chief ministers should belong to the assembly and not to the legislative council ... there is very strong opinion that no chief minister should come from the upper house'[2]. When Prime Minister Jawaharlal Nehru wrote this admonition to Sri Prakasa, the governor of Madras (as it then was), on 5 March 1952, he could scarcely have dreamt that a day would come when a prime minister of India would stand for a Rajya Sabha election, and this after becoming prime minister without a seat in parliament. Nehru was not in favour of 'a non-member being elected leader', either.

The rules have been bent over decades. H.D. Deve Gowda was sworn in as prime minister on 1 June 1996. Only three months later and a month before the election commission announced, on 2 September, its schedule for six by-elections to both houses of parliament (three to each house), reports began to appear that Gowda was closely surveying the Rajya Sabha route. Significantly, he had still not resigned his seat in the Karnataka assembly.

After the election commission's announcement similar reports flew thick and fast culminating in the Karnataka Chief Minister, J.M. Patel's announcement, on 10 September, that the prime minister indeed will seek election to the Rajya Sabha from his State. He added that this is a 'temporary decision' and he would seek election to the Lok Sabha after the UP polls.

[1] *The Statesman*, 19 September 1996.
[2] S. Gopal (ed), *Selected Works of Jawaharlal Nehru*, Second Services Jawaharlal Nehru Memorial Fund and Oxford University Press, vol. 17, p. 345.

No reasons were cited. The irrelevance of the UP polls to such a decision is obvious. This course will do worse than damage Gowda's prestige and credibility; it will also damage the prestige and authority of the office of the nation's chief executive. We have come to this sorry pass because breaches of the rules were condoned in the past. That chief ministers were imposed on States by the party's central leadership was bad enough. Worse still, the nominee did not have a seat in the state legislature.

In 1971 the report of the Committee of Governors, appointed by the president, deprecated this practice. It noted that the Constitution does permit appointments of such a person as minister, but said 'The chief minister, however, occupies a more conspicuous and important position, and the convention needs to be developed that an elected member should be chosen as leader of the group or groups claiming to form the government.' It however watered down this salutory advice by adding this preposterous qualification: 'If, in very exceptional circumstances, a person, who is not already elected, is chosen as leader and is invited to be the chief minister, he must stand for election within the shortest possible time ...' Even so, they clearly meant election to the assembly, not the council.[3]

The relevant and rather quaintly worded constitutional provision is Article 75(5) which reads: 'A minister who for any period of six consecutive months is not a member of either house of parliament shall at the expiration of that period cease to be a minister.' A warning and a word of advice, from judges of the United States' Supreme Court come to mind. The warning: The worst way to read a Constitution is to read it literally. The advice, 'It is a Constitution that we are expounding'.

The constituent assembly debates show that this provision was not meant for the prime minister at all but for ministers other than the prime minister. Its counterpart for the States is Article 164(4). Dr B.R. Ambedkar explained its raison d'être on 31 December 1948 when a member objected to it: 'It is perfectly possible to imagine that a person who is otherwise competent to hold the post of a minister has been defeated in a constituency ..., It is not a reason why a member so competent as that should not be permitted to be appointed a member of the cabinet on the assumption that he

[3]Report of the Committee of Governors, p. 34.

shall be able to get himself elected either from the same or another constituency.'[4]

The entire long paragraph of his exposition concerned appointment as 'a member of the cabinet', an institution that already existed, having been formed by the prime minister as its 'head' (Article 74(1)). For instance, Dr Ambedkar referred to such an appointee pending his election to parliament being 'prepared to accept the policy of the cabinet'. In this light, the view expressed earlier that the appointment as prime minister of one who is not a member of parliament is valid is not correct. For good measure, Dr Ambedkar stressed that this interim situation would not violate the principle of collective responsibility of the council of ministers to the Lok Sabha as Article 75(3) mandates. This suggests that the appointee's status is as a "member other than the 'head' of the cabinet".

Thus read, as, indeed, Article 75(5) should be read, the appointments as Prime Minister of both, P.V. Narasimha Rao and H.D. Deve Gowda were unconstitutional. The heavens would not have fallen had the Constitution had been followed. Granted that the leader of the Congress Party was tragically assassinated in the midst of the election campaign in 1991, the Congress parliamentary party could not have been so bankrupt in talent as not to find a leader from its members in the Lok Sabha. It is this silent encroachment on the spirit and letter of the Constitution that has brought the country to the present situation when its prime minister is trying desperately to delay and perhaps avoid popular verdict on himself.

Nehru's dicta were wholly in accord with the Constitution. They were fortified by yet stronger disapproval of events in Madras by President Rajendra Prasad, who had earlier served as president of the constituent assembly. In the first general elections in 1952, the Congress fared badly in Madras and was reduced to a minority. However, both, Governor Sri Prakasa and Rajaji were determined to keep the Communists out. The governor nominated Rajaji to the legislative council, whereupon he was elected leader of the Congress party on 31 March and was invited to form a government by his friend, Sri Prakasa, the following day, 1 April. The president thoroughly disapproved of this[5]. Incidentally, before his election as leader, Rajaji had gone so far as to suggest president's rule. Nehru's

[4]CAD, vol. vii, p. 1186

[5]S. Gopal, *Jawaharlal Nehru: A Biography*, Volume Two, 1947–1956, Delhi: Oxford University Press, 1979, p. 221.

admonition of 5 March was flouted. Sri Prakasa did not conceal his sleight of hand from the president. He felt, he wrote to Rajen babu, that 'in order that the matter may not look too obvious I should nominate two or three other persons along with him [Rajaji]'. One hopes that Mr Deve Gowda will not pick on this to declaim: 'And even in the great Nehru's days violations of the Constitution were not unknown'; implying, why pick on his all too humble self.

The chief executive, be he prime minister or chief minister, has the power to select his colleagues in the cabinet, advise the head of state to dismiss them, advise dissolution of the lower house, preside over the cabinet, besides the powers of patronage. It is absurd that he should not be a member of the house directly elected by the people to whom he is responsible and which alone controls the public purse.

He represents the nation in a real sense. What respect can he command in the eyes of the nation and the world outside if he is seen to be avoiding his own election by the people?

In Britain no peer has become prime minister since 1902. Richard Crossman's theory of 'prime ministerial government' may be an exaggeration but he was right in pointing out that some vital decisions were taken by prime ministers without consulting the cabinet, e.g. making the atomic bomb and launching attacks on the Suez. The least the people can expect is that so powerful an office be held by one who has faced the electorate.

India has not been particularly fortunate in the choice of its prime ministers since Jawaharlal Nehru breathed his last. Without exception, every one of those who followed left the office in a condition worse than when he or she came to occupy it. Bar only a few, whose political and personal protests were brushed aside, and very rightly too, by and large people overlooked the constitutional infraction in Deve Gowda's appointment as Prime Minister, as they had in P.V. Narasimha Rao's five years earlier. They hoped desperately that he would perform well and so make a success of the job of holding the BJP at bay.

His conduct and performance since have been sadly disappointing. If he has any desire to wipe out corruption, it remains one of Deve Gowda's best kept secrets. He has neither the capacity nor the desire.

A prime minister's entry into Parliament by the back door would reduce the office of the prime minister of India to a state where it would not be worthy even of a politician who demeans himself thus to hold it. However, in the fullness of time the office will undoubtedly recover. The politician's prestige will not.

20
Rajya Sabha: Clog or Rubber Stamp?[1]

This will probably be the fifth time that, following a government's defeat in the elections to the Lok Sabha, the elated spirits of its victorious successor are somewhat dampened as it wakes up to the fact that it faces a Rajya Sabha in which it has no majority. This happened in 1977, 1980, 1989, 1986 and now in 1998. The 1996 precedent is, perhaps, not so apposite as the Congress supported the United Front Government from outside. In the other cases the upper house came to life and made its presence felt, not always wisely.

On 11 April 1977, the Congress, smarting under a humiliating defeat, persisted in its amendments to the Government of Union Territories (Amendment) Bill and the Delhi Administration (Amendment) Bill which totally defeated the objects of the Bills. The Bills sought an extension to the life of the legislative assemblies of Goa, Daman & Diu, and Mizoram by seven months and of the Delhi metropolitan council by four months, respectively. The amendments sought to extend the terms of all these bodies to six years. These were clearly 'wrecking amendments', as they are known in parliamentary parlance. Not surprisingly, the mover of the Bills, the union Home Minister, Charan Singh, refused to proceed with them.

The Janata Party government faced enormous difficulties in implementing its electoral pledge to repeal the 42nd Amendment to the Constitution enacted during the Emergency, for which it

[1] *The Statesman*, 1 May 1998.

has received an unambiguous mandate from the people. Eventually a compromise was arrived at and its worst features were removed. Indira Gandhi did not have to face such a situation for long after her return to power in January 1980. Biennial elections to the Rajya Sabha were due that year. She sacked nine state governments in February. The 1977 precedent is relevant because now, as then, there is a deep divide between the government and the Opposition; a divide which, despite profuse assurances, the government has widened by one action after another; appointment of a party man as governor to an Opposition-ruled State (Bihar), in the teeth of the Sarkaria Committee Report, is the latest in the sorry series.

The Opposition would, however, be ill-advised to borrow a leaf from the Congress's black book, nor need it play second fiddle to the government. The Rajya Sabha has a role to play in our constitutional set up and its significance is best understood in the light of authoritative dicta by the framers of the Constitution.

The BJP, on its part, would do well to bear in mind that in a Rajya Sabha of 245 members its strength, allies included, is less than one third. The Congress(I), the UF, and Independents are more that twice as many; not to forget the BJP's 13 vote majority in the Lok Sabha. The biennial elections to the Rajya Sabha will be held on 20 May when the final picture will emerge.

The Rajya Sabha's status is in stark contrast to that of legislative councils in the states and its relationship with the Lok Sabha is quite different from that between a State's legislative assembly and its legislative council. A deadlock between the two houses of parliament is to be resolved by majority of members both present and voting at a joint sitting of the two houses, as provided in Article 108 of the Constitution, though the Lok Sabha controls the government of the day and the public purse to the complete exclusion of the Rajya Sabha. The latter, however, has a function as a second chamber in a federation. However, a State assembly has only to pass the Bill a second time for its will to eventually prevail (Article 197). The assembly can even secure the abolition of the council altogether by a two-thirds vote and a majority of the total membership of the assembly provided parliament so agrees. Such a law is not regarded as an amendment of the Constitution (Article 169).

Two authoritative expositions are relevant. When the constituent assembly discussed the report of the Union Constitution committee, presided over by Jawaharlal Nehru, N Gopalaswamy Ayyangar, a senior member, explained in detail the raison d'être of the Rajya Sabha, on 28 July 1947, in these terms:

The need for a second chamber has been felt practically all over the world wherever there are federations of any importance. After all, the question for us to consider is whether it performs any useful function. The most that we expect the second chamber to do is perhaps to hold dignified debates on important issues and to delay legislations which might be the outcome of passions of the moment until the passions have subsided and calm consideration could be bestowed on the measures which will be before the legislature; and we shall take care to provide in the Constitution that whenever on any important matter, particularly matters relating to finance, there is conflict between the house of the people and the council of states, it is the view of the house of the people that shall prevail. Therefore, what we really achieve by the existence of this Second Chamber is only an instrument by which we delay action which might be hastily conceived, and we also give an opportunity, perhaps, to seasoned people who may not be in the thick of the political fray, but who might be willing to participate in the debate with an amount of learning and importance which we do not ordinarily associate with a house of the people.'[2]

Note the somewhat apologetic tone. Members' disquiet was sought to be allayed two years later by the chairman of the drafting committee on 20 May 1949 when the provision for resolution of deadlock between the two houses of parliament came up for discussion on 20 May 1949. Members voiced the fear that the Rajya Sabha might thwart the will of the people expressed in the Lok Sabha which is directly elected. Dr B.R. Ambedkar assured them:

With regard to the observations that have been made by several speakers regarding the provisions contained in Article 88 [the equivalent of Article 108 of the Constitution, in the draft], all I can say is, there is some amount of justification for the fear they have expressed, but as other members have pointed out, this is not in any sense a novel provision. It is contained in various other Constitutions also and, therefore, my suggestion to them is to allow this Article to stand as it is and see what happens in course of time. If their fears come true, I have no doubt that some honourable member will come forward hereafter to have the Article amended through the procedure we have prescribed for the amendment of the Constitution.'[3]

[2]CAD, vol. iv, p. 876.
[3]CAD, vol. viii, p. 183

That surely is not all. The Rajya Sabha is very much a council of States, its original designation vis-à-vis the house of the people (the Lok Sabha). That its members are elected by the legislative assemblies of the states is not without significance even if they are not equally represented in the council as in the US Senate but according to the size of their population.

The Rajya Sabha is not only a house for second thoughts but also a guardian of State's rights. Article 249 of the Constitution empowers parliament to legislate with respect to a matter in the State list if the council of states has declared by a resolution, supported by not less than two-thirds of the members present and voting, that 'it is necessary or expedient in the national interest' that parliament should legislate on that matter.

When this provision was debated in the constituent assembly on 13 June 1949, Mr T.T. Krishnamachari, a member of the drafting committee, fully shared the disquiet expressed by members of the assembly on two grounds. One was the possibility of abuse of such a unique provision. The other was the universal trend of the Centre amassing power in all federations. If the provision was adopted none the less, it was because the assembly accepted the Rajya Sabha as a reliable check on abuse of Article 249. As Krishnamachari put it, the Centre would be 'empowered by the council of States in which the component States are adequately represented and that act of empowering parliament is by a two-thirds majority, which implied that the States agree to the Centre attracting to itself that power.'[4] Implicit in this is recognition of the Rajya Sabha as a representative of the States and its vote as the collective will of the States.

There is yet another indication of their awareness of that. It was the constituent assembly itself functioning as parliament, before the first general election in 1952, which enacted the Representation of the People Acts 1950 and 1951. The union law minister who piloted the measure was Dr B.R. Ambedkar, one of the principal architects of the Constitution. The language used in Section 3 of the Act of 1951 for prescribing qualification for membership of the council of states is significant: 'A person shall not be qualified to be chosen as a representative of any state in the council of states unless he is an elector for a parliamentary constituency in that State.' This requirement has been evaded by shoddy methods. Section 3 envisages

[4]CAD, vol. viii, p. 803.

a member of the Rajya Sabha as 'a representative' of the State to which he belongs. In contrast, Section 4 which prescribes qualificaticns for membership of the Lok Sabha, speaks simply of a person to be chosen 'to fill a seat in the house of the people'. He is required to be a voter in 'any' parliamentary constituency in the country. A person must be 'ordinarily resident in a constituency' of the assembly in order to qualify for enrolment as a voter in that assembly constituency and thus in the parliamentary constituency of which it is a part. In December 1993, the Chief Election Commissioner, T.N. Seshan, read the Riot act on this. True to form he did nothing about it. Unless the abuses that have crept in of persons living in Delhi and pretending to be voters elsewhere is set right, the Rajya Sabha will not work effectively as a guardian of the states' rights, a necessary role in a federation. A nameplate or even the ownership of a house does not make it one's 'dwelling house', still less confer 'ordinary residence' there as the law itself makes clear. People have lied on solemn declarations to enter the Rajya Sabha, thus brazenly deceiving the nation.

The Rajya Sabha must assert itself as a 'house of correction'. Its function is improvement of legislation passed by the lower house, not obstruction. If a question of principle arises, it must dig in its heels, without shutting the door to a fair compromise at a joint sitting of the house of the people and the council of states.

21
'Strangers' in the Rajya Sabha[1]

The Rajya Sabha elections are over but the issue of MPs securing election by false declarations on their 'ordinary residence' cannot be brushed aside. It concerns both our federalism and the probity of public life. However, consistently with our political culture, rather than addressing themselves to such basic issues, politicians talk of changing the law to legitimize the fraud of the past and subvert for the future what is left of the Rajya Sabha.

The Representation of the People Act, 1950 (on delimitation of constituencies and preparation of electoral rolls, etc.) and the Representation of the People Act, 1951 (qualification of membership of legislatures, conduct of elections, etc.) were piloted in parliament by a law minister, Dr B.R. Ambedkar, who had served as the chairman of the drafting committee of the constituent assembly.

The Act of 1951 requires mandatorily (Section 3) that a member of the council of states (Rajya Sabha) must be 'an elector for a parliamentary constituency in that state' because, as that provision puts it, he is to be 'chosen as a representative' of that very 'state'. In deliberate contrast, a member of the house of the people (Lok Sabha) may be 'an elector for any parliamentary constituency'. The country's unity is recognized; so is its diversity.

The upper house is not only a forum for second thoughts. As Sir John Marriott's classic, *Upper Chambers*, says, 'whatever be the case with unitary states, the bicameral system is essential to the successful working of a genuinely federal system.'[2] Indeed, 'bicameralism is an essential attribute of federalism'. In the

---

[1] *The Statesman*, 24 February 1994.

[2] John A.R Marriott, *Second Chambers*, 2nd edn, Oxford: Clarendon Press, 1927, p. 228

constituent assembly, Mr N. Gopalaswamy Ayyanger remarked, on 28 July 1947, that 'the need for a second chamber has been felt practically all over the world wherever there are federations of any importance'.

Recognition of the Rajya Sabha's role as a guardian of States' rights and as a monitor of the working of India's federalism is reflected in Article 249 of the Constitution. It empowers parliament to legislate on a matter in the state list provided the Rajya Sabha had permitted this. It can do so by a resolution supported by not less than two-thirds of the members present and voting, declaring that 'it is necessary or expedient in the national interest' that parliament should legislate on that matter. Such legislation, like any other, is passed by both houses, but the green signal is given by the Rajya Sabha alone. The Acts of 1950 and 1951 carried out this scheme. The statutes must be read in the context of the Constitution.

While the Act of 1951 mandatorily prescribes that a 'representative of the State' in the Rajya Sabha must also be a voter in that State, the Act of 1950 and the rules made under it prescribe a detailed procedure for enrolment as voter in an assembly constituency. The electoral roll for every parliamentary constituency consists of the electoral rolls of all the assembly constituencies in that parliamentary constituency'.

Two basic principles are laid down by Sections 17 and 18 of the Act of 1950. No person shall be entitled to be registered in the electoral roll for more than one assembly constituency or in its roll more than once. Two conditions are prescribed by Section 19 for enrolment; namely, a minimum age of 18 years and that the person 'is ordinarily resident in a constituency'. Thereupon, he shall be entitled to be registered in the roll 'for that constituency'. Such residence must obtain at the time of enrolment ('is ordinarily resident').

There is a plethora of judicial dicta on when a person can be said to be 'ordinarily resident'. They all stress the intention to reside, not mere ownership of a house. Section 20(1) of Act of 1950 plugged this one loophole which would strike anyone who falsely wished to claim that they were 'ordinarily resident' at a given place. It says in so many words that 'a person shall not be deemed to be ordinarily resident in a constituency on the ground only that he owns, or is in possession of, a dwelling house therein'. Yet, astonishingly, this is precisely the one ground advanced in recent years by almost all the delinquents to claim ordinary residence.

When the claims by these public figures are tested against well known, established facts of their residence, what emerges is a concord of cynics whose members, transcending political differences, are united by a common disdain for the law. Successive chief election commissioners have shut their eyes to it. The law became a mere 'technicality'. Even persons of outstanding personal integrity like Dr Manmohan Singh were lured into this by party managers. It is to Mr Seshan's credit that he sounded the tocsin on 28 December 1993.

Incidentally, Section 20(7) empowers the government to prescribe, in consultation with the election commission, rules amplifying the test of ordinary residence, so that 'if in any case a question arises as to where a person is ordinarily resident at any relevant time, the question shall be determined with reference to all the facts of the case and to such rules ...' Section 23(1) of the Act enables any person whose name is not included in the electoral roll of a constituency to apply to the electoral registration officer for the inclusion of his name in that roll. Section 22 empowers that officer, whether on his own motion or on an application made to him, to amend, delete, or transpose an entry in the electoral roll on the ground *inter alia* that the person is 'not entitled to be registered in that roll'.

Section 31 of the Act of 1950 makes it a criminal offence to make false declarations in connection with, *inter alia,* the inclusion or exclusion of any entry in or from an electoral roll. That is, 'a statement or declaration in writing which is false and which he either knows or believes to be false or does not believe to be true'. The offence is punishable with imprisonment for a term that may extend to one year or with fine or both. Section 468 of the Criminal Procedure Code prescribes one year as the period of limitation for cognizance of such an offence by a court. Section 469 adds that the period of limitation commences on the date of the offence.

The Registration of Electors Rules, 1960, made under the Act of 1950, provide the details. Briefly, every application for inclusion of a name in an electoral roll must be signed by the person who desires his name to be included and also countersigned by another person whose name is already included in the roll in which the claimant desires his name to be included. Such an application must be in a prescribed form, Form 6 (Rules 13 and 26). One has only to read Form 6 to be stuck by the gravity of the offence and the brazenness of the offenders.

Any 'request' for inclusion of a name in an electoral roll is followed by statements of fact which the applicant is required to 'declare to the best of my knowledge and belief'. One of the statements is that 'I am ordinarily resident at the address given above'. Similarly, statements are required as to non-inclusion or exclusion of the name elsewhere. His espousing voter is required to 'support this claim and countersign it.'

Both, however, are put on clear notice by an emphatic note at the foot of Form 6. It reads: 'Any person who makes a statement or declaration which is false and which he either knows or believes to be false or does not believe to be true is punishable under Section 31 of the Representation of the People Act, 1950.'

However, this offence also falls within the ambit of Section 199 of the Penal Code and constitutes the offence of giving 'false evidence', as defined by Section 193, which is punishable with a 7-year term and is not subject to any period of limitation.

On 22 December 1993, the Election Commission (EC) reminded the chief electoral officers in states about the correct legal position. On 28 December it cited seven union ministers and 13 other Rajya Sabha members who, according to the records, appeared 'prima facie' to have violated the law: 'presumed' to have got elected on 'bogus and false entries' in the electoral rolls. The list comprised only persons elected after 1 January, 1988. Electoral registration officers (EROs) were directed to take corrective action under Section 22. The EC also suggested penal action.

These specific cases have since been highlighted. On 9 February the EC directed the ERO of Hassangarh in Haryana not to take a decision on the application of the union minister of state for law and justice, Mr H.R. Bhardwaj, to delete his name from the electoral rolls there because it had been found during its inquiry that Mr Bhardwaj continued to be registered as an elector from two constituencies, one in Madhya Pradesh (from where he was elected) and the other in Haryana.

On the same day, the EC directed the ERO, Gurgaon, to reconsider the status of Mr Dinesh Singh, the minister for external affairs, as a voter there since his registration was done on the basis of 'tenuous facts'. Considering the reports sent by the ERO and the information available to it, the EC concluded that on 19 April 1993, while filing the application for registration as a voter in village Dhankot of the Gurgaon assembly constituency, Mr Dinesh Singh had hired one room, a garage, and a kitchen but had no intention of becoming 'ordinarily resident' at the place. The ERO, the EC observed, had failed to examine whether Mr Dinesh Singh was also 'ordinarily resident' in village Kunda in Partapgarh district of Uttar Pradesh where he was earlier registered as a voter.

On 11 February 1994 the Maharashtra election department informed the EC that Mr Ghulam Nabi Azad, the Tourism Minister, was not qualified to be elected to the Rajya Sabha from the state and his name had, accordingly, been deleted from the list of voters. Dr D.K. Shankaran, Chief Electoral Officer of the State, revealed that following the EC's directives, 'the Assistant Returning Officer Washim examined relevant documents from 1980' and found that Mr Azad was not ordinarily resident in Washim. On 17 February a senior official told the press that the state's election department is contemplating penal proceedings against Mr Azad for furnishing 'false' information.

However, there is one cause célèbre which has not received the attention it merits. It concerns none other than the president of the BJP, Mr Lal Krishn Advani. His name was included in the electoral roll of Lashkar assembly constituency in Gwalior district while he was a Rajya Sabha MP from Gujarat. A local journalist and Congress leader, Mr Surya Prakash Johri, filed a complaint in 1982 before the judicial magistrate seeking to initiate action against Mr Advani and Mr Amal Chand for 'submitting false statements'. It was alleged that Mr Advani had applied for the inclusion of his name in the electoral roll of Lashkar though he had never stayed there or in Gwalior.

The additional sessions judge, Gwalior, not only upheld the magistrate's decision but also directed that, besides charges under Section 31 of the Act of 1950, charges under Section 193 of the penal code should also be framed against Mr Advani. He further quashed the order acquitting Mr Amal Chand and directed the framing of charges against him too.

The two moved the Gwalior bench of the Madhya Pradesh high court to quash the sessions court's orders. The high court rejected their petition last August. Mr Justice V.D. Gyani upheld the session court's direction to frame charges against both Mr Advani and M Amal Chand. He rejected Mr Advani's contention that charges unde Section 193 of the IPC cannot be framed against a person who ha already been charged under Section 31 of the Act of 1950.

The election commission must fully examine the three cases of Mr H.R. Bhardwaj, Mr Dinesh Singh, and Mr Ghulam Nabi Azad and must pursue cases against all those who were elected this month to the Rajya Sabha from states where they were not 'ordinarily resident'. As well as prosecutions under Section 31 of the Act of 1950 and Section 199 of the penal code, such MPs are liable to be unseated on an election petition filed in the high court, Section 100 of the Act of 1951 lists the grounds for declaring an election to be void. One of them is 'that on the date of his election a returned candidate was not qualified'. Ano·l er is improper acceptance of a nomination paper that materially affects the election. Under Section 81 an election petition can be filed not only by any candidate·but also by any voter within 45 days of the poll.

22
Parliament in Peril [1]

A n incompetent, uneducated, and irresponsible Opposition has dealt a severe blow to India's parliamentary democracy. Undoubtedly, there is an unanswerable case for a thorough and independent inquiry into the Telecom scandal and into the charges levelled against the minister for communications, Mr Sukh Ram. That Messrs Chandra Shekhar and George Fernandes rushed to his defence in a macabre performance, at a joint press conference on 21 December 1995 can help little to repel the charges. A probe alone can.

Someone else, who alone could have helped in resolving tangle, did not. Having spent his entire political life in the service of, successively, two autocrats, it is not fair to expect Mr P.V. Narasimha Rao to show outstanding qualities of leadership at this age. Even so, his studied absence from parliament throughout the crisis into which it was plunged was highly improper. When at last he spoke, on 22 December 1995, it was to his partymen. He has revealed a cynicism that is all too natural in the head of government whose career has been marred by one scandal after another.

Direct Action

None of this however can affect the incontestable fact that the crisis into which both houses of parliament were plunged, for nearly a fortnight, was entirely of the Opposition's making. No Opposition party in parliament has a right to insist on the acceptance of any of

[1]An earlier version of this article was published in the *Statesman*, 3 January 1996.

its demands, no matter how reasonable, as a precondition to its participation in its proceedings, least of all to so obstruct them as to render its functioning impossible. Parliament is not an arena for civil disobedience or direct action or *dharna*. The spectacle of leaders of the Opposition making merry while performing *dharna* at the main gate of Parliament was a revolting one.

It is very doubtful if any of these blissfully ignorant souls had a clue about the implications of their behaviour. One of them, who once enjoyed high respect for commitment to parliamentary values, Mr Atal Behari Vajpayee, has revealed that the opportunism that prodded him to go along with the forces of Hindutva, while emitting occasional cries of anguish, has goaded him to join the merry crowd with equal abandon.

To think that this was the MP who, during a similar but much more brief crisis in 1974 in the Tulmohan Ram case, made little secret of his disapproval of *dharnas* in the house. The Opposition then won, albeit at a very high price, an important concession. The government belatedly agreed to permit it to study the official records. The precedent has since been followed in the States as well.

The provocation then was grave. On 9 September 1974, the union home minister, Mr Uma Shankar Dixit, had solemnly promised the Lok Sabha that he would report to it 'after the investigation is over'. A couple of hours before parliament's winter session began on 11 November, a charge-sheet was filed in court so that government could argue in the house that since the licence scandal was now sub judice, parliament could not discuss it. (The sub judice rule has been invoked repeatedly and deserves a closer look.) Interestingly, during the interval, the home portfolio was transferred from Mr Dixit to Mr Brahmananda Reddy in order to save the former from embarrassment.

In the case in point the government proposed, at a fairly early stage, inspection of the relevant files by party leaders, debate in the two houses, and a decision on the mode of inquiry thereafter. Since the offer was made by Mr V.C. Shukla, minister for parliamentary affairs, the Opposition's wariness was understandable. Not so its total rejection, least of all its demand of a prior 'commitment' to the establishment of a joint parliamentary committee (JPC) or, for that matter, any committee of parliament.

In doing so, it revealed its abysmal ignorance of the importance of parliamentary debate. 'We don't want a debate for debate's sake',

Mr Vajpayee said on 19 December while the Left Front and Janata Dal's memorandum to the president, on 22 December, 4 queried: 'Can we remain supine spectators to the process of parliamentary proceedings being reduced to desicating debates, particularly when the government has, time and again, cynically tried to sweep a succession of scandals under the carpet ?'

The implication is plain. Since debates do not yield the result desired by the Opposition, it will prevent parliament from functioning. There is a certain contempt for debates per se, as if they are an exercise in futility. However, a parliamentary debate has a direct impact on the minds of the public. No wonder then that Indira Gandhi even when she lifted pre-censorship during the Emergency, was careful to retain it for three topics. One of them was proceedings in parliament.

Vigorous Debate

Vigorous debate in parliament can well be complemented by mass meetings outside, by protest marches and demonstrations. Dr B.R. Ambedkar is relevant not only as a champion of the *dalits* but, no less, as an architect of the Constitution. His speech in the constituent assembly on 25 November 1949, as it was about to conclude its task, is of enormous relevance. He posed a question of vital importance and provided its answer which we have forgotten to our great loss:

If we wish to maintain democracy not merely in form, but also in fact, what must we do? The first thing in my judgment we must do is to hold fast to constitutional methods of achieving our social and economic objectives; ... It means that we must abandon the method of civil disobedience, non-cooperation and satyagraha .... Where constitutional methods are open, there can be no justification for these unconstitutional methods. These methods are nothing but the grammar of anarchy and the sooner they are abandoned the better for us.'[2]

Dr Ambedkar was speaking of conduct outside parliament. His warning is all the more applicable to conduct within it. Parliamentary tradition recognizes obstruction as a permissible tactic but within the rules. It has 'quite a respectable history', Jennings recalled.'Party

[2]CAD, vol. xii, p. 978.

warfare is essential to the working of the democratic system. Yet it will not function if it is carried to extremes. A government in control of both houses could effectively stifle the Opposition. An Opposition that would not accept the majority rule could make the parliamentary system unworkable. In practice, government is by consent and opposition by agreement.'[3] Public opinion is the referee of both sides.

What Jennings added in the concluding pages of his classic *Cabinet Government* is very pertinent:

The function of parliament is not to govern but to criticize. Its criticism, too, is directed not so much towards a fundamental modification of the, government's policy as towards the education of public opinion ... the government governs and the Opposition criticizes. Failure to understand this simple principle is one of the causes of the failure of so many of the progeny of mother of parliaments and of the supersession of parliamentary government by dictatorships.'[4]

Greater Clarity

The same idea was expressed with even greater clarity by the philosopher–politician A.J. Balfour, in a conversation with his niece Blanche Dugdale on 25 April 1925:

I doubt if you would find it written in any book on the British constitution that the whole essence of British parliamentary government lies in the intention to make the thing work. We take that for granted. We have spent hundreds of years in elaborating a system that rests on that alone. It is so deep in us that we have lost sight of it. But it isn't so obvious to others. These peoples—Indians, Egyptians, and so on—study our learning. They read our history, our philosophy, our politics. They learn about our parliamentary methods of obstruction, but nobody explains to them that when it comes to the point all our parliamentary parties are determined that the machinery shan't stop. 'The king's government must go on', as the Duke of Wellington said. But their idea is that the function of opposition is to stop the machine. Nothing easier of course, but hopeless.[5]

We do not have to go far to see what rejection of this principle

[3]Jennings, *Cabinet Government*, p. 16.
[4]Ibid, p. 472.
[5]Blanche E.C. Dugdale, *Arthur James Balfour*, (London: Hutchinson, 1936), p. 364 'Their idea is that the function of opposition is to stop the machine'

entails. Parliamentary democracy is in siege in Bangladesh because the Opposition simply would not let the government govern. In Pakistan, Mr Nawaz Sharif refuses to accept his defeat in the elections; as Mrs Benazir Bhutto did before him. We are fortunate that the essential probity of our electoral process is not questioned, but we have been through nearly two decades of sharp political polarization that has exacted its toll. Our parliamentary process has suffered in consequence.

23
Inquiries by Parliamentary Committees[1]

P eople who do not know any better blame the parliamentary system. Dr B.R. Ambedkar had foreseen this. He told the constituent assembly, on 4 November 1948, when he moved that the draft Constitution be taken into consideration: 'If things go wrong under the new Constitution, the reason will not be that we had a bad Constitution. What we will have to say is that man was vile.'[2] A year later he was to remark: 'However good a Constitution may be, it is sure to turn out bad because those who are called to work it happen to be a bad lot.. Who can say how the people of India and their parties will behave ?'[3]

The short answer is that they have so behaved as to confirm the doubts of men like Balfour. It was bad enough for the Opposition to hold parliament to ransom because its demand was not accepted. It was worse still that the demand was for a joint parliamentary committee (JPC) which was most unlikely to complete its job before the general elections. What else was this but crass opportunism ?

Only an uneducated Opposition would demand a JPC on the telecom scandal or, for that matter, any other scandal. The one on the banks scam succeeded in exceptional circumstances; not least because of the personality of its chairman, Mr Ram Niwas Mirdha. It is a disused and rightly discarded instrument. The reasons are set out authoritatively in the report of the Royal Commission on Tribunal of Inquiry (1966) headed by an eminent jurist, Sir Cyril

[1] The Statesman, 4 January 1996.
[2] CAD, vol. vii, p. 44.
[3] CAD, vol. xii, p. 975.

Salmon. Formerly, select parliamentary committees of inquiry were set up. The Marconi scandal put an end to that.

The postmaster-general, Herbert Samuel, accepted the tender of the British Marconi Company to set up an imperial chain of wireless telegraphy, on 7 March 1912; subject to parliamentary approval. Its chairman was Godfrey Isaacs, brother of the attorney-general, Rufus Isaacs (later Lord Reading). The American Marconi Company, which was financially independent of the British company, issued new shares. Godfrey placed a block of them in England. Rufus refused to buy them but another brother Harry did. Rufus, however, later took a chunk of them from Harry after due inquiries of the independence of the American concern. Also, Rufus sold some shares to Lloyd George and the Master of Elibank. As prices soared, Rufus sold out most of his shares. His colleagues sold some of theirs and bought some again as an investment.

Soon charges were aired that the PMG had made heavy payments to the company in order to enrich his colleagues. Samuel himself moved for the appointment of a select committee of the Commons. Unfortunately, during the debate, Rufus, while denying any investment in the English company, did not mention investments in the American one. Nor, on his advice, did Lloyd George. They intended to mention it to the committee. The committee's report, on 13 June 1913, exonerated all three unanimously of corruption, but a minority report accused them of having committed a 'grave impropriety' and of having 'been wanting in frankness and respect for the House of Commons'. The committee of 14 members, excluding the chairman, split along party lines, 8–6, so did the house: 346–268.[4]

That was enough to destroy this mechanism when, in 1921, grave charges were made against officials of the ministry of munitions. Parliament enacted the Tribunals of Inquiry (Evidence) Act, 1921, on which our Commissions of Inquiry Act, 1952 is modelled. The Salmon Commission strongly argued against the committees and for probes by 'tribunals free from political influences'. It strongly favoured recourse to tribunals on 'matters of vital public importance concerning which there is something in the nature of a nationwide crisis of confidence. In such cases we

[4]G.R. Searle, *Corruption in British Politics*, 1895–1930, Oxford: Oxford University Press,1987, pp. 172–200.

consider that no other method of investigation would be adequate.'[5]

Unfortunately, by 1987 commissions of inquiry had fallen into disrepute thanks to the Thakkar commission on Indira Gandhi's assassination, the Thakkar–Natarajan commission on Fairfax, the Ranganath Misra commission on the Delhi riots of 1984, and some others. On 14 December 1987, Mr V.P. Singh revealed in the Rajya Sabha how judges were selected for the Fairfax commission in his presence. Mr P. Shiv Shankar brought along a list of the desirables to the office of the prime minister, Rajiv Gandhi, amongst whom the selection was made. The solution lies in insisting on the appointment of the judge by common consent; in reforming the commission, not in discarding it in favour of something far worse.

While in Britain the ministers, Lloyd George and his colleagues, were grilled by the committee, the Indian JPC cannot summon ministers and is hopelessly dependent on the speaker under the rules of procedure of the Lok Sabha. He appoints its chairman (Rule 258), determines disputes as to relevance of a witness or a document (Rule 270), and on 'procedure or otherwise'. He can also issue directions to regulate the procedure and organize the committee's work (Rule 283). Can anyone be in any doubt as to what this spells for any JPC in the context of 1995–6 as against that of 1992–3 ? There will be disputes galore.

It is preposterous to suggest that the prime minister's proposal to Mr Atal Behari Vajpayee on 20 December of 'an agency outside parliament' was an 'insult' to parliament. The Act of 1952 itself empowers the Lok Sabha to set up a commission of inquiry. Whether the prime minister would have accepted such a body is another matter, but that was no reason for not pressing for it within parliament and outside. Even in the USA, where party discipline is lax, the Senate Whitewater Committee tends to divide on party lines. The Opposition's insistence on a JPC was, to say the least, foolish if not cynical. One is inclined to suspect it was the latter, for cynicism alone can explain the destructive streak it exhibited in the infamous fortnight of December 1995.

[5]Royal Commission on Tribunals of Inquiry, 1966, HM SO, London, Cmnd. 3121, p. 16, para 27

24
The Speaker[1]

Even those who disapprove of his politics admire Atal Behari Vajpayee as the parliamentarian par excellence. It is a thousand pities that he should have commenced his second tenure as prime minister with a blow that inflicts damage on the values on which parliamentary democracy rests: the trust and confidence between government and the Opposition and the impartiality of the speaker, which is ensured by his election by consensus. They have been damaged to no gain. The government suffered in esteem; the speaker's office, in its standing; and parliament itself in its prestige. That was evident in the uproarious scenes on 24 March 1998 at the very moment Mr G.M.C. Balayogi of the TDP was elected defeating the Congress–UF candidate, Mr P.A. Sangma.

A grave disservice has been done to Mr Balayogi himself. For the first time in the life of the Lok Sabha, the election of its speaker was followed by a cacophony of voices. He needs a good deputy speaker to guide him. He has an onerous task ahead of controlling a house in which discipline and decorum have been declining steeply over the past three decades.

By an instructive coincidence, on that very day Kesri Nath Tripathi gave his expected ruling as speaker of the UP assembly on the defection of the BSP MLAs to the BJP five months ago. This is what Rajiv Gandhi's anti-defection law has accomplished. It put a premium on the politicization of an office which was never too far above the muddy waters of Indian politics. The BSP leader, Kanshi Ram, realist to the core, had asked for a change in the holder of the office of speaker along with transfer of power by the BSP to the

[1] *The Statesman*, 5 April 1998.

BJP in UP last year. Beneath the cynicism lay recognition of a sound principle: the speaker must not be a stooge of the government.

Paragraph 6 of the Tenth Schedule to the Constitution, embodying the anti-defection law, makes the speaker the sole judge of disputes arising under it. Paragraph 7 barred the jurisdiction of the courts but it was unanimously struck down by the Supreme Court in 1992. However, the five-judge bench split narrowly on the reasons for the decision.[2] Three judges were content to let their ruling rest on the narrow ground that a constitutional amendment, which made any changes, *inter alia,* in Chapter VI of the Constitution needs prior ratification by at least one-half of the states. Articles 226 and 227 conferring writ jurisdiction on the high court fall in this chapter. So does Chapter IV of Part V on the Supreme Court, another part so entrenched. Admittedly there was no such ratification.

The majority held Paragraph 7 to be severable from the rest. The minority (Justices L.M. Sharma and J.S. Verma) disagreed and also held that conferment on the speaker of the power to decide disputes was violative of a basic feature of the Constitution and therefore unconstitutional. Justice Verma's judgment (on behalf of L.M. Sharma J and himself) was realistic and, in a sense, prophetic:

It is only by a fair adjudication of such disputes relating to validity of elections and subsequent disqualifications of members that true reflection of the electoral mandate and governance by rule of law essential for democracy can be ensured. In the democratic pattern adopted in our Constitution, not only the resolution of election dispute is entrusted to a judicial tribunal, but even the decision on questions as to disqualification of members under Articles 103 and 192 is by the president/governor in accordance with the opinion of the election commission. The constitutional scheme, therefore, for decision on questions as to disqualification of members after being duly elected, contemplates adjudication of such disputes by an independent authority outside the house, namely, president/ governor in accordance with the opinion of the election commission, all of whom are high constitutional functionaries with security of tenure independent of the will of the house ... It is undisputed that the disqualification on the ground of defection could as well as have been prescribed by an ordinary law made by parliament under Article 102(1)(e) and 191(1)(e) instead of by resort to the constituent power of enacting the Tenth Schedule.

[2] *Kihoto Hollohan* vs *Zachillu & Ors,* (1992) Supp. (2) SCC 651.

He added, delicately

The Speaker's office is undoubtedly high and has considerable aura with the attribute of impartiality. This aura of the office was even greater when the Constitution was framed and yet the framers of the Constitution did not choose to vest the authority of adjudicating disputes as to disqualification of members to the speaker; and provision was made in Articles 103 and 192 for decision of such disputes by the president/governor in accordance with the opinion of the election commission. The reason is not far to seek. The Speaker being an authority within the house and his tenure being dependent on the will of the majority therein, likelihood of suspicion of bias could not be ruled out. The question as to disqualification of a member has adjudicatory disposition and, therefore, requires the decision to be rendered in consonance with the scheme for adjudication of disputes. Rule of law has in it firmly entrenched, natural justice, of which, rule against bias is a necessary concomitant; and basic postulates of rule against bias are: *nemo judex in causa sua*—'.

A judge is disqualified from determining any case in which he may be, or may fairly be suspected to be, biased, and it is of fundamental importance that justice should not only be done, but should manifestly and undoubtedly be seen to be done.

Justice M.M.Venkatachaliah's judgment (on behalf of K Jayachandra Reddy and S.C. Agarwal JJ and himself) provides a classic case of wilful judicial refusal to reckon with the realities and, instead, seek solace in rhetoric. He quoted G.V. Mavalankar, the first speaker of the Lok Sabha and, incidentally, the only one for whose removal a motion was moved by over 50 members. That was on 18 December 1954. Far smaller men followed him. The quotations from Mavalankar, Jawaharlal Nehru, and Erskine May were on the significance of the office in theory. They sound cruel when applied to the modern breed of Kesri Nath Tripathis.

Yet, the quotes were sufficient for Venkatachaliah, to say 'It is inappropriate to express distrust in the high office of the speaker, merely because some of the speakers are alleged, or even found, to have discharged their functions not in keeping with the great traditions of that high office. The robes of the speaker do change and elevate the man inside.'

By then (18 February 1992) Venkatachaliah could not but have known that it was not just 'some speakers' who had acted in a partisan manner; partisanship was the norm. The office had been systematically battered. A Speaker of the Lok Sabha, G.S. Dhillon, descended from the chair straight to the government benches in 1976 by the grace of the Prime Minister, Indira Gandhi. Nor must the claims to undying fame of P.H. Pandian, Speaker of the Tamil Nadu assembly, be overlooked. Balram Jakhar's tenure in the speaker's office (January 1980–9) was marred by gross partisanship and an unconcealed ambition for office as union minister. Speaker Shivraj Patil's ruling on 1 June 1993 on the split in the Janata Dal was a disgrace.

'Confidence in the impartiality of the speaker is an indispensable condition for the successful working of the procedure, and many conventions exist which have as their object not only to ensure the impartiality of the speaker but also to ensure that his impartiality is generally recognized'[3] asserts Erskine May's classic on *Parliamentary Practice*. In India, this 'indispensable condition' clearly does not exist and has not existed for many years. Our parliamentary system is manifestly flawed.

Prime Minister Vajpayee can institute two reforms. One is to vest the jurisdiction to try disputes under the anti-defection law in the election commission. The other is to force an all-party accord on the speaker. Nearly 30 years ago, on 13 March 1967, Madhu Limaye wrote to Indira Gandhi putting forward a proposal for securing the speaker's impartiality. The speaker must, upon election, resign from his party and declare his impartiality in the house. While in office, he should abstain from participation in controversies and should contest elections only as a non-party candidate, while the other parties should not put up a candidate against him. After retirement, the speaker should be given pension for life and barred from holding any public office, save as president.

One doctrine deserves speedy burial: the speaker's office is a gift in the hands of the ruling party. The *Economist* of 19 November 1994 wrote: 'Over the grey men, the placemen and the hired men who characterize the present House of Commons, a star shines. Betty Boothroyd, the speaker, dominates a difficult house to a degree that her immediate predecessors never attained.' She was elected in 1992 with the support of the Conservatives though she belonged to the Labour Opposition. 'She won because 74 Tories rightly rebelled at the thought of someone who had just left the cabinet—

[3]Erskine May, *Treatise on the Law, Privileges, Proceedings and Usage of Parliament*, 20th edn, (London: Butterworths, 1983), p. 235.

the government's unofficial candidate, Peter Brooke—sitting in the speaker's chair and posing as a neutral arbiter of proceedings.'

In India, such a revolt would be unthinkable and the language the *Economist* used would be regarded as breach of parliamentary privilege by speakers, most of whom are no more than instruments of the government's will. These are the very men who will act as judges on issues of free speech in the name of 'parliamentary privilege'.

25
Parliamentary Privileges[1]

'Freedom of the press is the ark of the covenant of democracy because public criticism is essential to the working of its institutions. Never has criticism been more necessary than today when the weapons of propaganda are so strong and so subtle.' When the Supreme Court of India delivered these ringing words in the newsprint policy case in 1972,[2] it was, perhaps, unconscious of the irony that it had itself created the gravest menace to press freedom by its ruling in the *Searchlight* case in 1958 that the privileges of legislatures, elected by the people of India, override the fundamental rights of their masters, the people themselves

In 1964 the court sought to recapture the genie it had let loose only when the Uttar Pradesh assembly went on the rampage and attempted to arrest two high court judges. It now ruled that the fundamental rights to personal liberty (Article 21), to freedom from arbitrary arrest (Article 22), and to move the Supreme Court for the enforcement of the fundamental rights (Article 32) do prevail over the privileges. The court however resisted the logic of its own reasoning and chose wilfully not to pronounce on the crucial question whether the precious fundamental right to freedom of speech and expression— Article 19(1)a—also prevails over the privileges. This it refused to decide despite repeated instances of gross abuse of legislative privileges and the first press commission's reference to them in 1954. The privileges are archaic, uncertain, and repressive.

On 24 April 1992 the Supreme Court stayed till further orders the warrants of arrest and production issued by the Speaker of the

[1] *Frontline,* 22 May 1992.
[2] *Bennett Coleman & Co.* vs *Union of India* AIR 1973 SC 106.

Tamil Nadu assembly, R. Muthiah, against K.P. Sunil, former correspondent of the *Illustrated Weekly of India,* on 20 April. There was justified national outrage against the speaker's action and the court's order came as a relief. That very day, however, when his attention was drawn to the report of the Supreme Court's stay order, Muthiah said, 'the warrant is there. Police will take action'

On 27 April he went further still. He declared that the Supreme Court's order bound neither him nor the house and directed the commissioner of police and the secretary of the assembly not to heed the court's notice on its stay order. (He also ordered the issue of arrest warrants against editors of two Tamil dailies).

The speaker and the leader of the house, V.R. Nedunchezhian, propounded the pernicious doctrine that courts should not 'interfere' in the 'affairs' of the assembly. This challenge to the courts' right and duty of judicial review is menacingly reminiscent of the words used by H.R. Gokhale, Union Law Minister, during the Emergency. Replying to the debate in the Lok Sabha on the infamous 42nd Amendment on 28 October 1976, he said, 'We are really trying to save them [the judges] from the temptation of intruding into powers which do not belong to them'. Conscious that the courts would strike down as unconstitutional the bar on judicial review he sought to impose, he threatened that it would be 'a bad day for the judiciary of this country'.[3]

By now, instances of legislatures' and their speakers' refusal to heed court orders have become alarmingly common. The committee of the Tamil Nadu assembly decided to ignore the notice issued by the Supreme Court on 4 June 1987 to the secretary of the assembly while granting a stay order to the editor of *Dinakaran,* K. Kesavan, against the committee's notice requiring him to appear before it on 5 June.

The Andhra Pradesh Legislative Council summoned Ramoji Rao, chief editor of *Eenadu,* to appear before it to receive admonition on 28 March 1984. He moved the Supreme Court which issued a stay order against any warrant of arrest in pursuance of the summons. It also issued a notice to the council. However, in deliberate disregard of the court's order, the council chairman asked the commissioner of police to produce the editor before the house on 28 March. The court passed yet another order on 27 March, this time to the

---

[3] *Lok Sabha Debates,* Fifth Series, vol. lxv, no. 4, 28 October 1976, Col. 10.

commissioner, restraining him from arresting Ramoji Rao. Undeterred, the council chairman directed the commissioner to ignore this order too. The deadlock was resolved only when Chief Minister N.T. Rama Rao advised the governor to prorogue the Council on 30 March 1984.

'No constitutional government can work in any country', Dr. B.R. Ambedkar warned in the constituent assembly on 14 October 1949, 'unless any particular authority remembers the fact that its authority is limited by Constitution and that if there is any created by the Constitution which has to decide between that particular authority and any other authority, then the decision of that authority shall be binding upon any other organ.' That authority, he clearly indicated, was the judiciary.[4]

How, then, has it come about that while the court's power to strike down Acts enacted by parliament and state legislatures is not challenged, each house of the country's many legislatures now feels itself free to order, by a mere *resolution,* the arrest of any citizen anywhere in the wide land and to cock a snook at the courts if they order a stay?

This grotesque situation has come about because of the founding fathers' misplaced faith in the commitment of legislators to the rights of citizens. The fence began to devour the grass. This is how it happened. Article 105(1) says that subject to the provisions of the Constitution and to the rules of procedure 'there shall be freedom of speech in parliament'. Sub-clause 2 confers immunity on MPs against judicial proceedings in relation to speeches and votes in the house.

Sub-clause 3 is crucial. 'In other respects, the powers, privileges and immunities of each house of parliament, and of the members and the committees of each house, *shall be such as may from time to time be defined by parliament, and, until so defined, shall be those of the House of Commons of the parliament of the United Kingdom,* and of its members and committees, at the commencement of this Constitution.' Note its temporary character 'until so defined' and the mandate to codify the privileges ('shall be ... defined by Parliament by law').

Members of the constituent assembly deeply resented the reference to the British House of Commons in the Constitution of an independent India. On behalf of the drafting committee, Sir Alladi Krishnaswami Aiyar assured them: 'If you have the time and

4CAD, vol. x, p. 269.

if you have the leisure to formulate all the privileges in a compendious form, it will be well and good. There is nothing to fetter the discretion of the future Parliament of India. *Only as a temporary measure*, the privileges of the House of Commons are made applicable to this House'[5] (emphasis added, throughout).

It was on the faith of this explicit assurance that on 19 May 1949 the assembly adopted the provision. Article 194 contains identical provisions for State legislatures. However, on 16 October 1949 R.K. Sidhva reviewed the issue. He had studied the subject and found the privileges perilously vague. 'Until two or three years after the formation of parliament these privileges may not be framed.' Dr. Ambedkar informed the house that he had since obtained a copy of South Africa's Act defining the privileges. 'It might be possible later on for our own parliament to embody the privileges.'

The president of the assembly, Dr Rajendra Prasad, referred to the incorporation, by reference, of the privileges of the British House of Commons and delivered this sage warning. 'So, *it is only a temporary affair*. Of course, the parliament may never legislate on that point and it is therefore for the members to be vigilant.'[6] Little did he reckon with the day when the apex court of the country would not only take away all need for vigilance but provide them with incentive for aggrandizement by mere inaction. The court ruled in the *Searchlight* case that Article 19(1)(a), embodying the fundamental right to freedom of speech and expression, 'must yield' to Article 194(3). This, in its view, was the 'only way of reconciling' the two. It ruled also that the Commons 'had at the commencement of our Constitution the power or privilege of prohibiting the publication of *even a true and faithful report of the debates* or proceedings that take place within the house.'[7]

It was admitted by Chief Justice S.R. Das, who delivered the majority judgment, that if parliament and the state legislatures were to define the privileges by 'law', that law, like any other, would be subject to the fundamental rights. He also remarked: 'It may well be that it is precisely the reason why our parliament and state legislatures have not made any law.' Their cynicism thus stands exposed. Unlike India, Britain does not have a written Constitution that fetters the powers of parliament on grounds of the fundamental rights of the citizen.

[5]CAD, vol. viii, p. 149.
[6]CAD, vol. x, p. 374.
[7]*M.S.M. Sharma v S.K. Sinha*, AIR 1959 SC 395.

In a masterly dissent, Justice K. Subba Rao remarked on the irony of Das's interpretation: a law made by an Indian legislature would be subject to fundamental rights; but not so the temporary application of the privileges of a foreign legislature. Even the doctrine of harmonious construction mandated that the right of the citizen prevailed over the privileges of the legislatures they elected. He ruled also that in 1950 the House of Commons 'had no privilege to prevent the publication of the correct and faithful reports of its proceedings.' The chief justice had relied on old, obsolete precedents., Referring to Das's judgment, Subba Rao warned that 'the reasoning adopted therein would unduly restrict and circumscribe the wide scope and content of one of the most cherished fundamental rights, namely the freedom of speech in its application to the press.' He was proved right.

Until then the view universally held was that the rights prevailed over the privileges. In 1954 the Supreme Court itself had accepted a habeas corpus petition by G.K. Reddy, then of the *Blitz*, and set free its assistant editor, D.H. Mistry, who had been arrested in Bombay on the orders of the UP Speaker.[8] Now *Searchlight* opened a new vista of power. The politicians were not slow to exploit it.

In 1964 the UP Assembly sent Keshav Singh to prison for contempt of the house. A few days later it ordered the arrest and production of two high court judges of the Lucknow bench, who had granted him bail, and his advocate who had presented the bail application. The judges rushed to the Allahabad high court with writ petitions. A full bench of 28 judges admitted the petitions and granted interim stay of the assembly's order. The president averted an uglier situation by seeking the Supreme Court's advisory opinion on the legal questions.[9]

A special bench of seven judges ruled, by 6–1, that:

1. 'The content of Article 194 (3) must ultimately be determined by courts and not by legislatures' (their spurious and novel claim to be judges of their own power was rejected); 2. The writ jurisdiction of the high courts under Article 226 is not subject to the privileges; 3. The fundamental right to move the Supreme Court for the enforcement of the fundamental rights, embodied in Article 32, is not subject to the privileges, either—it is an 'absolute constitutional right'; 4. The guarantee of personal liberty embodied in Article 21 applies when the legislatures exercise their powers

---

[8]*G.K. Reddy v Nafisul Hasan*, AIR 1954 SC 636.
[9]President's Reference No. 1 of 1964, AIR. 1965 SC 745.

in respect of their privileges; and, 5. Article 212(1) exempts from judicial scrutiny only irregularities in legislative proceedings. But if the impugned procedure is illegal and unconstitutional, it would be open to be scrutinized in a court of law.'

Attacks on the judiciary would fall in this category because of the bar imposed by Article 211. Thus, the doctrine propounded by Muthiah and Nedunchezhian on 27 April is legal nonsense.

Unfortunately, the court stopped here. It did not proceed to rule, as it *ought* to have, that the fundamental rights, particularly the right to free speech (Article 19(1)(a)), prevail over the privileges. It said:

We do not propose to enter into a general discussion as to the applicability of all the fundamental rights to the cases where legislative powers and privileges can be exercised against any individual citizen of this country. We are dealing with this matter on the footing that Article 19(1)(a) [freedom of speech] does not apply and Article 21 [right to personal liberty] does. If a citizen moves this court and complains that his fundamental right under Article 21 had been contravened, it would plainly be the duty of the court *to examine the merits of the said contention,* and that inevitably raises the question as to whether the personal liberty of the citizen has been taken away according to the procedure established by law.

The court asked a pertinent question: *'was it the intention of the Constitution to perpetuate the dualism which rudely disturbed public life in England in the seventeenth, eighteenth and nineteenth centuries?'*

The court pointed out that while the British parliament originated as a high court of parliament, the Indian legislature did not, and many privileges had fallen into desuetude. Three points deserve particular note. First, the legislatures' rules of procedure are 'law' and, therefore, subject to fundamental rights. The committees of privileges are however creatures of the rules. Their composition and procedure are, therefore, wide open to challenge on the ground that they do not guarantee fairness and impartiality as Article 21 requires.

Secondly, that a general warrant (one which cites no reasons) issued by a legislature for the arrest of a citizen who is not a member of the house for contempt is *not conclusive.* The court has the right and a duty to examine its validity 'and to pass the interim orders prohibiting the further execution of the impugned orders'. That includes grant of bail. In sum, *the legislature is not the sole judge of its privileges.* It forms part of the law of the land and the courts will consider that law like any other.

Finally, the court pointed to 'the uniform practice which the House of Commons has followed for more than a century past' to file a return before the courts. 'It is *not disputed* that whenever commitment orders passed by the House of Commons are challenged in England before the courts at Westminster, the house *invariabl'* makes a return ....' Indian legislatures however refuse to do that while claiming the privileges of the Commons. They rely on the *Searchlight* ruling and flout the UP ruling because it was an 'advisory opinion', as if the law it declared was not binding.

In an able study, *Parliamentary Privileges and the Press* by Prof. M.P. Jain commissioned jointly by the Press Council of India and the Indian Law Institute,[10] the author records that 'Since 1965, a new trend has been visible in the legislature–court equation in privilege matters. A view 'ias now come to be held that if any question is raised in a court as egards the legislative privilege, it will itself be a breach of privilege for any member or the speaker of the house to defend the position of the legislature. Before 1965, invariably in all cases arising in the courts concerning privilege matters, the legislature defended its position before the courts.' This trend was set by the UP assembly's committee of privileges pronouncing the Supreme Court's opinion to be wrong.

In the quarter century and more since the Supreme Court's halting attempt to undo the wrong it had done, the attitude of legislatures, both at the Centre and in the States, has not changed. All that parliament did was to wipe out the explicit reference to the House of Commons and retain it by implication. A cosmetic sham. The 42nd Amendment enacted in 1976 during the Emergency simply said that the privileges shall be those 'at the commencement' of the amendment itself.

This made matters worse still. The obligation to codify was deleted. Instead, the amendment added: '*and* as may be *evolved* by such house of parliament from time to time'. This had the effect of empowering the house to *add* to its privileges, something the House of Commons admittedly cannot do. Now, by a mere resolution a house could 'evolve', a new privilege 'from time to time'. The 44th Amendment enacted in 1978 deleted the additional power to 'evolve', *re-inserted* the duty to define privileges by law, but added that the privileges 'until so defined, shall be those ... immediately before' the 44th Amendment, that is, as in 1976–7 which takes us

[10]N.M. Tripathi Bombay, 1984

to those between 1950–76; *in short, the privileges of the Commons frozen as of 26 January 1950.*

Such is the state of Article 105(3) and 194(3) today. There has however been one development of seminal importance whose impact on the law of privileges is yet to be understood. In 1978 the Supreme Court ruled, in Maneka Gandhi's case, that when Article 21 says that 'no person shall be deprived of his life or personal liberty except according to procedure established by law', it does not mean any procedure and by any law. It must be a procedure fair and reasonable and the 'law' must be one which also satisfies the tests of Article 19.[11] Thus, an action that violates the right to free speech, guaranteed by Article 19(1)(a), is also violative of Article 21. *The Supreme Court has also ruled that in any event Article 21 prevails over the privileges.* The select committee on parliamentary privileges set up by the House of Commons reported in December 1967 that 'the present procedure for dealing with complaints does not manifestly comply with the ordinary principles of natural justice.'[12]. *Since we still follow that procedure, it stands condemned under the Maneka Gandhi case ruling.*

Incidentally, neither in *Searchlight* nor in the UP case did the Supreme Court refer to the constituent assembly debates. That salutary practice has come into vogue recently. In 1954 the first press commission commented on 'oversensitiveness on the part of legislatures to even honest criticism' and urged codification of privileges. In 1982 the second press commission endorsed the plea. So did the press council at its meeting on 28 December 1982.

We however witness a strange phenomenon of pupils excelling teachers. On 28 March 1987, the speaker of the Tamil Nadu assembly felt free to condemn S. Balasubramaniam, editor of *Ananda Vikatan*, unheard. He was imprisoned. On 5 July 1987, a notice of breach of privilege was given against Justice B. Lentin of the Bombay high court merely because he had made a statement denying the allegations made in the Maharashtra assembly that he had received information from the Opposition. On 7 April 1988, the mover, Keshavrao Dhandge, hurled abuses at the judge in the assembly.

In Britain, however, the trend is in the opposite direction. 'I am ashamed of parliament and want sincerely to apologise to my constituents and the country. They elected me to do a serious job,

[11]*Maneka Gandhi v Union of India* AIR 1978, S.C. 597.
[12]Report of the Committee on Parliamentary Privileges, HMSO, London; Dec. 1967, p. x, para 22.

not to be part of an idiotic circus' said Norman Atkinson, a Labour MP in Britain, in a message to his constituents on 19 July 1966. In the same vein Bernard Levin wrote in *The Times* (London) of (9 December 1975) regarding 'the curious passion the House of Commons seems to have for making a collective ass of itself'. Neither was hauled up for contempt of parliament. In India it is unthinkable that anyone making such remarks about parliament or a State legislature would escape punishment. The cartoon *Ananda Vikatan* published was far more restrained than that which *The Times* (London) published with impunity on 20 April 1988.

Truth is a perfect defence to a charge of contempt of court. 'Indeed, it would be a public duty to bring the relevant facts to light' if the integrity of a judge is impugned, said Lord Justice Salmon.[13] Truth is an equally perfect defence to a charge of contempt of the legislature.

MPs *debate random breath testing*

---

[13]Report of the Interdepartmental Committee on the Law of Contempt as it affects Tribunals of Inquiry; (Chairman: The Rt. Mon. Lord Justice Salmon); HMSO, London; June 1969; Cmnd. 4078; p. 15, para 36. He cited in support the famous Australian Case *The King v. Nicholls*, 12 C.L. Rao 280 at p. 286.

26
Press Leaks and Parliamentary Privilege[1]

I f the chairman of the joint parliamentary committee on the banks scam, Mr Ram Niwas Mirdha's press conference on 13 August 1992 was intended to reassure the press and the public that they would not be kept in the dark about the JPC's deliberations, his remarks have done the exact opposite. The proceedings would be *in camera* and Mr Mirdha would brief the press 'whenever necessary', that is, whenever he deems it necessary. He will be the judge of what the people are entitled to know.

It is unthinkable that the people of the USA would have accepted such a claim by Senator Sam Ervin who presided over the Watergate hearings. Eighty years ago in Britain the committee on the Marconi scandal heard evidence in public. Here, while the JPC's work would be secret, the government would be free to influence public opinion not only by its pronouncements but even be selective publication of the very documents it had submitted to the JPC. Mr Mirdha said that the papers presented to it would 'be sort of privileged' but it would be left to the government to decide whether it wanted to share information with the press on these matters. One would have thought that the decision on publication should, if at all, lie with the JPC.

The JPC consists of 30 members not all of whom can be expected to keep a stiff upper lip. As the proceedings get under way, leaks will occur. They did even in the tightly controlled JPC on Bofors which the Opposition had boycotted. The press, to its credit, reported the proceedings on 18 September 1987, when the quick

[1] *The Statesman*, 26 August 1992.

change artists of Bofors, Messrs Per Ove Morberg and Lars Gothlin, performed before the JPC. Its chairman, Mr B. Shankaranand, cautioned the members against such 'indiscretions' which, he warned, constituted a breach of privilege of parliament.

Since Mr Mirdha also has spoken of confidentiality and privilege, it is only right that he be enlightened that neither the press nor the people of the country can compromise on their fundamental right to freedom of speech and expression and its corollary, the right to know. They cannot accept any authority as the sole judge of what they are entitled to know. Quite apart from the fact that parliamentary privileges are subject to these rights, as they must be, the content and application of the privileges themselves have undergone radical change in Britain, whose law on parliamentary privileges our Constitution borrowed, pending their codification. Unlike India, Britain does not have a written Constitution nor a Bill of Rights which even parliament may not abridge.

There is a resolution of the House of Commons of 21 April 1837: 'That ..., the evidence taken by any select committee of this house, and the documents presented to such committee, and which have not been reported to the house, ought not to be published by any member of such committee or by any other person.'[2] The practice today, a century and a half later, is different. Reputed journals like the *Economist* and *The Times* (London) have published draft reports of select committees with impunity. The old law has become unenforceable like any archaic, anachronistic law. The leaks come from members of the committees. Journalists refuse to reveal the sources. The privileges committee and the House of Commons are principled enough not to punish the press when they are unable to identify the main culprit.

The present practice is well set out in the evidence which *The Times*' lobby reporter, Mr Richard Evans, gave to the committee of privileges on 15 April 1966. He was asked: 'How often did you breach privilege in the course of last year?' The candid answer was: 'I have not kept count, but several times, and so have other newspapers.'

The new practice was set in the last decade. Leaks have been of

---

[2]Second Report from the Committee of Privileges Session 1994–5, Premature Disclosure of Proceedings of Select Committees, 23 July 1985, HMSO, London, p. iv.

two kinds: of the evidence and of the draft report prepared by the chairman which he proceeds to 'negotiate' with his colleagues. The House has taken a sensible view of its privileges. On 6 February 1978, it approved a recommendation by its committee of privileges that, in general it should exercise its penal jurisdiction '(i) as sparingly as possible, and (ii) only when satisfied that it was essential to do so in order to provide reasonable protection for the house and its officers from obstruction or threats of obstruction causing or likely to cause substantial interference with the performance of their functions.' The test, in short, is the likelihood of 'substantial interference' with the work.

The Economist was the first ranking journal to breach the dam of archaic privilege in 1975. It published the chairman's draft report for the select committee on wealth tax 1974–5. As a direct consequence of the leak, the committee was unable to agree on a report. Both the editor and the correspondent refused to reveal the source. The committee of privileges recommended the exclusion of both from the precincts of the house for six months. The house rejected this recommendation by a vote of 64 to 55.

It also ignored another recommendation which is of direct relevance to us. Incredibly, our parliament and state legislatures cannot impose a fine for breach of their privileges, though they can send persons to prison, simply because the House of Commons never enjoyed this power. The committee of privileges recommended legislation to fill the lacuna. The House of Commons declined. Our legislatures can acquire the power when they codify the privileges in a statute.

Before long *The Guardian* and *Daily Mail* emulated the example set by *The Economist* A decade later came the next major assault, this time by *The Times.* On 6 March 1985, it published the draft report of the chairman of the home affairs committee on a sensitive subject: the special branches of the police. The committee of privileges was prompt in submitting its report on 27 March, only to find to its dismay that its own deliberations had been published by *The Times* on 22 March.

This report is a noteworthy document. It fairly recognized that editors and writers had been asked to disclose their sources 'but in each case they have, in accordance with the tenets of their profession, refused'. The tenets were thus fully recognized. It recalled that 'in the absence of knowledge of the original perpetrator of the disclosure, previous Committees of Privileges (with one exception) have not been willing to recommend imposing any penalty on editors or journalists for the publicity of that disclosure. They have confined themselves to condemning, sometimes in strong terms, such contempts of the House on the part of both the original disclosure and the journalists.' That exception was The *Economist*. The committee recognized 'the near impossibility of enforcing those rules' of 1837. It, therefore, decided to consider the matter in greater detail. It did so but its report (23 July 1975) persisted in the quest for plugging the leaks.[3]

There were however two notable gains. One was the honest recognition that 'all those questioned on this—both from the select committee side and the press—agreed that members of the select committees themselves were the principal sources of leaks'. The other was the unanimity in the media including the BBC. Only 'the national interest' would deter them from publishing information, not parliamentary privilege. 'They began by questioning the need for any rule of privilege at all in relation to the proceedings of select committees' and urged its abolition or substantial modification to bring it into line with current practice. In practice, it was said, privileges in this matter was unworkable.

Grenada Television was blunt: 'Confidentiality is a legitimate interest of MPs. Disclosure is the legitimate business of the media.' On its part, the committee recommended that 'the ultimate criterion in all such cases lies ... in the effect of the leak on the public interest'. On 16 March 1986, the House of Commons accepted these recommendations.

Meanwhile, on 16 December 1985, *The Times* had published the contents of yet another draft report (of the environment committee on radioactive waste). This time the committee of privileges recommended, on 1 May 1986, the exclusion of the lobby reporter, Mr Richard Evans, from the precincts of the house for six months and reduction of the lobby passes issued to *The Times* by one for six months. On 21 May 1986, the Commons voted not to impose any penalty at all by 158 votes to 124. The prime minister, Mrs Margaret Thatcher, voted with the majority. This in a case of deliberate 'breach' of privilege, and despite the fact that *The Times* had struck a defiant note on 9 May in a leader entitled 'Pride and

[3]Ibid.

Privilege'. Its central point was that the press is as good a judge of public interest as government or parliament.

One wishes the JPC success, but a member who is baulked in his attempts to unravel the truth there will be provoked to alert the press to the fact, and the press will be guilty of a sordid betrayal if it did not publish that information.

27
Defections (1967–1997)[1]

It is preposterous to suggest that the clamour for reform of the anti-defection law is motivated by a desire to do the BJP down. The sheer grossness of events in Uttar Pradesh from 19 to 27 October 1997, when its chief minister Kalyan Singh rewarded all the 37 MLAs who had defected to his party with posts in his jumbo council of ministers of 93, was enough to impart an edge to the demand for checks on the vice. The call was often heard in the past in similar circumstances.

All the principal Opposition parties met on 7 July 1982 to call for legislation on defections following Bhajan Lal's display in May of sheer virtuosity in the craft in tandem with Governor Tapase. Kalyan Singhs's stunning performance puts the Haryana affair in the shade. On 3 November he doled out portfolios with utter contempt for critics not unmixed with a puckish sense of humour. Hari Shankar Tiwari, a contractor who faces 24 criminal cases, was awarded science and technology. A well-known liquor baron, Jitendra Kumar Jaiswal, was entrusted with culture.

The moment has surely come to review the law. It would however be a shame if the opportunity is squandered away through partisanship or in quest of perfect solutions or in escapism. On 10 July 1982, Indira Gandhi poured scorn on the pleas of a fractured Opposition. On 31 January 1985, Rajiv Gandhi rushed through an admittedly defective law in order to freeze his majority while facilitating splits in the Opposition. The only changes in the situation since are the Congress (I)'s readiness for change and the BJP's reluctance to countenance it.

[1] *The Statesman*, 11 and 12 and 13 November 1997.

It is a game two can play. Statistics prepared by the union home ministry for the period from March 1967 to February 1968 showed that every party lost more than it gained from defections. The Congress for instance, secured 139 but lost 175 MLAs; the Jana Sangh won three and lost 16. While there were 542 cases of defection in the entire decade and a half from the first general election of 1952 to the fourth in 1967, there were at least 438 of them in the 12 months following it. That the conversions were not due entirely to honest changes of opinion is evident from the fact that out of 210 defectors from Bihar, Haryana, Madhya Pradesh, Punjab, Rajasthan, Uttar Pradesh and West Bengal, 116 secured office in the ministeries their defections helped to bring into being. There were also multiple acts of defection by the same person or group.

This is what we are up against. The situation has not improved over the past three decades. No law can instil political morality, but it can provide deterrents against its violation. It must be followed up by legislation in related spheres—electoral reforms, law on democratic functioning of parties, and constitutional reform. None of these, however, should retard reforms of more immediate concern. The best must not be made enemy of good, nor should the minimum checks necessary for effectiveness be abandoned in order to secure a consensus. Borrow the best from all previous ventures, the existing law included. A survey of the three decade-old efforts is very educational.

No committee set up since Independence had a more distinguished composition or enjoyed wider support than the committee of defections. The fourth general election (1967) battered the Congress monolith and let loose defectors all over the north. On 8 December 1967 the Lok Sabha unanimously adopted the following resolution: 'This house is of opinion that a high-level committee consisting of representatives of political parties and constitutional experts be set up immediately by the government to consider the problem of legislators changing their allegiance from one party to another and their frequent crossing of the floor in all its aspects and make recommendations in this regard.'

Jayaprakash Narayan, H.N. Kunzru, M.C. Setalvad, C.K. Daphtary, and Mohan Kumaramangalam were among its members. The chairman was Home Minister Y.B. Chavan. No committee has been better served by background material. The home ministry submitted papers on 'Defections', 'The Nature and Character of

Representation in the Democratic System', and a couple of related issues while the law ministry submitted a note on the constitutional and legal aspects. If defection is to be visited with legal consequences, it must be adequately defined to cover the vice, and sufficiently precisely to pass muster in the courts, but it should not include in its sweep legitimate activity. Definition of the offence lies at the heart of the problem.

Jayaprakash Narayan (JP) participated in the proceedings for the first time on 14 July 1968. Chavan deferentially invited him to speak first. By then the lawyer–members of the committee, headed by one of the finest law ministers we have had, P Govinda Menon, submitted their report on 5 July. They strongly recommended legislation under Articles 102(1)(e) and 191(1)(e) of the Constitution, to disqualify defectors form membership of parliament and the state legislatures. (These provisions empower parliament to make laws prescribing disqualifications for membership of both.) They recommended also disqualification for six years if acceptance of illegal gratification is proved and a constitutional amendment 'with a view to limiting the size of the Council of Ministers'.

JP said that, as the minutes record, 'if a representative, who had been elected on the ticket of a party, changed his affiliation, he should go back to the electorate and get its approval for his conduct'. He was realistic about the situation: 'the less said about conscience the better, only in rare circumstances had it played any part.' He was right. Massive conversions followed by quick rewards are unheard of elsewhere.

Yet, the law must not expose the honest dissenter to punishment. Two definitions were formulated; one, by the lawyers' group and another by JP. The lawyers defined a defector as one who 'renounces (whether by words, conduct or in any other manner); ... allegiance to, or association with such political party' on whose symbol he had fought the election.

This was wide enough to cover, subterfuges. The expression, 'by words, conduct or in any other manner' took care of that. JP proposed a definition which, unfortunately, omitted this expression but rightly excluded those expelled from a party: one who 'voluntarily renounces allegiance to or association with such political party, provided his action is not in consequence of a decision of the party concerned.' An expellee is no defector.

JP proposed this definition on 8 August. S.N. Dwivedi and

Madhu Limaye supported him on condition that the party accepting a defector should lose its symbol. On 28 September the committee 'endorsed' JP's definition. Its report dated 7 January 1969 was a pathetic confession of failure. It could not agree on the proposal to disqualify defectors or on the size of the council of ministers. It agreed unanimously on the need to limit the size and relate it to the total strength of the legislature. Bereft of the spirit of compromise, its members split in several groups on the actual size.

There was, however, absolute unanimity on the basic principle that 'a defector should be debarred for a period of one year or till such time as he resigned his seat and got himself re-elected, from appointment to the office of a minister' or any public office including one in a state corporation. This was the one recommendation which was ignored in all the three subsequent exercises in legislation. Its efficacy cannot be in doubt. Defectors want immediate returns.

Having split the Congress in 1969, Indira Gandhi had no use for the report. Interest was revived later thanks to no small extent to Jayaprakash Narayan's campaign. On 16 May 1973, the Constitution (32nd Amendment) Bill was moved in the Lok Sabha. It sought to amend Articles 102 and 191 to disqualify, respectively, an MP or MLA 'who voluntarily gives up his membership of the political party by which he was set up as a candidate' or if he violates the party whip.

An exception to both was made: a split in the 'political party'. It was clearly implied that a split in a legislature party was in consequence of one in the parent organizational wing. As with the other acts of disqualification, any dispute was to be decided by the president under Article 103 which contained the proviso: 'Before giving any decision on any such question the president shall obtain the opinion of the election commission and shall act according to such opinion.' Article 192 contains a similar proviso for the governor vis-à-vis MLAs.

This Bill contained two other provisions very relevant today. No prime minister or chief minister can hold office longer than 'six consecutive months' unless he is elected to the Lok Sabha or the assembly, as the case may be.

In an article in his journal *Everyman's* (8 September 1973) JP 'welcomed' the Bill as 'a step in the right direction' while pointing out 'some serious defects'. They concerned the wide sweep of the provision concerning whips and imprecise definition of splits. Mergers were not reckoned with either. JP revealed that P Ramamurthy of the CPM and he were the only members to support the lawyers' recommendation on disqualification. This Bill did not find its way to the statute book and lapsed, as did the Janata Party's Constitution (48th Amendment) Bill moved in the Lok Sabha on 18 August 1978.

In form it differed from the 1973 Bill. The law was to be in the Tenth Schedule to the Constitution. Both, the 'original political party' and the 'legislature party' were clearly and separately defined. The definition of defection was however no different. A valid split in the legislature party must explicitly be one 'as a result of a split in the member's original political party'. Unlike the 1973 Bill, it prescribed a minimum: 25 per cent of the legislature party. The election commission was left free to decide disputed cases.

In form the Constitution 52nd Amendment Act, 1985 emulated the 1978 Bill but with one radical departure. For the first time a politician, the presiding officer of the legislature, who mostly belongs to the ruling party, was made judge in cases of dispute arising under a vital part of the Constitution, its Ten Schedule, involving complex issues of law. Rajiv Gandhi freely admitted its shortcomings. He told the Lok Sabha on 30 January 1985: 'There are lots of areas in this Bill which are grey. We are covering new ground which may be [sic] not covered anywhere else in the world. So, there will be shortcomings in the Bill.' The Congress parliamentary party asserted itself for the first and last time and secured the deletion of a clause disqualifying a party expellee from membership of the legislature. It was supported by NTR alone and still exists in Kashmir's anti-defection law, the 7th Schedule of its Constitution.

Rajiv Gandhi thought that was one way of dealing with topplers, little realizing that they work in secret. He admitted that

One lacuna comes out and that is that if the house—either this house or a State legislature—is not in session and there is a defection or a split or however it may be defined, but the government is seen to lose its majority, then there would be a long time before the next session was to be called and this could lead to a lot of horse trading ... and hopefully we will be able to put some time-limit, possibly a minimum time-limit, between the suspicion of a government losing its majority and the test of its strength in the House. We will see whether this can be put in, either in this Bill, may be in the next session, or, if it has to be put in elsewhere, we can do it there as well.

The promise was not kept.

He told the Rajya Sabha on 31 January that the speaker was made judge so that decisions on disputes will be 'quick'. In the nature of things, they cannot be. The Members of Lok Sabha (Disqualification on ground of Defection) Rules, 1985 lay down the procedure for inquiries.

We must take the law as it stands and improve upon it. Its defects are twofold: in what it omits and what it provides. The time has surely come to embody in a suitable form, the rule suggested authoritatively by all the bodies concerned: the speakers' conference (1968), the administrative reforms commission (1969), the governors' committee appointed by the president (1971), and the Sarkaria commission (1988); namely, 'Where the governor is satisfied, by whatever process or means, that the ministry no longer enjoys majority support, he should ask the chief minister to face the assembly and prove his majority within the shortest possible time.' It is possible to achieve unanimity on this rule. The clause on splits is defective since it refers to a legislator who 'makes a claim' that he and his associates 'constitute the group representing a faction which has arisen as a result of a split.' Defectors however assert that they are the party and the others constitute 'the faction'.

The definition suggested by the lawyers group and ignored by the draftsmen of the Act would cover all subterfuges. It refers not to giving up of 'membership' of the party, a narrow concept, but to one who 'renounces (whether by words, conduct or in any other manner) allegiance to or association with' the party. The expression within brackets ropes in all turncoats including those who undermine the party within and outside the house by speech or conduct. The election commission should decide disputes. Writs against its decisions will be to high courts as well as the Supreme Court.

The report of the all-party committee on electoral reforms (May 1990) recorded that its Congress member H.K.L. Bhagat was 'strongly opposed to any change in the present law.'[2] All other members were 'unanimously of the view' that it should be changed in three respects: the whip, whose disobedience entails disqualification, should be confined to a motion of confidence or 'a motion

[2]Report of the Committee on Electoral Reforms, Ministry Reforms, Ministry of Law and Justice, GOi, May 1990.

amounting to no-confidence or Money Bill or motion of vote of thanks to the president's address'; the speaker should cease to be judge and the jurisdiction be transferred to the election commission; and the law should cover nominated members too.

The first point has been taken care of by the Supreme Court in its judgment in *Kihoto Hollohan v Zachillha and Others* delivered on 18 February 1992 construing the Tenth Schedule.[3] Three of the five judges of the constitution bench—Justices M.N.Venkatachalaiah, K.J. Reddy, and S.C. Agarwal—upheld the validity of the Act but held that Paragraph 7 of the Schedule, which bars the jurisdiction of the courts, is invalid. Any amendment of the Constitution which *inter alia*, affects the powers and the jurisdicion of the Supreme Court and high courts requires ratification by at least one-half of the states. This was admittedly not done.

The two judges in the minority, Justices L.M. Sharma and J.S. Verma, declared the entire Act to be invalid. One ground was that the offending provision (Para 7) was not severable from the rest. They held too that as the tenure of the speaker is dependent on the continuous support of the majority in the house, he does not satisfy the requirement 'of such an independent adjudicatory authority' and his (the speaker's) choice 'as the sole arbiter in the matter violates an essential attribute' of the basic feature of the Constitution. They added, 'democracy is a part of the basic structure of the Constitution and free and fair elections with provision for resolution of disputes relating to the same as also for adjudication of those relating to subsequent disqualification by an independent body outside the house are essential features of the democratic system.'

Accordingly, an independent adjudicatory machinery for resolving disputes relating to the competence of members of the house is envisaged 'as an attribute of this basic feature'. According to the minority judgement, all decisions rendered by several speakers must also be declared a nullity and liable to be ignored.

However, the majority ruled also that the provision concerning whips must not affect freedom of speech guaranteed to legislators by Articles 105 (1) and 194 (91). A whip whose violation entails disqualification 'would have to be limited to a vote on a motion of confidence or no confidence in the government or where the motion under consideration relates to a matter which was an integral policy

[3]*Kihoto Hollohan v Zachillu & Ors.* (1992) Supp. (2) SCC 651.

and programme of the political party on the basis of which it approached the electorate.'

Even in 1992 it was unrealistic of the majority to believe that 'the robes of the speaker do change and elevate the man inside'. Recent events have proved the truth of the minority's view. The speakers' tenure is dependent 'on the will of the majority therein'. For different reasons both the majority and the minority held that the ouster of judicial review under Paragraph 7 is unconstitutional. No opinion was expressed on the meaning of a split.

Thus, as a result of the ruling, the provision concerning whips has been 'read down' and shorn completely of its undemocratic content. The speaker remains judge but his decisions can be challenged in courts. It is pointless to continue with an innovation that has failed to accomplish its stated objective, speed, is incongruous and as experience has proved, is also open to grave abuse. The election commission is a far better judge.

That leaves us with the much abused provision concerning splits. On 2 November 1997, the speaker of the Lok Sabha, P.A. Sangma, asked a question that is on everyone's lips: 'What kind of law is this that if you defect individually, you are committing an illegal act, and if you defect in group of one-third, you are not accused of any illegality.' Is this however what the law really provides ? Paragraph 3 reads: 'Where a 'member' of a house makes a claim that he and any other members of his legislature party constitute the group representing a faction which has arisen as a result of a split in his original political party and such group consists of not less than one-third of the members of such legislature party.'

The splitters must not be less than one-third of the members of the 'legislature party', but the law refers to and separately defines 'legislature party' and the 'original political party' for good reason. The provision regarding splits (Paragraph 3) refers to both. It speaks of a legislator claiming that he and his colleagues of 'his legislature party, constitute the group representing a faction which has arisen as a result of a split in his original political party.' In plain words, there must first be a split in the party organization. The one in the legislature party must have 'arisen as a result' of the split in the organization.

Chandra Shekhar however explicitly declared on 5 November 1990 that the split was 'only in the Janata Dal Parliamentary Party, not in the Janata Dal itself'. He added pointedly that he had not derecognized S.R. Bommai as the Dal's president. On a plain reading of Paragraph 3 this was not a valid split at all, quite regardless of the numbers involved. Why blame the law for its perversion at the hands of politicians and the arbiters, themselves politicians, they appoint?

Those who drafted and enacted the law were aware of what splits meant: open debate in the party organization, failure to reconcile the differences, and the break. This is what happened in the three great splits: in the CPI in 1964; the Congress in 1969 and 1978; and the Janata Party in 1979 and 1980, not to forget the many splits that Lohia and his followers forced in the Socialist Party. Legislators who emerge out of the blue to knock at the doors of the governor or the speaker, keeping the party in the dark throughout, to claim a split are not splitters under Paragraph 3 at all. They are defectors or conspirators and clearly do not comply with the conditions laid down.

Is it fair, as some now suggest, to disqualify all splitters, even those who honestly, openly differ and part company? This was one of the reasons why the committee on defections did not accept its lawyers' suggestion on disqualification. 'The proposal would have the effect of freezing the political parties in their present state and thereby hinder their organic growth which was an essential part of democratic process.'

The problem can be resolved by introducing two changes. One is to redraft Paragraph 3 to make more explicit the requirement of a prior split openly arrived at in the 'original political party'. This can be done by a proviso: 'Provided that the split in the legislature party shall have arisen as a result of a prior split in the original political party owing to irreconcilable and publicly expressed differences of opinion.' This is, doubtless, open to much improvement.

The other solution is to bar all who split, lawfully or not, from public office for a year. The defector wants instant reward and will be deterred. The honest dissenter will not lose his seat in the legislature and will not mind the sacrifice of public office. No reform will make sense unless it incorporates the one provision on which the hopelessly divided committee on defections agreed unanimously.

On whether a split is a single event or a prolonged affair we have two conflicting rulings by speakers of the Lok Sabha. One, by Rabi Ray on 11 January 1991, which was widely hailed; the other by Shivraj Patil on 1 June 1993, which was as widely attacked. L.K. Advani characterized it as 'erroneous'.

Ray disqualified those who belatedly joined the splitters. Shivraj Patil kept open house for all from 1992 till his ruling on 1 June 1993, thus extending the mantle of protection to all who 'had left the Janta Dal in stages in 1992 right till his ruling. He went to the absurd length of holding that the legislature party cannot expel a member. On one point he was very right. 'It is more apt to have the cases involving the interpretation of the Tenth Schedule decided by the Supreme Court or high court judges.'

Though the committee's report and the Tenth Schedule are dated, neither should be rejected out of hand. A new committee will be an invitation to chaos. The situation demands a practical approach. Two omissions in the law must be repaired. One is to make the floor test obligatory, the other to bar defectors, splitters, or others, from public office. Amendments to the Tenth Schedule are necessary in three major respects: make the election commission rather than the speaker judge in cases of dispute; bring Paragraph 2 (1) (b) on whips in line with the Supreme Court's judgement; and redraft Paragraph 3 on splits to remove all ambiguity on two points. First, a split is a single event, albeit in consequence of several events; but late entrants do not qualify. Second, it must be an open affair publicly aired in the main party organization for the people to see.

28

Expulsions and the Law on Defections[1]

If there was any doubt as to Mr Shivraj Patil, the Speaker of the Lok Sabha's thinking when, in his famous order of 12 August 1992 he raised seven questions on the effect of expulsions from a party on its total strength in the Lok Sabha, they were removed on 17 August when he met the Opposition leaders. He now flatly asserts that even though a political party might have the right to expel its members, he, as the speaker, did not recognize expulsion in the house. The Janata Dal did not reply to the queries which it found 'bizarre'.

Mr Patil facetiously argued that the anti-defection law, embodied in the Tenth Schedule to the Constitution, did not contain any provision for expulsion of an MP from his party. Not surprisingly, even Mr L.K. Advani, the leader of the Opposition in the Lok Sabha, thought that Mr Patil was propounding a 'dangerous doctrine'.

Quite regardless of his final order, Mr Patil's doctrine deserves to be exposed as spurious. He was a member of the Rajiv Gandhi government which introduced the anti-defection law in January 1985. It is incredible that he has forgotten that, originally, the Bill contained three grounds on which a legislator can be deemed a defector and unseated: voluntary renunciation of membership, defiance of the party whip, and expulsion from the party. The first two figure in the law. The last was dropped.

Clause 2(1)(c) of the Bill reads: 'If he has been expelled from

[1] *The Statesman*, 20 August 1992.

such political party in accordance with the procedure established by the Constitution, rules or regulations of such political party.' Rajiv Gandhi was keen on this clause, so was Mr N.T. Rama Rao and the AIADMK. For the first and last time in the Rajiv era, however the Congress parliamentary party asserted itself at its meeting on 30 January 1985, and got the government to drop a clause that would have reduced legislators to bondsmen. The victory swept Mr Bhagwat Jha Azad off his feet and, holding Rajiv Gandhi's hand, he declaimed: 'It is Jawaharlal Nehru speaking through Rajiv Gandhi.' He and many others came to know better.

In 1987, Rajiv Gandhi expelled Mr V.P. Singh from the party the day after he had offered to resign. The other members expelled were Mr Arun Nehru, Mr Arif Mohammed Khan, and Mufti Mohammed Sayeed. No show cause notice was given. No hearing was accorded.

This notwithstanding, the first five of Mr Shivraj Patil's seven questions to the Janata Dal were to 'enlighten' him, seek to ascertain under what provisions of the Tenth Schedule or the rules made under it or the rules of procedure of the house or any other law can a member of a party be expelled by it, and by what procedure. The sixth question was equally absurd: 'does the expulsion affect his status as a member in the Lok Sabha ?'

The short answer to all these queries cannot possibly be unknown to Mr Shivraj Patil. The expulsion of a member of a political party is governed by the common law regulating all voluntary associations, be they clubs or political parties. The expellee has a right to challenge it in the courts. Mr Ajit Singh did just that. The Delhi high court rejected his plea.

The expelled member does not lose his membership of the house, as is clear from the fact that Clause 2(1)(C) was dropped. However, unless the expulsion is set aside by the courts, the expellee does lose his membership of the party. He is no longer amenable to its whip and cannot be counted among the members of the political party.

Since the clause was dropped, the speaker cannot judge the validity of an expulsion. That decision lies as before with the courts and the courts alone. The speaker is appointed the adjudicating authority only under the anti-defection law, and he is concerned with the two grounds alone: violation of the whip and renunciation of membership.

Once he is faced with expulsions which have not been set aside by courts, the aggrieved person is entitled, if he succeeds, to restoration of membership as well as damages; the speaker has no option but to regard the member as 'unattached'. He can neither be unseated by the law nor be reckoned to be a member of his former party. If it issues a whip to him thereafter, he is entitled to ignore it without losing his seat. The speaker will not regard it as a case of violation of the whip and unseat him.

His own directions tell him what to do. Direction 120 empowers him to recognize groups or parties 'for the purpose of functioning in the house'. Direction 121 lays down three criteria for such recognition: announcement of a distinct programme at the time of the general elections 'organization both inside and outside the house' and at least one-tenth of the membership of the house. If these criteria are not met, the members are treated as 'unattached.'

This is how Mr Ajit Singh and three other expellees from the Janata Dal on 26 December 1991 were regarded when the speaker allotted separate seats to them on 6 January 1992. Four other Janata Dal MPs expelled in July 1991, were accorded the same status. It will not do for Mr Shivraj Patil to say now, as he does, that he was not determining their status but gave them separate seats for the purpose of the functioning of the house. Direction 120 uses precisely that language. Implicit in his according the eight expellees separate seats was his acceptance of the fact of their expulsion with the obvious consequence from which he now seeks to resile—that they could no longer be regarded as members of the Janata Dal. Mr S. Jaipal Reddy's claim that in January Mr Patil accepted the expulsion rings true.

Had the Dal issued a whip to them thereafter, they could have ignored it. Likewise, they cannot gang up with any of the remaining members of the party to lend them the numerical strength of one-third of the party. This is what the eight expellees did on 7 August when they joined hands with 12 defectors to claim that the total of 20 was more than one-third of the 51 members of the Janata Dal that day. The speaker raises one pertinent query, the last of his seven. Can a party expel some members 'to see that the group separating from the original parent party may not have one-third of the members of the party?' This refers to the motivated expulsion at the moment of the split itself in order to reduce the number of splitters proper. This is precisely what the Congress (I) did in Nagaland in May 1990, when 12 of its 35 members broke away. It expelled two of them. The speaker disqualified the remaining 10.

The Janata Dal adopted this ploy on 5 November 1990, the day it split, when it expelled 25 of its members in the Lok Sabha. The speaker, Mr Rabi Ray, wisely declined to act on such an expulsion in his famous ruling on 11 January 1991, for which he won deservedly high praise.

In total contrast, the eight expulsions in the case in point took place in two instalments in December 1990, and July 1992, well before the Holiday Inn breakfast meeting on 7 August preliminary to the parade before Mr Shivraj Patil. If he is to treat it all as a split, he has to abandon the settled law on expulsions and propound new doctrines. The election commission had turned down Mr Ajit Singh's plea that he represented the original Janata Dal. Not only Mr Shivraj Patil, but many others too would do well to reckon with a factor that has been glossed over, reducing the anti-defection law to a farce. A split is not exempted only because the splitters constitute one-third of the membership. The law requires much more besides Paragraph 3 of the Tenth Schedule which envisages 'a faction which had arisen as a result of a split in his [the legislator's] original political party', and this faction is not less than one-third of the 'legislature party'. In sum, the split in the 'legislature party' must have arisen as a result of a split in 'the original political party'.

Those who rush at midnight to Raj Bhavan, or suddenly surface from Holiday Inn one fine morning are not splitters. They are defectors. What the law envisages is open debate and split in the organization, as in the Congress in 1969 and in the Janata party in 1990, and a split in the legislature party in consequence.

Incidentally, the mover of the piece of legislation, Rajiv Gandhi, was quite clear on one point in his speech in the Rajya Sabha on 31 January 1985:

'The decision should be automatic and the operation of the Bill should be quick so that there is no time in which horse-trading can take place.' Defection is a single act. So is a split.

Recent events have only confirmed the wisdom of the minority judgment of the Supreme Court on the law. Justices L.M. Sharma and J.S. Verma pointed out that the speaker's 'tenure being dependent on the will of the majority therein [in the house], likelihood of suspicion of bias could not be ruled out'. Rather than set up an appellate authority over him, would it not be sensible to empower the courts to try disputes summarily on affidavits within a fixed time, on a priority basis ?

The speaker is only a designated authority to decide disputes under the Tenth Schedule. In that capacity the curbs on criticism imposed by the archaic privileges do not apply, but they do affect him all the same. A little over a year after he assumed office as speaker, Mr Shivraj Patil has wantonly damaged his credibility for partisan ends.

29

The Speaker on the Law of Defection[1]

On 31 January 1985, Rajiv Gandhi claimed in the Rajya Sabha:

What we have tried to do in this Bill is to make it as black and white as possible so that there are no grey areas where somebody has to take a decision. The decision should be automatic, backed by a sequence of events which are on record, so that there is no debate about it. We also thought that the operation of the Bill should be quick so that there is no time in which horse–trading can take place and there is no time for a problem to arise. That is why we left this to the chairman [of the Rajya Sabha], or to the speaker' [of the Lok Sabha or as the case may be, the State Assembly].

All he conceded was that 'there may be shortcomings', but promised despatch, effectiveness, precision, and fair play.

On 7 August 1992, 20 MPs of the Janata Dal applied to the speaker, Mr Shivraj Patil, for separate seats provoking from the Dal the charge of defection. It took Mr Patil nearly 10 months to give his ruling on 1 June 1993. The law was supposed to curb the menace of defections. The net result of his ruling is to legitimize it. Men who suddenly emerged from the famous breakfast meeting at the Holiday Inn in Delhi on 7 August and claimed a split in the party are defectors. The essence of a party split is open debate prior to the parting of ways.

Like Rajiv Gandhi, Mr Patil says that 'the law is not happily worded nor free from lacunae'. It has 'defects too' and 'does not provide for coping up with the situations that arise' in dealing with

[1] The Statesman, 25 and 26 June 1993.

defections. He would rather that the judges decided cases under the law, which is embodied in the Constitution. 'The advantages in giving these cases to the Judiciary to decide are many ...The speaker or the chairman may or may not be endowed with legal acumen and proficiency in law ... The responsibility to interpret the Constitution of India is that of the Supreme Court or the high courts. It is, therefore, more apt to have the cases involving the interpretation of theTenth Schedule [to the Constitution] decided by the Supreme Court or high court judges.'

Mr Patil's remarks show how unreal were the encomiums showered on speakers last year by Justices M.N. Venkatachaliah, K.J. Reddy, and S.C.Agarwal of the Supreme Court while upholding the conferment of judicial powers on them. In contrast, Justices L.M. Sharma and J.S. Verma pointed out that since the speaker's tenure depends on the majority in the house, the 'likelihood of suspicion of bias could not be ruled out'.The majority cautiously struck down the ouster of courts' jurisdiction, by Paragraph 7 of the Tenth Schedule, on the narrow ground that the amendment to the Constitution had not been ratified by one-half of the states that the Constitution requires. Mr Patil suggests that this omission be remedied. If it is, the provision is liable to be struck down again; this time on the ground that it violates one of the basic features of the Constitution: judicial review.

Mr Patil's ruling on the merits of the case only fortifies his own observations and those of Justices Sharma and Verma on making the speaker the judge in defection cases.The ruling is bizarre in its reasoning and harmful in its legal consequences.The facts are simple. On 26 December 1991, the Janata Dal expelled Mr Ajit Singh and three others from its 59-strong parliamentary party. Four others were expelled on 19 July 1992, a total of eight expellees.

On 17 July, four others had violated the Dal's whip by abstaining from voting on the no-confidence motion against the government. On 7 August these four plus the eight expellees met eight other members at the famous breakfast and claimed to have split the party validly with the charmed fraction of one-third of 59. The Dal, however, contended that since the eight expellees had ceased to be party members earlier, the splitters were at best 12 in a party of 51; rather, eight out of 47 since four had incurred disqualification by violating the whip on 17 July.Thus, apart from the eight expellees, the rest were defectors.

Mr Patil, however, applied a different arithmetic based on a novel and startling proposition of law: namely, that no party can expel a member from its legislature party. Therefore, the eight expellees could lawfully join the rest to make up the total. The four violators of the whip, he held, were of course liable to disqualification. However the disqualification—hold your breath—took effect only from the date of his order ten months later. The net effect ? On 7 August, these four admitted violators of the law, plus the eight admitted expellees could join eight others to constitute a group of 20; one-third of the Dal's 59 members and lawful splitters all. Mr Patil has truly made a mockery of the law by his forced, tortuous reasoning. To begin with, the law condones a genuine split but not wholesale defection by one-third of the party. The difference is obvious. The Communists (1964), the Congress (1969), and the Janata (1980) split after public airing of disputes.

Paragraph 3 of the Tenth Schedule envisages 'a faction which has arisen as a result of a split in his [the legislator's] original political party', and this faction or group is not less than one-third of the 'legislature party'. In sum, the split in the 'legislature party' must have arisen as a result of a split in 'the original political party'. There must be two splits. The law separately defines the legislature party and its parent, the original political party. Those who rush at midnight to the Raj Bhavan, or suddenly surface from Holiday Inn are not splitters but defectors.

Mr Patil disdains to quote Paragraph 3. He repeatedly provides his own summary, omitting the split in the original party: 'The legislator can vote as he likes in violation of the whip issued to him if one-third members of his party in the legislature wish to vote along with him differently from the direction given by the party.' At one place he avers that the speaker 'has to decide if the political party had split outside the legislature', but only to hold a few paragraphs later that 'it is not necessary for him to find out if the political party splitting outside the Parliament has one-third members of the party in the parliament or not'.

In a statement filed by the Ajit Singh group it was claimed that they had split from the Janata Dal on 5 February 1992, and were, indeed, the 'original' Dal. The Dal latched on to this and argued that in that event, since there were only four of them on that day, they should be disqualified. Mr Patil had a clear duty to ascertain precisely when the Dal split as a political party, for on that depends the validity of the consequent break up of its legislature party. All he asserts is that from all the material he could 'hold that Janata Dal Political Party had split before 7 August 1992'.

If the speaker is to thus legitimize the defections on 7 August 1992 from the Janata Dal's legislature party, how could he include the eight expellees in the total of 20 splitters ? Simple. By holding that 'it is not correct and legal to hold that if a member of a party is expelled from its primary membership he loses his membership of his legislature party'. It is one thing to assert that by expelling a member the party cannot unseat a legislator elected by his people. Rajiv Gandhi's Bill had a clause to this effect [Clause 2(1)(c)]. It was dropped as a result of protest in the Congress parliamentary party meeting on 30 January 1985. What Mr Patil has however held is that expulsion of a member does not mean that 'he loses his membership of his legislature party'.

Mr Patil could not have forgotten that his party had expelled Messrs V.P. Singh, Arun Nehru, Arif Mohammed Khan, and Mufti Mohammed Sayeed in 1987. Does his ruling imply that they could have demanded the right to participate in the Congress (I) parliamentary party's meetings despite the expulsion? What is the legal basis for the ruling? Paragraph 63 of the ruling deserves quotation *in extenso* to demonstrate Mr Patil's approach: 'In this respect, Explanation (a) to Para 2(1) is relevant: '(a) an elected member of a house shall be deemed to belong to the political party, if any, by which he was set up as a candidate for election as such member'. This is a constitutional status given to the member which cannot be taken away from him by expulsion.' It is surely absurd to regard the legislator's membership of the party as a 'constitutional status' by virtue of explanation (a) and that he cannot be divested of that status by the expulsion. All that, it says is that he shall 'be deemed to belong to the political party' if he was elected as its candidate. It does not mean he shall always remain a member of it notwithstanding expulsion.

Why does Mr Patil totally omit the crucial qualifying words in the 'explanation' ? They are 'for the purposes of this sub-paragraph' and they belie his interpretation. These words are a reference to sub-para I of Paragraph 2 listing the two kinds of defection: 'voluntarily' giving up party membership and flouting the party whip. It is 'for the purposes of this sub-paragraph' that explanation (a) says that he shall 'be deemed' to be a member of the party on whose ticket he was elected. It does not spell an unbreakable link with the party at all. Indeed, in Paragraph 71 of his ruling Mr Patil himself recognizes that 'the Tenth Schedule applies to his duties and rights as the legislator. It does not apply to his rights and duties as a party member.' How, then, does he hold that expulsion does not mean 'he loses his membership of his legislature party' and that such membership is 'a constitutional status'?

Yet, heedless of the contradiction, Mr Patil holds (Paragraphs 143–6) that MPs cannot be 'legally and validly' expelled from their party outside or from the legislature party. In his view, that would 'defeat the provisions of the Tenth Schedule'. Expulsions do nothing of the sort. They do not entail loss of membership of the legislature but of the party. It is unthinkable that in India political parties should be divested of the right to expel members according to their Constitution. Mr Patil's ruling on this point is based on pure *ipse dixit* and forced misconstruction based on a patent misquotation of 'Explanation (a)'. Sad to add, it is also based on ignorance of the fundamentals of the law of political parties.

The framers of the Constitution and of legislation based their efforts on existing law. Mr Patil breezily dismisses the submission that the relationship of a member to his party is identical to 'the relationship between the members of a club and the club'. He ought to know that the law is the same for all voluntary organizations, be they political parties or clubs. The law of tort in respect of wrongful expulsion is identical in relation to both.

The Supreme Court of India ruled in the famous Sadiq Ali case, arising out of the Congress split in 1969, that the jurisdiction of the election commission under the Election Symbols (Allotment and Reservation) Order is confined only to resolving disputes over the allotment of the election symbol in the wake of a split in the party. Disputes over property, the Supreme Court ruled, are for the civil courts to determine.

No less absurd is Mr Patil's assertion that his ruling 'shall be operative from the date of the decision and not retrospectively'. The law gives him no such latitude. Paragraph 2 says that a legislator 'shall be disqualified' if he commits either of two offences: abandonment of party membership and or defiance of the whip. The speaker comes in under Paragraph 6 if any question arises as to whether a member of a house 'has become subject to disqualification' under the law.

He is thus asked to determine whether, on the basis of the member's misconduct, the disqualification has already accrued; whether he 'has become subject' to it under the law does not fall within the purview of the Speaker's ruling. Mr Patil's ruling protects the four admitted violators of the whip on 17 July 1992, till his ruling on 1 June, 1993. Of course, one consequence of his blanket of protection is that they could be counted with the other 16 to account for 20 on 7 August 1992.

It is an altogether inept and shoddy performance. Its only redeeming feature is the admission of defects in this self-serving law. Mr Patil recommends a committee 'to give a comprehensive report for overcoming the difficulties and defects of the law within a short period'. It is a sound suggestion. Meanwhile, if three moderate reforms are carried out the vice will be considerably curbed . First, debar anyone changing political affiliation from public office for a year. As I have noted earlier the honest convert will not be deterred. The turncoat will be. He wants instant reward. Secondly, a motion of no-confidence must name the alternative prime minister or chief minister in 'the constructive vote of no-confidence' as Article 67 of Germany's Basic Law calls it. Lastly, the legislature alone must decide whether the government commands majority support, not the governor.

30
Resignation of Disqualified Ministers[1]

P rime Minister Chandra Shekhar has only a few days between now and 21 February when the budget session of parliament begins, to avert a major confrontation with the speaker of the Lok Sabha, Rabi Ray. On 11 January 1991 the speaker disqualified eight Janata Dal (S) members of the Lok Sabha under the anti-defection law of whom as many as five are ministers. Foremost among them is the Minister for External Affairs, V.C. Shukla. When parliament meets the speaker will act on his ruling and treat all the eight disqualified members, the five ministers included, as 'strangers' in the house. On the other hand, the prime minister has rejected the resignations offered by the ministers and asserted that they can remain in office for another six months.

This squarely raises the question whether the constitutional provision (Article 75(5)) which disqualifies a minister who is not a member of parliament for six consecutive months applies only to one who is initially not an MP or is applicable also to one who subsequently incurs a disqualification. The latter view has never occurred to any one in these last 40 years. If the speaker rejects it, the prime minister will either suffer a humiliation or defy the speaker.

Neither the soundness of the ruling of 11 January nor the impartiality of the speaker was challenged by anybody. The prime minister's reaction to it was instant and incredible. It would have 'no effect at all' on the functioning of his government. Evidently he was prepared for it and had decided on his response in advance.

[1] *Sunday Mail*, 17 February 1991.

The Minister for Parliamentary Affairs, Satya Prakash Malaviya, revealed the line the government had decided to adopt: 'There is no need for the affected ministers to resign from the council of ministers because under the constitutional provisions, a non-member can continue as minister for six months.'

The ministers resigned but the prime minister declined to accept the resignations. Not only the opposition parties but even the Congress, on whose support the government exists, criticized it. What is more, Deputy Prime Minister Devi Lal also joined in the criticism. He met Chandra Shekhar on 15 January and asked him to drop the five ministers. He went a step further and even impugned their credentials. They had never been dissidents in the Janata Dal; had not attended the meeting at his residence on 5 November where the split was announced; and their names were not included in the list that Chandra Shekhar submitted to the speaker on 6 November. They had joined the Janata Dal (S) only to become ministers. Their plan had misfired. There is every reason to believe that the Tau was voicing the feelings of a significant section of the Janata Dal (S).

Therefore you have this section of the Janata Dal (S), the Congress, the Janata Dal, the BJP, the CPI, and the CPM, and indeed, public opinion at large is opposed to the continuance in office of these five.

Let us turn to the constitutional position. Article 75(5) reads: 'A minister who for any period of six consecutive months is not a member of either house of parliament shall at the expiration of that period cease to be a minister.' Do these words support Chandra Shekhar's contention ? It is by now well-settled by rulings of the Supreme Court that in cases of doubt the debates of the constituent assembly are relevant and can be referred to, to resolve the controversy.

Article 75 figured as Article 62 in the draft Constitution. An authoritative exposition of clause (5) was provided in the constituent assembly by none other than the chairman of its drafting committee, Dr B.R. Ambedkar, on 31 December 1948. His exposition shows Chandra Shekhar to be wholly in the wrong. The exemption clause was envisaged for ministers who initially lack the qualification of membership of parliament and not for those who had the requisite qualification but subsequently incurred a disqualification, for example, under the election law.

Dr Ambedkar's exposition is so lucid, comprehensive, and relevant that it bears quotation *in extenso:*

With regard to the second point, namely, the qualifications of ministers, we have three amendments.

The first amendment is by Mohammad Tahir. His suggestion is that no person should be appointed a minister unless at the time of his appointment he is an elected member of the house. He does not admit the possibility of the cases covered in the proviso, namely, that although a person is not *at the time of his appointment* a member of the house, he may nonetheless be appointed as a minister in the cabinet subject to the condition that within six months he shall get himself elected to the house.

The second qualification is by Prof. K.T. Shah. He said that a minister should belong to a majority party and his third qualification is that he must have a certain educational status.

Now, with regard to the first point, namely, the no person shall be entitled to be appointed a minister unless he is at the time of his appointment an elected member of the house. I think it forgets to take into consideration certain important matters which cannot be overlooked. First is this—it is perfectly possible to imagine that a person who is otherwise competent to hold the post of a minister has been defeated in a constituency for some reason which, although it may be perfectly good, might have annoyed the constituency and he might have incurred the displeasure of that particular constituency. It is not a reason why a member so competent as that should be not permitted to be appointed a member of the cabinet on the assumption that he shall be able to get himself elected either from the same constituency or from another. After all the privilege that is permitted is a privilege that extends only for six months. It does not confer a right to that individual to sit in the house without being elected at all.[2]

It never crossed his mind that the provision would or could be pressed into service by disqualified MPs. The Constitution itself lays down separately the qualifications for membership of parliament in Article 102. Apart from the named qualifications and disqualifications *both* provisions empower parliament to add to them. The election law prescribes disqualification on the ground of corrupt practices. Can it be argued that if the disqualification were to be for less than six months a minister could have continued and sought re-election ? Incidentally, will the three non-ministers also cling to their seats on the strength of the argument

[2]CAD, vol. vii, p. 1186.

which the prime minister advances to enable the five ministers to continue in office?

On the strength of Dr. Ambedkar's exposition, it would be open to any citizen to move any of the high courts for a writ for *quo warranto* against the five ministers challenging their continuance in office. Also, it would be open to the speaker, indeed it would be his bounden duty, to ask the ministers to leave the house since they are no longer its members. He has to act on his own ruling of 11 January, after all.

The only remedy open to the ministers is to move the courts, but in that event too they will have to resign from the government. Why? Because the government, reversing its stand, filed a solemn affidavit in the Delhi high court to declare that 'Parliament is supreme and no court can decide an issue pertaining to this house.' These very words were used by the prime minister in the house on 9 January. Will he go back on them now if the speaker implements his ruling and shows the ministers the door?

31

The *Sub Judice* Rule: Throttling Parliament[1]

The last session of parliament saw a curious application of the *sub judice* rule by the presiding officers of both its houses. Mr I.K. Gujral complained in the Rajya Sabha, on 5 December 1995, that the house had been denied an opportunity to discuss the nexus between criminals and politicians as someone had gone to court on the matter. He had a point. The press and the public discussed the matter freely, but parliament was stifled.

On 13 December 1995 the government cited the writ petitions in the Supreme Court on its telecom policy to argue that the matter was sub judice. The speaker of the Lok Sabha, Mr Shivraj Patil, said that a joint parliamentary committee would not be appropriate since the court was seized of the matter. On 15 December, the Supreme Court passed interim orders in the case. It directed the parties to refrain from giving any publicity outside, as the court was looking into the issues raised. The court, however, said that this direction should not be understood as barring any discussion on the subject in parliament.

The court was being helpful, but surely the rules are by now well settled. First, it is most unseemly of litigants and, more so, their advocates to give interviews to the media on pending cases; more often than not, on the very steps of the court before TV cameras.

[1] *The Statesman,* 7 March 1996. I am indebted to a characteristically erudite memorandum by the Clerk of the House of Commons appended to the Second Report from the Committee of Privilege, Session 1978–9 concerning, (1) Publication of the Proceedings of the House and, (2) Application of the Sub Judice Rule on 20 April 1978, 23 March 1979, HMSO London.

Secondly, all public discussion is not barred because a litigation is pending. Lastly, the *sub judice* rule does not bar parliamentary discussion in all cases, contrary to the current impression.

Parliament has been aptly called the 'grand inquest of the nation'. It imposes on itself rules of fair play in its deliberations out of respect for the rights of the citizens and the judiciary. One such rule is the sub judice rule, however phrased. Rule 186 of the rules of procedure of the Lok Sabha lists the grounds that render a motion inadmissible. One of them, (viii), is that 'it shall not relate to any matter which is under adjudication by a court of law having jurisdiction in any part of India'.

Rule 352 says that 'a member while speaking shall not ... refer to any matter of fact on which a judicial decision is pending'. Likewise, a question 'shall not ask for information on a matter which is under adjudication by a court of law ...' Rule 41(2) (xviii).

The law of contempt of court, surely does not bar all public discussion of such matters. In the famous *Sunday Times* case, Lord Diplock observed that

Discussion, however strongly expressed, on matters of general public interest of this kind is not to be stifled merely because there is litigation pending arising out of particular facts to which general principles discussed would be applicable. If the arousing of public opinion by this kind of discussion has the indirect effect of bringing pressure to bear upon a particular litigant ... this must be borne because of the greater public interest in upholding freedom of discussion on matters of general public concern.[2]

Mr A.R. Mukerjee, who served as secretary to the West Bengal legislative assembly, points out in his able work on parliamentary procedure, 'only those comments which may amount to a contempt of court will not be allowed to be made in the House',[3] for otherwise it would lead to the absurd result of members of parliament enjoying less freedom of speech than the citizens.

This is however precisely what successive chairpersons of both houses of parliament did. In one case, pure deceit was allowed to pass muster. In the Tul Mohan Ram case the government filed a charge sheet a couple of hours before parliament was to begin its

---

[2]*Attorney-General v Times Newspapers Ltd.* (1974) A.C. 273.

[3]A.R. Mukherjee; Parliamentary Procedure in India; Oxford University Press; Third Edition, 1983; p. 182.

winter session on 11 November 1974 and argued that the licence scandal could not be discussed because it was now sub judice. This was stratagem to wriggle out of its solemn 'promise' to the Lok Sabha on 9 September 1974 that 'after the investigation is over, the first thing we will do is to come to parliament ... It is only after that, according to the wishes of Parliament, that we will proceed.' The public and the press could freely discuss the matter. Parliament was throttled, exasperated, MPs resorted to unparliamentary forms of protest in the house.

Respect for a former chief justice of India led to neglect of the outrageous ruling given by Mr M. Hidayatullah as Vice-Chairman of the Rajya Sabha, on 13 March 1980, disallowing a motion expressing disapproval of the president's proclamation dissolving nine state assemblies on the ground that it was sub judice.

Three petitions challenging the action filed in Bombay, Allahabad, and Lucknow, rendered it a 'matter which is under adjudication'. Anyone can thus silence parliament by moving the courts in good time. The law certainly does not permit such stratagems to succeed.

In Britain the sub judice rule rested upon practice until it was codified in a resolution of the House of Commons on 23 July 1963. It forbade references to 'all matters awaiting or under adjudication in all courts', civil and criminal. This was however 'subject always to the discretion of the chair'. It was relaxed on 28 June 1972 by another resolution. It permitted reference to matters 'under adjudication in all civil courts, including the National Industrial Relations Court, in so far as such matters relate to a ministerial decision which cannot be challenged in court except on grounds of misdirection or bad faith, or concern issues of national importance such as the national economy, public order or the essentials of life.'

A memorandum submitted by the clerk of the House of Commons to the Select Procedure Committee of 1971–2 referred to the attitude taken by past speakers in relation to criminal cases and the sub judice rule and observed: 'It would appear that greater importance has been attached to criminal cases than to civil cases.'

The result was well summed up by that great authority on constitutional law, Professor S.A. de Smith. The rule had been narrowed to enable the speaker to admit questions in his discretion though they relate to matters pending adjudication in a civil court, if the issue raised concerns a matter of national importance or the exercise of a Minister's discretion challengeable only on narrow grounds before the court.'[4]

Writ Petitions

This undoubtedly applies to all writ petitions, especially one challenging imposition of president's rule. Writ petitions answer de Smith's description perfectly. They challenge the exercise of a minister's discretion, whether on grounds of mala fides or misdirection.

The 1972 resolution said that 'in exercising its discretion the chair should not allow reference to such matters if it appears that there is a real and substantial danger of prejudice to the proceedings'. This is the very test applied in cases of contempt of court: a real and substantial danger of prejudice to the court proceedings. The risk is greater in trials by jury and almost nil when questions of law, which are to be decided by trained judges, are discussed in public. Discussion of such issues in the press is permissible under the law of contempt even if a case is pending.

There are instances of speakers of the House of Commons altogether waiving the sub judice, rule. One concerned the editor of the *Yorkshire Miner*, Mr Maurice Jones. Charged with an offence and released on bail, he fled the country. As the speaker noted, on 21 July 1977, the matter was clearly sub judice under the Resolution of 1963 (the Lok Sabha rules use almost identical language). He however exercised his discretion and waived the rule. It would not, he ruled, 'for the immediate future, govern any other proceedings in the house connected with the charges against Mr Jones'.

The rules of procedure have been framed by the house itself. The Constitution guarantees 'freedom of speech in parliament'. The rules must be recast in the light of changes in British rules after 1963.

[4]De Smith, p. 305.

32

President, Prime Minister and Parliament[1]

The chairman of the Rajya Sabha, Mr R.Venkataraman, and the Speaker of the Lok Sabha, Mr Balram Jakhar, are very much mistaken if they think that their rulings on 20 and 19 March 1987 respectively, will be accepted as the last word on the prime minister's accountability to parliament for the performance of his constitutional duties towards the president, especially as they have ignored the explicit assertion of Dr B.R. Ambedkar that the task of overseeing the performance of those duties falls squarely on parliament. It is its duty and its right.

Addressing the constituent assembly on 31 December 1948, Dr Ambedkar pointed out that there were two ways of enforcing the rules of parliamentary government.

One way is to permit the court to enquire and to adjudicate upon the validity of the thing. The other is to leave the matter to the legislature itself and to see whether by a censure motion or a motion of non-confidence, it cannot compel the ministry to give proper advice to the president and impeachment to see that the president follows the advice by the ministry. In my judgment, the latter is the better way of effecting our purpose and would be unfair, inconvenient, if everything done in the house is made subject to the jurisdiction of the Court ....'.[2]

This passage is decisive. It is not referred to in either ruling. Mr Venkataraman rightly regards Dr Ambedkar as 'the architect of our Constitution' and the president–prime minister relationship as 'a

[1] *The Indian Express,* 26 March, 1987.
[2] CAD, vol. vii, p. 11.

nexus which is at the very heart of governance under the cabinet system'. Rulings that ignore the most authoritative exposition on a matter of the utmost importance stand exposed for their fatal error.

If the background and the aftermath of Dr Ambedkar's exposition are recalled, the error will be seen to be graver still. The drafting committee had envisaged two Instruments of Instructions for the guidance of the president and the governors embodying the 'conventions of responsible government'. Dr Ambedkar was explaining his amendment which said that 'in the choice of his ministers, and the exercise of his other functions under this constitution, the president shall be generally guided by the instructions set out in Schedule IIIA [embodying the Instrument], but the validity of anything done by the president shall not be called in question on the ground that it was done otherwise than in accordance with such instructions'.

Mr Naziruddin Ahmed pleaded for the deletion of the bar on judicial review. Dr Ambedkar declined. He wanted 'to leave the matter to the legislature itself' with unfettered power of debate on the subject 'whether by a censure motion or a motion of no-confidence'. He was anxious lest 'any recalcitrant member may run to the Supreme Court and by a writ of injunction against the speaker prevent him from carrying on the business of the house unless that matter is decided'.

Exemption from judicial review imposes a greater duty on the speaker to ensure that the legislature is not prevented from discharging the duty which Dr Ambedkar so clearly envisaged for it.

The aftermath makes it all the more incumbent upon him. The Instruments of Instructions were dropped as being 'unnecessary and superfluous'. The conventions of the parliamentary system were well known. Dr Ambedkar asked his colleague on the drafting committee, Mr T.T. Krishnamachari, to explain to the assembly, which he did: 'It has now been felt that the matter should be left entirely to convention rather than be put into the body of the Constitution as a Schedule in the shape of Instrument of Instructions.' The provisions of the Constitution were thus adopted on the definite understanding that the conventions would be followed. It is not open to the president or the prime minister to ignore them merely because the Instrument was deleted. The Supreme Court recognized them in the very judgment that Mr

Venkataraman cited. This fortifies the scheme of responsible government that Dr Ambedkar envisaged: it is for parliament to ensure that the Conventions of the parliamentary system are followed. However, on the crucial point the matter was not left to convention at all. Article 78 of the Constitution declares in detail the 'duties of prime minister as respects furnishing of information to the president etc.'.

Is a parliament which has been advisedly charged with the power and the duty of enforcing the 'obligation of the minister to follow the directions given in the Instrument of Instructions' and 'to compel the ministry to give proper advice to the president' precluded from discussing any failure on the part of the prime minister to discharge a duty imposed by a constitutional provision despite the publication of credible reports of such a lapse?

This is the question facing us today. Neither ruling cares even to reckon with it. Mr Venkataraman says that 'the first and essential question that arises for consideration is whether any matter communicated or purported to be communicated by the head of state to the head of government and vice versa may be raised in the house of parliament'. This is palpably wrong. The prime minister twice claimed in parliament on 2 and 4 March 1987 that there has never been any failure to keep the president informed on matters of national interest. The president's letter contradicting this claim in detail is a published document. It reveals a prima facie case of violation of Article 78.

Publication last July of the Tamil Nadu Governor Mr S.L. Khurana's reproachful letter to the Chief Minister of the State, Mr M.G. Ramachandran, dated 20 May 1986 and his reply ten days later raised an identical issue. Nobody talked of subversion of official secrets then. It is pointless to harp on the confidentiality of exchanges between the heads of state and government. MPs are not seeking publication of confidential exchanges. They are only taking cognizance of credible, published material that reveals grave lapses.

Both rulings rely on the rule that no one shall 'use the president's name for the purpose of influencing the debate'. It is based on British parliamentary practice and its object is not to stifle debate but the opposite: to ensure freedom of debate by protecting the independence of parliament from the intrusion of the crown. As Erskine May puts it, 'the irregular use of the queen's name to influence a decision of the house is unconstitutional in principle and inconsistent with the independence of parliament'[3] The very language of the rule is reminiscent of the days when the crown's placement in the Commons would use its name to bribe or intimidate members and prevent a free debate on a Bill or resolution.

The rule cannot be invoked when a member alleges, not that the crown supports or opposes a given proposition, but that the prime minister has failed in his duties to the head of state.[4] Since the practice of weekly consultation between the two and the regular furnishing of minutes of cabinet meetings and other state papers to the queen has been meticulously followed, there has not been cause for complaint against the prime minister in the House of Commons. Two precedents however clearly suggest that should the occasion arise, complaints can be made in parliament and the speaker will not prevent them from being voiced on the ground that 'I do not allow the name of the monarch to be brought here in any form and by anybody', to use Mr Jakhar's expression.

Mr Venkataraman revealed that 'a set of relevant queries was posed to Sir Kenneth Bradshaw, clerk of the House of Commons on the subject'. The texts of the queries, as well as the answers must in fairness be published in full, as they invariably are in British parliamentary reports.

Mr Venkataraman had sought the opinion in a public capacity. Those two precedents are cited by Sir Kenneth. However, Mr Venkataraman paraphrases one and quotes only partially from the other. 'The only occasion in this century when the discussions between the monarch and the prime minister were shared with the British parliament was during the course of a substantial debate of a legislative nature, namely, on the Abdication Bill, 1936.' This paraphrase harps on the aspect of confidentiality and ignores that of accountability. In fact, the matter was raised by Churchill in the House of Commons three times before the abdication. He was sore with Prime Minister Stanley Baldwin for not being understanding enough with Edward VIII. On 3 December 1936 he asked the prime minister whether any constitutional difficulty had arisen. Baldwin declined to reply 'at this stage'. The following day, both Churchill and Attlee raised the issue. The prime minister stated the legal position. On 7 December Churchill pleaded that no 'irrevocable

[3]Erskine May, *Parliamentary Practices*, London: Butterworth, 20th edn, p. 428).

[4]Conduct of the prime minister vis-à-vis the head of state can be scrutinized on introduction of a proper motion. (May, p. 430.)

step' be taken before parliament was consulted. He was shouted down by the prime minister's men. On none of the three occasions did the speaker prevent him from raising the issue.

In our context, would parliament be precluded from discussing credible reports of a president wishing to resign in despair because the prime minister does not consult him at all?

The other precedent is illuminating. On 20 July 1986, *The Sunday Times* carried a report quoting 'sources close to the Queen' to the effect that 'she is dismayed by many of Mrs Thatcher's policies'. The points of discord were listed. None implied any failure in consultation.

It is pointless for Mr Venkataraman to quote Sir Kenneth to the effect that 'no debate took place ... and no questions were *tabled*' [*sic*]. Questions were asked in the Commons on 22 July by the Liberal Leader, Mr David Steel, hours before the prime minister's regular weekly audience with the queen. Mrs Thatcher alluded to this fact. She stonewalled as several MPs joined Mr Steel and declined to answer any questions about the queen, pointedly noting however that there were 'no complaints about how the government is running the affairs of this country'.[5]

Two features are worthy of note. The issue was reported differences of opinion between the prime minister and the queen, not any failure to consult the queen. Nonetheless, the speaker, Mr Bernard Weatherill, did not intervene at all. Had the issue been one of any lapse on the part of the prime minister she could not have got away with evasion and the furore would have been overwhelming. In India we have the explicit Article 78.

One wonders what became of Mr Venkataraman's quest, as he revealed on 17 March for Canadian and Australian precedents. On 30 June 1926 in Canada and on 11 November 1975 in Australia there was 'mention of the governor-general's name' in debates on a motion of no-confidence in the prime minister.

These cases totally refute Mr Jakhar's thesis that 'even during the discussion on a motion of censure or non-confidence in the ministers the name of the president, the relationship between the president and the prime minister or the council of ministers ... cannot be allowed to be brought in to influence the debate'.

This is a gross misconstruction of the rule regarding misuse of

[5]Official Report, 22 July, 1986; cols. 176–8.

the president's name, but under Rule 352(v) 'the conduct of persons in high authority' can be discussed: the president's by way of impeachment, and the prime minister's on a censure motion. Can the former be impeached for violating the Constitution but the latter not be censured for the same offence because that would 'bring in the name of the president'? If the rulings are allowed to stand, the prime minister will not be accountable to parliament and, through it, to the nation in relation to his duties to the president. Devoid of this sanction, Article 78 will be reduced to naught and the parliamentary system will be in peril.

33

Discussing the Conduct of the President or Governor[1]

The Tamil Nadu assembly set a most unfortunate precedent when, on 19 April 1995 it adopted a motion, for suspension of Rule 92 (vii) of its rules of procedure in order to discuss the conduct of the state's Governor, Dr Chenna Reddy. The motion was moved by none other than the leader of the house, Mr V.R. Nedunchezian. It of course had the full support of the chief minister, Miss Jayalalitha. Well before that, both Dr Chenna Reddy and Miss Jayalalitha had amply demonstrated their contempt for propriety and their unfitness for public office. It is sad that things have come to such a sorry pass in Madras. The motion is far too important to be ignored.

Rule 92 (vii) says that 'A member while speaking must not ... (vii) reflect upon the conduct of the president or any governor or any court of justice or use the governor or the president's name for the purpose of influencing the debate'. If this rule can be suspended to discuss the conduct of the governor, what is there to prevent discussion of the conduct of the president?

There is a similar provision in Rule 352 (v) and (vi) of the rules of procedure and conduct of business in the Lok Sabha: 'A member while speaking shall not ... (v) reflect upon the conduct of persons in high authority unless the discussion is based on a substantive motion drawn in proper terms.' An Explanation adds that 'the words 'persons in high authority' mean persons whose conduct can only be discussed on a substantive motion drawn in proper terms under

[1] *The Statesman,* 11 and 12 May 1995.

the Constitution or such other persons whose conduct, in the opinion of the speaker, should be discussed on a substantive motion drawn up in terms to be approved by him.'

Under the Constitution (Article 121) the only persons whose conduct cannot be discussed in parliament except upon a motion, and that too for their removal, are judges of the Supreme Court and the high courts. The president and the governors fall under the category of 'other persons' in 'high authority' whose conduct can be discussed only on the basis of a substantive motion. Clause (vi) of Rule 352 provides that an MP shall not 'use the president's name for the purpose of influencing the debate'. This is to ensure the independence of MPs, a far cry from the days when the crown had its stooges in the House of Commons.

Once Rule 92 (vii) was suspended, the Tamil Nadu assembly proceeded to discuss the alleged attack on the governor's car by AIADMK volunteers near Tindivanam on 10 April. Miss Jayalalitha read out her letters to the president and the prime minister in refutation of the 'misreporting' by the governor, and proceeded to demand his recall by the president. On 26 April the rule was again suspended by the assembly before it adopted a resolution proposing amendment of Article 155 of the Constitution making consultation with the chief minister of the state mandatory before a governor is appointed. It added that 'the government of India be moved to recall Dr Chenna Reddy, governor of Tamil Nadu and to replace him by another appointee after prior consultation with the State government'.

None of the grievances aired in the assembly on 19 and 26 April at all warranted the drastic step of suspension of Rule 92 (vii). That apart, there are some grave misconceptions on the permissible limits of discussion in the legislature of the conduct of the head of state in a parliamentary democracy and also of the conduct of the head of government towards the head of state. The rules of procedure of parliament only reflect the substantive law of the Constitution. In every parliamentary system, the head of state acts on the advice of his ministers. Accordingly, it is they, not he who are responsible to parliament for the actions of the government. 'The head of state is entitled to be properly informed by his ministers, especially by the prime minister.'

A singularly brazen instance of gross misconstruction of the rules, in sheer partisanship on the part of the presiding officer of the legislature, when the issue of the relationship between the president and the prime minister arose, was provided by Mr R.Venkataraman in his ruling as Chairman of the Rajya Sabha on 20 March 1987.

If this ruling is treated as good precedent, parliament will never be able to hold a prime minister to account for failing to fulfil his constitutional obligations towards the president, especially the duties to keep him informed (Article 78) and, indeed, to act with rectitude.

The facts were all too clear. Rajiv Gandhi was permitted to assert in parliament, twice, on 2 and 4 March 1987, that there had never been any failure on his part to keep President Zail Singh informed. Publication in the press on 13 March of the full text of a letter by the president to the prime minister, challenging his claims, proved what everyone knew: Rajiv Gandhi had lied to parliament. The issue was not the mere confidentiality of the correspondence between the two but a wider one, namely, the prime minister's violation of his duties towards the president under Article 78.

I am in a position to confidently expose a grave impropriety Mr R. Venkataraman committed in delivering his ruling. He flouted the established practice in regard to advice sought and received from the Clerk of the House of Commons by its speaker and by speakers of parliament of commonwealth countries. They are treated as confidential. Mr Venkataraman violated the confidence and, worse, misquoted the advice given by Sir Kenneth Bradshaw, the clerk of the House of Commons, by quoting selectively the parts that he felt supported his own conclusions and omitting what did not.

He told the Rajya Sabha that 'a set of relevant queries' was posed to Sir Kenneth. 'The answers are revealing', but he did not reveal them in full as he ought to have done if he decided to quote them at all. Sir Kenneth was quoted only on two points: the confidentiality of the correspondence between the queen and the prime minister and on the 'leaking' of her views on sanctions against South Africa in July 1986.

The clerk, strictly sticking to the record, said that no debate took place in the House of Commons and no questions were tabled. *Sir Kenneth did not however stop at these two points, as, indeed, he could not possibly have in fairness.* He stated the law succinctly as it was set out in Erskine May's *Parliamentary Practice*[2]. The law is that whereas there are limits on what may be asked in questions regarding

[2]20th edn, 1983.

communications between the prime minister and the queen, and prohibitions on the use of the queen's name to influence debate[3], *the conduct of the prime minister could be effectively scrutinized and debated on a properly drawn up substantive motion*[4]. *Ministerial accountability to parliament is thereby unimpaired in respect of the prime minister's conduct in advising the Crown. This crucial and most relevant part was not revealed to the Rajya Sabha.*

It is unthinkable that Rajiv Gandhi would have offered the presidency to Mr Venkataraman in June 1987 had the latter not saved his bacon in the Rajya Sabha on that fateful 20 March 1987. There was a sequel to this two years later.

In 1989, Rule 196 of the Lok Sabha's rules of procedure was amended to add further conditions to the admissibility of a motion. One of them, significantly, was this sweeping clause (xvii): 'It shall not refer to or seek disclosure of information about matters which are in their nature secret such as cabinet discussions or advice given to the president in relation to any matter in respect of which there is a constitutional, statutory or conventional obligation not to disclose information.' This is subversive of the very basis of the prime minister's accountability to parliament. Dr B.R. Ambedkar told the constituent assembly on 31 December 1948 that there were two ways of enforcing the rules of parliamentary government: through the courts or the legislature. Accordingly, the courts—but only the courts—are barred by Article 74(2) from inquiring 'whether any and if so what, advice was tendered by ministers to the president'.

Parliament and state legislatures were advisedly not mentioned; because, Dr Ambedkar opted for the other option: 'The other is to leave the matter to the legislature itself and to see whether by a censure motion or a motion of non-confidence, it cannot compel the Ministry to give proper advice to the President and impeachment to see that the President follows the advice by the ministry.'[5] The fundamental principle is ignored in the 1989 amendment, Clause (XVII) of Rule 196, clumsily worded as it is. A partisan chairperson like Mr Venkataraman can latch on, however untenably to the 'conventional obligation not to disclose information'.

[3]Ibid., p. 428.
[4]Ibid., p. 430.
[5]CAD; vol. vii, p. 11.

There is, on the contrary, a clear constitutional obligation to reveal to parliament whether or not the president is being properly advised and informed. The courts have also expanded the scope of judicial review. The privy council ruled in 1979 that a writ of mandamus can be issued to ministers to compel them to advise the head of state to revoke a proclamation of Emergency which cannot be sustained in law.[6] The Supreme Court ruled in 1994 that while Article 174(2) bars the courts from inquiring into the advice tendered to the president, it is open to them to examine the material on which the advice was based.[7]

The powers of parliament and the State legislatures on this matter are far wider than those of the courts. No one is immune to accountability under the Constitution. A procedural rule that constricts such accountability is unconstitutional. Properly read, the rules of procedure do permit discussion on substantive and proper motions of the conduct of both the heads of state and of government, with due propriety and decorum and when the situation warrants such discussion. The language must be precise and dignified and the debate limited to its terms. The speaker must ensure all this. To suspend the rules is to proclaim freedom from the constraints and values that they embody.

[6] *The Cheng Poh* vs *Public Prosecutor, Malaysia* (1979), 2 WLR. 623 at 634.
[7] *S.R. Bommai* vs *Union of India* (1994), 3 SCC 1.

34

Bribing Legislators During the Raj[1]

It is an offence under the penal code to bribe or offer to bribe a minister, a civil servant, or a voter. It is not an offence, however, to bribe a legislator be he an MP or an MLA, nor is this an offence under the Prevention of Corruption Act, 1988. It was not so under the Prevention of Corruption Act, 1947. Behind this mess lies a history, and that history should prompt us to ask whether corruption is after all in our genes for, even in the halcyon days of the freedom movement, bribing legislators was not an unknown sport.

On 16 August 1924, the private secretary to the viceroy, G.F. de Montmorency wrote to Sir James Crerar, the home member, about queries sent by the governor of Bengal: 'Lord Lytton at various times informed His Excellency the Viceroy of cases of corruption connected with the legislative council which have come to his notice.' He added:

'These consist in: (1) offers to pay sums to Muhammedan members of council to abstain from voting in the division on ministers' salaries; (2) actual payments made to members of the legislative council to vote with the Swaraj Party; (3) offers to members of the legislative council of salaried posts in the corporation on the condition of abstention from voting with the government; (4) monthly payments to nominated members of the legislative council to absent themselves during portions of sessions when important debates were to take place.

The times have changed, but the modus operandi of politicians has remained constant. The letter continued:

[1] *The Statesman*, 26 August 1995.

Lord Lytton has enquird privately from His Excellency as to the means by which corruption of this kind can be stopped. He has been advised that prosecutions are not likely to succeed ... He also enquires whether it is possible to appoint by any existing law or by special enactment of a statutory commission to enquire into the alleged prevalence of corruption in Bengal with power to summon witnesses, take evidence on oath, call for production of documents, banking accounts, etc.

H.E. wishes the suggestion to be examined both from the point of view of what machinery exists for the purpose of enquiries of this nature under present law and from the point of view of what machinery could be crea ed.

The Viceroy replied:

The legal position is very anomalous. Under the law in India it is an offence to bribe a voter; but the tender of a bribe to or the receipt of a bribe by a member of a legislature in order to induce him to vote in a particular way is not an offence under the criminal law. These acts are dealt with in England by parliament itself as a question of privilege. I am having the question of necessity of the recognition of privileges for Indian legislatures considered and the dominion and the colonial and foreign Legislation on the point examined ...'

A Bill was drafted, the Legislative Bodies Corrupt Practices Bill, as Dr Salil Kumar Nag records in his book *Evolution of Parliamentary Privileges in India till 1947.*[2] It sought to penalize the offer to and receipt or demand of a bribe by a legislator in connection with his functions as such. Introduced in the central legislative assembly on 25 August 1925, it was referred to a select committee. The opinion of 'local' (provincial) governments was sought. Predictably, opinion was divided. Pandit Motilal Nehru endorsed the principle but had reservations on the provisions of the Bill.

The Report of the Reforms Enquiry Committee (1924), popularly known as the Muddiman committee, recommended such legislation:

We are given to understand that there are at present no means of dealing with the corrupt influencing of votes within in the legislature. We are unanimously of opinion that the influencing of the votes of members by bribery, intimidation and the like should be legislated against. Here, again, we do not recommend that the matter should be dealt with as a breach of

---

[2]Salil Kumar Nagi, *Evolution of Parliamentary Privileges in India till 1947,* (Delhi: Sterling Publishers, 1978), a work of good archival research.

privilege. We advocate that these offences should be made penal under the ordinary law.'[3]

Among the members of the committee who joined in the unanimity were Tej Bahadur Sapru, P.S. Sivaswamy Aiyer, M.A. Jinnah, and R.P. Paranjpye.

The Royal Commission on Standards of Conduct in Public Life (1974–6), headed by a distinguished jurist, Lord Salmon, summed up the law in Britain: 'Neither the statutory nor the common law applies to the bribery or attempted bribery of a member of parliament in respect of his parliamentary activities.' It is regarded as no more than a breach of privilege.[4]

In 1984 a Constitution bench of five judges to the Supreme Court ruled in the Antulay case that an MLA is not a 'public servant' as defined in Section 21 of the Indian Penal Code.[5] The Court had ruled to the same effect in 1979 in the Karunanidhi case.[6] Section 2 of the Prevention of Corruption Act, 1947 said that for the purposes of that Act, the meaning of 'public servant' was as defined in Section 21 of the IPC. Section 2 (c) of the Prevention of Corruption Act, 1988 itself defines 'public servant' elaborately, consciously departing from the definition in Section 21 of the IPC. Thus Clause (viii) of Section 2 includes in the definition 'any person who holds any office by virtue of which he is authorized or required to perform any public duty'.

A legislator does perform a public duty, but does he hold an 'office'? The Salmon Commission was of the view that he does not. 'Nor does membership of parliament, as such, constitute public office for the purposes of the common law'. If the definition in Section 2 of the Act of 1988 does not apply, neither does Section 13 of that Act dealing with 'criminal misconduct by a public servant'.

---

[3]Report of the Reforms Enquiry Committee, 1924, GOI, Central Publications Branch, Calcutta, 1925, p. 75. para 91.

[4]Royal Commission on Standards of Conduct in Public Life (1974–6), Report, July 1976, HMSO, London, Cmnd 6524, p. 98: para 307.

[5]*R.S. Nayak v A.R. Antulay* (1984) 2 SCC 183.

[6]*M. Karunanidhi v Union of India* (1979) 3 SCC 431.

35
Bribery and MPs[1]

This is a charter for freedom of speech in the house. It is not
a charter for corruption', Lord Salmon, remarked during
the debate in the House of Lords on the presentation of the
Report of the Royal Commission on Standards in Public Life (1976),
over which he had presided. He was referring to Article 9 of the
Bill of Rights (1688): 'That the freedom of speech and debates or
proceedings in parliament ought not to be impeached or *questioned*
in any court or place out of parliament.' Article 105(2) of the Indian
Constitution is based on that rule which has been handed down
the centuries but with a significant modification. No MP shall be
liable to legal proceedings 'in respect of anything said or any vote
given by him in parliament'. It is more narrowly worded than Article
9; there is no stipulation that speeches shall not be 'questioned'.

The Salmon report was of the view that, without any detailed
discussion, neither the common law nor the Prevention of
Corruption Act, 1906, as it stood, 'applies to the bribery or attempted
briber' of an MP 'in respect of his parliamentary activities'. These
offences formed part of the law of parliamentary privilege. It said
in the good British manner, now slowly going out of vogue: 'With
the most genuine respect to the committee of privileges and the
select committee on members' interests, we do not consider that
they provide an investigative machinery comparable to that of a
police investigation. We have had frequent occasion to comment
on the complexity of most investigations into serious corruption,
and the special expertise that is necessary for this type of inquiry'.

Experience of two decades in Britain and of recent months in

[1] *The Statesman*, 25 and 26 December 1996.

India have proved the truth of these remarks. Parliamentary committees are notoriously partisan, especially when the stakes are high. Parliament did nothing after the disclosures of the Jain diaries in 1991. As police investigations gathered speed, however, thanks to whiplashes regularly administered by the Supreme Court, moves began to secure amendment of the law in a direction opposite to that recommended by the Salmon report and a high-powered Indian committee, namely, the Reforms Enquiry Committee headed by Sir Alexander Muddiman.

In 1988 parliament enacted the Prevention of Corruption Act to replace the Act of 1947. It departed *consciously* from the definition of 'public servant' in the old Act and in Section 21 of the Penal Code. It inserted an altogether new category in Section 2(c)(viii): 'any person who holds an office by virtue of which he is authorized or required to perform any public duty'. Legislators do perform public duties, in law at least. Two views are possible on whether they hold an office. On 5 May 1993 a division bench of Orissa high court held in Habibullah Khan's case that an MLA is a 'public servant' within the meaning of this clause. On 2 February 1995, the Supreme Court dismissed his appeal on another ground while 'assuming ... that the MLA is a public servant within the meaning of Section 2(c)(viii) of the Act'. An assumption, not a ruling, but the court would not have made any such assumption had it appeared to be altogether wrong.[2]

The recent moves are designed to set all this at naught and bring the existing cases against politicians to a grinding halt, for explicit exclusion of MPs and MLAs from cases that would arise in the future, besides being unconstitutional, will only build up pressure for its extension to pending cases as well. At a time when corruption laws are being tightened all over the world, India will provide a unique illustration of their dilution. It will be a step in the teeth of reports by eminent jurists and for the protection of politicians as the dragnet is beginning to close on them. Marx would not have approved of such 'class consciousness'.

Bribery was rare in the British parliament. Recent disclosures suggest that it is not quite as rare any longer. On 10 July 1994, *The Sunday Times* hit the news stands with a story headlined: 'Revealed: MPs who accepted £1,000 to ask a parliamentary question.' On 20

---

[2]*Habibullah Khan v State of Orissa*, (1993) G. LJ 3604 and (1995) 2 SCC 437.

October *The Guardian* came out with similar disclosures. The rate fittingly was double because the MPs had been allegedly paid by the owner of Harrods, Mohammed Al-Fayed.

During the debate in the House of Commons on 25 October 1994, the prime minister, John Major, announced the appointment of a committee as a standing body with these terms of reference: 'To examine current concerns about standards of conduct of all holders of public office, including arrangements relating to financial and commercial activities, and make recommendations as to any changes in present arrangements which might be required to ensure the highest standards of propriety in public life. For these purposes, public life should include MPs.' It was headed by Lord Nolan, a Law Lord.

The first Nolan report, entitled *Standards in Public Life* was published in May 1995. It noted that the Commons' procedures for self-policing had 'over recent years ... appeared to be less than satisfactory. It noted 'the inevitable tendency for party politics to influence decisions on matters of conduct.'[3]

Sir William Wade, 'the leading constitutional lawyer', wrote to the committee pointing out that till the Parliamentary Elections Act, 1868, election petitions were tried by the house itself. Later, they were 'transferred to election courts manned by high court judges, much to the benefit of justice'. Privileges were surrendered to the law. The committee noted the inaction on the Salmon report and considered that 'it would be unsatisfactory to leave this issue outstanding when other aspects of the law of parliament are being clarified. We recommend that the government should now take steps to clarify the law relating to the bribery of or the receipt of a bribe by' an MP. In the context of its remarks, and of the recent disclosures, the report clearly suggested clarification to include MPs within the sway of criminal law, not exclude them.

The Nolan report recommended this despite another recommendation for injecting an independent element *within* parliament: the parliamentary commissioner for standards. The office is held by Sir Gordon Downey.

The select committee on standards in public life was set up by the House of Commons to consider the first Nolan report. On 6

[3]Standards in Public Life: First Report of the Committee on Standards in Public Life, May 1995, HMSO, London, Cmnd 2850–51.

July 1995, this committee said, in its first report: 'In the interests of members, as well as in the wider public interest, it is important that the extent to which the actions of members are subject to the law of bribery should be clarified as soon as possible.'

That very month, July 1995, besides the select committee, the government also gave its response to the first report of the Nolan committee. 'The government reaffirms its commitment to consolidate the laws on corruption and welcomes the opportunity to clarify the law relating to the bribery of or receipt of a bribe by a member of parliament alongside that consolidation.'

Meanwhile, the committee of privileges had reported, on 3 April 1995, on a complaint concerning *The Sunday Times* report of 10 July 1994: 'We doubt whether it is possible to say that the offering or making of a payment in exchange for the tabling of a parliamentary question could never constitute the offence of bribery at common law, or fall within the definition of bribery in parliamentary law.' It did not consider the legal issue to be relevant to the matter it was considering.

Appended to this report were two cameos: erudite memoranda by the then clerk of the house, Clifford Boulton, in August 1994 and by the Attorney-General in September 1994. Both referred to a case, decided in 1992, in which charges were brought against an MP and others for receipt of benefits as an inducement to show favours as an MP. There was no reference to proceedings in parliament. Deficiencies in the prosecution evidence led eventually to the charges being dropped. Before this however legal argument was heard on whether an MP was subject to such charges in common law. Justice Buckley ruled that he was. That an MP 'against who there is a prima facie case of corruption should be immune from prosecution in the courts of law is to my mind an unacceptable proposition at the present time. I do not believe it to be the law. The committee of privileges is not well equipped to conduct an enquiry into such a case nor is it an appropriate or experienced body to pass sentence.'

The attorney-general was of the opinion that there was 'support for the view of Buckley J. in authorities in three Commonwealth jurisdictions'. He cited three rulings in Australia and Canada and considered the effect of Article 9 of the Bill of Rights on the production of evidence as to what happened in the house. Article 105 of our Constitution poses no problem on this score. It differs from Article 9, as we have noted, Lord Salman had no difficulty on this point: 'To my mind, the Bill of Rights ... has no more to do with the topic which we are discussing than the Merchandise Marks Act. The crime or corruption is complete when the bribe is offered or given or solicited and taken.' The attorney-general, however, concluded that 'the position at common law is not settled'.

The law in the USA was laid down by the Supreme Court in 1972 in a case concerning a former Senator, Daniel Brewster, who had been charged with accepting bribes for favours as a member of the Senate. He challenged it on the ground that it violated Article 1, Section 6 of the Constitution protecting members of Congress in respect of votes or speeches in Congress. The court ruled (6–3) that the provision did not prevent indictment and prosecution for taking bribes, and that such conduct is not part of any legislative process or function.

Chief Justice Warren Burger pointed out that the clause was not for the personal benefit of a member 'but to protect the integrity of the legislative process'. Bribery destroys the integrity. The clause comes in if evidence of the vote is essential to the prosecution case, but 'there is no need for the government to show that appellee [the Senator] fulfilled the alleged bargain. Acceptance of the bribe is the violation of the statute, not performance of the illegal promise. Taking bribe is, obviously, no part of the legislative process or function; it is not a legislative act.'[4]

It is not an act in the course of a legislator's duty. Here again Article 1, Section 6 says that speech should not be 'questioned'. Article 105 says no such thing.

In Australia, Section 73A of the Crimes Act makes an MP who asks for or receives or offers or agrees to ask for a benefit, in return for the exercise of his duties as MP, liable to a sentence of two years' imprisonment. Article 119 of Canada's criminal code provides a maximum of 14 years in jail for that offence.

The British parliament is itself 'The high court of parliament'. Not so the Indian Parliament, as the Supreme Court ruled in the UP high court judge's case in 1965.

It offends the guarantee of equality (Article 14) in the Constitution that, while bribing a voter, civil servant, judge, and minister is

[4] *United States v Brewster* 33 L. 2nd ed., 507.

an offence in law, bribing a legislator is not. Such a law would be patently unconstitutional. Three great democracies have laws treating bribery of legislators as criminal offences as well as breaches of privilege. Only the UK does not, for entirely historical reasons which do not apply to India. What is so unique about the Indian MP to afford him such protection?

36
Bribes in Parliament: A Shocking Ruling by the Supreme Court[1]

In the nearly half a century of its existence, few rulings of the Supreme Court incurred such odium, and so deservedly, than that so merrily handed down on 17 April 1998 in the Jharkand Mukti Morcha case. *P.V. Narasimha Rao v State* (CBI/ SPE) (1998) 4 SCC 626. It holds that legislators, MPs or MLAs, who take bribes enjoy constitutional protection from prosecution for their crimes. Lesser mortals however who offer the bribes do not, and this in the name of free speech and free vote in the house.

Nothing short of an inescapable juristic compulsion, such as fidelity to a text that permits no other interpretation but this one, which is as preposterous as it is subversive of public probity, should constrain any judge to pronounce such a ruling. In a judgment of compelling logic and incisive analysis, Justice S.C. Agrawal, with whom Justice A.S. Anand concurred, had not the slightest hesitation in spurning such a conclusion. It was adopted ardently by Justice S.P. Bharucha in a judgement with which Justice S. Rajendra Babu concurred.

Justice G.N. Ray tipped the precarious balance by agreeing with the latter justices. It is a ruling that cries for reversal by a larger bench, for it comes at a time when, as Indira Gandhi once said of corruption, legislators' venality is a global phenomenon. Witness recent events in the US and UK. Not even the most olympian detachment of judges can justify indifference to the stark realities of life.

[1] *The Statesman*, 31 May 1998.

There was unanimity on one question alone: namely that an MP is a 'public servant' as defined by Section 2(c) of the Prevention of Corruption Act, 1988. On the follow up however the Bench split once again. Is a sanction required for the prosecution of this exotic tribe of 'public servant'? If so, by whom? for, unlike the civil servant, the legislator is not removable by any single, superior appointing authority.

Justices Agrawal and Anand held that the omission of an explicit sanction provision for MPs did not exclude them from the Act; rather, the omission means that 'there is no limitation on the power of the court to take cognizance' of the offence. The sanction provisions in Section 19 of the Act do not apply to a legislator. Only the permission of the presiding officer of the house to which he belongs is necessary. Justice G.N. Ray agreed with these judges on this point, yielding a majority of 3–2.

The minority view expressed by Bharucha J. is that MPs and MLAs, though public servants, cannot be prosecuted for the grave offences under the Act 'because of want of an authority competent to grant sanction thereto'. Such a narrow, hyper-technical approach is wholly innapproapriate in a court charged with the task of finally interpreting the law of the land. As a judge of the US Supreme Court once remarked, 'It is a *Constitution* that we are expounding'. It is, however, precisely this narrow approach, redolent of the privy council of old, that led Barucha J. to confer the mantle of immunity on the corrupt MP.

Article 105(2) of the Constitution declares: 'No member of parliament shall be liable to any proceeding in any court in respect of anything said or any vote given by him in parliament or any committee thereof and no person shall be so liable in respect of the publication by or under the authority of either house of parliament of any report paper, votes or proceedings.' Can an MP be prosecuted for accepting a bribe to speak or vote in a particular way? Likewise, to refrain from speaking or voting? Article 105(2) clearly does not apply to silence bought through corrupt means.

The provision has a long history behind it. Justice Agrawal's survey brought out only too clearly that the modern trend is to confine the traditional immunity so as not to allow it to be abused as immunity for bribery. Twenty years ago, in July 1976, a Royal commission on Standards of Conduct on Public Life, chaired by Lord Salmon, submitted its report. During the course of the debate in the house of lords, Lord Salmon said: 'To my mind equality before the law is one of the pillars of freedom. To say that immunity from criminal proceedings against anyone who tries to bribe a member of parliament and any member of parliament who accepts the bribe, stems from the Bill of Rights is possibly a serious mistake.' After quoting the Bill of Rights, Lord Salmon continued: 'Now this is a charter for freedom of speech in the house. It is not a charter for corruption. To my mind, the Bill of Rights, for which no one has more respect than I have, has no more to do with the topic which we are discussing than the Merchandise Marks Act. The Crime of corruption is complete when the bribe is offered or given or solicited or taken.' Article 105(2) is based on the British Bill of Rights.

In 1992 Justice Buckley held 'That a member of parliament against whom there is a prima facie case of corruption should be immune from prosecution in the courts of law is to my mind an unacceptable proposition at the present time, I do not believe it to be the law'. In Australia, Canada, and the US the trends have been unmistakably in this very direction 'Most countries treat corruption and bribery by members of parliament as a criminal offence rather than as breach of privilege', Gerrard Carney concluded in his survey of Commonwealth MPs.

That is precisely what we are talking about. Chief Justice Warren Burger of the US Supreme Court said, 'taking a bribe is obviously no part of the legislative process or function; it is not a legislative act. It is not, by any conceivable interpretation, an act performed as a part of or even incidental to the role of a legislator.' Mark the emphasis: 'by any conceivable interpretation'.

Justice Bharucha's survey covers the same ground as Justice Agrawal reproducing ritualistically dicta by Salmon and Burger without the least influence on his stance. Our judges must surely be alive to the nature of proceedings for breach of parliamentary privilege. In India even the process of impeachment of a Supreme Court judge was subverted in parliament by an unofficial whip. The shield against prosecution is intended to preserve the integrity of the legislative process; not to enable its subversion.

Consider this test propounded by Justice Agrawal:

There may be an agreement whereunder a member accepts illegal gratification and agrees not to speak in parliament or not to give his vote in parliament. The immunity granted under Article 105(2) would not be available to such a member and he would be liable to be prosecuted on the charge of bribery in a criminal court. What would be the position if the agreement is that, in lieu of the illegal gratification paid or promised, the member would speak or give his vote in parliament in a particular manner and he speaks and gives his vote in that manner? It is difficult to conceive that the framers of the Constitution intended to make such a distinction in the matter coming up before the house.'

To Justice Bharucha: 'The important public interest protected by such privilege is to ensure that the member or witness at the time he speaks is not inhibited from stating fully and freely what he has to say. If there were any exceptions which permitted his statements to be questioned subsequently, at the time when he speaks in parliament he would not know whether or not there would subsequently be a challenge to what he is saying.' Surely only a guilty conscience would feel so inhibited while speaking? His answer to that is one that can be given in and of any situation and is no guide to construction—what of trumped up charges of bribery. A judge clearly fails to perform the judicial function of balancing competing values when he rejects one totally and, that too, grave public harm.

In his view, the words 'in respect of' in Article 105(2) 'must receive a broad meaning. The alleged conspiracy and agreement had a nexus to and were in respect of those votes and that the proposed inquiry in the criminal proceedings is in regard to the motivation thereof.' Inappropriate even in statutory interpretation, this is grotesque in constitutional construction.

It is Justice Bharucha approach to precedents that causes disquiet. He prefers a dissent in the US Supreme Court to the majority ruling that negates his view. The 1992 English case is brushed aside 'For the first time in England, Justice Buckley ruled in *R. V. Currie* that a member of parliament who accepts a bribe to abuse his trust is guilty of the common law offence of bribery. The innovation in English law needs to be tested in appeal.' Would his lordship have followed the appeal court's ruling if it went against his view? This is sheer subjectivity in excelsis.

One aspect of Justice Bharucha's Judgment has escaped notice. He has gratuitously ventured into a highly complex and controversial field of parliamentary privilege of direct bearing on press freedom. His excursion is as uninformed and wrong as it is unnecessary.

III

THE STATES

37
The Governor[1]

I t would be a thousand pities if the wide acclaim that greeted
the appointment of the Sarkaria commission on centre–state
relations were to be dissipated by a narrow approach on its terms
of reference or its composition. Consultation with the chief
ministers, particularly of the non-Congress (I) state governments,
will be in keeping with the appropriately non-partisan character of
the entire exercise whose magnitude brooks no underestimation. It
will, in effect, be the first authoritative review of the working of
the constitution in the last three decades and it cannot evade the
gross abuse of the one institution on whose impartiality the
autonomy of the states and the soundness of centre–state relations
depend: the governors.

The reports of the Administrative Reforms Commission (ARC)
(1969) as well as the Centre-State Relations Inquiry Committee
(1971), set up by the Tamil Nadu government and headed by Dr P.V.
Rajamannar, discussed the governors' pivotal role in considerable
detail. Over a decade has elapsed since, and that too a decade that
witnessed the intensification of party warfare to an unprecendented
degree, and with it a distortion of centre–state relations in which
abuse of the institution of governor as a non-partisan instrument of
the ruling party at the centre played a crucial role.

The union home minister, Mr P. C. Sethi, recalled in the Lok
Sabha on 12 April 1983, that the ARC had come to the conclusion
that no constitutional amendment was necessary for ensuring
harmonious relations between the centre and the states. True enough,
but with two important qualifications. First, the ARC's chairman,

[1] *The Indian Express*, 25 April 1983.

Mr K. Hanumanthaiya, pointedly remarked in his letter to the Prime Minister, Mrs Indira Gandhi, forwarding the report in June 1969: 'It is not in the amendment of the constitution that the solution of the problems of the centre–state relationship is to be sought, but in the working of the provisions of the constitution by all concerned in the balanced spirit in which the founding fathers, intended them to be worked.'[2]

Within weeks, after this, the spirit was under attack by the genie let loose by the split in the Congress party. Where is the spirit today? In 1967 Mrs Gandhi warmly spoke of a 'more vigorous practising federalism with multiple parties and coalitions in power'. Five years later, on 3 February 1972, she insisted that it was necessary that the State government should be 'in tune' with the government at the Centre, accept its policies, and be willing to implement its programme.

The ARC's reaction to such a claim, had it been made before it, can easily be imagined. Even without it, the ARC had no hesitation in recommending that 'guidelines on the manner in which discretionary powers should be exercised by the governors should be formulated by the Inter-State Council and, on acceptance by the union, issued in the name of the president. They should be placed before both houses of parliament.[3] This is the second qualification with which the ARC's rejection of constitutional amendment must be read.

Yet, when a plea for such guidelines was made at the recent governors' conference, the government quietly abandoned the ARC and relied, instead, on the report of the governors' committee. In his address to the governors on 9 April 1983, President Zail Singh referred to that report and said, 'In our constitution, there is no power vested in any authority to issue any directions to the governor or lay down any code or rules for this guidance.'

The ARC had squarely met such a legalistic objection and answered it. 'Though the constitution does not provide for the issue of any instrument of instructions, there seems to be no bar to agreed guidelines being issued. The guidelines must command general acceptance.'[4] That is the essence of the matter; namely, the expression

[2]Administrative Reforms Commission (ARC), *Report on Centre–State Relationships*, (Delhi: GOI, Manager of Publications, Delhi, June 1969), p. ii para 2.

[3]Ibid, Recommendation 9, p. 25.

[4]Ibid, p. 25.

of a national consensus. The procedure for recording it is of secondary importance, whether by a decision of the inter-state council or of parliament. In Canada's history 'conventional understandings' are fairly common.

The report of the Committee of Governors (1971) itself came fairly close to suggesting a procedure for evolving a body of precedents. 'A special wing may be set up in the president's secretariat which would ascertain all the facts and circumstances relating to each situation which may arise from time to time requiring action by a governor in the exercise of his powers and the reasons for the action taken by him in a particular situation.'[5] These would then be 'confidentially' communicated to the governors. The objects were 'to help establish a degree of uniformity' in the treatment of similar situations and 'perhaps even, in some cases, certain norms of action based on accepted canons of interpretation of the constitution'.

Canons of parliamentary government are not much in doubt. The draft constitution contained some of them in an Instrument of Instructions for governors. The Instrument was not eventually adopted but not for the reasons President Zail Singh mentioned, namely, because as head of State, the governor 'would have to act according to the provisions of the constitution and his oath of office in the light of the circumstances obtaining at the time when a question came up for decision'. Neither the constitution nor the oath imply that a governor can ignore the conventions of parliamentary government or militate against the codification of the guidelines. The governors' committee itself was set up 'to study and formulate norms and conventions governing the role of governors under the constitution.'

There were two reasons why the draft instrument of instructions was abandoned, as mentioned by Dr B.R. Ambedkar in the constituent assembly on 11 October 1949. 'There is no discretion in the governor and there is no functionary under the constitution who can enforce this.'[6] Time has proved the view to be wrong. Evidently, the doctor was overstating the position, for earlier on 30 December 1948, he had told the assembly that 'under a parliamentary system of government, there are only two prerogatives which the

[5]Report of the Committee of Governors, p. 11.
[6]CAD, vol. x, p. 115.

king or head of the state may exercise. One is the appointment of the prime minister and the other is the dissolution of parliament ... the position of the governor is exactly the same as the position of the president.'

It is precisely in regard to these two matters, concerning the reins of power, that criticism of the governors' conduct in the course of all these years has been strongest and most justified. Governor Tapase's legerdemain last year, when he asked Mr Devi Lal to present his supporters before him on 24 May 1982, and proceeded to swear in his rival, Mr Bhajan Lal, the day before, is only the worst in a sordid series. It is unlikely that Mr Tapase or his predecessors in impropriety would have acted the way they did except at the Centre's behest.

This is the nub of the matter. A state's autonomy comes to naught if its people's mandate can be defied or ignored by a central appointee. The very possibility of the ruling party at the centre being able to manipulate the selection of the chief minister or the dissolution of the state legislature, not to forget the imposition of central rule, has an unhealthy impact on state politics and engenders alienation from New Delhi.

The correct position was excellently summed up by Mr G.S. Pathak, a distinguished constitutional lawyer, in a speech at New Delhi on 3 April 1970, as vice-president:

In the sphere in which he (the governor) is bound by the advice of the council of ministers, for obvious reasons, he must be independent of the centre. There may be cases where the advice of the Centre may clash with the advice of the State council of ministers. In the sphere in which he is required by the Constitution to exercise his discretion, it is obvious again, that it is his discretion and not that of any other authority and, therefore his discretion cannot be controlled or interfered with by the centre.'[7]

This is why the governor's independence is indispensable to a state's autonomy.

On 4 May 1979 the Supreme Court ruled in Dr Raghukul Tilak's case:

it is not material that the governor holds office during the pleasure of the president. It is a constitutional provision for determination of the term of

---

[7]White Paper on the office of the Governor: Constitutional Position and Political Perversion, Government of Karnataka, Sept. 1983, p. 21.

office of the governor and it does not make the government of India an employer of the governor ... this office is not subordinate or subservient to the government of India. He is not amenable to the direction of the government of India nor is he accountable to them for the manner in which he carries out his functions and duties. He is an independent constitutional office which is not subject to the control of the government of India. He is constitutionally the head of the State ...'[8]

Experience has however amply demonstrated that the governors cannot fulfil this role so long as they hold office, as they do now, entirely 'during the pleasure of the president'. Some safeguards are necessary to ensure their independence, whether by constitutional amendment or otherwise. The ARC recomended that 'a person should not be appointed as governor for more than one term. Such a restriction is necessary in order to safeguard his independence and impartiality against being jeopardized by expectations of patronage.'

The ARC's study team, headed by Mr M.C. Setalvad, had gone a step further. 'No person who is appointed governor should take part in politics after his appointment as such', not even after retirement.[9] To these may be added Mr K. Subba Rao, a former chief justice of India's suggestion that a governor should be ineligible for any other office under government after retirement and should be irremovable from office on any ground other than proven misbehaviour or incapacity after inquiry by the Supreme Court.

[8]*Hargovind Pant* vs *Dr Raghukul Tilak*, AIR 1979 SC 709.
[9]ARC, Report of the Study Team, Centre–State Relationships, 1967, vol. i, p. 287

38

Dismissing Governors[1]

When on 5 August 1983 Ramakrishna Hegde, as Chief Minister of Karnataka, lamented at a seminar on centre–state relations in Bangalore that 'even the governor has become a glorified servant of the Union', there was quite a stir. The Karnataka government backed up the charge with a 'White Paper on the Office of the Governor'.

The resignation of Surjit Singh Barnala as Governor of Tamil Nadu on 13 February 1991, in protest against his transfer to Bihar, and the dismissal the same day of the Bihar Governor, Mohammad Yunus Saleem, for reading to the state assembly an address containing criticism of the imposition of president's rule in Tamil Nadu, reveal the steep decline in norms.

The facts of the two cases are shocking. Viewed against the background of the debasement of the office as established by the constitution, they suggest that we are not very far from the collapse of the system. In the case of Barnala, he refused to send the kind of report on the state of law and order in Tamil Nadu which the centre would have liked. President's rule was imposed by the Centre on the strength of its own assessment without the backing of the governor's report as is usually the case.

Barnala deserves credit for his independence. Sadly, he tripped at this point. He ought to have resigned instantly when the centre took over the state's administration. Instead, he not only continued in office but declared himself comfortable in the chair he occupied. The centre was not however to be diverted from its course. Barnala discovered the bitter truth many before him had learnt to their

[1] *Frontline*, 2–15 March 1991.

cost: confronted with a grave moral wrong, one must not compromise.

Barnala's replacement is Bhishma Narain Singh, a senior Congress(I) leader. Such an appointment on the eve of the elections to the state assembly cannot but cause disquiet.

Yunus Saleem's case is gross. His remarks in a press interview reveal the pattern of conduct followed by the government of India. 'I had refused to succumb to the pressures of Prime Minister Chandra Shekhar and other union ministers from Bihar to give a report against the Laloo Prasad Yadav government. How could I say that the law and order situation in Bihar was deteriorating?'

His charges are very specific and uncontroverted: 'The prime minister had earlier asked me not to summon the House when the chief minister was seeking a vote of confidence.' No prime minister has a right to direct a governor as to how he should exercise his discretion as head of a State, least of all in a matter in which the governor is bound by the advice of the chief minister.

Impropriety was matched by indignity. The union home secretary had the gall to ring up the governor at around midnight and ask him to resign. He called again the following morning and seven more times later. What business does a secretary to the government have to ask a governor to resign? The only person entitled to do that is the president and no one else. The governor's address contained these words: 'This government [of Tamil Nadu] had a full majority in the assembly and the governor had also not indicated any possibility of any constitutional crisis. This action hits at the democratic principles and also attacks the constitutional autonomy of the states. Therefore, our government expresses annoyance over this action.'[2]

The constitutional position in regard to these two cases is not in doubt. There is a specific provision in the Constitution (Article 222) for the transfer of a judge from one high court to another Significantly, there is no provision at all for the transfer of a governor from one state to another. There is provision only for a person to serve as governor 'of two or more States' (Article 158–3A). The president is empowered by Article 160 to 'make such provision as he thinks fit for the discharge of the functions of the governor of a state in any contingency not provided for in this chapter' (on

[2]See interview, *Frontline*, 2 March 1991, pp. 36–7.

governors). Transfers cannot fall within this provision because they are not executed to meet any unforeseen 'contingency'. In any event, the power to transfer must itself be conferred on the president in the first instance. In the absence of such power, a transfer is in effect demission of one office and acceptance of another. For both, the consent of the governor is indispensable. An enforced resignation in such circumstances is nothing other than recourse to extra-constitutional pressure, a virtual dismissal.

This brings us to the issue of the power of dismissal. The governor holds office 'during the pleasure' of the president, but so do the prime minister and other members of the union council of ministers (Article 75–2), as also every member of the armed forces and of the civil service (Article 310). The expression 'pleasure of the president' does not confer a carte blanche or serve as a sanction for arbitrary behaviour. One governor, a jurist, who was faced with the prospect of dismissal let it be known that he would go to court. He was left alone. In the light of a series of rulings by the Supreme Court a governor can challenge his dismissal on the ground that it was arbitrary, without due cause or that the principles of natural justice were not complied with.

No less clear is the constitutional position in regard to the address to the house. Sir Ivor Jennings's authoritative opinion in his classic *Cabinet Government* is: 'As to the queen's speech, it has been universally accepted since 1841 as the statement of ministerial policy, for which the sovereign accepts no personal responsibility.'[3] The governor cannot criticize an action of the president taken in his individual discretion, such as appointing the prime minister. He has every right to criticize an action of the union government taken, as all such action is under the constitution, in the name of the president, provided, in turn, that the governor himself speaks officially on behalf of the state government and not for himself personally as, say, in a public speech. To deny this right is, in effect, to deny the states the right to censure the union in a major policy statement to the state legislature.

Dharam Vira's refusal, as Governor of West Bengal, to read certain portions of the address prepared by the Ajoy Mukherjee ministry is no precedent. It was not because the address criticized the Centre but because it condemned *him*. His memoirs, *Reminiscences*, are quite

---

[3]Jennings, *Cabinet Government*, p. 402.

clear: 'My own attitude was simple and clear. Parliamentary government, with all its practices and conventions, had been in existence for centuries. But never in its history has any head of the government been faced with the problem of having to read self-condemnatory material.'[4] The Union only came in incidentally. Moreover, legal proceedings concerning the earlier dismissal of the United Front government, which he was asked to criticize, were pending in the Supreme Court.

In January 1968, Kerala Governor V.Viswanathan was alleged to have altered the address that the cabinet had approved. He omitted the word 'ideological' from a sentence which spoke of harmony in the council of ministers despite 'ideological differences' among its members. He was also alleged to have dropped criticism of the Centre's action in raising the price of rice allotted to Kerala.

However, a year later in January 1969,Viswanathan did criticize the Centre 'for neglecting the State in matters of location of central sector projects and allocation of financial resources'. Professor W.H. Morris-Jones, commented on the episodes in India in these faultless terms: 'It is, therefore, beyond doubt that the governor cannot alter the speech prepared for him by the cabinet, if the cabinet is not willing to incorporate the changes suggested by the governor.'

In the brief three months of its existence, the Chandra Shekhar government's treatment of governors and states ruled by Opposition parties has been grossly improper. The Janata Dal government headed by V.P. Singh treated Congress(I) state governments properly but blotted its copybook by using Governor Bhanu Pratap Singh to impose president's rule in Karnataka for partisan ends.

It was perfectly justified in sacking the likes of Kumudben Joshi, governor of Andhra Pradesh, whose conduct was notoriously partisan. But the *en masse* change of governors was totally unjustified. Mufti Mohammed Sayeed, as Home Minister, brought no credit to the government when he went so far as to say on 17 January 1990 that 'governors are after all the representatives of the centre'. It is this pernicious doctrine which governed the policies of Indira Gandhi and Rajiv Gandhi towards the states and governs those of Chandra Shekhar too. That the Mufti said it so brazenly shows that the Janata Dal was not free from blemish either, despite its otherwise creditable record in this sphere.

[4]Dharma Vira, *Reminiscences*, (Delhi:Vikas, 1990), p. 116.

The committee of governors appointed by the president considered the subject in its report entitled 'The Role of Governors', submitted in 1971. It said the governor's functions as head of a state were laid down in the Constitution itself and he 'is in no sense an agent of the president'[5] His oath of office requires him to 'preserve, protect and defend the Constitution and the law'. It added that 'there is no power vested in any authority to issue any directions to the governor or lay down any code or rules for his guidance.'

The framers of the Constitution were quite clear as to the status of the governor. Addressing the constituent assembly on 31 May 1949, T.T. Krishnamachari, member of the drafting committee, said, 'I would at once disclaim all ideals, at any rate so far as I am concerned, that we in this house want the future governor who is to be nominated by the president to be in any sense an agent of the central government. I would like that point to be made very clear, because such an idea finds no place in the scheme of government we envisage for the future.'[6]

Indira Gandhi dismissed Tamil Nadu Governor Prabhudas Patwari on 26 October 1980 without showing any cause. As H.M. Seervai wrote in his work, *Constitutional Law of India:*

'a responsible union ministry would not advise, and would not be justified in advising, the removal of a governor because in the honest discharge of his duty, the governor takes action which does not fall in line with the policy of the union ministry. To hold otherwise would mean that the union executive would effectively control the State executive which is opposed to the basic scheme of our federal constitution.'[7]

Governors like Jagmohan in Kashmir in July 1984 and Ram Lal in Andhra Pradesh in August 1984 willingly carried out the centre's wishes in unconstitutionally sacking a ministry without allowing it to test its strength in the assembly.

There is another aspect, no less grave. The power of dissolution in the head of state is to be exercised on the advice of the head of government, though on the basis of settled norms. It is a potent and necessary weapon for use by the head of government against topplers. A study entitled *Politics of President's Rule in India* by Dr J. R. Siwach of Kurukshetra University said that advice for

[5]Report of the Committee of Governors, pp. 8–9.
[6]CAD, vol. vii. pp. 459–60.
[7]Seervai, 3rd edn, 1984, p. 1725.

dissolution by a non-Congress chief minister 'was rejected in all the cases where the Congress party was keen on forming the government'.

Unless the Constitution is amended to ensure better appointments and greater independence, the office of the governor will be damaged beyond repair. One reform is to make it obligatory for the president to appoint as governor one from a panel of names recommended by a committee consisting of the prime minister, the vice-president, and the chief minister. Another is to give the governor security of tenure and make him irremovable except by impeachment.

The Sarkaria commission's two recommendations are neither bold nor adequate. One is to prescribe a procedure for consultation with the chief minister before appointing the governor. On dismissal, the 'governor should be informally apprised of the grounds of the proposed action and afforded a reasonable opportunity of showing cause against it.'[8] However, a governor, like any other functionary, has a right to go to court against arbitrary dismissal, but this has not proved a strong check. The report suggests that the governor's reply should be examined by an advisory group consisting of the vice-president and the speaker of the Lok Sabha or a retired chief justice of India. 'After receiving the recommendation of this group, the president may pass such orders in the case as he may deem fit'. It does not require submission of the recommendation to parliament or that it should be binding on the government. This recommendation is of little help. The only remedy is to make the governor irremovable, save, by impeachment.

[8] Report of the Commission on Centre–State Relations, p. 127, para 4.8.08.

39

Appointment of a Chief Minister[1]

Nearly four decades after the establishment of our republic, it is incredible that people should be so woefully ignorant of established norms and well-known precedents of parliamentary practice. When MGR died on 24 December 1987, Governor S.L. Khurana faced a situation no different from that faced by other heads of state in the country when the head of government died in office.

He did what they had done: swear in the seniormost cabinet member as acting head of government and wait for the election of the leader of the ruling party. It so happened that in this case the party split exactly a week after MGR's death. Few were surprised, though the governor had then to decide prima facie which was the larger group in the ruling party. He had little choice. Janaki Ramachandran was backed by 97 identified MLAs in a legislature party of 131. He rightly asked her to step into MGR's shoes.

However, while doing so Khurana made one cardinal error. He gave her three long weeks in which to satisfy the final test, that she enjoyed the confidence of the majority in the assembly of 234 members in which 12 seats are vacant. She obviously needs the support of 15 more. Where she obtains this from remains to be seen. The Congress(I) has 64 members, the DMK has 12, CPI(M) 4, CPI 2, Janata 3, Forward Bloc 2, the Republican Party 1, Muslim League 2, Independent 1, and there is Speaker Paul Hector Pandian.

However, when a respected journal argues that 'there was no

[1] *The Week*, 24 January 1988.

basic explanation [by the governor] of the way and means through which a strength of 112 would be produced', one wonders what yardsticks people use since the rival faction has only 30-odd members. It is absurd to say that 'the governor entertained the notion of a de facto split in the AIADMK'. A latent reality, the split became public when, on 31 December, the rival factions convened separate meetings through different party functionaries.

The precedents are clear. When B.C. Roy, chief minister of West Bengal, died on 1 July 1962, Governor Padmaja Naidu sought the advice of President Radhakrishnan who happened to be in Calcutta. His advice was sound. 'Just swear in the seniormost member of the cabinet and ask the Congress legislature party to elect a new leader.'[2] In May 1964 he acted on his own advice when Jawaharlal Nehru died. Tragically, he had to repeat the procedure on Lal Bahadur Shastri's death in January 1966. On both occasions, G.L. Nanda was sworn in as acting Prime Minister. Unfortunately, Giani Zail Singh departed from this course on Indira Gandhi's assassination on 31 October 1984.

As it happened, just a few days earlier, on 21 October 1984 *The Sunday Times* (London) published an article in which the writer reported Attorney-General Sir Michael Havers' weighty opinion on the proper way in which the British government would have acted if the IRA's bomb had killed Prime Minister Margaret Thatcher and her senior cabinet ministers when it exploded at the Grand Hotel in Brighton on 12 October 1984.

He said that within hours 'the remnants of the Thatcher cabinet would have gathered under tight security' in London. The chairman of the Conservative Party in the House of Commons, known as the 1922 committee, and, of course, the Queen would have been alerted. 'The priority would be to select a new leader of the party so that he could be summoned to Buckingham Palace to kiss hands and be asked to form a government.'

However until that election took place, Deputy Prime Minister Lord Whitelaw would have been asked 'to take control of the government'. By the evening of 12 October a new prime minister would have been sworn in. 'Of course the new prime minister would have been temporary; he would have stood down as soon as

[2]Michael Brecher, *Succession in India*, (London: Oxford University Press, 1966), p. 35.

the Tory party had held a leadership election.' By 22 October, ten days later, the nominations for the leader's election would have closed, Sir Michael remarked. The result would have been announced by 25 October, within a fortnight of the 'tragedy'. Sir Michael said that 'it would be desirable to have this settled as soon as possible and I think this time scale is acceptable'.

What if the Conservatives had lost their wafer-thin majority in the Commons as a result of the bombing? According to the attorney-general, this would only have entailed greater delay but no more than that. 'We might have had to take more sounding among the Tory MPs over who they would find acceptable. But we would have managed.' There would have been a brief truce between the parties after the tragedy to allow time for a general election to be held since the majority in the House of Commons was in issue.

Indeed, when C.N. Annaduri died on 3 February 1969, V.R. Nedunchezhian was appointed acting chief minister. He duly resigned, on 9 February 1969, on M. Karunanidhi's election as party leader. This precedent is very relevant. Let us apply it to the facts of the MGR succession. When he died on 24 December the Governor properly invited V.R. Nedunchezhian, leader of the house and seniormost minister, to form a government 'till the election of a new leader by the party in majority in the assembly'.

On 29 December Khurana asked him to convene the party meeting by 3 January at the latest. Nedunchezhian did not object even then. However, on 31 December, the day the party split with both factions meeting separately and electing rival leaders, Janaki Ramachandran and V.R. Nedunchezhian, the latter wrote to the governor saying 'there is a great difficulty in calling for a meeting of the legislature party to elect a leader at which there can be a free and fair election'. Therefore, instead of the party meeting which he had promised to face, he asked the governor 'to permit me to continue as the chief minister till the legislative assembly of our state is called to meet where I will be able to establish that I command a majority'. On that very day he also said, according to UNI, that no time limit had been fixed to elect a party leader. This was not true.

On New Year's day 1988, after he had been asked to convene a party meeting by 3 January, Nedunchezhian wrote to the governor to say that Miss Jayalalitha had called a meeting of the MLAs at 11 a.m. the next day in her capacity as general secretary with his concurrence. On 2 January Jayalalitha informed the governor of

V.R. Nedunchezhian's election. Significantly, she did not mention how many MLAs had met and declared their support. Of all the politicians in Madras, she is known to be the most efficient and meticulous. V.R. Nedunchezhian also wrote the same day to challenge the validity of the rival's meeting and to intimate his own election as party leader and Jayalalitha's as general secretary.

On 3 January Governor Khurana announced his decision at a press conference. He had received a communication from Mrs Ramachandran that day to the effect that 97 MLAs supported her and elected her as leader. 'I took steps to interview individually each of them and I was satisfied that all the 97 MLAs were supporting Mrs Janaki Ramachandran; as such out of 131 MLAs belonging to the AIADMK, Mrs Janaki Ramachandran commands a clear majority.'

The conclusion is flawless, but he tripped badly. While stipulating the condition that she must win a vote of confidence in the assembly, he solicited her convenience about how much time she needed. Instead, he ought to have stipulated how much time he thought proper to grant her. It should have been no more than ten days at the very maximum, preferably a week. The governor's excuses for this lapse do not hold water. Mrs Ramachandran said she would prove her majority 'as early as possible, but not later than three weeks from the time of her assuming office as chief minister', which she did, only on 7 January. In other words, she can remain chief minister without the assembly meeting for a month and four days after MGR's death. This is sheer nonsense.

It is difficult to understand the governor's remark that Mrs Ramachandran should be given 'sufficient opportunity' to prove her majority in the house. He revealed, in his letter to Jayalalitha on 8 January, that Mrs Ramchandran had asked for four weeks but it was reduced to three at his instance. He irrelevantly cited eight holidays including that for Pongal during this period and the preparation of the governor's address. Surely, the new chief minister knows her late husband's party programme. The issue is one of confidence in her. Both factions were agreed on MGR's programme. The governor stumbled badly.

The governor is right in saying that he need not 'go into the controversy raised by each of the groups' concerning the other's meeting. 'What is material is my personal satisfaction of the majority support claimed by the two groups.'

V.R. Nedunchezhian justified his volte-face by quoting from

the report of the Committee of Governors (1971). All it says is that the leader of the largest party has no 'absolute right' to be called to form a government. The others could have drummed up majority support through an alliance. Indeed, V.R. Nedunchezhian's references are all to the N. Bhaskara Rao situation when an elected chief minister is being toppled. In such cases, of course, it is the assembly, not the governor, that must decide. Here however, Mr Nedunchezhian had agreed to seek a party vote but failed to muster more than 30-odd votes despite tall claims of 70-odd, and then sought an assembly vote.

True, the report of the Committee of Governors found the Raj Bhavan parades 'distressing'. They are improper for toppling a chief minister but could become unavoidable in the appointment of one. V.R. Nedunchezhian fell in the latter category though he claimed belatedly to fall in the former. All the instances he cited in his memorandum of 6 January are those of loss of majority subsequently, not of disputed majority initially.

Jayalalitha's letter of protest to the governor on 6 January significantly pleaded for dissolution of the assembly: a tacit admission that she did not enjoy a majority there.

Finally, one quibble needs to be disposed of. The test is not absolute majority in the house but a stable majority. The report of the Committee of Governors says:[3] It is 'a person most likely to command a stable majority'. The report goes on to say[4] that even a party in a minority in the house, like Indira Gandhi's Congress(I) in 1969, can be asked to form a government 'provided the governor is satisfied that such a minority party leader will be able to command the support of other parties in the assembly'. In plain words, the majority means majority of those present and voting. No head of state has the right to ask for an absolute majority

---

[3]Ibid, p. 28.
[4]Ibid, p. 31.

40

Chief Ministers: An Endangered Species?[1]

In the light of Veerendra Patil's recent experience, some might be tempted to regard chief ministers as an endangered species; a tribe subject to pressures from their central leadership as well as the government of India, regardless of which party runs it. The fact that Veerendra Patil is only the latest in a long series of chief ministers whose resignations from office Rajiv Gandhi, and his predecessor Mrs Indira Gandhi, felt free to demand at whim for two decades, fortifies the impression.

So does the contrast across the border where a Nawaz Sharif could cock a snook at Benazir Bhutto and Nawab Akbar Bugti could call her names. This does not however reckon with powerful chief ministers we have today like Jyoti Basu, M. Karunanidhi, and Mulayam Singh Yadav. To Mr Laloo Prasad Yadav goes the credit for demonstrating that a chief minister who is in earnest about doing his job soon also acquires political clout. Even in the worst days of the blighted decade of Indira Gandhi–Rajiv Gandhi rule in the eighties, Ramakrishna Hegde could stand up to the Centre and so could NTR, not forgetting Sheikh Abdullah.

Nonetheless, it would be wrong to overlook the fact that the chief minister, even at the best of times, wields less power than that envisaged for him/her by the framers of the constitution. This is only partly due to the aggrandizement of power by the centre at the expense of the states. There are also other factors besides which are often overlooked.

[1] *The Indian Express*, 21 October 1990.

It is a complex situation. There is the tradition of the Congress prior to independence when the centralized high command laid down the law and the premiers of the provinces, as they were called, held office only as participants in the freedom struggle. There were powerful personalities like Rajaji and Pandit Gobind Ballabh Pant but there was never any question as to where the real power lay. K.F. Nariman did not realize that and lost out to a lesser known figure, B.G. Kher, in the bid for the premiership of Bombay. N.B. Khare became prime minister of Central Provinces but received the order of the boot from the high command in a year's time when he overreached himself. In Madras, T. Prakasam was taught the same lesson in 1947.

The status of the chief minister since Independence accurately reflects the quality of our parliamentary democracy and of our party system; specifically, the procedures which our parties follow in awarding party tickets to candidates in assembly elections. If the MLAs are handpicked by the central leadership of the party with an eye to retaining control over the chief ministership, then the person elected can not possibly aspire to be his own man. This stark political reality of highly centralized political parties warps the working of a federal constitution.

This constitutional position itself is not in doubt. The framers of the constitution sought to establish the parliamentary system both at the centre and in the states. The constitutional provisions concerning the president, the prime minister, and the union council of ministers are exactly identical to those concerning, respectively, the governor, the chief minister, and the states' council of ministers, with but one difference: the governor reports to the president on matters concerning the state, and the president can by proclamation impose president's rule on the state. Only in some states is the governor conferred special responsibilities in relation to specified matters and the power to act in his individual judgment in relation to them; for instance, in Sikkim and Nagaland.

For the rest, as the chairman of the drafting committee, Dr B.R. Ambedkar, told the constituent assembly, on 30 December 1948, 'The position of the governor is exactly the same as the position of the president' as constitutional head of State. He was speaking specifically on the sensitive topic of dissolution.

Within the range of subjects allotted to the state by the constitution, the chief minister has the same authority as the prime minister has at the centre. That constitutional position has been made to stand on its head by the politics of our country. The prime minister, even when he is not the party president, has enormous influence on the party's functionaries. vis-à-vis chief ministers. He can bring pressure to bear by invoking the Centre's considerable powers in regard to licensing of industrial projects and sanctioning of State projects.

By and large, constitutional proprieties were observed in the Nehru era, but some grave lapses were made in those formative years for which the country has had to pay a heavy price. Some of these lapses were treated as precedents by Mr Nehru's successors. It is altogether wrong to regard that period as one studded with men like Dr B C Roy, Rajaji, and Pandit Pant as Chief Ministers. It not only had people like Sardar Partap Singh Kairon and Bakshi Gaulam Mohammed but others who were simply mediocre. The Congress high command did a lot of politicking but with one difference, Mr Nehru would not flout either the constitution or the party's opinion, whether at the centre or in the states. The question always remains: does the democratic experience rest on the forbearance of the leader or the strength of the democratic urges in the people?

Consider just two grave lapses of that period. One concerns the very first instance of imposition of president's rule after the constitution came into force. It was on Punjab on 16 June 1951. One fine day the prime minister told President Rajendra Prasad that the Chief Minister, Dr Gopichand Bhargava would resign and that no Congressman should thereupon from a government.

The president's note in his diary on this is of abiding relevance:

I abhor the idea of suspending the constitution and taking over the administration of a state in this manner. The ministry in the State had the confidence of the assembly and it could have continued to rule the state if the Congress parliamentary board had not forced it to resign ... the question arises whether the government could be run through persons authorized by the constitution or on the advicse of the Congress which had no constitutional locus standi. It would be a dangerous precedent to run a government on the advice of an extra-constitutional authority when the constitutional apparatus was in existence. The Congressmen may like it today, but a time could come when a different set of people would be in power.

He ended this prophetic note with the lament: 'It is a precedent which will do no good, it would be harmful in the future'.[2]

So it proved to be. President's rule was imposed a number of times only in order to resolve party wrangles or to take advantage of an opposition party's wrangles.

President's rule in Punjab once again, in 1966, in Andhra Pradesh in 1973; in Uttar Pradesh in 1973 and 1975; and in Orissa in 1976 are instances of the first kind. The Congress high command wanted to evict an incumbent chief minister of its own party for its own ends. The imposition of President's rule in Karnataka in April 1989 and on 10 October 1990 are clear cases of exploiting an opposition's feuds. In both categories, democratically elected chief ministers were sacked by the Centre, and democracy as well as federalism reduced to naught. Dr Rajendra Prasad's warning proved prophetic.

Another grave lapse in the Nehru era was that regarding Mr Morarji Desai. He lost in the 1952 general elections. Mr Nehru nonetheless pressed that he should not resign but seek re-election. Even the constitution of the state's Congress legislature party was amended to get Mr Desai elected as its leader after he had got himself elected to the legislative council.

Professor Stanley A Kochanek has ably described the state of the office of the chief minister during Mr Nehru's premiership in his classic, *The Congress Party of India*.[3] The parliamentary board functioned as umpire in State politics. There were three broad patterns. If the legislature party was united, it was left free to elect its leader: Y.B. Chavan, K. Kamaraj, and B.C. Roy were outstanding examples. A divided party was given guidance. If one faction was dominant, its leader was not elected after the centre's preference was clearly shown. Kairon and Sanjiva Reddy belonged to this category, but a 'broad based' cabinet was imposed on them as the price of central support. In the third case of an even split, informal soundings were taken and the favourite got elected. S.R. Kanthi in Mysore and B. Jha in Bihar reaped the fruits of this approach.

In short, the power of the centre depended on the unity of the state party. Nehru preferred unity and disliked intervention. Mrs Gandhi and her son sedulously disrupted it to augment their own

[2]Valmiki Choudary, *President and the Indian Constitution* (Delhi: Allied, 1985), p. 80.

[3]Stanley A. Kochanek, *The Congress Party of India*, (New Jersey: Princeton University Press), 1968.

power. In 1972, central ministers were sent down as 'readymade' chief ministers: Nandini Satpathy in Orissa, S. S. Ray in West Bengal, and P.C. Sethi in Madhya Pradesh. The limit was reached during the Emergency when the Congress general secretary, Mr A.R. Antulay declared on 17 December 1976 that those appointed by the 'National' leader 'to discharge certain duties like chief ministership can expect only cooperation of colleagues and other Congressmen but not loyalty. Loyalty is not divisible ...' It belonged to Mrs Gandhi alone. The constitutional office of the chief executive of the State was reduced to retainership of the party leader.

The Janata era saw a different spectacle. The Bharatiya Lok Dal, led by Charan Singh, and the Bharatiya Jana Sangh constituents, struck a deal parcelling out some states and got their nominees elected as leaders in seven states.[4]

On 21 June 1977 State legislators met to elect their respective leaders on the basis of 'consensus' in Orissa, Haryana, and Madhya Pradesh. Popular elections were held in Uttar Pradesh, Bihar, Rajasthan, and Himachal Pradesh. Later, Charan Singh and the Jana Sangh fell out and in 1979 their rift and the factionalism in the Janata Party generally led to the ouster of the chief ministers of UP, Bihar, Himachal Pradesh, and Haryana. The party president, Chandra Shekhar, was very much privy to Devi Lal's ouster from the chief ministership in Haryana and to the election of his successor Mr Bhajan Lal, a crony of his, who jilted the Janata in 1980 and crossed over to the Congress (I). In contrast, the National Front made no attempt to control elections to the leadership of State legislature parties.

The crux of the matter is that our system of awarding party tickets to candidates for elections is fundamentally undemocratic. Organizational elections are not held. A party cabal controlling the party purse awards 'tickets' to its favourites unless the State's leader has clout enough to get his men in. In the UK it is the constituency party which has a powerful say in the selection of the candidate.

The existing system can be made to work only if certain norms are obeyed. First and foremost, the legislature party must be absolutely free to elect its leader without any central guidance. The shoddy practice of the party asking the fuhrer to nominate his man for state leadership shows the discordance between our political

[4]See C.P. Bhambhri, *The Janata Party*, (Delhi: National Publishing House, 1980), p. 42.

culture and our democratic constitution. Secondly, the leader elected by a free vote must be free also to select and drop his cabinet colleagues. Finally, the chief minister must be allowed to use the weapon of dissolution as much as the prime minister is able to.

Constitutionally, the norms and conventions that govern the prime minister's advice to the president with regard to dissolution govern, no less, the chief minister's advice to the governor. In practice the governor has governed himself by the Centre's advice. We must not underestimate the net impact of all these distortions. It is nothing short of an atrophy of parliamentary democracy in the States.

41

The States and Lok Sabha Polls[1]

The Bharatiya Janata Party (BJP) discovered at the very moment of its triumph the truth of the old saying that allies can be more troublesome than adversaries. No sympathy should be wasted on a party which, in its desperate quest for power, cobbles together an alliance of rag, tag, and bobtail. Pledged to provide stable government, the BJP is faced with insistent demands from its allies to destabilize State governments. What will they not ask for themselves if the BJP's position becomes weaker still? The demand was made in the first flush of victory, before the reins of power touched their hands. This reveals a lot about their allies.

The BJP's election manifesto (1998) pledges that it 'is committed to take necessary steps to prevent misuse of Article 356 of the Constitution'. The 1996 manifesto said: 'The BJP will implement the main recommendations of the Sarkaria commission, such as: ... (b) ending the misuse of the Article 356 to dismiss state governments and dissolve state assemblies. We will explore the possibility of making it mandatory for the union government to seek parliament's approval by two-thirds majority for dismissal of state governments.'

Curiously, on her return to Chennai, Jayalalitha made the ouster operation legally impossible. She embroidered the pejorative 'anti-national' with the specific but puerile charge that the DMK government is 'encouraging, aiding and abetting' extremists, particularly Pakistan's ISI. The charge is not one of negligence but of conscious complicity. This is very much open to judicial scrutiny. The centre will have to make it stick in the courts if it invokes Article 356.

[1] *The Statesman*, 22 March 1998.

All the nine members of the Bench of the Supreme Court ruled unanimously in Bommai's case that although Article 74(2) bars judicial review so far as the advice given by the council of ministers is concerned, it does not bar scrutiny of the material on the basis of which the advice was given. This is true of advice on any matter. On Article 356, specifically, the court ruled that a proclamation made under it is subject to judicial review. The material on the basis of which such a proclamation is made will have to be produced in court.[2]

The Sarkaria commission cited among the cases in which Article 356 cannot be used, one 'Where Article 356 is sought to be invoked for superseding the duly constituted ministry and dissolving the state legislative assembly on the sole ground that, in the general elections to the Lok Sabha, the ruling party in the state has suffered a massive defeat'. Two judges (P.B. Sawant and Kuldip Singh) 'endorsed' this explicitly. A.M. Ahmadi and K. Ramaswamy endorsed the principle drawing attention to the federal principle. B.P. Jeevan Reddy and S.C. Agrawal, with whom S.R. Pandian agreed, did not deal with this specific situation. Their construction of Article 356 however rules out its application to such a case. Thus, the Bommai case renders action of the kind that the BJP's allies demand as unconstitutional.

It is unnecessary in this context to deal with the implications of the electoral verdict in Bihar, Tamil Nadu, Haryana or, for that matter, Rajasthan and Maharashtra. They nowhere approach those of the 1977 Lok Sabha elections in the wake of the Emergency. That verdict by itself is not however relevant as the Supreme Court pointed out while upholding the president's proclamations issued on 30 April 1977, when the Janata Party was in office, in respect of nine states: Haryana, Himachal Pradesh, Punjab, Uttar Pradesh, Rajasthan, Madhya Pradesh, Bihar, Orissa, and West Bengal. That action has been misunderstood by many. It has also been deliberately misrepresented by some others to justify similar action by Indira Gandhi on her return to power. The proclamation she got issued on 17 February 1980 was also in relation to nine States: Punjab, Uttar Pradesh, Rajasthan, Madhya Pradesh, Bihar, Orissa, Gujarat, Maharashtra, and Tamil Nadu.

It is necessary to deal with both cases in detail in order to explode the myths in relation to both. The proclamation of 1977 was upheld

[2] *S.R. Bommai & Ors.* vs *Union of India* (1994) 3 SCC 1

by a seven-member bench of the Supreme Court unanimously in
State of Rajasthan vs *Union of India*[3] In Bommai's case, Justice Sawant
noted that that ruling did not support dismissal of a state government
'however complete the defeat may be' because, as Justices P.N.
Bhagwati and A.C. Gupta clearly said in the 1977 case:

We have no doubt at all that merely because the ruling party in a state
suffers defeat in the elections to the Lok Sabha or for the matter of that,
in the panchayat elections, that by itself can be no ground for saying that
the government of the State cannot be carried on in accordance with the
provisions of the Constitution.

The federal structure under our Constitution clearly postulates that
there may be one party in power in the State and another at the centre. It
is also not an unusual phemomenon that the same electorate may elect a
majority of members of one party to the legislative assembly while at the
same time electing a majority of members of another party to the Lok
Sabha ... even if it were indicative of a definite shift in the opinion of the
electorate, that by itself would be no grounds for dissolution, because the
constitution contemplates that ordinarily the will of the electorate shall
be expressed at the end of the term of the assembly and a change in the
electorate's in between would not be relevant.

Why, then, did they uphold the proclamation? 'The situation here
is, however, wholly different. This is not a case where just an ordinary
defeat has been suffered by the ruling party in a state at the elections
in the Lok Sabha. There has been a total rout of candidates belonging
to the ruling party. In some of the plaintiff-states, the ruling party
has not been able to secure a single seat ... It is symptomatic of
complete alienation between the government and the people.'

In 1977, five States in the entire northern belt—Haryana, Punjab,
Himachal Pradesh, Uttar Pradesh and Bihar—did not return a single
Congress candidate to the Lok Sabha which prompted a columnist
to remark that a truck driver could have driven all the way from
Amritsar to Calcutta with little fear of knocking down a Congress
MP; except, in West Bengal and Orissa, which he overlooked, where
they returned three and four out of a total of 42 and 21 respectively,
and in Rajasthan and Madhya Pradesh, one each.

Contrast this with the results in the Lok Sabha elections in 1980.
In Punjab, Orissa, and Gujarat the Congress(I) won all the seats bar
one in each. The verdict in the other six States, while undoubtedly

[3]*State of Rajasthan* vs *Union of India* (1977) 3 SCC 592.

in favour of the Congress(I), was not such as to qualify as total rejection of the Opposition. Bihar returned 30 Congress(I) candidates out of 54; Madhya Pradesh 35 out of 40; Maharashtra 39 out of 48; Rajasthan 18 out of 25; Tamil Nadu 20 out of 39; and Uttar Pradesh 51 out of 85. The observations of Bhagwati and Gupta are, therefore, all the more apposite in all these cases. Of the nine states which the 1980 proclamation covered, only in Gujarat, Punjab, and Orissa did the Janata Party suffer a rout of the dimensions of 1977. Even had that debacle occurred however it would not in itself suffice to warrant imposition of president's rule. Bhagwati and Gupta spoke in a certain context. Murtaza Ali Fazal Ali described it in precise terms:

Summarizing the position, in short, it is clear—(1) that a grave emergency was clamped in the whole country; (2) that civil liberties were withdrawn to a great extent; (3) that important fundamental rights of the people were suspended; (4) that strict censorship on the press was placed; and (5) that the judicial powers were crippled to a large extent.

In the new elections the Congress party suffered reverses in the nine States and the people displayed complete lack of confidence in the Congress party. The cumulative effect of the circumstances mentioned above may lead to a reasonable inference that the people had given a massive verdict not only against the Congress candidates who fought the elections to the Lok Sabha but also against the policies and ideologies followed by the Congress governments as a whole, whether at the centre or in the states during the 20 months preceding the elections.

In these circumstances it cannot be said that the inference drawn by the home minister that the state governments may have forfeited the confidence of the people is not a reasonable one or has no nexus with the action proposed to be taken under Article 356 for dissolution of the Assemblies.

It was, clearly, 'the cumulative effect of the circumstances', and not the mere defeat of the Congress that weighed with the court.

There are five distinct features which make the 1977 and 1980 situations fundamentally different, quite apart from the qualitatively different electoral verdict in these cases. First, in 1977 the assemblies of all the nine states, bar only two, had completed the five-year term for which the people had elected them in 1972. The UP and Orissa assemblies were elected in 1974. The seven others owed their extension for another year to the hated 42nd Amendment to the Constitution which was pushed through parliament when the fraudulent emergency was in force, the opposition leaders behind bars, and the press under censorship. The Janata Party sought and won a mandate 'to rescind the 42nd Amendment' in terms of its manifesto.

Morally, they had not a leg to stand on. That the assemblies did not reflect the popular will was tacitly conceded by the chief minister of Maharashtra, Mr S.B. Chavan when, on 30 March 1977, he remarked a propos dissolution: 'how can I hand over the state assembly on a silver platter to the Janata Party?' Similar considerations, no doubt, motivated the other chief ministers to reject the very idea of dissolution of the assemblies in order to hold fresh elections.

Secondly, a proclamation of emergency makes India a unitary state. The Lok Sabha elections in the situation as it existed in 1977 reflected rejection of the state governments, no less. Related to this is the third feature. The country went to the polls to give its verdict on the emergency and the excesses that followed in its train. Congress(I) state governments were not lagging behind in their enthusiasm to perpetrate those excesses in order to please Indira and Sanjay Gandhi.

Fourthly, the emergency itself; not as an excess which it was, but as a seismic event on which the people had a right to give an opinion in a federation at both levels of government, national and state, since the states were accomplices in the fraud and the excesses. Fresh elections to invite their verdict would have been necessary even if the assemblies had been elected just a day before the fraudulent proclamation of emergency of 25 June 1975. Britain went through two general elections in one year. First, on 10 January 1910 when the House of Lords rejected the budget; and, next, on 28 November 1910 on the Bill that sought to curb the power of the House of Lords. Was the Emergency of lesser importance and consequence to our nation? Such an event is all too rare in a nation's history. When it occurs the people are entitled to give their verdict as soon as possible. Indira Gandhi sacked the nine governments for no cause and on no issue at all; in one case (UP's), on the basis of sheer falsehood.

The last feature is overlooked by all sides. The Janata government asked the chief ministers to advise their respective governors to dissolve the assemblies. They could have continued to remain in office during the polls, an option Indira Gandhi would never have dreamt of giving her opponents.

The Union Home Minister, Charan Singh's letter to the chief ministers dated 18 April 1977 set out 'the most unprecedented political situation ... the resultant climate of uncertainty' and concluded: 'I would, therefore, earnestly commend for your consideration that you may advise your governor to dissolve the state assembly in exercise of powers under Article 174(2)(b) and seek a fresh mandate from the electorate. This alone would, in our considered view, be consistent with constitutional precedents and democratic practices.'[4]

This was absolutely incontrovertible. These were chief ministers whose electoral mandate had expired; who formed part of the emergency set-up, with all that it entailed; an event of gravest consequence that occurs but rarely had shaken the nation; and the party that had inflicted the wrong on the nation had been savagely defeated at the national polls. Nonetheless, they refused to face their masters because, as S.B. Chavan blurted out, they were certain of defeat at their hands. The situation in 1980 was fundamentally different. The two cases bear not the slightest resemblance except for the fact that in each case the party in power at the centre had lost.

One other neglected feature brings out the difference starkly. On 31 January 1980 Sanjay Gandhi charged that in Narainpur in the Deoria district of UP, where some disturbances had occurred on 14 January 1980, 'every village woman was raped and every house had been looted'. It had 650 adult women and 160 huts and houses. Indira Gandhi said: 'I doubt if there has been any other instance of such magnitude since independence.' It affected 'India's name nationally and internationally'. She visited Narainpur on 7 February and said that the State government had no right to exist. 'There are few parallels in the world to the Narainpur episode'. On 5 February, the state government set up a commission of inquiry. This did not prevent Indira Gandhi from imposing president's rule along with the other eight states on 17 February. On 7 February she had said 'Why should we not take advantage of other parties' failures?'

Justice H.C.P Tripathi of the Allahabad high court submitted his report on 2 July 1981 but it was tabled in the assembly only on 30 August 1982. He found not a single instance of rape or of death

[4]Ibid. Quoted in full in the judgements.

by police beating or of looting. Sanjay had gone so far as to allege that people were compelled to urinate in one another's mouths when they asked the police for water.[5] No such falsehood was purveyed by the Janata government in 1977. It was a straightforward action.

Indira Gandhi's vendetta was not confined to selecting exactly nine states against the Janata's nine. It went further still. On 1 February 1980 a spokesman of the prime minister's office said that reports had reached her from UP, Rajasthan, Madhya Pradesh, and other States of massive programmes of demolition of houses and of forced sterilizations and that she had asked their chief ministers to look into the matter immediately. Sonia Gandhi's election campaign clearly reveals that in her efforts to imbibe the values of the Indira Gandhi and Rajiv Gandhi *parivar*, mendacity has not been neglected.

If in 1980 A.B.A Ghani Khan Choudhury talked of throwing the West Bengal government into the sea, on 2 December 1984 Pranab Mukherjee said 'The centre will consider whether the Left Front government should be allowed to continue in office if the Congress(I) gets a majority of the Lok Sabha seats in West Bengal'.

In 1998 we find in George Fernandes, Jayalalitha and Chautala politicians of the same outlook. 1998 is not however 1980 or even 1991 when the DMK government was sacked by a pliable Chandra Shekhar at Rajiv Gandhi's behest. The Supreme Court's ruling in Bommai case makes all the difference, as does the far greater popular awakening today.

---

[5]For a full discussion of the episode, see A.G. Noorani, *Indian Affairs: The Political Dimension*, Konark, 1990, pp. 17–20.

42
President's Rule[1]

I ndira Gandhi returned to power in January 1980 and a new political climate began when she set about planting favourites in key places to perform hatchet jobs there. One of them, Jagmohan, of emergency fame, assumed office as Lt-Governor of Delhi on 17 February 1980, a Sunday. Ten days later, he issued an order under Section 238(I) of the Punjab Municipal Act, 1911 and superseded the New Delhi Municipal Committee with immediate effect. His predecessor had appointed its members for a year's term with effect from 4 October 1979. A full bench of the Delhi high court dismissed writ petitions challenging the action. The Supreme Court reversed the decision on appeal.

The Court said:

A committee so soon as it is constituted, at once assumes a certain office and status, is endowed with certain rights and burdened with certain responsibilities, all of a nature commanding respectful regard from the public. To be stripped of the office and status, to be deprived of the rights, to be removed from the responsibilities, in an unceremonious way as to suffer in public esteem, is certainly to visit the committee with civil consequences. In our opinion the status and office and the rights and responsibilities to which we have referred and the expectation of the committee to serve its full term of office would certainly create sufficient interest in the municipal committee and their loss, if superseded, would entail civil consequences so as to justify an insistence upon the observance of the principles of natural justice before an order of supersession is passed.'[2]

The Order was held to be 'vitiated by the failure to observe the

[1] *The Statesman*, 11 and 12 August 1997.
[2] *S.L. Kapoor* vs *Jagmohan & Ors.* (1980) 4 SCC 379

principles of natural justice'. The judgment was delivered on 18 September 1980. The NDMC's term was anyway to expire on 3 October 1980. The petitioners did not insist on reinstatement. They had won a resounding moral victory. The judgment was based on the principles of administrative law that require strict observance of the principles of natural justice for such executive action. They apply if a state government supersedes a municipal body. Apparently, they do not apply if the government of India ousts an elected state government and imposes direct central rule through a presidential proclamation under Article 356 of the Constitution.

In 1993, a nine-member bench of the Supreme Court was set up to consider the ambit of Article 356 anew. As many as six opinions were delivered, yet nor one could say with certitude whether the principles of administrative law on the validity of executive action apply to judicial review of so drastic a power as imposition of president's rule in the states. Distilling the law from the six opinions requires talent not dissimilar to that required in scriptural exegesis.[3] In a notable ruling in 1980, the privy council applied the principles in a case concerning the exercise of emergency powers in Malaysia.[4]

The Supreme Court could well have read into Article 356 the conditions for the exercise of the power it confers which its sponsors had mentioned in the constituent assembly. It did not. In the circumstances, constitutional amendment remains the only course. A broad consensus on this emerged on 10 May and 17 June 1997 in the standing committee of the Inter-State Council. According to the Union Home Minister, Indrajit Gupta, the major safeguards that are proposed to be adopted are: parliament's approval before, rather than after, the State government's dismissal; a show cause notice by the Union to the delinquent government citing the grounds for the threatened action and seeking a reply within a week; and ratification of the president's proclamation by a two-thirds vote by both house of parliament, not by a mere majority vote. This would entail some approval by the Opposition. There was a setback on 8 July when this body 'more or less exhausted' the possibility of a consensus on 'adequate safeguards' and left the matter to be resolved by the Inter-State Council on 17 July, 1997 which failed to evolve a consensus.

[3] *S.R. Bommai* (1994) 3 SCC 1.
[4] *Teh Cheng Poh* vs *Public Prosecutor, Malaysia* (1980) AC 458.

These are by no means radical proposals. Spain's constitution permits provincial councils to form autonomous communities. They enjoy greater safeguards of autonomy under a unitary constitution than our states do under our federal constitution. Article 155 of the Spanish Constitution reads:

If an autonomous community does not fulfil the obligations imposed upon it by the constitution or other laws, or acts in a way seriously prejudicing the general interests of Spain, the government, after lodging a complaint with the president of the autonomous community and failing to receive satisfaction therefore, may, following approval granted by an absolute majority of the Senate, take the measures necessary in order to compel the latter forcibly to meet said obligations, or in order to protect the above-mentioned general interests.

It provides for a notice plus prior approval of the Senate.

Article 356 is based on the notorious Section 93 of the Government of India Act 1935 which provided for 'governor's rule' in the provinces just as Section 45 provided for the governor-general's rule at the centre (the federal part, however, never came into force). Initially, the draftsmen of our constitution provided for an elected governor. It was the threat to 'the peace and tranquillity' which was to trigger off action by the governor. Both decisions were reversed. Governors were not to be elected but appointed by the president who would step in at the outset if there is need for Central action on grounds other than threat to the peace.

While discussing amendments to Article 356 in order to check abuse of power, two distinct aspects must be borne in mind. One is procedural: the show-case notice and ratification by parliament. The other and neglected aspect is the substantive one. The crucial expression in Section 93 was adopted bodily and unwisely; 'a situation has arisen in which the government of the province cannot be carried on in accordance with the provisions of this Act' which served as the Constitution of India from 1 April 1937 to 25 January 1950. It lends itself readily to abuse, almost invites it.

H.N. Kunzru's request for clarification was brushed aside by Ambedkar in August 1949: 'Everybody must be quite familiar with its *de facto* and *de jure* meaning'. Its de facto application has cost us dear.[5]

[5]CAD, vol. ix, pp, 176–7.

The Joint Parliamentary committee of the British parliament on the Government of India Bill observed:

It is proposed to give the governor power at his discretion, if at any time he is satisfied that a situation has arisen which for the time being renders it *impossible* for the government of the province to be carried on in accordance with the provisions of the Constitution Act, to assume himself by proclamation all such powers vested in any provincial authority as appear to him to be necessary for the purpose of securing that the government of the province shall be carried on effectively ...'[6]

Similar language was used by Alladi Krishnaswamy Ayyar in the constituent assembly on 3 August 1949: 'It is only when there is a failure or *breakdown* of the constitutional machinery that the union government will interfere.'[7] The then Secretary of State for India, Sir Samuel Hoare, told the House of Commons on 13 March 1935 that he was 'contemplating *the last emergency, when the whole machinery or government has broken down*'.[8] In India, Article 356 is a weapon of first resort.

Replying to the debate in the constituent assembly on 4 August 1949, Ambedkar said: 'In regard to the general debate which has taken place in which it has been suggested that these articles are liable to be abused, I may say that I do not altogether deny that there is a possibility of these articles being abused or employed for political purposes. But that objection applies to every part of the Constitution which gives power to the Centre to override the provinces.' This was sheer facetiousness. Surely the ease with which it could be abused and the consequences of abuse were far greater in this case.

He added:

The proper thing we ought to expect is that such articles will never be called into operation and that they would remain a dead letter. If at all they are brought into operation, I hope the president, who is endowed with these powers, will take proper precautions before actually suspending the administration of the provinces. I *hope* the first thing he will do would be to issue a mere warning to a province that has erred, that things were not happening in the way in which they were intended to happen in the constitution. If that warning fails the second thing for him to do *will be to*

[6]*Joint Committee on Indian Constitutional Reform Session 1933–4*, vol. I, pt I, Report HC 5, HMSO, London, p. 60, para 109,

[7]CAD, vol. ix, p. 150.

[8]299 *House of Commons Debates*, 13 March, 935, vol. 463

order an election allowing the people of the province to settle matters by themselves. *It is only when these two remedies fail that he would resort to this article.'*

In the context, 'would' clearly implies 'should'.[9]

It would be perfectly legitimate in constitutional interpretation to read these two conditions into Article 356; namely, notice or warning plus dissolution of the assembly and polls, without, however, sacking the state government, before invoking Article 356. It bears mention that those who put Indira Gandhi's action in dismissing state assemblies in 1980 on a par with Charan Singh's action in 1977 forget that his letter to the chief ministers on 18 April 1977, asked them only to face the people at the hustings. Nearly all had overstayed their term and, in any case, a radically new situation had been created by the emergency, its gross abuses, and the 42nd Amendment. Charan Singh explicitly asked the chief ministers to 'advise your governor to dissolve the state assembly in exercise of the powers under Article 174(2)(b) and seek a fresh mandate from the electorate'. *Meanwhile they were not asked to resign. They could have continued to remain in office during the polls.* Indira Gandhi's victims were given no such option. The chief ministers of 1977 preferred to be sacked rather than face the polls honourably.

The Sarkaria report recommended *inter alia* 'a warning' and incorporation in the president's proclamation of 'the material facts and grounds' for the action in order 'to make the remedy of judicial review on the grounds of mala fides a little more meaningful'. This should be ensured by constitutional amendment, it said. Thus, on at least three points, there exists a clear and strong consensus in favour of a constitutional amendment: a warning followed by a show-cause notice; recital of 'the material facts and grounds' in the proclamation which, shockingly, is now not the case; and more stringent conditions for its ratification by parliament. The Chief Minister of Tamil Nadu, Mr M. Karunanidhi, rightly insists that the warning should come only from the union; not the governor.

All these affect procedure. The vice in the substantive provision, taken over from the Act of 1935, remains. The expression should be repealed and substituted by the words: 'a breakdown of the constitutional machinery such as to render government according to the provisions of the constitution impossible'.

[9]CAD, vol. ix, pp. 176–7

This is not a radical change either. It only expresses the intention of the framers of Section 93. Those who aped it in Article 356 had shown less concern for its abuse than the British did. On 13 July 1933, the Secretary of the State for India, Samuel Hoare, had to face members of the British as well as Indian delegations to the Round Table Conference in defence of his proposals. Among them were lawyers of the stature of Ambedkar, C.P. Ramaswamy Aiyar, Hari Singh Gour, M R Jayakar, Tej Bahadur Sapru, Abdur Rahim, and Zafrulla Khan. Hoare was grilled by Rangaswami Iyengar. The entire exchange bears quotation *in extenso.*

I am putting it to you because you have amongst the special responsibilities put down the responsibility that in the event of a breakdown of the constitution (that is, in the event of a breakdown of the constitution, to use the words of the First Round Table Conference, on account of the difficulties which the legislatures or the executives make in preserving the constitution and working along constitutional lines), the governor or the governor-general, as the case may be, will immediately suspend the constitution and assume the responsibility for the administration. What I am saying is that, when you have got that provision and in all cases where a ministry fails to grapple with cases of grave menace to peace and tranquillity, would not it be a case of breakdown, and is it not therefore unnecessary to have a clause to give him special responsibility to prevent grave menace to peace and tranquillity?'

The answer was:

No I would not at all agree with that point of view. I think there are many intermediate stages before a breakdown comes about, and I think it may well be that by one or other of those means: finding an alternative minister, finding an alternative ministry, possibly by having a dissolution the governor may reach a situation in which the breakdown clause will not come into operation.' ... I regard the breakdown clause *as the final and ultimate sanction,* and I think there ought to be many of these other stages before the breakdown actually takes place.'[10]

On 14 August 1947, a day before India became independent, the governor-general promulgated the India (Provisional Constitution) Order 1947, in exercise of his powers under Section 8(2) of the Indian Independence Act, 1947, adopting the Act of 1935, with

[10]Secretary of State Sir Samuel Hoare's evidence on 11 July, 1933 on Proposals for Indian Constitutional Reforms Cmnd Paper 4268 of 1933, p. 67.

important modifications, as a provisional constitution while the constituent assembly was at work on a new constitution.

This Order omitted the hated Section 93 completely. Thus, from 15 August 1947 till 25 January 1950, the country was governed without any provision in its constitution for governor's rule or governor-general's rule. This period witnessed communal riots, refugee influx, the CPI's revolt pursuant to its Second Congress's decision at Calcutta in February 1948, rebellion in Telangana, and much else besides. *Section 93 was proved to be dispensable.*

If Article 356 is nonetheless to be retained, it must be amended to include stringent safeguards against its abuse. The governor is nobody's 'agent', as the Supreme Court has ruled. Notice to the erring State must go from him who is to act on its failure: the president, on the advice of the council of ministers, not the governor.

The governor can write to the chief minister as any head of state can to the head of government, as presidents have done to prime ministers in the past, but a notice envisaging central rule must come from the centre alone and should be sent directly to the State government, not through the governor.

Let it be remembered that the entire exercise is about amending Article 356. The Inter-State Council secretariat put forth before the council on 17 June a 'Proposed consensus Paper'. Item 8 of the proposed amendments referred to a situation 'in case no single party obtains majority in the house ...' This is insolently preposterous. Andhra's chief minister, N Chandrababu Naidu, rightly said 'The guideline for formation of government is not an integral part of Article 356. It need not be incorporated'.

Tailpiece

Alas, as Foreign Secretary, Hoare came to grief. In December 1935 he entered into a pact with the French Foreign Minister Pierre Laval in Paris to partition Abyssinia, giving its fertile lands to Mussolini's Italy. A leak, unusual in those days, wrecked the scheme and Hoare's career. When he went to King George V to surrender the seals of office, the king told him: 'No more coals to Newcastle no more Hoares to Paris.' The king complained to his successor. Anthony Eden, while narrating the story: 'The chap didn't even laugh.'

43

The President and the Bommai Case[1]

On 25 June 1975, what option did President Fakhruddin Ali Ahmed have, under the constitution, when Prime Minister Indira Gandhi asked him to sign a proclamation of emergency under Article 352 which was manifestly, palpably fraudulent?

It was based on the ground that the country's security was threatened by 'internal disturbance'. As the Shah Commission's report showed, neither the intelligence bureau, nor the governors nor the union home ministry had submitted any reports to warrant that conclusion. Nor did Fakhruddin Ali Ahmed ask for them. Like Barkis, he was very 'willin'! Had he had the spine, however, what constitutional alternatives did he have?

As originally enacted, Article 74(I) read: 'There shall be a council of ministers with the prime minister at the head to aid and advise the president in the exercise of his functions.' Authoritative dicta in the constituent assembly and successive rulings of the Supreme Court established beyond doubt that the provision sought to establish the British parliamentary system in which the head of state was bound by the advice of his council of ministers subject to recognized exceptions.

It is accepted, for instance, that the crown in the UK is entitled to dismiss a ministry which seeks to subvert democracy. A fortiori, the elected president of India who takes an oath, prescribed by Article 62, to 'preserve, protect and defend the constitution' and is liable to be impeached, under Article 61 read with Article 56(I),

[1] *The Statesman,* 12 and 13 July 1998.

'for violation of the constitution'. These provisions do not make him a super prime minister, but they do bind him not to be privy to a manifest violation of the constitution and to exert himself, within the limits of his recognized discretionary powers, to prevent it. Fakhruddin Ali Ahmed could and should have dismissed Indira Gandhi, spoken to the nation exposing her plans, invited the Opposition to form a government, instantly dissolved the Lok Sabha and, thus, invited the nation's verdict.

Article 74(I) was amended during the emergency by the 42nd Amendment to read: 'There shall be a council of ministers with the prime minister at the head to aid and advise the president who shall, in the exercise of his functions, act in accordance with such advice.' We have, however, its sponsor, the Union Law Minister H.R. Gokhale's acknowledgement in the Lok Sabha on 29 October 1976 that this amendment 'only reproduces the position which has always been there all along'. In other words, it did no more than make explicit what was already implied. Ergo, the recognized discretionary powers survived.

The logic was accepted by the Janata Party government which had attacked Fakhruddin Ali Ahmed for signing the proclamation of emergency. That is why the 44th Amendment to the Constitution which it sponsored (1978), made no change in Article 74(I). It only added a proviso to it: 'Provided that the president may require the council of ministers to reconsider such advice, either generally or otherwise, and the president shall act in accordance with the advice tendered after such reconsideration.'

This proviso applies, however, to the president's reservations or objections on the merits of the advice. It applies, perhaps, also to advice of doubtful constitutional validity. The president ought to act on advice reaffirmed after the reconsideration he had sought. It can never apply to advice which is inherently, palpably, demonstrably violative of the constitution. For example, Article 85(I), while empowering the president to summon each house of parliament, enjoins 'but six months shall not intervene' between the last sitting in one session and the first sitting in the next session. The president is bound to reject the council of ministers' advice to call the next session after six months in order to tide over its political difficulties.

Citing this apt illustration, the late H.M. Seervai, after a thorough survey of case law, expressed the view that 'it is a necessary implication of Articles 60 and 61 that if the council of ministers should advise the president to take action which is contrary to the constitution and the law, or which the ministers are driven to admit is contrary to the constitution and the law, the president should reject such advice and, if necessary, dismiss the ministry which persists in its advice. If in the event he is unable to form another ministry he can direct a dissolution of the house of the people and order a fresh general election'.[2]

Another jurist, M. Hidayatullah, a former Chief Justice of India, described in his memoirs, *My Own Boswell*, how he dealt with the bank nationalization bill when he was asked to sign his assent as acting president. 'The president has certain responsibilities under the Constitution and I wanted to study the Bill before I assented to it ... Unless it was intrinsically wrong or offended the Constitution or procedural rules, the president was bound to assent to it'.[3]

President Shankar Dayal Sharma rejected the prime minister's advice that certain people be nominated to the Rajya Sabha because they did not fulfil the qualifications prescribed by Article 80(3): 'special knowledge or practical experience in respect of such matters as the following namely—literature, science, art and social service'. He went a step further. The newspapers of 21 March 1996 reported that the president had returned two ordinances sent for his signature. One sought to shorten the period for election campaign to two weeks and the other, to make reservations for Dalit Christians.

President Sharma's letter to Prime Minister P.V. Narasimha Rao cogently set out the reasons for his refusal to sign them into law. 'I would like to inform you that independent of the relative intrinsic merits of the ordinances proposed, promulgating these ordinances would appear to be inappropriate and contrary to the canons of constitutional propriety in view of circumstances existing at this particular juncture'.[4]

The ordinances clearly did not conform to the conditions laid down in Article 123: 'circumstances exist which render it necessary for him [the president] to take immediate action'.

Far more stringent are the conditions laid down in Article 356 and far more consequential is a proclamation made by the president under that provision. It enables him to sack an elected state government, prematurely dissolve an elected state assembly, and

[2]Seervai, 4th edn, 1993, vol. 2, p. 2049.
[3]M. Hidayatullah, *My Own Boswell*, Arnold–Heinemann, 1980, p. 242.
[4]*The Times of India*, 21 March 1996.

bring the state under direct central rule, reducing its autonomy to naught. The precondition must be honestly fulfilled if such a drastic action is to be valid: 'a situation has arisen in which the government of the state cannot be carried on in accordance with the provisions of this Constitution'. The word 'cannot' implies impossibility of governance; not difficulty no matter how serious.

Now however it is universally accepted that Article 356 has been systematically abused all these years. Presidents who put their signatures to those proclamations, very many, indeed, most of which were manifestly unconstitutional, bear a heavy responsibility for the wrongs to which they were a party.

President K.R. Narayanan won deserved acclaim for his rejection, on 21 October 1997, of the advice of the council of ministers to impose president's rule in Uttar Pradesh, asking it to reconsider the advice. The following day, the council of ministers decided that 'proceedings under Article 356 need not be undertaken'. Would he have been constitutionally bound to sign the proclamation under Article 356 if the council of ministers had, instead, persisted in its advice? Of course not.

This would have been the clear constitutional position even before the Supreme Court's rulings on 11 March 1994 in the Bommai case.[5] Those rulings make the constitutional position clearer still. Nine judges sat on the Bench which heard the case. Six judgments were delivered on a host of the issues involved. This makes the task of inferring the majority ruling on each issue difficult, though not impossible.

In a brief judgment Justice S. Ratnavel Pandia agreed with the joint and detailed judgment of Justices P.B. Sawant and Kuldip Singh on certain points and on others with the joint and detailed judgment of Justices B.P. Jeevan Reddy and S.C. Agrawal. This is the liberal majority in a broad sense.

To these judgments add one more, briefly in concurrence, by Justice A.M. Ahmadi; Justice K. Ramaswamy wrote a detailed judgment. Justices J.S. Verma and Yogeshwar Dayal wrote a joint judgment but confined to a few points. A majority ruling on crucial points can be culled out from these judgments.

It has taken quite a while for the implications of the rulings in the Bommai case to seep in. What has been totally overlooked,

---

[5] *S.R. Bommai & Ors. v Union of India v Ors.* (1994) 3 SCC.

however, is the fact that they affect the president directly and fortify him in asserting his legitimate discretionary powers. Fundamentally, the court has made judicial review of a proclamation under Article 356 vastly more effective than in the past. As a direct result, while a high court or the Supreme Court's invalidation of and strictures on a proclamation will undoubtedly affect the prestige of the government of India, in an obvious case of abuse the president's prestige will not escape unaffected. People will legitimately ask why he put his signature on a proclamation so obviously unconstitutional.

R.Venkataraman, who blows hot air on constitutional proprieties these days after demitting the office of president in 1992, earned a deserved stricture from the Supreme Court in 1994 in the Bommai case in relation to the proclamation of 21 April 1989 imposing president's rule in Karnataka. It was obvious to all that it was a gross abuse.Venkataraman reserved his criticisms of Rajiv Gandhi for his memoirs. In office he readily did whatever Rajiv bade him to do. Justices Jeevan Reddy and S. C. Agrawal held the action to be 'mala fide and unconstitutional'. Imagine its impact on the prestige of the office of the president and on the incumbent who signed it if he were still in office.

Two other proclamations Venkataraman had signed were also struck down; one relating to Nagaland (1988) and the other to Meghalaya (1991).The Supreme Court has asserted that the courts have a right to: (1) call for the production of records on the basis of which union council of ministers advised the president; (2) to restrain the dissolution of the assembly prior to parliamentary ratification of the proclamation (3) order revival of the assembly and the restoration of the government, even after parliament has approved the proclamation, if the court finds them to be unconstitutional; and (4) to grant interim relief to prevent the holding of elections to the assembly which might defeat a legal challenge to the proclamation under Article 356 by which the assembly had been dissolved. Any chief minister dismissed from office under Article 356 can rush to the high court and secure these reliefs.

Authorities on constitutional law have written of the embarrassment caused to a head of state if he refused dissolution to the prime minister in office but grants it to his successor who, however, is defeated in the elections. It is the prime minister whose advice was rejected who returns to office. A similar predicament awaits a president whose proclamation under Article 356 is nullified and the dismissed chief minister is restored to office along with the revival of the dissolved Assembly.

The gravest source of embarrassment however lies in the production of the records before the courts. Article 74(2) says that 'the question whether any, and if so what, advice was tendered by ministers to the president shall not be inquired into in any court'.

Justices Sawant and Kuldeep Singh ruled:

The validity of the proclamation issued by the president under Article 356(1) is judicially reviewable to the extent of examining whether it was issued on the basis of any material at all or whether the material was relevant or whether the proclamation was issued in the mala fide exercise of the power. When a prima facie case is made out in the challenge to the proclamation, the burden is on the union government to prove that the relevant material did in fact exist; such material may be either the report of the governor or other than the report. Article 74(2) is not a bar against the scrutiny of the material on the basis of which the president had arrived at his satisfaction.'[6]

Justice K. Ramaswamy observed:

By operation of Article 74(2) only the actual advice tendered by the council of ministers gets immunity from production and court shall not inquire into the question whether and if so what advice was tendered by the minister. In other words, the records other than the advice tendered by the minister to the president, if found necessary, may be required to be produced before the constitutional court.'[7]

Justice Jeevan Reddy and S.C. Agrawal held to the same effect:

Article 74(2) merely bars an enquiry into the question whether any, and if so, what, advice was tendered by the ministers to the president. It does not bar the court from calling upon the union council of ministers [union of India] to disclose to the court the material upon which the president had formed the requisite satisfaction. The material on the basis of which advice was tendered does not become part of the advice. Even if the material is looked into by or shown to the president, it does not partake the character of advice. Article 74(2) and Section 123 of the Evidence Act cover different fields. It may happen that while defending the proclamation, the minister or the official concerned may claim the privilege under Section 123. If and when such privilege is claimed, it will be decided on its own merits in accordance with the provisions of Section 123'.[8]

[6]Ibid., p. 148.
[7]Ibid., p. 182.
[8]Ibid., p. 297.

It will be decided by the courts themselves.

Justice Rathnavel Pandia agreed with this conclusion.[9] Thus, a clear majority of six judges in the nine member bench ruled that the material submitted by the government of India to the president can be called for and examined by the courts. Any claim to privilege will also be decided by the courts.

Moreover, no court can fail to take judicial cognizance of claims of deals for sacking state governments or of the fact that a report under Article 356 has emanated from a governor who belongs to the ruling party at the centre which is opposed to the ruling party in the state. Mr Sunder Singh Bhandari's appointment as governor of Bihar was in flagrant breach of the recommendation of the Sarkaria commission.

Once the doors to judicial review are thrown open, everything will be exposed to the scrutiny of the courts and to the glare of public opinion. No government of India can act as arbitrarily as was the case with governments in the past. This does not weaken the authority of the president. It fortifies it.

[9]Ibid., p. 65 (Para 2)

44

The Centre and Law and Order in the States: Article 355[1]

Article 355 was not entirely born in sin, but it was conceived in murky circumstances. In 1948 the process of democratization of the erstwhile princely states had not gone far. The maharajas acceded to the Indian Union in 1947 by signing Instruments of Accession embodying, what they thought were, cast-iron guarantees. They wanted much more, besides. They wanted the Union to protect their thrones lest neighbouring provinces of the former British India or their own people rose in revolt in the altered circumstances. They planted the embryo of Article 355.

The drafting committee of the constituent assembly nursed it and delivered the baby to a surprised assembly. In 1998, Union Home Minister L.K. Advani, finds it a handy weapon with which to meddle in the affairs of states ruled by non-BJP governments. Article 355 reads: 'It shall be the duty of the union to protect every state against external aggression and internal disturbance and to ensure that the government of every state is carried on in accordance with the provisions of this constitution.'

No such provision existed in the draft constitution which the committee submitted to the president of the assembly, Rajendra Prasad, on 21 February 1948. It was published in *the Gazette of India Extraordinary* on 26 February 'for general information'. (That issue of the gazette is now a collector's prize). Article 356, which provides for the imposition of president's rule, did figure in the draft as Article 278. Evidently, none of the distinguished members considered Article 355 to be necessary.

[1] *The Statesman*, 17 July 1998.

The draft constitution elicited notes and memoranda from various individuals and parties. An early response came in the form of a long memorandum signed by the Dewan of Jaipur, V.T. Krishnamachari, the Dewan of Rampur, B.H. Zaidi, Sardar Singhji of Khetri, and Sardar Jaidev Singh. The draft conferred on the union emergency powers of 'an extraordinary nature' which 'do not find any parallel whatsoever in any other federal constitution', they rightly complained. What of the union's duties? 'There is no reference anywhere in the draft to the obligations which necessarily devolve on the union government in such cases.'[2]

Remember, this idea had never occurred to any of the representatives of the provinces. The memorandum suggested insertion of 'a specific clause' in the constitution on these lines: 'It shall be the duty of the union to protect every state against external aggression and, upon a request from the executive government of a state, to protect or restore the duly constituted authorities of that state in the event of domestic violence or insurrection.'

On 24 March 1948 just three members of the drafting committee, including the chairman, B.R. Ambedkar, considered *inter alia* the Maharajas' memo and agreed to insert a new clause which read: 'It shall be the duty of the Union to protect every state against external aggression and domestic violence'[3] One would have thought that this was implicit in the Union's duty to protect the entire country against external aggression and armed insurrection. This decision was reaffirmed in October 1948.[4] Little did Their Highnesses imagine that the vital condition they had stipulated— a prior 'request' from the state government for protection against domestic violence—would be dropped while accepting their bright suggestion.

The constitution of the United States contains precisely such a condition in a stringent form in Article IV, Section 4: 'The United States shall guarantee to every state in this union a republican form of government, and shall protect each of them against invasion, and on application of the legislature or of the executive (when the legislature cannot be convened), against domestic violence.' Section 119 of the Australian Constitution also contains that condition. 'The Commonwealth shall protect every state against invasion and,

[2]B. Shiva Rao, *Framing of India's Constitution*, vol. iv, pp. 210.
[3]Ibid., p. 403.
[4]bid., pp. 367–8.

on the application of the executive government of the state, against domestic violence.'

Ambedkar moved for the adoption of the new provision Article 277 A (Article 355, now) in the constituent assembly on 3 August 1949 together with provisions for imposition of president's rule in the states in Article 278 (now Article 356). He referred to the American and Australian constitutions and said:

All that we propose to do is to add one more clause to the principle enunciated in the American and Australian constitutions; namely, that it shall also be the duty of the union to maintain the constitution in the provinces as enacted by this law. There is nothing new in this and, as I said, in view of the fact that we are endowing the provinces with plenary powers and making them sovereign in their own field, it is necessary to provide that if any invasion of the provincial field is done by this centre, it is in virtue of this obligation.

He proceeded to elucidate the provisions for president's rule. Article 355 and 356 go together.[5]

Article 352 which empowers imposition of Emergency in the country used the words 'internal disturbance' in glaring contrast to 'public order' which is exclusively a state subject. Its abuse by Indira Gandhi in 1975 prompted their replacement, in 1978 by the 44th Constitution Amendment, by the words 'armed rebellion'. She had, through the 42nd Amendment (1976), inserted a new provision, Article 257A, empowering the centre to deploy any central force 'for dealing with any grave situation of law and order in any state'. This was deleted by the 44th Amendment.

The Sarkaria report's comments show how wide off the mark Advani is when he tries desperately to press the words 'internal disturbance' in the service of the BJP's agenda. It said that the expression 'conveys the sense of "domestic chaos" which takes the colour of a security threat from its associate expression "external aggression". Such a chaos could be due to various causes. Large-scale public disorder which throws out of gear the even tempo of administration and endangers the security of the state, is, ordinarily, one such cause.' These comments were made in the section of the report dealing with the 'scope and effect' of Article 355. Imposition of president's rule need not necessarily follow from deployment of central forces in such extreme cases unless the chaos has also led to a 'breakdown of the constitutional machinery of the state', as the report puts it.[6]

On 9 July 1998 the Chief Minister of West Bengal, Jyoti Basu, asked the Prime Minister, Atal Behari Vajpayee, to convene at the earliest a meeting of chief ministers to discuss the correct import of Article 355. He said he had already written to him to ask for a meeting of the inter-state council. Significantly, while each of the BJP's election manifestos of 1989, 1991, and 1996 pledged the establishment of the council to settle all inter-state and centre–state disputes', the pledge was omitted in the 1998 manifesto as well as in the so-called National Agenda.

Experience has shown that the council is too frail a reed to rely upon. Far more effective is the safeguard of public opinion. In 1969 the DMK government of Tamil Nadu set up the Rajamannar committee on centre–state relations. Its report (1971), an extremely able document, went a long way in alerting public opinion, so did the Janata Party government of Karnataka's white paper on the Role of Governors (1983).

As the *primus inter pares,* Jyoti Basu might convene a conference of chief ministers of non-BJP governments to consider the Centre's menacing stand on Article 355. The West Bengal government might place before it a document analysing its implications very much on the lines of its famous memorandum on Centre–State relations published two decades ago. An informed appeal to public opinion will not go in vain. It is the people who are the masters, not the transient ministers in New Delhi. They live on borrowed time, all the time.

[6]Report of the Commission on Centre–States Relation, vol. 1, p. 168.

45

Parliament and Law and Order in the States[1]

I t is singularly unfortunate that, in breach of the rules of procedure of the Lok Sabha and its established practice, the speaker of the Lok Sabha, Mr Shivraj Patil, allowed the Union home minister, Mr S.B. Chavan, to make a statement on 3 August 1993, on the incidents in Calcutta on 21 July. Mr Chavan alleged, in the main, that there was 'excessive use of force by the police'. This is but an aspect of 'public order' which, like the 'police', is exclusively a state subject; unless, of course, the centre's armed forces are involved.

As that authoritative work, *Practice and Procedure of Parliament*, by Messrs T.N. Kaul and S.L. Shakdher, says:

The special type of federal polity adopted by the constitution of India dictates certain norms to be followed in the field of centre–State relations and determines and delimits the jurisdiction of the union parliament in matters like law and order which are appropriately in the province of states' responsibility. There are certain areas however, where the special responsibility of the union parliament is attracted as, for instance, in the matter of welfare of Harijans, even though the central government may not be directly involved. In many border line areas, each case has to be decided on merits. But in case of doubt, it would be most advisable to exercise utmost care and generally, to err in favour of States' autonomy'.[2]

[1] *The Statesman*, 11 August 1993.
[2] See M.N. Kaul and S.L. Shakdher, *Practice and Procedure of Parliament*, Lok Sabha Secretariat, 4th edn, (Delhi: Metropolitan 1991), p. 935–6. The quotation in the article is, however, taken from the text in the third edition.

A whole set of rules (Rules 41 (viii); 58 (iii); and 186 (xiii), respectively), bar questions, adjournment motions and other motions if the subject 'is not primarily the concern of the government of India'. The constitutional position is clear beyond doubt. 'Public order' and 'police' are both exclusively state subjects. (Entries 1 and 2 of state list). This is subject to one exception; namely, the use of the armed forces of the union 'in aid of the civil power' is not involved. If the army, the CRPF or the BSF need to be deployed, it ceases to be an exclusively state subject. The 42nd Amendment removed all doubt. Entry 2A of the union list now covers 'deployment of any armed forces of the union ... in aid of the civil power'.

However, this amendment inserted also Article 257A which read: 'The government of India may deploy an armed force of the union or any other armed force subject to the control of the union for dealing with any grave situation of law and order in any state.' This was advisedly deleted by the 44th Amendment. All we now have is Article 355, which says that 'it shall be the duty of the union to protect every state against external aggression and internal disturbance and to ensure that the government of every State is carried on in accordance with the provisions of this constitution'. The repeal of Article 257A is very significant.

There is a world of difference between a 'grave situation of law and order'—which is deleted—and 'internal disturbance' which remains. It means a disturbance so serious as to affect the very governance of the state; a disturbance which the state government cannot control. The phrase 'internal disturbance' has this meaning; and it was originally used in Article 352, as a condition for a proclamation of emergency. It has been substituted by the expression 'armed rebellion'. The scheme of the constitution becomes clear if the document is read as a whole. Public order is exclusively a state responsibility unless: (a) central aid is sought by the state government, or (b) the breaches of public order have become so grave and prolonged as to amount to the 'internal disturbance' contemplated by the founding fathers.

On 4 August 1949, Dr Ambedkar told the constituent assembly that Article 355 and its corollary Article 356 (president's rule) cannot be invoked to cure 'misgovernment' in the states: 'Whether there is good government or not in the province is not for the centre to determine, I am quite clear on this point'[3] This was the basis on which the provision for president's rule was adopted by the assembly.

The Sarkaria commission, despite its centrist bias, emphasized:

It is important to distinguish 'internal disturbance' from ordinary problems relating to law and order. Maintenance of public order, excepting where it requires the use of the armed forces of the union, is the responsibility of the states (Entry 1, List II). That being the case, 'internal disturbance' within the contemplation of Article 355 cannot be equated with mere breaches of public peace. In terms of gravity and magnitude, it is intended to connote a far more serious situation. The difference between a situation of public disorder and 'internal disturbance' is not only one of degree but also of kind. While the later is an aggravated form of public disorder which *endangers the security* of the state, the former involves relatively minor breaches of the peace of purely local significance ... Internal disturbance' [has the] ... characteristics of domestic chaos and *inter alia* endangers the security of the State.[4]

Even a partisan view of the events of 21 July 1992 in Calcutta cannot support the charge that they endangered 'the security of the state'. The centre's responsibility was not attracted even by the farthest stretching of the provisions of the constitution. If, nonetheless, the union home minister, Mr Chavan, chose to descend on Calcutta, it was only to indulge in petty politicking with the authority of his office.

The facts are gross. Aided by lumpen elements, Miss Mamata Banerjee publicly declared that her aim was to lay 'siege' to Writers' Building, the headquarters of the state government. Breaches of prohibitory orders under section 144 of the CrPC were the least of the offences committed. The casualty figures are significant: 12 died in police firing while 65 were admitted to the city hospitals. Of these, while 12 had bullet injuries, 19 were injured by bomb splinters, one by pellets, and all others in brickbatting; 88 policemen were injured, 21 officers and 38 policemen were hospitalized.

As Mr Somnath Chatterjee noted, on 3 August Mr Chavan visited 'only injured Congress activists and not wounded policemen'. Nor had he a word of criticism of the fact that his partymen 'were armed with pipe guns and bombs'. Mr Chatterjee can hardly be faulted

[3]CAD, vol. iv, pp. 176–7.

[4]Report of the Commission on Centre-State Relations, part I, p. 170, para 6.3.13.

for alleging that Mr Chavan's 'offensive is in retaliation to the no-trust motion', for Mr Chavan's statement in Calcutta on 1 August and in the Lok Sabha on 3 August fully confirm the charge.

Mr Chavan had the temerity to ask West Bengal's chief minister, Mr Jyoti Basu, to hold a judicial inquiry into the police firing on 21 July while he has turned a deaf ear to all appeals for the judicial probe into the systematic killing of persons taken into custody by his paramilitary forces in Kashmir. The deliberate torching of homes in Sopore and Lal Chowk—which were never witnessed even in Punjab—call for judicial inquiry at the highest level. Not content with this, Mr Chavan hinted that the centre could undertake a judicial probe on its own but preferred the state to take this action.

Mr Chavan would do well to remember the warning delivered by the Sarkaria report. If, by reason of Entry 45 in the Concurrent list, the centre can institute inquires into matters in the state and Concurrent lists, 'on parity of reasoning, a state government also is competent to set up a Commission for Inquiry into charges of corruption against union ministers in respect of any matter in (State) list II, if not in respect of any matter in (Concurrent) list III.' Since 'abuse of power' and 'favouritism' are forms of corruption recognized by several commisions of inquiry, Mr Chavan should not provoke West Bengal to set up a commission of inquiry into his own conduct in Calcutta on 1 August.

This is by no means the first instance when, to use Mr Jyoti Basu's words, Mr Chavan 'has spoken like a Congressman, but not as a responsible home minister'. There is however something far worse about the episode that deserves note. It marks a revival of the practice which Mrs Indira Gandhi and Mr Rajiv Gandhi had nourished: the abuse of the centre's powers for partisan ends in the states. The most notorious instances were Mrs Gandhi's exploitation of the disturbances in Narainpur in Uttar Pradesh in February 1980 and Mr Gandhi's of the Karamchedu incidents in Andhra Pradesh in July 1985.

Mr Chavan has accused the Calcutta police of 'excessive use of force', the West Bengal government of intolerance and of politicizing the state police. The state of the CBI should deter him from casting this particular stone. That apart, two questions demand an answer. One is constitutional, the other political. First, what right has any minister of the government of India at all to go to a state on inspection after incidents of the kind that occurred on 21 July?

Related to this is the question of whether the centre has any right whatever under the constitution even to call for reports on such matters that the constitution does not make it a monitor. It establishes a federal polity. The political question is: Would Mr Chavan have performed thus unless he had been put to the job by Prime Minister Narasimha Rao? This does not augur well for the future.

46
The Centre's Fact-finding
Teams in the States[1]

Public memory is proverbially short. On 7 October 1992 the newly constituted Rapid Action Force (RAF) became operational under the command of the Central Reserve Police Force which had been set up under the CRPF Act, 1949. The RAF's specific task was to assist in quelling those communal riots where central help became necessary.

A mere five days later, on 12 October 1992, the BJP general secretary Pramod Mahajan went so far as to declare that the BJP-ruled states would not allow the RAF into their territories. He told mediapersons at Aurangabad that the party top brass had decided to ban the RAF's entry in Uttar Pradesh, Madhya Pradesh, Himachal Pradesh, and Rajasthan. He cited two reasons. One was the likelihood of its abuse by the centre for political ends. The other was that law and order is a purely state subject under the constitution.

The BJP-dominated government at the Centre needs to be reminded today of its stand on the RAF as it faces pressures from its partners in the rag-tag and bobtail alliance to use central power to destabilize the state governments to which they are opposed. The centre is in a fix. Gone are the days when Article 356 of the constitution, which provides for the imposition of president's rule in the states, can be abused for partisan ends. The Supreme Court's ruling in the Bommai case put an end to that in six significant ways.[2] First, the court is far more alert than ever before to perceive

---

[1]This article, written in the context of the BJP sending a fact-finding team to Tamil Nadu in 1998, was published in *Frontline*, 3 July 1998.

[2]S.R. Bommai (1994) 3 SCC 1.

mala fides, in view of a sustained record of sheer abuse of Article 356.

Secondly, it has construed the crucial test prescribed by Article 356, 'a situation has arisen in which the government cannot be carried on in accordance with the provisions of this constitution' to mean the virtual impossibility of, not difficulty in, governance.

Thirdly, it has not only reasserted but widened the ambit of the power of judicial review to a degree that provides a deterrent against abuse. The court can call for the files. Article 74(2) says that 'the question whether any, and if so what, advice was tendered by ministers to the president shall not be inquired into in any court'. The Supreme Court has ruled that this exempts from judicial scrutiny only the advice proper but *not the material on which the advice was based*. Ergo, it can call for the files to examine for itself whether the material was germane to Article 356 or reflected mala fides. (The centre's claim of privilege will itself be subject to judicial determination.) The implications are obvious. The centre's calculations will be exposed to the glare of publicity.

Fourthly, a state assembly cannot be dissolved until each house of parliament has ratified the president's proclamation as clause (3) to Article 356 requires. This gives the State government precious time to act.

Fifthly, while no interim injunction can be granted against the promulgation of the proclamation, an interim injunction can be granted against elections being held to the assembly pursuant to the proclamation in order to avert a fait accompli.

Lastly, even if the proclamation is ratified by parliament and the assembly dissolved, the high courts and the Supreme Court have the power not only to set aside the order of dissolution and order the revival of the assembly *but also order the restoration to power of the dismissed state government*.

Since invoking Article 356 is now a daunting task, the BJP regime has taken recourse to pressure tactics. It has arrogated to itself the right to monitor the 'law and order situation in the states' and to send with fanfare, not unmixed with intimidatory hints, teams of officials to call the state government to account. Tamil Nadu was the first in the series, but it is unlikely to be the last. The states are put in a bind. If they refuse, à la Pramod Mahajan in 1992, they will be seen by many as putting themselves in the wrong. If they receive the visitors, they risk an adverse pre-arranged verdict. Thanks to upright officials, the ploy did not work in Chennai. Next time, the team will be carefully selected.

Constitutionally, the Centre has no business sending such investigative teams at all. It might be asked that if a team of journalists or civil libertarians can go and inspect the state of things in a State or city—as, indeed, they *ought* to do in the Shiv Sena's fiefdom, Mumbai—why cannot the government of India? The answer is simple. Governments are creatures of the constitution and must act within the limits it prescribes.

The first two entries in the state list of topics of legislation are relevant. The first reads thus: 'I. Public Order (but not including the use of any naval, military or air force or any other armed force of the Union or of any other force subject to the control of the union or of any contingent or unit thereof in aid of the civil power.')

The second reads: 'Police (including railway and village police) subject to the provisions of Entry 2A of List 1.' Under entry 2A of List 1, the Union list, the centre has authority over 'deployment of any armed force of the union or any other force subject to the control of the union or any contingent or unit thereof in any state in aid of the civil power, powers, jurisdiction, privileges and liabilities of the members of such forces while on such deployment.'

These entries make public order and police *exclusively* a state subject,—unless the situation deteriorates to such a degree that Central aid becomes necessary.

As the Sarkaria commission said, 'A state government has the sole responsibility for maintaining public order except where the use of the armed forces of the union is called for.' Sections 129 and 130 of the Criminal Procedure Code enable states to seek the aid of the armed forces of the union to disperse an 'unlawful assembly,' a riotous mob.[3]

It is very significant that Article 257A, which was inserted in the constitution by the 42nd Amendment during the emergency in 1976, was deleted by the 44th Amendment enacted in 1978. It read: 'The government of India may deploy any armed force of the union or any other force subject to the control of the union for dealing with any grave situation of law and order in any state.' This was deleted deliberately. All we now have is Article 355, which says

[3]Report of the Commission on Centre-State Relations, p. 197, Para 7.3.02.

that 'it shall be the duty of the Union to protect every State against external aggression and internal disturbance and to ensure that the government of every state is carried on in accordance with the provisions of this constitution.'

There is a world of difference between the expressions a 'grave situation of law and order,' which was deleted, and 'internal disturbance which the state government cannot control'. The phrase 'internal disturbance' was used in Article 352 originally as a condition for the proclamation of a state of emergency. It has been substituted by the expression 'armed rebellion'.

Doubtless, Entry 2A read with Article 355 empowers the centre to send its forces of its own accord and deploy them even against the wishes of a state government; provided, however, that the situation is one of 'internal disturbance'. However, it has no right to invoke Article 356 in such a situation unless the governance of the state is rendered impossible and there is a collapse of the constitutional machinery. Central forces are sent to aid, not to supplant, a state government.

The Sarkaria report's observations are very apt. Even when it lawfully sends its force, the centre 'cannot assume the sole responsibility for dealing with an internal disturbance by superseding or excluding the state police and other authorities responsible for maintaining public order. Neither can the union government deploy, in contravention of the wishes of a state government, its armed forces to deal with a relatively less serious public order problem which is unlikely to escalate and which the state is confident of tackling.'

These dicta must be read in the context of the fundamentals of India's federal polity which Dr B.R. Ambedkar expounded in the constituent assembly. He said on 4 August 1949: 'Whether there is good government or not in the province is not for the centre to determine. I am quite clear on the point.' A day earlier, on 3 August 1949, when the provisions for president's rule in the states came up for discussion, Dr Ambedkar was at pains to emphasize: 'I think it is agreed that our constitution, notwithstanding the many provisions which are contained in it whereby the centre has been given powers to override the provinces, nonetheless is a federal constitution and when we say that the constitution is a federal constitution it means this, that *the provinces are as sovereign in their field which is left to them by the constitution as the centre is in the field which is assigned to them.'*[4] Hence the necessity for explicit provisions concerning union intervention, in Article 356 of the constitution (emphasis added, throughout).

When the constituent assembly had completed its deliberations, Dr Ambedkar replied to the debate on 25 November 1949.

He said:

'As to the relations between the centre and the states, it is necessary to bear in mind the fundamental principle on which it rests. The basic principle of federalism is that the legislative and executive authority is partitioned between the centre and the ctates, not by any law to be made by the centre, but by the constitution itself. This is what [the] Constitution does. *The States under our constitution are in no way dependent upon the centre for their legislative or executive authority. The centre and the states are coequal in this matter.'*[5]

No administrative practice can override the constitution. Some day, a state might well question the right of the union home minister or the home secretary to call for reports from them on the law and order situation. The rules of procedure of both houses of parliament bar questions, adjournment motions and other motions if the subject is 'not primarily the concern of the government of India', for instance, law and order in a state. It is time that, as in the days of Indira Gandhi and Rajiv Gandhi, the states ruled by parties other than those in power at the centre get together and assert the states' rights under the constitution.

[4]CAD, vol. ix, p. 133.
[5]CAD, vol. xi, p. 976.

47
The Army and Law and Order[1]

The Defence Minister, Mr Sharad Pawar's sharp criticism, on 28 July 1991 of the frequent deployment of the army on the request of the state governments to quell disturbances has been widely welcomed. It would however be unfortunate if matters are allowed to rest where they are without devising checks against this pernicious practice.

The latest annual report of the ministry of defence for 1990–1 was published shortly after Mr Pawar spoke. Every such report has a chapter entitled 'Cooperation between armed forces and civil authorities', mentioning broadly the assistance that the armed forces render to civil authorities for the maintenance of law and order, of essential services, and in rescue and relief operations. The relevant chapter (XII) in the latest report makes particularly depressive reading. We may leave aside the special cases of Kashmir, Assam, Manipur, and perhaps even Meghalaya which was rocked by inter-tribal violence in September 1990.

Two case that the report cites however merit special notice: 'Army assistance was rendered to the state governments in Uttar Pradesh, Himachal Pradesh, Rajasthan, Punjab, Haryana, Bihar and Gujarat in the wake of widespread agitation against the implementation of the Mandal commission recommendations, during September–October, 1990.'

The other was: 'The requisite assistance was extended to the States of Rajasthan. Gujarat, Uttar Pradesh, Haryana, Bihar, Andhra

[1] *The Indian Express,* 30 August 1991.

Pradesh, Assam, and Jammu and Kashmir during the agitation arising out of the controversy relating to Ram Janmabhoomi–Babri Masjid dispute. Army also assisted civil authorities in the maintenance of law and order in Uttar Pradesh, Andhra Pradesh, and Gujarat during communal riots in December, 1990.' Both involved people's emotions and both were the result of sheer ineptitude by the governments concerned.

Lt. Gen, P.N. Hoon (retd) felt so strongly about this that, on 29 September 1990, he issued a statement from Chandigarh questioning the deployment of the troops for handling the students' agitation against the Mandal report. It was as cogently argued as it was strongly worded. He rightly pointed out that the sight of troops on the roads checking curfew passes of people, including women and children, and performing traffic duties adversely affected the public image that the army enjoys as a force. The army should be brought out only under extreme circumstances as when anti-national forces threaten to destroy the country's fabric and the police and paramilitary forces fail to pacify or curb the situation. Lt. Gen. Hoon said it was sickening to find jeeps with mounted machine guns flitting around the countryside trying to frighten school and college students.

The army was trained to 'shoot to kill' and it is grievously callous on the part of the civil administration to embroil it in such situations. What do the civil authorities desire to achieve? 'Get the problem off their hands and put it in the lap of the army? We all know that this gallant, disciplined force will carry out assigned tasks. Is it fair?' People in power should remember that the army does not carry 'lathis'.

The indictment was devastating and deserved. The defence ministry's report for 1989–90 reminds us that the army's assistance was invoked not only to control communal riots in Rajasthan and Bihar but also in the conduct of elections in Tamil Nadu, besides Nagaland and Mizoram. Previous reports tell the same uninspiring tale. The reports provide only the broad categories of assistance. Statistics fill in the details According to one estimate, between 1951 and 1970 the army was called upon to suppress domestic violence approximately 475 times, but between 1981 and 1985 it was deployed 369 times.

What checks does Mr Sharad Pawar propose to devise against the ready, escapist recourse to the services of the armed forces for quelling public disorder? He mentioned one. The state governments will be asked to bear the expenses of deploying the army whenever they call the army in their states. Few of them will however be deterred, for few are particularly oppressed by scruples about how the people's money is misspent. The malady is a grave one. As Mr Pawar pointed out, it saps the morale of the troops and also impairs the authority of the civilian administration.

Perhaps some norms could be devised to deter abuse of the present law which does make it all too easy for the states to call in the army.'It has become a fashion to pick up the phone and ask for deployment of the army', Mr Pawar ruefully recalled. Often troops were not even used. How easy it is to seek their help was well brought out in a report on one of our gravest riots ever when the army was not called in in time. It is the PUCL–PUDR report on the Delhi riots from 31 October to 10 November 1984, entitled 'Who are the guilty?' Failure to deploy the army in such a situation was culpable, especially since the law makes the deployment so easy.

Section 130(2) of the Code of Criminal Procedure, 1973, empowers the executive magistrate of the highest rank who is present to 'require any officer in command of any group of persons belonging to the armed forces' to disperse an unlawful assembly which poses a threat to 'public security', not 'law and order'. Sub-section (3) adds: 'Every such officer shall obey such requisition in such manner as he thinks fit' and enjoins him to use 'as little force and do as little injury to persons and property' as possible. Note, that the commanding officer, while bound to respond to the magistrate's requisition, is free to act in accordance with his own professional judgment. It is not open to the government to direct him how to accomplish the objective of restoring 'public security'.

Section 131 goes a step further. 'When the public security is manifestly endangered by any such assembly and no executive magistrate can be communicated with', any commissioned or gazetted officer of the armed forces can of his own account disperse the unlawful assembly with the help of the armed forces at his command. Once communication with the magistrate becomes practicable he must inform him of the action he had taken 'and shall thenceforward obey the instructions of the magistrate as to whether he shall or shall not continue such action'.

These statutory provisions are supplemented by the Defence Services' Regulations. They provide that 'when the services of troops are required by the civil authorities, the local military commander shall first obtain through authorized channels the approval of the central government to their employment.' If the government should refuse to accord its approval, is the local military commander absolved of his clear duty under the law Section 130(3) that he 'shall obey' the requisition by the magistrate? The regulations provide also that 'in case of an emergency, when reference to the central government would entail delay, the local military authority will comply immediately as far as possible with the demand, reporting its action at once through authorized channels for confirmation'.

There appears to be a conflict between Sections 130(3) and 131 of the Criminal Procedure Code and the Defence Services Regulations. In any event, Sections 130 and 131, which were first enacted in 1898, call for a review in consultation with the states and the defence services in the light of the actual practice in recent years. In Britain, when a chief officer of police believes that his force can no longer deal with a threat to public order, he contacts, not the armed forces, but the home office. The home secretary and the defence secretary put their heads together and decide on the request. In extreme cases, the prime minister and the cabinet take the decision. The armed forces then coordinate their operations with the police.

As Sir Robert Mark, the commissioner of the metropolitan police, explained authoritatively in 1976, 'such assistance was formerly sought by police from the magistracy rather than from the home office, but whatever the legal position the present practice reflects the emergence of a professional, well-organized police service'. In the nineteenth century the 'civil power' which could call in the armed forces was the local magistracy, not the home office. Sections 130 and 131, which are taken from the Criminal Procedure Code of 1898, reflect British practice in the nineteenth century.

A suitable revision of Sections 130 and 131 of the Code will provide a far more effective check. There is another aspect to the issue. The constitution makes public order exclusively a state subject but this does not include the use of any of the armed services of the union 'in aid of civil power'. The states are justifiably resentful of central encroachments into their domain. When however they invoke the aid of the armed forces they invite central intervention and cannot complain about it.

48

The Governor's Message to the Assembly and the Speaker[1]

'On a point of order, how will it explain the position of the governors and the ministers of the state where discretionary powers have been allowed to be used by the governors?' Interjected Mr Mohammed Tahir in the constituent assembly on 30 December 1948 just when Dr Ambedkar was elaborating on his remark that 'under a parliamentary system of government, there are only two prerogatives which the king or head of the state may exercise. One is the appointment of the prime minister and the other is the dissolution of Parliament.' In this context the doctor's reply to Mr Tahir is significant: '*The position of the governor is exactly the same as the position of the president*'.[2]

Those who are enthusing over the recent developments in UP, or who connive at skulduggery elsewhere, ought to bear Dr Ambedkar's dictum in mind. Apart from a few matters expressly mentioned in the constitution, the governor as head of state is bound by the same rules and conventions of the parliamentary system as those which apply to the president. Some precedents set in the states may be invoked at the centre. The moral stature of politicians is not much higher there than that of the breed in the states.

The UP governor, Mr Moti Lal Vora, enjoyed no higher power of dismissal of Mr Mulayam Singh Yadav as Chief Minister than does President Shankar Dayal Sharma in respect of Prime Minister P.V. Narasimha Rao. Mr Vora's tutors in New Delhi overlooked the

[1] This article was written in the context of the unsavoury events in the UP assembly in 1995, and was published in the *The Statesman*, 29 and 30 June 1995.
[2] CAD, vol. vii, p. 1158.

possibility of its citation as precedent by a president in the future.

In retrospect, it is clear that had he allowed Mr Yadav to prove his majority, albeit in a very short time, he would have deservedly been defeated. Instead, on 3 June 1995 Mr Vora dismissed him in flagrant violation of the Supreme Court's ruling in the Bommai case delivered only a year earlier by a nine-member bench.[3]

Of them, only five spoke on the floor test. Justice P.B. Sawant and Kuldip Singh said that 'that *alone* is the constitutionally ordained forum for seeking openly and objectively the claims and counter-claims' of support in the legislature. 'When such demonstration is possible, it is not open to bypass it and instead depend upon the subjective satisfaction of the governor *or the president*'. Note, that they properly placed the two on a par, as did Dr Ambedkar. They added: 'It is possible that on some rare occasions, the floor test may be *impossible*, although it is difficult to envisage such situation. Even assuming that there arises one, it should be obligatory on the governor, in such circumstances, to state in writing the reasons for not holding the floor test'. Exemption should, thus, be on the ground of impossibility, not difficulty. Impossibility of the legislature's democratic functioning might be a ground for president's rule. No such situation existed in Lucknow.

Justice B.P. Jeevan Reddy and S.C. Agrawal were of the same view. They pointed out that 'minority governments are not unknown', and said as emphatically as their other two colleagues, 'Wherever a doubt arises, whether the council ministers has lost the confidence of the house, the *only* way of testing it is on the floor of the house except in an extraordinary situation where because of all-pervasive violence, the governor comes to the conclusion— and records the same in his report—that for the reasons mentioned by him, a free vote is not possible in the house.'

Since Justice S. Ratnavel Pandian concurred with Justices Reddy and Agrawal, a majority of 5–4 gave the ruling. None of the others, bar one judge, spoke on it. By the established rules 'it must be taken that all of them agreed in it', as an English judge put it. There is a clear majority ruling on the floor test as the only one, bar very rare exceptions. This is 'the law declared by the Supreme Court' under Article 141 of the Constitution.

Justice K. Ramaswamy alone was of the view that 'the floor test

[3](1994) 3 SCC 1.

may be one consideration which the governor may keep in view. But whether or not to resort to it would depend on the prevailing situation. The possibility of horse-trading is also to be kept in view having regard to the prevailing political situation.' Indeed, in his view, 'a floor-test may provide impetus for corruption and rank force and violence by musclemen or wrongful confinement or volitional captivity of legislators occurs till the date of the floor test in the house, to gain majority support on the floor of the house.'

This is an accurate description of both: the violence let loose by Mr Mulayam Singh Yadav and the confinement by Miss Mayawati and the BJP of their legislators, whether in 'wrongful confinement or volitional captivity' as the judge so well expressed it. That should however prompt correction of the situation, not bending of the rules of the game. The malaise affects not only a vote of confidence but any vote on any matter on which feelings run high. The presidential system is no cure. In the parliamentary system governments are toppled by politicians of easy virtue; in the presidential system the entire edifice will collapse—they will not allow the passage of any budget or law, leaving the president high and dry.

We are up against an age-old truth: 'How can a representative assembly work for good if its members can be bought, or if their excitability of temperament, uncorrected by public discipline or private self-control, makes them incapable of calm deliberation, and they resort to manual violence on the floor of the house, or shoot at one another with rifles?' John Stuart Mill is not in fashion[4] but he is relevant. So is Dr Ambedkar: 'If things go wrong under the new constitution, the reason will not be that we had a bad constitution', he said in the constituent assembly on 4 November 1948. 'What we will have to say is that man was vile.'[5]

That vileness is not confined to any one state or region. Consider the occurrences in Tamil Nadu, for instance; nor is it absent in New Delhi which played its habitual role in Lucknow. The developments in UP after Mr Yadav's dismissal merit study because they raise vital issues of constitutional law and propriety.

On 4 June 1995 legislators gave three notices of motions for no-confidence against the UP Speaker, Mr Dhani Ram Varma. They

[4]John Stuart Mill, *Utilitarianism: Liberty, Representative Government*, Everyman's Library, 1968, p. 192.
[5]CAD, vii, p. 44

had ample reason to do so. The assembly was due to meet on 19 June. He claimed on that day that he had dismissed all of them earlier on 7 June. The secretary of the assembly, Mr Prem Chandra Saxena, circulated the 'agenda as amended by the speaker' listing only two items for the two-day special session; obituary references on 19 June and the vote of confidence in the government on 20 June. Missing were two others: the vote of no-confidence against the speaker and 'taking up of formal business of the government' though it had been listed by its law department. Twenty-one ordinances were involved.

The speaker set up on 17 June a panel of presiding officers for the Assembly comprising two members, both close to the former chief minister, having dissolved five days earlier the representative 10-member panel. He played similar tricks with the Business Advisory Committee. Faced with this situation, the governor sent a message to the Assembly, on 17 June, in purported exercise of his powers under Article 175(2), prescribing an agenda with the motion of no-confidence against the speaker as the first item and a rider that he should not occupy the chair while it was discussed. The vote of confidence in the government was to follow this.

The following day, Sunday 18 June the Business Advisory Commission, presided over by the speaker, sent the message back to the governor for review. He declined and returned it. 'My instructions are for the house and not for any individual. It is up to the house to take further action.' The atmosphere and the state of the service was well reflected in the remarks which the governor's principal secretary, Mr Sushil C. Tripathi, made on 18 June when asked how the impasse could be resolved: 'One way could be physically evicting Mr Varma', the speaker.

On 19 June, no sooner had the assembly met, Mr Varma declared: 'I hold the assembly session called on the advice of this unconstitutionally formed government as illegal and adjourn the house *sine die*,' and walked away. The assembly proceeded unanimously to elect a new presiding officer, Mr Barkhu Ram Varma of the BSP, to conduct the day's business. The Samajwadi Party members led by Mr M.S. Yadav, had walked out. Obituary references over, the assembly adjourned to the following day.

On 20 June the house unanimously adopted the motion of no-confidence against the speaker and removed him from office. It adjourned for an hour. Thereupon, the governor appointed Mr Barkhu

Ram Varma as the pro tem speaker under Article 180(1). The new speaker is to be elected at the next session of the assembly. The house reconvened and passed a vote of confidence in the Mayawati government. 249 of the 279 members present voted in favour.

There cannot be the slightest doubt as to the assembly's lack of confidence in Mr Dhani Ram Varma or its confidence in the Mayawati government. There is grave doubt on two constitutional issues—the validity of the governor's message on 17 June and the removal of the speaker on 20 June and, relatedly, the proceedings on 19 June. There is also grave disquiet at reported doctoring of the assembly's proceedings on 19 June in order to expunge from them the speaker's order adjourning the house on the ground that none had heard it. It was audible to all who had ears to hear and was reported verbatim by press persons present in the press gallery above.

No sooner had the speaker, Mr D. R. Varma, left the house on 19 June than Mr Rajendra Kumar Gupta, Parliamentary Affairs Minister in the BSP government, said: 'As the speaker had left the house for *unknown reasons* and the governor had sent a message for the conduct of the proceedings, I propose the name of Mr Barkhu Ram Varma.' Thereafter, the secretary of the assembly moved it for voice vote. The chair, already occupied by Mr Verma, declared the resolution passed. Another resolution stated that the house would meet the following day under his chairmanship. A third resolution, also adopted unanimously, rescinded the proceedings of the house after Vande Mataram had been sung, i.e. the speaker's order of adjournment. A Congress(I) MLA, Mr Pramod Tiwari, was the first to claim that the speaker's words could not be understood. The refrain was picked up at Raj Bhavan.

A ruling by the Supreme Court in the case concerning the crisis in Punjab in 1968 and by a full bench of the Madras high court in 1973 help to resolve both issues—the legality of the Governor's message and the removal of the speaker. The facts in both cases are relevant.

On 6 March 1968 two motions expressing lack of confidence in the speaker of the Punjab assembly, Lt. Col. Joginder Singh Mann, were admitted. He promised to fix a date for discussion. They very next day, however, he ruled them to be bad in law 'and should be deemed to have not been moved at all'. A pandemonium ensued. The speaker adjourned the house for two months, making the passage of the budget before 1 April impossible. He had been elected when the UF Ministry, led by Mr Gurnam Singh, was sworn in after the 1967 elections. The defection of 18 MLAs led to its replacement in November 1967 by the Gill ministry.

On 11 March the governor prorogued the house under Article 174(a). On 13 March he promulgated the Punjab Legislature (Regulation of Procedure in relation to the Financial Business) Ordinance. The following day he not only summoned the assembly to meet on 18 March but sent a message under Article 175(2) directing it to consider the financial business under four specified heads. The ordinance, overriding the rules, forbade adjournment of the house pending completion of the financial business except by a vote of the house itself. Any adjournment otherwise was to be 'null and void'.

When the assembly met on 18 March, the speaker read out the governor's message. The ordinance was placed on the table of the house. The speaker ruled that the house was prorogued, in law, on 18 not 11 March; accordingly, the summons to meet was void. The earlier adjournment stood. He left the house whereupon the deputy speaker occupied the chair. The financial business was completed; a resolution for the speaker's removal was moved and leave was granted.

The Supreme Court ruled that the assembly had been lawfully prorogued on 11 March and properly summoned. The speaker sought 'to nullify the ordinance by a ruling which he was not competent to give. Therefore, his ruling was not only not final, but utterly null and void and of no effect'. The continuation of the proceedings by his deputy was valid; so was the passage of the budget. 'The speaker was not sure of his own position in a house in which he had probably lost a sustaining majority', the court remarked.

The Supreme Court did not consider the validity of the governor's message since, evidently, no one contested it. Article 175(2) reads: '(2) The governor may send messages to the house or houses of the legislature of the state, whether with respect to a Bill then pending in the legislature or otherwise, and a house to which any message is so sent shall with all convenient despatch consider any matter required by the message to be taken into consideration.' There is a clear duty cast on the legislature to 'consider' the message; its freedom to decide on its contents is not curtailed. Article 86(2) has an identical provision with regard to the president and parliament. Rule 23 of the rules of procedure and conduct of business in the Lok Sabha obligates the speaker ('shall') to read the president's message to the house and give necessary directions in regard to the procedure to be followed for its consideration. He is empowered even to suspend or vary the rules to the extent this is necessary. Rule 21 of the UP Assembly's rules embodies a similar provision.[6]

The Madras high court ruled explicitly on the governor's message. It is a directive to all concerned, is at once a mandate and one pregnant with details as to the subjects to be discussed in the assembly session. Governor Vora's message of 17 June was, therefore, in order. It was addressed to the assembly. Neither the speaker nor the Business Advisory Committee had any right to return it, even for 'review'. The assembly alone could. The speaker was bound to read it to the house. Instead, he ruled that the government having been 'unconstitutionally formed', it could not advise the governor to summon it. Shades of the Speaker of the West Bengal assembly, Mr B.K. Bannerjee's ruling on the PDF ministry in 1967.

As a high authority, Bourinot, has viewed it: 'The speaker will not give a decision upon a constitutional question, nor decide a question of law though the same be raised on a point of order or privilege'.[7] The speaker can rule on matters of procedure, not on the constitutional validity of a Bill, still less of a ministry's assumption of power. That is for the courts of law to decide. Mr Dhani Ram Varma returned a lawful message, gave a grossly improper ruling on the ministry and did something else which Mr N.A. Palkhiwala has tellingly pointed out. He adjourned the house when a no-confidence motion against him was pending. 'He cannot prevent a discussion on the issue.' The adjournment had no legal force.

If the speaker's adjournment of the house on 19 June was an abuse of power, how valid was his removal? We must ignore any doctoring of the proceedings and proceed on the basis that he did adjourn the house. The Supreme Court, having ruled that the Punjab speaker's adjournment of the assembly was void, approved implicitly the continuance of the proceedings thereafter by his deputy.

The Madras precedent is far more direct. The ruling DMK split in 1972 when MGR left to form the ADMK. On 13 November 1972, the assembly met with Mr K.A. Mathialagan in the chair as its speaker. There were two motions before it, one of no-confidence in the government and the other for his removal, yet he adjourned the

[6] *The State of Punjab v Sat Pal Dang* AIR 1969, SC 903.
[7] A.R. Mukherjee, op. cit., p. 271.

house to 5 December. His sympahties with MGR were no secret. In all, 183 members signed a petition for his removal. The governor prorogued the assembly on 14 November which the speaker unsuccessfully challenged in the court. On 16 November notices of motions for the speaker's removal were given. On 28 November the governor summoned the assembly to meet on 2 December and the following day he sent a message to the assembly under Article 175(2) listing the business to be transacted. The assembly met on 2 December and notice of a censure motion against the government was given by MGR in the morning. The high court noted that there was pandemonium and confusion during the session. The speaker was aware of the motion for his removal. 'With this consciousness he occupied the chair and he has therefore to face the limitations of such occupancy', words which are very apt in the case of Mr D.R. Varma on 19 June. He was aware of the governor's message. 'It was therefore the primordial duty of the speaker ... to obey such a mandate.' Instead, he allowed MGR to move the censure motion against the Karunanidhi government.

The following observations by the court are very relevant to the UP episode:

A vacancy in the office of the speaker is created by Thiru N. Veerasami's rising after question hour and moving the resolution for removal of the speaker. ...The petitioner [the speaker], for reasons better known to himself did not allow such a motion. Under Article 181(I), at any sitting of the legislative assembly while any resolution for the removal of the speaker from this office is under consideration, the speaker shall not, though he is present, preside. In such contingency, the provisions of Article 180(2) shall apply in relation to every such sitting as if the speaker is absent. It is in those circumstances that the deemed vacancy was appreciated by the house and the leader of the house in consequence thereof sought the leave of the house through the deputy speaker for the latter to occupy the chair and conduct the proceedings thereafter.

The court ruled:

A resolution for the removal of the speaker becomes operative when a notice of motion for the removal of the speaker is given and is taken up for consideration. *Eo instanti* when such a resolution comes up for consideration there is a deemed vacancy under the provisions of the constitution and the speaker even though he is physically present is said to be constitutionally absent and cannot, therefore, be the presiding officer of the assembly from that moment .... He ceased to be a speaker when the motion for his removal was taken up for consideration.[8]

In this case, the speaker was physically present in the house and challenged 'parallel' proceedings by his deputy. In UP he gave a patently invalid ruling and quit. The UP assembly was as entitled to proceed further as were the assemblies of Punjab and Madras after their speakers' equally void rulings. In Madras the speaker's attempt 'to expunge certain proceedings from the Debates' was held to be 'without power'. Similar attempts in UP by others deserve censure.

What emerges from these three cases from 1968 to 1995 is the politicization of the office of the speaker, and it is in this highly politicized office that the anti-defection law consciously vests the power to decide disputes—in the interests of the ruling party.

[8]*K.A. Mathialagan v P. Srinivasan* AIR 1973 Madras 371 at 382 (Para 14)

49
Renewing President's Rule[1]

Regardless of the outcome of the recent parleys, the issues that arose in the constitutional crises in Uttar Pradesh in October call for close study. There is one sure test for judging the integrity and soundness of Governor Romesh Bhandari's report and the government of India's decision to impose president's rule in UP on 17 October 1996. Were a similar configuration of political parties to arise in the Lok Sabha after a general election, which of the imperfect options available could the president legitimately take?

As Dr B.R. Ambedkar authoritatively said in the constituent assembly on 30 December 1948 with regard to the appointment of the head of government and the dissolution of the legislature, 'the position of the Governors is exactly the same as the position of the President'.

Unlike Pakistan's constitution, there is no provision in ours for President's rule at the Centre. In UP the option of president's rule was constitutionally not available on 17 October either. President's rule was proclaimed in the State on 18 October 1995. It could not be extended beyond a year whether directly or deviously by revoking the old proclamation and issuing a new one.

As it originally existed, Article 356 of the Constitution, which empowers the imposition of president's rule in a state, consisted of four clauses. It was to be a weapon of last, not first, resort after all avenues had been explored and popular government in the state 'in accordance with the provisions' of the constitution had proved impossible; not difficult. Clause (4) gave the president's proclamation

[1] *The Statesman*, 11, 12 and 13 November 1996.

a term of six months since its ratification by the second of the resolutions by each house of parliament. It could be extended repeatedly, for the same period, 'but no such proclamation shall in any case remain in force for more than three years'.

The 38th Amendment to the Constitution added Clause 5 to provide that the president's 'satisfaction' as to the conditions in the state 'shall be final and conclusive and shall not be questioned in any court on any ground'. It came into force on 1 August 1975. The 42nd Amendment, (18 December 1976), substituted in Clause (4) the term of one year in place of six months but without altering the outer limit of three years. On 30 April 1979, the 44th Amendment did away with many of the excesses perpetrated on the constitution during the emergency. The period of six months was restored in Clause (4). Clause (5), which sought to bar judicial review, was deleted. In its place was substituted a new Clause (5) which is very relevant. It forbade parliament from passing any 'resolution with respect to the continuance in force of a proclamation' approved by it earlier 'for any period beyond the expiration of one year from the date of issue of such proclamation' unless both the two specified conditions were met: a proclamation of emergency in operation in the country or in any part of the state plus a certificate by the election commission that the continuance of president's rule 'is necessary on account of difficulties in holding general elections' to the state assembly. The maximum limit of three years remained.

It is a well established rule of interpretation that where a law permits something to be done subject to certain conditions only, it cannot be evaded by doing the act in any other manner, let alone deviously. The 44th Amendment was enacted in the climate of 1979 to curb abuses of Article 356. That is why the 59th Constitution Amendment had to be enacted on 30 March 1988 in order to provide that Clause (5) would not apply to the president's proclamation issued on 11 May 1987 in relation to Punjab. It was not revoked and issued afresh, as in UP the Constitution was amended.

There is a perfect analogy for this restraint: the ordinance making power of the president (Article 123) and the governors (Article 213), when the legislature is not in session. Every ordinance must be ratified by both its houses. It 'shall cease to operate at the expiration of six weeks from the reassembly' of the legislature if it took no action on the ordinance. Ordinances came to be repromulgated by Bihar for years together in disregard of constitutional limitations.

In a unanimous judgment delivered in 1986 on behalf of a constitution bench of five judges of the Supreme Court, Chief Justice P.N. Bhagwati called it 'a colourable exercise of power on the part of the executive to continue an ordinance with substantially the same provisions beyond the period limited by the constitution, by adopting the methodology [sic] of repromulgation. It is settled law that a constitutional authority cannot do indirectly what it is not permitted to do directly.' Constitutional limitations cannot be evaded by recourse to 'any subterfuge'.[2]

The constitution lays down a time limit of six weeks for legislative enactment of an ordinance. The government cannot ignore that by its repromulgation. 'It would enable the executive to transgress its constitutional limitations in the matter of law-making in an emergent situation and to covertly and indirectly arrogate to itself the law-making function of the legislature.' Such a power would enable the government 'to continue to regulate the life and liberty of the citizens through [an] ordinance made by the executive'. Article 356 requires stricter interpretation, as an emergency provision that prevents or ousts a popularly elected government in a state.

The Kerala high court's ruling that a proclamation can be issued under Article 356 though the state is already under president's rule was given in 1965 before Clause (5) was added in 1979. It is a judgment of a single judge and reeks of error. He held that the proclamation is not open to judicial review, which is not good law. Besides, he ruled that it can be challenged only by impeaching the President. His appreciation of the facts was also wrong.[3]

President's rule was imposed in Kerala on 10 September 1964 because none of the parties could form a government. Elections to the assembly, held on 4 March 1965, yielded an inconclusive verdict. The CPM's claim to form a government, with 40 in a house of 134 members was supported by the SSP (13), CPI (3) and five others. It was also prepared to support an SSP government. The Congress (36) resisted the claim. The Kerala Congress (24) and the Muslim League (6) were together prepared to form a coalition, 29 members of the CPM were in detention. The high court's finding that 'none of the parties was able to secure a working majority of seats' was irrelevant. A fundamental error lay in ignoring the rule that the

[2]*D.C. Wadhwa v State of Bihar & Ors.* (1987) 1 SCC 378 at 394.
[3]*K.K. Aboo v Union of India,* AIR 1965 Ker. 229.

issue was for the elected assembly to decide, not Governor Mr Ajit Prasad Jain, a partisan Congressman.

On 24 March 1965 the proclamation of 10 September was revoked and a fresh one promulgated under Article 356 the same day. The action was strongly criticized in parliament, in the press, and by academics. A distinguished member of the constituent assembly, Mr K. Santhanam, prophetically said: 'If every time there is no majority president's rule is automatic, the constitution must be deemed to have broken down and all those who are against democracy in India will rejoice. This may become a major feature in the political evolution of India during the next decade or two in those states and some time or the other it may happen even at the centre.'

Remarks made by Mr Era Sezhiyan, who rendered yeoman service during the emergency, fit the UP case to perfection:

When the elected representatives were there it would have been wiser and constitutionally correct to allow a ministry to be formed and the assembly to meet. Then if somebody brings forward a no-confidence motion and the ministry falls, you can say that such and such party claimed that it could run the government but it has not got the full confidence of the assembly. Without going through all that democratic process we cut short the way by hasty assessments and astrological predictions and we rushed to the conclusion that there is no other go but to usher in president's rule .... So whether the single party is able to command a majority inside the house, whether the largest party though in a minority, should be allowed to form a government, and whether that government will be stable are all matters which should have been left to the legislature to decide and not to be decided by the predictions of astrologers like Ajit Prasad Jain.

Predictions of stability are not for governors to make. The assembly was dissolved without being summoned to meet.

Even more to the point is the case of West Bengal. The United Front government collapsed when Ajoy Mukherji resigned as Chief Minister on 16 March 1970. The Deputy Chief Minister, Jyoti Basu, as leader of the largest party (80 in a House of 280), staked his claim to form a Government. He insisted however that his strength should be demonstrated in the assembly rather than in Raj Bhavan. He rejected the governor, S.S. Dhavan's demand for evidence of majority support. Some constituents of the United Front, who were 110-strong, declared that they would not support the CPI(M). So did groups in the Congress (55 members).

Thus, 165 in a house of 280 were opposed to the CPI(M). Mr Basu counted on revolts in the ranks of the former United Front. The governor demurred: president's rule was imposed on 19 March and the assembly was suspended. As J.R. Siwach points out in his excellent work, *Politics of President's Rule in India,* 'there are many instances where the governors and *raj pramukhs* have appointed the leaders of the largest party in the assembly without compelling them to prove their majority in the Raj Bhavan. This was done in Madras, Orissa, Travancore Cochin and Pepsu in 1952, and again in Orissa in 1957; in Madhya Pradesh in 1962; in Rajasthan in 1967; and in Pondicherry in 1974.

As in West Bengal, the Opposition in Madras, in 1952, with a strength of 166 approached the governor to show that the Congress party led by C. Rajagopalachari did not have a majority in the assembly but still Sri Prakasa, the then Governor, appointed the leader of the Congress party as chief minister.

Similarly in Rajasthan, in 1967, Dr Sampurnanand appointed Mohan Lal Sukhadia, not because he had the majority but because he was the leader of the largest party in the assembly of Rajasthan. If the same course of action had been adopted in West Bengal, there was a possibility that Basu too, like Sukhadia, would have proved his majority in the assembly. If he did not have a majority, he would have been thrown out of office within a fortnight because the Assembly was due to meet within this period to pass the budget.[4]

Governor S.S. Dhavan of West Bengal had gone so far as to write to leaders of various parties: 'I shall be obliged if you kindly give me your reasons why you think it would be illegal and immoral if I allow Mr Jyoti Basu, leader of the largest single party in the legislative assembly, to form a ministry and then force the legislative assembly with a demand for seeking confidence of the majority to enable the opposite parties to move a motion of no-confidence against the new ministry.' He showed their replies to Basu on 18 March. It was a novel as well as an unreliable course to adopt. The fundamental flaw, of course, was that the assembly was not permitted to pronounce its verdict. It was dissolved on 30 July 1970.

In UP, results of all the 424 out of 425 seats for which the polls were held were out by 11 October at the latest. So were the parties'

[4]See J.R. Siwach, *Politics of President's Rule in India,* Indian Institute of Advanced Study, Simla, 1979, pp. 39–44 for a survey of the abuse of Art. 356 in the interests of the Congress.

reactions. The BSP–Congress alliance (67+33) demanded unconditional support for Mayawati as Chief Minister. The Samajwadi Party (110) would have none of it. The Janata Dal (seven) reluctantly concurred. The BJP (174) did not support her claim either. On 12 October the CPI-M (four) asked the BSP to declare in writing that it would have no truck with the BJP as a preliminary to talks between the United Front and the BSP. There were 13 Independents and other small groups. Only a major climbdown by one of the three major parties (BJP, BSP, and United Front) could have resolved the impasse or defections enough for any of them to achieve a majority (213).

It bears emphasis that not till 16 October did the BSP formally stake a claim to form a Government, and it did so after it became known that the governor had already recommended president's rule. By then Mayawati had informed the governor over the telephone that the BSP was not supporting the BJP nor would it do so in the future.

On 16 October the governor said in statement to the press: 'The BJP has stated that they will prove their majority on the floor of the House. They, however, did not inform how they will get the majority. As the BJP was not in a position to indicate from where they will secure the necessary support, the governor called the major parties to ascertain their respective positions.'

It is recorded that the other two groups (the United Front and BSP–Congress) could claim 234 members plus the support of 10 others. 'All of them were common on one ground that they would not support the BJP. As such, they maintained there was no way that BJP would get a majority without indulging in horsetrading', concluding that the governor was 'evaluating the positions of the respective parties and to see how best a stable government can be provided within the framework of the constitution'. That very day (16 October) the union cabinet decided to accept the governor's report and 'reimpose' president's rule. His proclamation was issued on 17 October, after revoking the earlier one of 18 October 1995 which was to expire that day.

The election commission fully cooperated in this disgraceful drama. Having sat for a whole week over it, the commission issued only on 17 October, just before the president's fresh proclamation, its notification under Section 73 of the Representation of the People Act, 1951 constituting the state assembly. The president suspended the assembly.

Romesh Bhandari was explicit in his justification of his action to the press on 18 October: 'If today some leader approached me with the support of 213 legislators I would hold the swearing-in ceremony without any delay.' This was sheer constitutional illiteracy. No head of state in a parliamentary democracy has a right to insist on majority support if the electorate returns a hung legislature. This view cannot pass muster in any court of law. A fortnight later, he said, on 1 November: 'I can invite a party which shows support of even 200 MLAs, if not 213'. Why 200? and not 190, or 180, or 174? On 7 November in New Delhi, obviously at the instance of his mentors, Bhandari reverted to his insistence on a majority.

He said on 18 October that he had 'tried to find out from them [BJP] as to how they would manage to fill up the gap of 32 MLAs'. They said they would prove their majority in the assembly—as had Jyoti Basu in 1970 and rightly so. Bhandari said that nothing was impossible in politics; things could change. Such pop philosophy from persons temperamentally disposed to non-reflective pursuits can be very amusing. The contradiction is obvious. He did not leave it to the assembly to decide on the possibilities. He changed his views on a minority government because his benefactors in Delhi had changed their policy.

Bhandari was wrong in characterizing the situation as 'unprecedented'. So was the Union Home Minister, Indrajit Gupta, in holding that there was no alternative to president's rule. There was an invitation to the largest party, the BJP, to form a government. Neither its politics nor its spurious claims to morality should affect judgment on constitutional questions. The constitution is a sacred document.

The vice president of the BJP in UP, S.S. Bhandari, gave the game away on 28 October. The BJP 'never took the first option, that is forming our own government, seriously'. How would it acquire a majority? He meaningfully replied that the constitution 'only requires 50 per cent of those present and voting'.

Nonetheless, on 17 October the BJP's claims were wrongly rejected. Probably more nonsense has been said and written on the weight to be given to claims by the largest single party in a hung legislature than on any other topic of constitutional law. Not one authority supports the so-called 'objective' (i.e. mechanical) test. A party that has 40 members in a house of 100 has a weaker claim than one which has 35 but enjoys support from the rest and a fortiori if the 40 are rejected by all. The logic was reflected in the queries that the chief whip of the Conservative Party put to its MPs in 1963 on Harold Macmillan's resignation as prime minister to ascertain the consensus: '1. Whom would you like to see in office? 2. Do you want any runners-up? 3. Is there anybody you would rather not see in office?'

The report of the Committee of Governors (1971) was of the view that there is

no absolute right as leader of the largest single party or group to claim that he should be entrusted with the task of forming a government to the exclusion of all others. The relevant test is not the size of a party but its ability to command the support of the majority in the legislature. It may be that a party, though leading in relative strength in a legislature, may not be able to obtain the support of other members. In contrast, a numerically smaller party may command majority support with the help of other parties or groups.

Hence, the success of some minority governments.

The draft Instruments of Instructions to the president and governors were dropped, but they enunciated a good test: commission one who is 'most likely to command a stable majority' as prime minister and chief minister and as his colleagues those who will 'best be in a position collectively to command the confidence' of the legislature. It has to be a tentative view. The verdict is for the legislature alone to give. The head of state short-lists the claimants. This is where the test of largest single party comes in. If not inflexible, it is not irrelevant either. It is a rule of thumb guide when the legislature is badly hung and a decision has to be made. If an alternative majority group exists, the claim is defeated. If it does not, as in UP, the largest party must be invited and the assembly asked to pronounce on its claims.

No president or governor has any right to pre-empt the verdict of the house by giving his own. In a similar situation at the centre, the BJP would have been called. In UP, Romesh Bhandari and his mentors in New Delhi had ready recourse to Article 356. That was constitutionally simply not an option at all.

The Supreme Court's ruling in the Bommai case is clear, Justices P.B. Sawant and Kuldip Singh said: 'The assessment of the strength of the ministry is not a matter of private opinion of any individual, be he the governor or the president. It is capable of being demonstrated and ascertained publicly in the house ... such private assessment is an anathema to the democratic principle.' This was said apropos the ouster of an existing government. The basic principle however applies also to the initial decision to appoint a new prime minister and chief minister, subject to the verdict of the house. For, they added, the governor must keep on exploring all possibilities: 'Even if this meant installing the government belonging to a minority party, the governor was duty-bound to opt for it so long as the government could enjoy the confidence of the House.' On this, the house alone can finally pronounce.[5]

Justices B.P. Jeevan Reddy and S.C. Agrawal held the same view while declining to express any opinion on the initial appointment. Justice S. Ratnavel Pandian concurred. Two other judges were silent (Justices J.S. Verma and Yogeshwar Dayal). Justice K. Ramaswamy alone rejected the floor test. Thus, a majority (5–4) accepted it.

Sloth, among other things, accounts for the fact that every time such issues arise, Indian lawyers and politicians regard them as novel and glibly propound their own *ipse dixit* with supreme confidence. We however have precedents of over a century and a half to draw upon not only from the UK but also from Canada and Australia, including those set in their many provinces. It may surprise some to know that there have been cases when a newly elected legislature was too divided even to elect a speaker. None of their constitutions is disfigured with provisions for central rule or preventive detention.

On 2 November 1908 general elections in Newfoundland resulted in a tie, 18–18. The prime minister, Sir Robert Bond, wrote to the governor asking whether the proper course would not be 'for the governor to convene the legislature and immediately dissolve it'. The governor refused to grant dissolution until it had been made clear that an alternative did not exist. *The assembly must be allowed a chance to do business, he ruled firmly.* Sir Robert replied that he was prepared to resign if the legislature rejected him, but would the governor, then, grant dissolution to his successor who was also certain to be rejected?[6]

On 25 February, the governor invited Sir Edward Morris to form a government. To neither prime minister would he promise a dissolution. On 30 March the house met but could not elect a speaker. It was prorogued. The following day Sir Edward advised dissolution. The governor suggested a compromise between the

[5](1994) 3 SCC 1 at 127.
[6]Forsey, op. cit., p. 60.

two politicians so that the budget could be passed, but Sir Robert insisted on restoration to office. The governor granted dissolution to Sir Edward on 9 April, a good few months after he had rejected his rival's advice for dissolution.

On 19 February 1859 the new assembly of Prince Edward Island was also unable to elect a speaker. Dissolution was granted at once to the existing government.[7] In UP, under president's rule, no one existed to secure that. The proper course on 17 October would have been to invite the BJP and give it, in the circumstances, no more than a very few days to secure a vote of confidence. On its failure the process should have been repeated. Only at the end of it all should president's rule have been proclaimed since in such a situation no party is entitled to stay in power to conduct the elections. This course can yet be followed.

The election commission acted improperly in delaying the notification constituting the assembly. This is linked to an important question. When does the anti-defection law begin to operate after a general election? Para 2 of the Tenth Schedule to the Constitution says that 'a member of the house belonging any political party shall be disqualified from being a member of the house, (a) if he has voluntarily given up his membership of such political party' or defies its whip in the house.

This implies three things. The house must exist; the candidate elected must have acquired its membership; dissociation from his party must be subsequent to that. He cannot be disqualified if he has turned coat before the house is constituted or before he has become a member of it in law. The law speaks of 'a member of the house belonging to any political party', not a candidate elected on a party's ticket switching sides.

When is a house constituted? Section 73 of the Representation of the People Act, 1951 provides a clear answer. The election commission notifies it in the *Official Gazette* 'as soon as may be', after the results of the elections of all the constituencies where the poll was held have been declared by their returning officers. 'The names of the members elected for those constituencies and upon the issues of such notification that house or assembly shall be deemed to be duly constituted.' Given the provisions of the defection law, no election commission with any sense of responsibility would delay

[7]Ibid., p. 277.

this notification for a whole week as the three performers on the commission did in UP.

When does an elected candidate become 'member' of the house? Section 67A of the Act says that 'for the purposes of this Act' the date on which a candidate is declared by the returning officer to be elected shall be the date of his election. This does not carry us far. Rule 66 of the Conduct of Election Rules 1961, made under the Act, require the returning officer to grant the elected candidate a certificate of election in Form 22. This form certifies that a candidate 'sponsored by' a named party 'to have been duty elected ... *to be* a member' of the Lok Sabha or assembly. The language is apt. The returning officer's certificate necessarily precedes the election commission's notification.

Dr Ambedkar however said in the constituent assembly, on 19 May 1949, that 'There are certain, what I may call, ceremonies that have to be gone through before a duly elected candidate can be said to have become a member of parliament. One such thing which he has to undergo is the taking of the oath... That is the sequence of events—election, taking of the oath, becoming a member ....'[8]

Dr Ambedkar tripped badly when he said 'that is the provision'. He was speaking on Article 81 in the draft constitution which became Article 99 as adopted. It clearly implies membership *prior* to the oath. Article 104 punishes a person who 'sits or votes as a member' of the house unless he has complied with Article 99. But Article 99 says: 'Every *member* of either house of parliament shall, before taking his seat make and subscribe' to the prescribed oath. Thus only a 'member' can take the oath. The Act of 1951 was also piloted in parliament by Dr Ambedkar.

The late. H.M. Seervai was strongly against reference to the constituent assembly debates in interpretation of the constitution. The better course is to rely on them to understand the text; especially one adopted on the basis of certain understandings. For instance, parliamentary conventions. But the debates cannot control a text as explicit as Article 99. It is submitted that while a candidate is declared elected '*to be* a member' of the house by the returning officer, he acquires membership of it when the house is duly constituted by the election commission and takes his seat as a member when he takes the oath. The defection law begins to operate when the house is constituted, not when he takes the oath.

[8]CAD, vol. viii, p. 131.

50
The High Court's Judgment on Renewal of President's Rule[1]

High praise is due to Justices B.M. Lal, B. Kumar, and M. Katju of the Lucknow bench of Allahabad high court for their unanimous rulings on the three substantive issues involved in the case concerning the validity of the proclamation imposing president's rule in UP on 17 October 1996. It would however have been better if the unanimity had been expressed in a single judgment rather than in three separate concurring ones.

The issues were whether the proclamation violated Clause (5) of Article 356 which lays down an outer limit of one year unless both the conditions are met for a valid extension; namely, that a proclamation of emergency is in force in the whole or any part of the state plus a certificate from the election commission that continuance of president's rule 'is necessary on account of difficulties in holding general elections' to the state assembly.

Admittedly, neither condition was fulfilled in this case. The answer to this issue, therefore, turned on whether the proclamation was in truth not a fresh one at all, regardless of the form, but in fact a devious extension of the earlier one promulgated on 18 October 1995. They ruled that it was.

The second issue was whether it was promulgated in colourable exercise of power, for extraneous reasons, and was mala fide in law. They ruled again that it was. The third issue was whether, in the circumstances, the governor was bound to invite the largest single party, the BJP, to form a government. The bench ruled that he was

[1] *The Statesman*, 7 and 8 January 1997.

not. Mr Romesh Bhandari is unwise to flaunt this as vindication, for all the three judgments censure his conduct and, at one remove, that of his mentors in New Delhi.What is more, the judges overlooked that, while the arithmetical test in its rigidity has no support from any authority, it need not be discarded altogether either. It is a rule of thumb helpful in an uncertain situation.

It is important to stress this because, while avoiding the rule altogether, the bench stumbled on an innovation and, in gross error, faulted the governor for not adopting that unprecedented course when it should have censured him for not inviting the single largest party. The innovation was a summons to the state assembly to meet and elect a chief minister whom the governor would then invite to form a ministry. The bench fell between the stools as it were.While insisting that the aspirant to power should convince the governor of his majority support—and thus minimizing the floor test—it went to the other extreme and ruled that the floor test should precede and not follow the invitation to form a ministry, which is the course adopted in all parliamentary democracies save where the constitution provides otherwise. The bench need not have travelled as far as Japan to find such a provision. Our neighbour Pakistan has it, emulating Germany.

Two fundamentals emerge in the final result. The bench has upheld the respect for constitutional limitations. Sadly, however, it has missed a fine opportunity for upholding the principle that the governor's satisfaction, at best tentative, need not hinge on actual proof of majority support but on prima facie evidence.That is where the rule of thumb comes in.The final verdict is for the assembly to pronounce.

The election results were out on 10 October 1996.The election commission issued its notification under Section 73 of the Representation of the People Act, 1951 constituting the house a whole week later on 17 October. In fairness, the governor does not deserve criticism for not 'inviting' it to issue the notification. The election commission, a supposedly autonomous body then headed by MrT.N. Seshan, was clearly 'playing ball' with the centre. The commission should have been censured. Its notification preceded by just a few hours two proclamations by the president on the same day, 17 October; one to revoke the proclamation of 18 October 1995 and the other to impose president's rule anew, in form, but to extend it, in fact. All three, i.e. the notification and the two proclamations were, as lawyers say, 'parts of the same transaction'. Both were decided at a single meeting of the union cabinet.

Since the proclamation of 18 October 1995 was going to end on 17 October 1996, where was the need to revoke it hours before its expiry? It would have been more honest to issue a new one without the revocation. That would however have been a blatant breach of Clause (5) of Article 356. The government preferred a devious breach. Justice Lal drew pointed attention to the fact that Clause (5) was inserted by the Constitution 44th Amendment Act, 1978 in order to prevent the excesses of the past. The situation had not changed. No new grounds were available.

The situation that existed on 18 October 1995, a political deadlock, continued even while it was in force till its revocation. Nor was the test prescribed by Article 356 fulfilled. No situation existed to justify the opinion that UP could not be governed after 10 October 1996, 'in accordance with the provisions' of the constitution.

On 15 October Mr Romesh Bhandari wrote to the president to say that no party was in a position to form a stable government or to garner support without recourse to horse-trading. That was the day the BJP formally staked its claim to form a government for the first time. The following day Mr Bhandari recommended president's rule.

Justice Lal observed that the governor's letter of 15 October 'also reported to the President of India that till 15 October 1996 he did not go into the exercise of taking the initiative to have formal discussions with party leaders', a revealing admission indeed.

To continue, Justice Lal proceeded to record: 'However, the governor found no possibility of any party or group in a position to form a stable government and since the presidential rule was to expire on 17 October 1996, he submitted his report for suitable action or suitable direction ...' The following day he formally recommended president's rule.

The bench saw 'the entire file' and found no material to warrant president's rule. Justice Lal observed: 'The two letters, itself speak [sic] that the recommendations was made without exploring all possibilities ...'

So far, so good, The judge, with respect, rightly held that 'normally and not invariably, the largest party has to be invited'. he however erred in holding that 'it must be convinced to [sic] the governor that in whom he is ... confidence of appointing chief minister and council of ministers, must have a majority in the assembly'. This is simply not correct. For one thing, the test is not on an existing numerical majority in the house but of being able to command a majority there. For another, in a murky situation, someone has to be invited. Hence the rule of thumb: the largest party.

In the states, recourse is had to the easy option of president's rule, but what would the president do in an identical situation at the centre? The rules cannot be different. Nor was the judge right in refering to the anti-defection law in this context for that law surely applies to MPs as much as to MLAs. The crucial question is whether precisely in such a situation the leader of the largest party is bound to convince the governor of his ability to muster a majority by proving the grounds of his confidence. What alternative was available if the hideous provision for president's rule did not exist?

The answer that the bench provides is that the governor should have summoned the assembly under Article 174(1) and sent a message under Article 175 directing it to elect a chief minister whom he could then have sworn in as such. While it is true that a politician who is given a mandate to form a government acquires an advantage in horse-trading, the game can also be played if the assembly meets before the appointment of a chief minister.

A level playing field can be secured by this innovation as I suggested in an earlier article[2] apropos the Gujarat case. However, without either a constitutional amendment—or perhaps a constitutional convention openly proclaimed—a governor cannot be fairly blamed, as he is by the Bench, for not taking recourse to this admittedly novel procedure which, let it be said, is fully in conformity with the structure of the parliamentary system. A constitutional amendment is however advisable.

The bench referred to the Supreme Court's ruling in 1984 in P.M. Sukul's case that an MLA is entitled to vote as an elector for a Rajya Sabha seat during the interval between the due constitution of the house and its first meeting summoned by the governor. The governor however has no control over this process. As the court noted, the election is held by the returning officer appointed by the election commission and the election is a non-legislative function of the MLA outside the proceedings of the Assembly.

That cannot be said of the MLAs electing their chief minister

[2]Vide pp. 348–356.

by a majority vote as a body. If it is to be done outside the house by secret ballot, legislation is necessary. If within it, the house must be summoned. The judges consciously and completely ignored the fact that the governor had no power to summon the house since the proclamation of 18 October 1995 was in force and it had suspended 'the operation' of Articles 174(1) and 175 along with that of several others, as did its successor, the proclamation of 1996. This the bench knew for Justice Katju expressed the view that Article 174 'should not have been suspended'.

In fairness to Mr Romesh Bhandari, he cannot be blamed for not exercising a power that did not belong to him, yet this is what the justices did. Justice Lal held that 'invoking the provisions of Article 174 and 175, the governor, indeed could have asked the members of the legislative assembly to indicate a person in whom they have [sic] confidence so as to exercise his prerogative rights under Article 164 (1) to appoint chief minister' Between the declaration of election results on 10 October and imposition of president's rule on 17 October, Articles 174(1) and 175 were in suspension and the governor could not have invoked them.

The judge said that fears of a deadlock were unreal. 'This apprehension would only be sorted out when all legislators are given a chance to meet; assemble, discuss and reach some conclusion.' The logic applies also to the largest single party claiming that it would prove its majority in the house. Defections and horse trading can be checked if the election commission does its job impartially by prompt issue of the notification constituting the house. Thereupon anti-defection law begins to operate.

The bench was driven to this startling conclusion because it rejected a sound one: invite the largest party and give it but a short time to prove its majority in the house. On 22 October 1973 the chief justice of the Orissa high court and Justice S.K. Ray ruled that 'even assuming that the governor wanted to test the exact support, he should have called upon the leader of the Opposition to test his strength in the house itself'...[3]

In this case Mr Biju Patnaik had claimed support of 70 in a house of 140 on Mrs Nandini Satpathy's resignation. Had he failed to command a majority, president's rule could have been imposed. In the climate of 1973 the president's proclamation was regarded

[3]AIR 1974 Orissa 5.

as non-justiciable and constitutional conventions as unenforceable by the courts. The Supreme Court has ruled both notions to be wrong. While Justice Brajesh Kumar recognized that 'no doubt, the suggested procedure of election for C.M. would be a novel one since the British parliamentary history', Justice M. Katju said that he had not 'been able to find any precedent for such a course of action but in my humble opinion it is the only rational and democratic alternative left to the governor when faced with such a situation'.

Justice Kumar recorded the submission, but recorded too that 'virtually there was no formal parley between the governor and the leaders of political parties up to 15 October, 1996 as is indicated in the report of the governor itself. The election result was declared on October 10, 1996 Talks took place between the governor and the leaders only on October 16, 1996.'

Mr Romesh Bhandari, in his desire to please those who had made him governor of UP, simply aligned himself with Arthur Clough's famous lines *'Thou shall not kill; but needst not strive/officiously to keep alive.'* In truth he went beyond the lines. He wrecked democracy by deliberate delay.

The judge noted the affidavit of the state government on the governor's meetings with 'various members and political groups to explore the possibility of forming a government' in Para 14 and a similar claim in Para 29. Justice Katju's censure of Mr Romesh Bhandari is explicit: 'In my opinion both paragraphs 14 and 29 are vague. It is not clear what exactly did the governor do between October 10 and October 16, 1996.' The names of the interlocutors, the dates of the meetings, and the substance of the discussions was not mentioned in either paragraph 14 or 29. 'In the absence of these details, therefore, I am constrained to observe that the governor did not act with the promptness and despatch that the situation required'; a classic case of judicial understatement. On this point too all the three justices pronounced against Mr Romesh Bhandari.

51
Defections, Speaker and the Governor[1]

It is bad enough that political support is being sought by offering ministerial offices at the cost of the taxpayer, but what is worse is that individual members of the legislature have realized their own importance. They can interfere in administration with impunity and make demands which, even if they are unreasonable, can hardly be resisted by the chief minister ... Since the loyalty of its followers is so flexible, the exact majority of the ruling party is not of any consequence. Allegations have been made by the Opposition that the ministry is continuing 'in power through corruption, bribery, political victimization and distribution of offices ...'.

It would be hard to more accurately describe what happened in Lucknow in the days from 19 October 1997 when the BSP leader Miss Mayawati withdrew her support to the BSP–BJP coalition led by Chief Minister Kalyan Singh, and 27 October when he expanded his team of ministers to include all the 37 MLAs who had defected from rival parties to save his government on the vote of confidence in the state assembly on 21 October. As many as 19 of them are 'history-sheeters' in police records. Their conversion seemed as sudden and dramatic as that of Paul on the road to Damascus. Unlike the saint, however, theirs was not a conversion in response to a call of conscience. Their handlers in the BJP were privy to their plans for weeks while close colleagues in their own parties were kept in the dark till the last.

The passage quoted above was written three decades ago by

[1] *The Statesman*, 4, 5 and 6 November 1997.

B. N. Chakravarty, Governor of Haryana—the birthplace of 'aya rams, gaya rams'—in his celebrated report dated 17 November 1967 to President Zakir Hussain. Those who thought that the Jamuna afforded protection against the spread of the disease to Delhi were disillusioned when, on 5 November 1990, Chandra Shekhar split the Janata Dal to become prime minister four days later, with Rajiv Gandhi's support negotiated weeks earlier.

We have been warned that Kalyan Singh's techniques will, indeed, be adopted at the centre before long. His was not the act of a local rebel, enjoying as it did the full backing of the BJP's central leadership. Its president, L.K. Advani said on 26 October: 'If something similar happens in parliament, why should we be averse to the process?' As for the newcomers, 'the situation has been such that there could not have been any screening or selectivity in the matter'. The following day the official spokesman, Yashwant Sinha, said that the BJP 'has been forced to take extraordinary steps which cannot be judged by peacetime standards'. The implication is obvious: everything is fair in 'war'. The situation had been no different a week earlier yet he had twice, on 19 and 20 October, assured the public that there would be no horse-trading: 'Without indulging in horse trading it is still possible to enter into an honest, transparent, and open understanding.'

A.B. Vajpayee declaimed on 28 May 1996 that 'If power comes my way by breaking parties, I will consider it sinful to touch such power'. He was present at the swearing in of the defectors in Lucknow on 27 October and defended their induction in the ministry. They were not convicts after all, he said. The Vajpayee doctrine puts paid to the efforts to curb, if not eliminate, the role of criminals in politics.

The crisis in UP raises a host of constitutional issues: the governor's status; the ambit of his power to send messages to the state legislature; limitations on the imposition of president's rule; the president's relationship with his council of ministers; legal consequences of legislators' use of violence on the floor of the house and of the speaker's manifest lack of impartiality and reform of the anti-defection law.

It must be viewed against the background of events since 1989 when the Congress(I) was ejected from power in the elections to the state assembly. The National Front ministry lasted longer than V.P. Singh's government at the centre because Chief Minister

Mulayam Singh Yadav cast his lot with Chandra Shekhar in November 1990. Like him, he advised dissolution once the Congress(I) withdrew its support early in 1991. A BJP government came to power only to be sacked in December 1992 following the demolition of the Babri Masjid. The Supreme Court has yet to punish Kalyan Singh for his breaches of assurances to the court on sworn affidavits. Mulayam Singh parted company with Chandra Shekhar. His Samajwadi Party (SP) forged an alliance with Kanshi Ram's Bahujan Samaj Party (BSP) and formed the government after the 1993 elections. On 2 June 1995 the BSP withdrew its support and Mulayam Singh was sacked by Governor Motilal Vora the following day. His plea that his claim to support of the majority in the assembly be tested on the floor of the house was rejected. That wrong still rankles in his mind. Mayawati was appointed chief minister on 3 June with the BJP's support, besides that of some others. Only four months later, the BJP withdrew its support. President's rule was imposed on 18 October. The assembly was dissolved 10 days later.

Elections to the UP Assembly in October 1996 yielded an uncertain verdict. The governor, Romesh Bhandari insisted on proof of majority support by the parties as a precondition to the formation of a ministry. He did not take the initiative to explore the possibility of forming a government. The Deve Gowda government did the incredible. On 17 October 1996 the proclamation of 18 October 1995 imposing president's rule was revoked, moments before its expiry, and a fresh one issued under Article 356 in a disgraceful attempt to circumvent the one-year limit prescribed by its Clause (5). This was on Bhandari's recommendation.

On 19 December 1996, the Lucknow bench of the Allahabad high court struck down the proclamation as unconstitutional. It was revoked on 21 March 1997 when Mayawati formed the government with BJP support under their six-monthly power-sharing accord. The party position was as follows: BJP and ally 176 seats; the BSP 67 and its allies, the Congress(I) 33, the UF 134 (Samajwadi Party (SP) 110, Janata Dal 7, BKKP 8, Tiwari Congress 4, CPM 4, CPI 1), and Independents 14 in a House of 425.

As 'The State of Uttar Pradesh', Romesh Bhandari went in appeal to the Supreme Court against the high court's order. Mayawati did not withdraw the appeal when she became chief minister though she intended to. In recent discussion one fact has been overlooked.

While staying the high court's order, the Supreme Court directed that the state assembly should not be dissolved pending the hearing and final disposal of the appeal. Some who clamoured for the imposition of president's rule on 19 October, the day she withdrew support to the BJP–BSP coalition headed by Kalyan Singh, or the following day, overlooked the court's order. Those who did not suggested that the assembly be kept in 'suspended animation' so that Kalyan Singh's new supporters would get disenchanted and desert him.

The events of 20 and 21 October deserve careful analysis. By now the Tiwari Congress had joined the Congress(I) raising its strength to 37. On 20 October, 19 of them, led by Naresh Agarwal, presented themselves before the speaker, Kesri Nath Tripathi, in the evening as members of the UP Loktantrik Congress and declared their support to the Kalyan Singh government, three more followed hours later. So did three of the members of the Janata Dal. Agarwal said categorically that day that his party would 'join the government' as a 'coalition partner'.

Recognition was accorded instantly. The speaker said: 'I am fully satisfied with the provisions of the law [sic] under the Anti-Defection Act [sic] and the group of the Congress MLAs numbering 19 [sic] has been extended recognition as the UP Loktantrik Congress in the Vidhan Sabha.' He said too: 'I personally recognize each of these MLAs who have physically presented themselves and signed before me. Still, I have got the verification done by the assembly secretary, Prem Chandra Saxena.' He recognized a group of 19, not of 22.

While all this was on, came a visitor whose entry alone serves to completely destroy the speaker's position as judge under the anti-defection law. Its significance has been overlooked although it occurred in the open. *The Statesman's* Lucknow correspondent reported it in the issue of 21 October: 'Mr Kalyan Singh, who joined the group of 19 erstwhile Congress legislators at the residence of the speaker to finalize the strategy for tomorrow's special session of the house, told reporters that he would obtain more than the required number of 213 votes to prove his majority.'

The speaker is expected to act in a strictly quasi-judicial capacity under the law. The Supreme Court upheld his umpireship under the Tenth Schedule by a narrow vote (3–2) only on that basis. Yet, Kesri Nath Tripathi met Kalyan Singh in a strategy session, behind the back of the opposition, while he was holding 'hearings' as umpire on the application of recognition by the 19 Congress MLAs. He has, thus, hopelessly compromised his position and disabled himself in law from acting as umpire any longer in any of the proceedings under the Tenth Schedule to the Constitution. If he does, his conduct will be open to judicial censure even as his orders are open to judicial review under the Supreme Court's ruling. His chairmanship of the assembly however only the house can terminate.

The governor was not idle. He sent two reports to the president and a message to the assembly under Article 175 (2) of the Constitution g.ving these directives: 'The session will continue till the debate on the confidence motion and voting is completed. Voting will be done through lobby division.' He said he would appoint three observers— two independent and one official—to observe the proceedings.

The speaker, Mr Kesri Nath Tripathi, may be faulted for his language but not for his stand when he responded: 'The governor is living in a fool's paradise if he thinks that I would let the observers occupy seats in the house. His order in this respect is not binding.' Eventually, they sat in the governor's gallery. On the rest, Mr Tripathi said: 'I will abide by the Constitution and read out the message before the assembly. The house will decide whether to accept or reject the massage.' The Governor had no right to dictate terms to the assembly. The speaker was perfectly justified. The message was unconstitutional.

The assembly's proceedings on 21 October have been extensively reported. Eight features stand proved beyond doubt: (1) It was the Opposition, led by the Congress legislature party leader Pramod Tiwari, that initiated the use of violence; (2) Once the speaker summoned security personnel to the house—some in plain clothes were already present there—BJP MLAs went on a ferocious counter-offensive; (3) members of the Opposition who had stayed behind were beaten mercilessly. Urmila Yadav of the SP, who hid under the table as she bled profusely, was beaten with microphones 'even as she begged for mercy', two correspondents noted; (4) the security men locked up the Opposition in the lobby after driving them out of the house; (5) Voting took place after the Opposition had thus been forcibly ejected. It was not a voluntary walkout. Forty-five persons were injured, seven seriously; (6) non-members of the house, belonging to the BJP, were present while the fracas and the voting took place, two of whom were identified incontestably as Sunder Singh Bagel, MLC and Avadh Pal Singh, a former MLA; (7) 12

BSP MLAs, led by Markandey Chand, voted for the motion of confidence and were seen and identified by the press doing so besides the 22 of the Congress (I) of the Janata Dal and some Independents. The speaker later declined to take any notice of this.

In the circumstance, the vote (222 in favour, none against) is a palpable nullity in law. The BJP leader in charge of UP, Sunder Singh Bhandari, realized this when, in the hearing of press-persons, he angrily berated his colleagues for 'losing the cool and spoiling the game ... they have given the Centre enough reason to take action against us'.

Meanwhile, in Delhi, the Union cabinet's recommendation for imposition of president's rule, on 21 October, was returned by President K.R. Narayanan for its reconsideration on 22 October. The cabinet did not reaffirm its advice after reconsideration under Article 74 (1). It decided instead (22 October) that proceeding under Article 356 need not be undertaken'.

A fair number, like the highly respected CPI(M) leader, Harkishen Singh Surjeet, have argued that president's rule could and should have been imposed before the vote in the assembly. Others have said that the violence there on 21 October justifies such action. Neither argument is tenable in the light of the Supreme Court's ruling in the Bommai Case (1994). Five of the nine judges of the bench ruled that a vote in the assembly provides the sole acceptable test; the expressions used were 'alone' and 'the only way'. All five recognized exceptional situations. Two spoke of the note being 'impossible'; three others of 'all-pervasive violence'. On 19 and 20 October neither situation could have been contemplated save in the fevered brain of Romesh Bhandari, with bloodshed and the rest. For different reasons the vote on 21 October was nullity but it was no valid ground for imposition of president's rule.

In Gujarat, on 18 September 1996, it was the BJP government that had initiated recourse to violence with plain-clothes men entering the house at its behest to beat up the Opposition members. The legal maxim applies to all: no one can take advantage of his own wrong. In UP the Opposition cannot take advantage of its use of violence to secure Kalyan Singh's ouster, nor can the latter avail of similar conduct in retaliation to claim validity for the vote after forcibly locking up the Opposition in the lobby. A fresh vote is called for, and that after a prompt decision on the Oppositions applications under the anti-defection law.

The Supreme Court was unanimously of the view that while Article 74 (2) bars the court from inquiring into 'the question whether any, and if so what, advice was tendered by ministers to the president', it is no bar to the 'production of all the material on which the ministerial advice was based'. Governors' reports have been placed before parliament in many a case and published for all to read. As Justice P.B. Sawant said: 'the two houses of parliament would be entitled to go into the material on the basis of which the council of ministers had tendered' its advice. MPs can demand that Romesh Bhandari's many reports be placed before parliament. Claims of privilege against disclosure receive short shrift in parliament and in the courts. A majority ruled that a proclamation under Article 356 can be struck down not only on the ground that it was issued mala fide but also that it was based on no material at all or on irrelevant grounds.

Even if 'horse-trading' is alleged, Justice Sawant held in a very able judgment, 'the correct and proper course for him [the Governor] to adopt was to await the test on the floor of the house'. No proclamation under Article 356 could have passed muster in the courts whether made before or after the vote on 21 October. Article 356 envisages: 'the government of the state cannot be carried on in accordance with the provisions of the constitution'. In 1996, the Lucknow bench saw 'the entire file' and found no material to warrant presidents' rule. A similar scrutiny now would have greatly embarrassed all involved in the action.

The Union cabinet was unwise to advise the president as it did on 21 October, but wise not to persist in it once the president asked it to reconsider its advice. The cabinet and the nation owe a lot to President Narayanan. Advani's suggestion on 22 October that he refer the issue to the Supreme Court for its advisory opinion under Article 143 was sheer nonsense. The president cannot make such a reference except on his ministers' advice. Any other interpretation would reduce Article 74 to a nullity.

Both the governor and the speaker have disgraced themselves. The president's rejection of Bhandari's one-sided reports alone renders his continuance in office untenable. One point that deserves closer notice than it has received so far is the governor's message to the State legislature under Article 175 (2). It says: 'The governor may send messages to the house or houses of the legislature of the State, whether with respect to a Bill then pending in the legislature or otherwise, and a house to which any message is so sent shall with all convenient despatch consider any matter required by the message to be taken into consideration.' There is a similar provision for the president vis-à-vis either house of parliament in Article 86 (2). The constituent assembly adopted both without a debate on 2 June 1949 and 18 May 1949, respectively. They are modelled on Sections 63 and 20 of the Government of India Act 1935.

Article 175 (2) was first invoked in 1968 in Punjab in order to set at naught the speaker's adjournment of the assembly for two months making the passage of the budget before 1 April impossible. The governor prorogued the house, promulgated an ordinance forbidding its adjournment without completion of the financial business save by a vote of the house. He then summoned the assembly and sent a message directing it to consider the financial business. The Supreme Court upheld the ordinance but did not consider the validity of the message. The ordinance was decisive.

However, in 1973 a full bench of the Madras high court characterized the governor's message as 'a directive to all concerned, is at once a mandate and a mandate pregnant with details as to the subjects to be discussed in the assembly session'.[2] This was pure *obiter* and *ipse dixit* as well. The court had found that the draft agenda contained in the message had been seen by the petitioner (the speaker) and approved by the leader of the house. The list of business for the meeting of the assembly was circulated to all members. 'Even otherwise, the agenda having been prescribed by the governor in the message as above, it was not open to his speaker to bypass the same and introduce an irregular censure motion ..' That motion was in any case a breach of the rules of procedure. There was no discussion of the import of Article 175 (2).

The Constitution, like the Act of 1935, sought to incorporate British parliamentary practice which the high court did not pause to consider at all. Neither the British crown nor the president or the governor in India can prescribe an agenda to the legislature, let alone the form of voting.

Erskine May authoritatively explains the 'subject of such messages'. They pertain to 'important public events which require the attention of parliament, the declaration of a state of emergency' and the like. They arc 'additions to the royal speech'.[3] The use of

---

[2] *K.A. Mathialagan v P. Srinivasan*, AIR 1973 Madras 371 at 378, para 9.
[3] Erskine May, p. 628.

Articles 86(2) and 175(2) in the manner the latter was used in Punjab, Madras and in UP—in 1995 by MotilalVora and in 1997 by Romesh Bhandari—is contrary to the clear terms of the provision and is patently unconstitutional.

The speaker, Kesri Nath Tripathi, was required to consider two cases of defection. One was of 19, and later, of three Congress MLAs from their 37-member Party on 20 October. The other was of 12 of the 67 BSP members voting against the party whip on 21 October. On both, Tripathi has functioned as a defender, and promoter, of defections from those parties. His pronouncements reveal either crass ignorance of the law or a wilful determination to pervert it. This is proved from one pronouncement alone. The speaker said on 24 October: 'During the debate on the confidence motion, one BSP MLA, Mr Markanday Chand, had stated that 23 BSP legislators had broken away from the parent party ... to vote for the BJP ... However, these MLAs could not cast their vote ... Since Mr Chand's statement is part of the Assembly proceedings, I have decided to take cognizance of the same. Whenever the remaining MLAs present themselves before me for physical verification, I will take cognizance of the same.' There was, he added, no time-limit for getting a separate group recognized after it splits from a party. 'No one has come yet, but as soon as they come, I will give them recognition.'

This is declaring open season on defections in the future. Even a minimum number is not specified. Come one, come all is the message. No wonder then that on 27 October Kalyan Singh declared: 'There will be another expansion of the cabinet very soon.' The speaker and the chief minister have ever acted in tandem with each other. Tripathi's view that 'a split is a continuous process' makes a mockery of the minimum requirement of one-third of the members of the legislature party prescribed by Para 3 of the Tenth Schedule. He will close the account only once the stragglers add up to the minimum, no matter when.

This is in flagrant contradiction to a landmark ruling pronounced by one of the most impartial speakers of the Lok Sabha, Rabi Ray, on 11 January 1991. On 5 November 1990 the Janata Dal expelled 25 of its 140 Lok Sabha MPs in order to reduce the strength of the remaining 32 dissidents to less than one-third. This was after the split. It was a shoddy tactic. On 7 November, 30 MPs of the Dal voted against V P Singh's motion of confidence in the Lok Sabha. Seven others voted for it but, defying the party whip, voted for

Chandra Shekhar's motion of confidence on 16 November. Shakeelur Rehman joined his regime on 21 November when the cabinet was expanded.

Rabi Ray dismissed the petition in regard to those who had voted against the motion on 5 November. He disqualified the seven who voted for Chandra Shekhar on 16 November, V.C. Shukla being one of them, and Shakeelur Rehman as well. The leader of the Opposition, L.K. Advani, demanded the resignation from the council of ministers of those who had been disqualified as members of the Lok Sabha. His approval of the ruling was manifest.

In the instant case, one might ignore the three Congress MLAs who joined the 19 dissidents hours later on 20 October but the disqualification incurred on 21 October by the 12 BSP MLAs is incontestable. Those who join either group later will meet the same fate unless each splitting group constitutes one-third of the party.

No one condones the sheer obscenity of the practice, perfected by the BSP, of holding MLAs in bondage. The remedy is to apply for habeas corpus, not pervert the Tenth Schedule. Nor is it relevant that the government would have survived without the 12 votes. It is the breach of the constitution that is relevant. Having pronounced his views on the law at length, the speaker announced on 26 October that he would begin hearings on the fate of the 12 on 6 November. Significantly, he said that even if he disqualified the 12, the government's majority would not be affected. They were sworn in as ministers the following day.

The secretary of the assembly, Premchand Saxena, admitted on 25 October: 'No member of the BSP has written any letter regarding defection from his party.' The speaker himself said that day: 'There is still time. The strength of the new group will be determined when the defectors [sic] formally announce the split.' He called it a 'legal split' he explained because of Saxena's statement that more would follow.

The whole object of a lobby division, as distinct from a voice vote, is to identify who voted and how. Those in the press and visitors' galleries had no problem in this regard, but the speaker said that it was not possible to establish which MLA voted against the party whip since the party's name is not recorded. Worse, he asserted categorically on 25 October that 'It is a legal myth that crossing the floor by a legislator can invite disqualification'. Both statements make a mockery of Paragraph 2(1)(b) of the Tenth Schedule: 'if he votes ...'

A speaker can stall by sheer delay. One slept over a case for four months. Kesri Nath Tripathi has amply demonstrated that he will not be an impartial arbiter under Para 6 of the Tenth Schedule to the Constitution. Its wilful perversion by the speaker can justify the conclusion that 'the government of the state cannot be carried on in accordance with the provisions of this constitution' (Article 356). The same applies to another constitutional functionary, Governor Romesh Bhandari.

In the Kihoto Hollohan case (1992) three judges of the Supreme Court accepted the speaker as 'an independent adjudicatory authority', as the Constitution requires since the rule of law and democracy are part of 'the basic structure' of the constitution. The judges held that he is a political appointee and conferment of the adjudicatory power on him 'violates a basic feature of the constitution'.

There is another aspect which the Supreme Court glossed over when it pronounced on this law. A split is not a matter of mere numbers: one-third. Paragraph 3 of the Tenth Schedule clearly speaks of a split in the legislature party 'which has arisen as a result of a split in ... original political party', the organizational wing, as happened in the CPI in 1964 and the Congress in 1969. An open split on issues; not a sudden revolt by conspirators. The organization must split first and the legislature party splits as 'a result'. By this test there was no split in law either in the Congress or the BSP.

The CPI's articulate General Secretary A.B. Bardhan raised an important issue on 26 October. Legislators who indulged in violence are not prosecuted. 'Filing of criminal cases for such acts needs the speaker's permission which is usually not given and such violence, therefore, goes unpunished.' Neither the Criminal Procedure Code nor any other statute enjoins such a sanction. Nor does the law of parliamentary privilege. May's *Parliamentary Practice* says that 'criminal words in parliament' cannot be inquired into out of parliament. Articles 105(2) and 194(2) of the Constitution are to the same effect. However, 'criminal acts in parliament' are not immune to the judicial process. Assaults are not part of a 'proceeding in parliament'. In the famous case of *Bradlaugh* vs *Gossett*, Justice Stephen said that he 'knew of no authority for the proposition that an ordinary crime committed in the House of Commons would be withdrawn from the ordinary course of criminal justice . Any citizen can file an FIR in respect of the violence in the UP Assembly on 21 October and invite our legal system to rise to the challenge, or shall we wait till firearms are used in legislatures? Some years ago in Bombay, an MLA was prosecuted for assault in the assembly and sent to prison.

A simple reform of the anti-defection law can provide an effective cure, as the committee on defections recommended: bar the defector or splitter, from public office for a year. The honest convert will not be deterred; the turncoat will be. He wants instant reward, not a cheque post-dated by a year. Kalyan Singh and the BJP leadership have exploited the flaws in the system. Their adversaries have shown little interest in eradicating the flaws.

52

Dismissing a Chief Minister: The UP Case[1]

'Offer some plums before them; give a *laddu* to one, a *rasagulla* to another... members from Independents will join and you will then be able to produce a majority. Now, this is an insult to the constitution. This is a mockery of the constitution'. This mockery which Kailash Nath Katju, then Union Home Minister, so picturesquely described in the Lok Sabha on 19 November, 1954, is no longer an aberration. It is the norm of Indian politics. Elections to a new Lok Sabha should prompt serious reflection on the state of political morality in the country today.

We need to retrieve the constitution of India from the morass in which it was made to slide down since 1969 when the Congress was split. A constitution is rooted in a national consensus which comprises, besides its text, a host of conventions, tacit understandings and assumptions. Reactions to the recent crisis in UP reveal that the roots have become alarmingly weak. A consensus barely exists. No convention is too sacred to be violated for political exigencies. The office of the prime minister, the governor, and the speaker have been shorn of dignity and public confidence. The president alone kept his head, only to invite orchestrated opprobrium. There is not one politician in the country today who can be trusted to consistently stand by constitutional values or respect the rights of his opponents if it entails sacrifice of significant, though momentary, political gain.

Truth to tell, the present breed of the Indian politician does not

[1] *The Statesman*, 8, 9 and 10 March 1998.

share the outlook and ethos of the three principal founding fathers of the constitution: Jawaharlal Nehru, Sardar Patel and B.R. Ambedkar. This is particularly true of the likes of Kanshi Ram, Kalyan Singh, and Laloo Prasad Yadav. The rejection is manifested in two ways: disdain for constitutional morality and ignorance of and contempt for constitutional conventions.

While moving for the adoption of the draft constitution in the constituent assembly on 4 November 1948, Ambedkar quoted at some length George Grote, the historian of Greece, on constitutional morality. It means

a paramount reverence for the forms of the constitution, enforcing obedience to authority acting under and within these forms yet combined with the habits of free speech, of action subject only to definite legal control, and unrestrained censure of those very authorities as to all their public acts combined too with a perfect confidence in the bosom of every citizen, amidst the bitterness of party contest, that the forms of the constitution will not be less sacred in the eyes of his opponents than in his own.

Such confidence was not overly abundant even in 1948. Fifty years later it does not exist. Ambedkar was not unaware of its frail nature. 'Constitutional morality is not a natural sentiment. It has to be cultivated. We must realize that our people have yet to learn it. Democracy in India is only a top dressing on an Indian soil which is essentially undemocratic.'[2]

On 25 November 1949 when he moved 'That the constitution as settled by the assembly be passed', he said: 'However good a constitution may be, it is sure to turn out bad because those who are called to work it happen to be a bad lot ... It is, therefore, futile to pass any judgment upon the constitution without reference to the part which the people and their parties are likely to play'[3] The following day the president of the constituent assembly, Rajendra Prasad, pointed out that 'many things which canno: be written in a constitution are done by conventions. Let me hope that we shall show those capacities and develop those conventions.'[4]

For over four decades the Supreme Court has consistently recognized the conventions of the British parliamentary system as the ones on which rest important provisions of the constitution

[2]CAD, vol. vii, p. 38.
[3]CAD, vol. xii, p. 975.
[4]CAD, vol. xii, p. 993.

concerning the relationship between the head of state and the chief executive, at the centre as well as in the states: to wit, in *Ram Jawaya Kapur* vs *State of Punjab* (1955), *U.N. Rao v Indira Gandhi* (1971), *Samsher Singh* vs *State of Punjab* (1974), and *Supreme Court Advocates on Record Association* vs *Union of India* (1993). In the last case Justice Kuldip Singh aptly said 'Once it is established to the satisfaction of the Court that a particular convention exists and is operating then the conventions becomes a part of the 'constitutional law of the land and can be enforced in the like manner'.

For all that, there is a curious reluctance among judges, lawyers, as well as others concerned to probe into their import and scope. Specific issues *ipse dixit* are more convenient to research into than conventions. The court's ruling in the Bommai Case (1994) was given against a background that stretched over a quarter century since 1967, when non-Congress governments came to power. No one had bothered to question Sheikh Abdullah's dismissal from office as prime minister of Kashmir on 8 August 1953.

As far back as 11 November 1967, the Union Law Minister, P. Govinda Menon, said that 'the relative strength of the government in the legislature can only be tested on the floor of the house through a relevant vote and then the governor cannot take any cognizance of any charges in party or personal loyalties on the basis of public parade of its strength by the opposition'. These remarks were made in the context of the split in the UF ministry in West Bengal, led by Ajoy Mukerji, on 2 November. He was dismissed because he had sought a longer time frame for the floor contest than Governor Dharma Vira allowed. Opinion against the governors' arbitrariness hardened, and another authoritative pronouncement followed.

'In no circumstances should it be left to the governor to determine whether a chief minister continues to enjoy the support of the majority of the members or not. Even if the members make their opinion known to the governor in writing, it is the prerogative of the assembly to decide this issue.' This emphatic enunciation was made by Mr N Sanjiva Reddi on 6 April 1968 as speaker of the Lok Sabha in his presidential address to the 33rd Emergent Conference of Presiding Officers.[5]

In June 1969 the Administrative Reforms Commission recommended: 'when the governor has reason to believe that the ministry

[5]Maya Dube, *The Speaker in India*, (Delhi: S. Chand & Co., 1971), p. 292.

has ceased to command a majority in the assembly, he should come to a final conclusion on this question by summoning the assembly and ascertaining its verdict on the support enjoyed by the ministry.'[6]

The Committee of Governors set up by the president said in its report in 1971:'where the governor is satisfied, by whatever progress or means, that the ministry no longer enjoys majority support, he should ask the chief minister to face the assembly and prove his majority within the shortest possible time.'[7]

In 1984 three state governments were sacked in a row by the governors at the centre's behest: Nar Bahadur Bhandari in Sikkim by H.J.H Talyarkhan on 11 May; Farooq Abdullah by Jagmohan on 2 July; and N.T. Rama Rao by Ram Lal on 16 August. It is important to note that Ram Lal had to quit once NTR was restored to office. Will Romesh Bhandari follow this precedent?[8]

All this happened while the Sarkaria commission, set up in June 1983, was at work. Its report (1988) said 'Arid legality apart, as a matter of constitutional propriety, the governor should not dismiss a council of ministers unless the legislative assembly has expressed on the floor of the House [sic.] its want of confidence in it. He should advise the chief minister to summon the assembly as early as possible.' The chief minister should be allowed 'a reasonable time ... a period of 30 days will be reasonable unless there is very urgent business to be transacted such as passing the budget, in which case a shorter period may be indicated. In special circumstances, it may even exceed this period and go up to 60 days' (Para 4.11.13).[9]

The commission overlooked two factors and exceeded its remit. First, it is not arid legality but a fundamental of constitutional law that in such a situation the governor has no right to sack the chief minister on the basis of his own subjective satisfaction as to loss of majority support. Secondly, it is none of his business to set up, as it were, letter boxes on the gates of the Raj Bhavan to receive letters withdrawing that support. Unless dire urgency is disclosed or the loss is palpable, he ought firmly to direct the dissidents to the gates of the assembly, there to wait till it meets in due course. This is what B.K. Nehru very properly did as governor of Kashmir.

[6]ARC, p. 28, Rec. 11

[7]Committee of Governors, p. 45.

[8]White Paper on the Toppling of State Governments. Subversion of the Constitution, A Janata Party Publication, 1984.

[9]Report of the Commission on Centre–State Relations, p. 129.

The Supreme Court had all this material when it ruled in the Bommai case. Five of the nine judges on the bench ruled on the floor test. Four (Justices P.B. Sawant, Kuldip Singh, B.P. Jeevan Reddy and S.C. Agrawal) ruled it to be the sole acceptable test using expressions like 'alone' and 'the only way'. All five recognized exceptional situations, one of them to the point of rejecting the test as imperative. (K. Ramaswamy). However, the other four received the concurrence of Justice S. Ratnavel Pandian making it a clear majority (5–4) on the necessity of a floor test.

In 1995, only a year after the Bommai case, the court's ruling was flouted with impuni y by the Governor of UP, Motilal Vora. On 1 June the 18-month-old SP–BSP coalition, led by Mulayam Singh Yadav, broke up when the BSP withdrew its support. It won full support from the BJP. Mulayam Singh wrote to the governor drawing his attention to the court's ruling and saying that he would prove his majority when the Vidhan Sabha met. It had already been summoned to meet on 8 July. Vora was not prepared to give him more than ten days while Miss Mayawati staked her claim to form a ministry. On 2 June Mulayam Singh's supporters let loose terror at the guest-house where Miss Mayawati and some BSP MLAs were staying, an incident fully described in the Ramesh Chandra report. The BSP and the BJP kept their MLAs in 'volitional captivity'. In New Delhi on 3 June, a correspondent, Radhika Ramaseshan, heard the BSP leader Kanshi Ram direct Miss Mayawati over the phone: 'Mobilize a crowd of 5,000 partymen in Lucknow; requisition an army of Gujjar musclemen from western UP, arm them with high-powered weapons and not just licensed revolvers; let them loose on the streets and ask them to raise provocative slogans.' Vora sacked the chief minister after he refused to abide by his advice to resign and swore in Miss Mayawati later at night on 3 June.

Speaking in the Lok Sabha earlier that day, Atal Behari Vajpayee said:'A deadlock has been created there and the only solution is that the governor, who had appointed the chief minister, should withdraw his pleasure. The chief minister says he is prepared for a trial of strength on the floor of the Vidhan Sabha when it meets on July 8. But the chief minister who has lost majority support is banking on terrorizing MLAs into submission .... If such a chief minister is allowed to remain in power up to July 8, it will not be proper ...'

Ministries have not been sacked for outrages far worse than those on 2 June, e.g., the police firings on an unarmed crowd of Dalits in

Bombay under the Shiv Sena–BJP coalition. Vora was not without resource, including Central help, to ensure a free vote on 8 July when Mulayam Singh would have gone down to certain defect. He was, however, entitled to his day in court. The Supreme Court has yet to hear his petition.

Surely, corruption is no less revolting or consequential as terror. Vajpayee had no qualms about blessing with his presence the Kalyan Singh ministry's infamous expansion on 27 October 1997. All the defectors were appointed ministers including 19 'history-sheeters' in police records. Fasts unto death are more credible when they are undertaken in protest at the wrongs by one's own side. It was appropriate that the end of that charade was graced by the presence of R. Venkataraman, whose conduct was responsible for the Bommai ruling. All the three proclamations imposing president's rule—in Nagaland (7 August, 1988); Karnataka (21 April, 1989) and Meghalaya (14 October, 1991)—on which he had obediently put the rubber stamp of his signature as president were struck down by the court. S.R. Bommai, chief minister of Karnataka, took the matter to court as did the other two. In the Meghalaya case two of the judges found the material given to the president 'not only irrational but motivated by factual and legal malafides'. R. Venkataraman had evidently shut his eyes to them.

The 1995 precedent exposes Vajpayee's double standards but it does not justify Bhandari's action, either. His report to the president reeked of falsehood. Twelve out of the 22 members of the Loktantrik Congress (LTC) members 'came to see me around 13.30 hrs on 21 February to say that they had withdrawn from the Kalyan Singh ministry and staked a claim to form one under the leadership of Jagadambika Pal. Letters of support from leaders of BSP, the Congress, the Janata Dal and its breakaway faction, and personal endorsements by leaders of the CPM, CPI, and the BKKP followed. This added to 221 in an assembly of 424. Even including the 12 BSP defectors, the CM's strength had fallen to 197. He informed Kalyan Singh of the situation at 2.45 p.m., and the latter met him at 5 p.m. Mark these words: 'I informed Shri Kalyan Singh that they had clearly (*sic.*) lost the majority. It was not for me to do the count of heads. I have to go by what the leaders of the recognized political parties maintained.'

Kalyan Singh claimed that more than a third of the 22 LTC members were with him. Bhandari noted that two MLAs, Vivek Singh and Virendra Singh, had changed sides that very instant.

Moreover, how could he permit the 12 to speak for the entire LTC of 22? 'Under the Anti-Defection Law it is now accepted parliamentary practice that a letter from the leader of the party is accepted by the head of state signifying support or withdrawal. Only such splinter groups can he taken cognizance of whose status has been accepted by the speaker.'This is sheer nonsense.The law, embodied in the Tenth Schedule to the Constitution, envisages (para 8) framing of rules for reports by the leader of a legislative party for condoning violations of a whip and admission of new members. The head of state does not come in here. He comes in when a group claims majority support, a process in which, however, the speaker has no role. The obfuscation is deliberate. Even without the speaker's recognition of a split, it is open to the governor to reckon with it, if it is manifestly valid, leaving the speaker to decide the dispute later under the law. The practice of relying on letters of support by leaders to the governor precedes the anti-defection law. It has an obvious qualification: no such letter is reliable if the situation is uncertain or the writer's credentials dubious. The maximum strength he himself allowed the LTC was 'a total of 15 out of 22'.

Kalyan Singh rightly demanded that the issue be resolved on the floor of the assembly. To Bhandari this 'would mean giving an opportunity to a government which was already in a minority to test its strength on the floor of the house'. It is however precisely in a case where the government's majority is challenged that authorities have insisted, for over 30 years, that the house alone should give its verdict, not the governor. Bhandari chose wilfully to decide for himself that afternoon that the government was 'already in a minority' and arrived at the conclusion that in such a case he should not let the house decide; as if its verdict should be sought only in cases where the government's majority was unchallenged.This would be bad enough in any situation. It is unforgivable when loyalties were shifting rapidly before his own eyes.

From his basic premise the rest follows with equal perverseness. 'In the case of Shri Jágdambika Pal, the question would not be of filling a gap, but ensuring (*sic.*) that the support he claimed (*sic.*) would continue and would be reflected in the Assembly.' As he put it frankly, 'It would only be a question of keeping the flock together'. Bhandari's efforts were to assist this amorphous group of leaders in 'keeping the flock together'.Thereby 'a more stable government is possible'.

That Bhandari cited the 1995 precedent is understandable. What is unforgivable is his dishonest attempt to establish the irrelevance of the Supreme Court's ruling in the Bommai case. A chief minister can be sacked in one of two ways. One is by the president promulgating a proclamation under Article 356, whether on the governor's report or otherwise, imposing president's rule in the State. It entails dismissal of the state government. The other is by the governor's order. Article 164 (1) says that 'the ministers shall hold office during the pleasure of the governor'. The governor makes an order signifying his withdrawal of 'the pleasure'.

Bhandari argued, first, that the Bommai case related ' to the dismissal of a government under Article 356 of the Constitution. Here it was not a case of dismissing a government and imposing president's rule.' Realizing the disingenuousness of the distinction, he added: 'The essence of the Bommai judgment is that the establishment of a majority or otherwise must be determined on the floor of the house. The principle of the floor test should be invoked. I wished to adhere to that, particularly as Shri Kalyan Singh had also made a similar request.'

What, then, prevented him from acting on that 'principle', the 'essence of the Bommai judgment'? Incredibly, in the very next sentence he cited the 1995 precedent, 'the change of speaker' that followed in its train, and the LTC's demand for a similar change now. 'For this, a minimum notice of 14 days is required.'

The Supreme Court's ruling covered all situations of dismissal. As Justice P.B. Sawant said, 'in all cases where the support to the ministry is claimed to have been withdrawn by some legislators, the proper course for testing the strength of the ministry is holding the test on the floor of the house. That alone is the constitutionally ordained forum ...' He also brushed aside the pretext trotted out by governors of 'horse-trading going on between the legislators'. It is a game two can play; one side, to topple a ministry; the other, to ensure its survival. The latter enjoys an advantage. The cure lies in a better anti-defection law, not in abandoning democratic norms. The entire operation was conducted with the frenzy of a coup at night.

It is little realized that Bhandari's precedent, as that of Vora, imperils democracy at the Centre, no less. Article 75 (2) says 'the ministers shall hold office during the pleasure of the president', very much as Article 164 (1) says of the ones in the States. Ambedkar emphatically told the constituent assembly on 30 December 1948, apropos the discretionary powers, that as head of state in a parliamentary system 'the position of the governor is exactly the same as the position of the president'.

On 23 February the Lucknow bench of the Allahabad high court held the governor's action to be unconstitutional and ordered restoration of the dismissed government to office leaving it to the governor 'to summon the house if he thinks fit to have the vote of confidence tested'. It pointedly remarked on 'the hot haste of the governor's action on the eve of the Lok Sabha election scheduled to be held on February 22, 1998, a few hours later'.

Governor Bhandari's Report was a 'speaking order', as lawyers call it. Sadly, what was obvious to all was lost on the Supreme Court. On 24 February a three-member bench, comprising Chief Justice M.M. Punchi and Justices S.C. Agarwal and K.T. Thomas, made an order as astonishing in its implications as it was unprecedented. It ordered a quaint floor test on 26 February and also directed the assembly how to hold it, in palpable breach of the constitution, the rules of procedure, and the very fundamentals of the parliamentary system: 'The only agenda for the special session will be to have a composite floor test between the contending parties in order to see which of the two claimants for chief ministership has a majority in the house.'

If such an order were made on a full discussion of the law, it would have caused disquiet enough. Three judges of the court felt free thus to 'innovate' in an interim order, made after only a brief argument. The court ordered that 'no major decisions would be made by the functioning (*sic.*) government except attending to routine matters'. Its existence was thus recognized as prima facie valid. This was a government restored to office by a high court order which the Supreme Court did not overturn. It would have been appropriate to allow either side to table its motion, of confidence or no-confidence, leaving the house to be master of its established procedure. A 'composite' vote is appropriate in a club election. It is unheard of in legislatures which vote on motions after debate. Constitutions alone can provide for election of the chief executive as do those of Pakistan Articles 9 (2A) and 130 (2A) and Germany (Article 63). No court can. It is sheer usurpation of power for a court to command it by an order without the sanction of the constitution.

The constitution contains the most explicit provisions for occasions when an assembly votes as an electorate, whether in the election of the president (Article 55) or the Rajya Sabha (Article 80). The very expression 'composite floor test' does not exist in constitutional or parliamentary parlance. The constitution envisages legislators voting either at elections or in the house on a 'resolution'. It empowers (Article 208) the assembly to make rules of procedure, which thus enjoy constitutional sanction. Article 212 reads:

(1) The validity of any proceedings in the legislature of a state shall not be called in question on the ground of any alleged irregularity of procedure. (2) No officer or member of the legislature of state in whom powers are vested by or under this constitution for regulating procedure or the conduct of business, or for maintaining order, in the legislature shall be subject to the jurisdiction of any court in respect of the exercise by him of those powers.

If this bars judicial intervention after the event, except in the case of a sheer nullity in the procedure so does its intervention before the event; especially by prescribing an 'innovation' devoid of legality.

It fell to the Speaker of the UP assembly, Kesri Nath Tripathi, to spell out the detailed procedure for the new-fangled 'composite floor test' on 26 February. He had a ballot box placed near his podium. MLAs were called constituency-wise. They signed a register, the counterfoil of the ballot paper, as also the ballot paper, while marking their preference on it. It was neither a secret ballot nor proper voting in a division following parliamentary debate. Kalyan Singh secured 225 votes against Jagdambika Pal's 196. Twenty LTC members voted for the chief minister.

The Supreme Court resumed hearing of the case on 27 February and ordered 'we are of the view that the impugned order of the high court directing the Kalyan Singh ministry to be put back to office should be hereby made absolute subject of course to democratic discipline.' The high court, far from shutting out the floor test, had suggested it. The Supreme Court could and should have affirmed the high court order on 24 February on a perusal of Bhandari's report alone in the light of the Bommai case. Instead of quashing Bhandari's order of dismissal it characterized the Kalyan Singh government a 'functioning' one—another 'innovation'—and decreed a 'composite vote'. Is this a precedent which it wishes the high courts to follow?

The court noted, pointedly, that the speaker's failure over four months to rule on the legality of the split, claimed by 12 BSP defectors from a party of 66, had been severely criticized. 'We, however, reserve any comments on this aspect in view of the wide margin of win by Kalyan Singh.' That is less material than the patent illegality. Twelve votes would not have made any difference to his survival but the episode does bear on the governance of the state and on the machinery of the law.

The anti-defection law is part of the Constitution (Tenth Schedule) and makes the speaker sole judge of disputes (para 6). Surely. 'a situation has arisen in which the government of the State cannot be carried on in accordance with the provisions of this constitution' within the meaning of Art. 356, if the speaker deliberately and persistently flouts the law; just as much as it would were the chief minister or governor to do so.

On 20 October 1997 the speaker had held a strategy session with the chief minister and hopelessly compromised his position. On 24 October he cited a statement by a BSP MLA, Markanday Chand, who said that 23 BSP members 'had broken away from the party'. The speaker ruled: 'I have decided to take cognisance of the same.' He had of course no right to do so. Four months rolled by and the claim remains unfulfilled yet Kesri Nath Tripathi refused to disqualify the 12 defectors, trotting out one false excuse after another: 'I have already asked for verification', he said on 24 October. There was, he asserted, no time limit to do so. 'No one has come yet, but as soon as they come, I will give them recognition.' In his view 'split is a continuous process'. He held a charade of hearings in November 1997. The last hearing was held on 25 February when he reserved his ruling. Kesri Nath Tripathi has made a mockery of the constitution. The sponsor of the Tenth Schedule, Rajiv Gandhi, said in the Rajya Sabha on 31 January 1985: 'The decision should be automatic ... so that there is no debate about it ... the operation of the Bill should be quick so that there is not time in which horse-trading can take place.' Kesri Nath Tripathi has demonstrated that while he sits in the speaker's chair the constitution simply cannot work in Uttar Pradesh.

As for the president, it is too late in the day for anyone to question his rights in the matter. Some of the protesters have themselves gone to the Rashtrapati Bhavan in the last few decades to urge him to bridle the prime minister of the day or, more to the point, about partisan governors. Leaks there have been since the fifties about differences between Rajendra Prasad and Jawarlal Nehru and their respective successors. In 1987 there were leaks about those between the queen and Margaret Thatcher.

Governors are appointed by and hold offices during 'the pleasure of the president'. President Narayanan would have been within his rights in issuing a formal communiqué on the lines of that issued by President Shankar Dayal Sharma on 20 April 1996 in a similar situation: a prime minister who, for his own political ends, shut his eyes to a governor's manifest misconduct and failed in his duty to the president and to the nation. That communiqué recorded: 'The president is yet to receive any advice of the union cabinet relating to the Governor of Himachal Pradesh [Sheila Kaul]'. It set out the gist of the discussions between the president and the prime minister, quoted from his letter to the latter, seeking the latter's advice and said that they were published 'in view of certain erroneous reports and speculation in a section of the press'.

In the case in point, it is not the press but politicians who have been culpable, not least Vajpayee for betraying confidence. Others went so far as to censure the president. President Narayanan owes it to himself and to the nation to publish his letters to the prime minister, Inder Kumar Gujral, who served him and the nation so poorly in this affair. The nation has a right to know the truth.

53
Dismissing a Chief Minister: The Gujarat Case[1]

L urking in the subconscious of Indian judges, lawyers, and
politicians is the ghost of Alhaji Adegbenro. For quite some
time he exercised a baleful influence on New Delhi as it
abused Article 356 of the Constitution (president's rule). Little help
was needed; the ghost provided it in plenty. It must be exorcized for
good.

On 21 May 1962, Chief Akintola, Premier of Western Nigeria,
filed a suit in the high court against the governor, Sir Adesoji Aderemi
and another for 'declaration that there is no right in the defendant
to relieve the plaintiff of his office as premier of the Western Nigeria
under Section (5) 33 (10) of the Constitution of Western Nigeria
in the absence of a prior resolution/decision of the Western House
of Assembly reached on the floor of the house to the effect that the
plaintiff no longer commands the majority of the members of the
House of Assembly.' Another prayer was an injunction restraining
the Governor from acting in violation of this 'right'.

Section 33(1) said that ministers held office 'during the governor's
pleasure', as in our constitution, but, unlike ours, a proviso was added
forbidding the governor from dismissing the prime minister 'unless
it appears to him that the premier no longer commands the support
of a majority ... '

Within hours of the suit being filed the governor sacked the
prime minister and appointed Adegbenro in his place. The prayers

[1]This article written in the context of the dismissal of the Suresh Mehta
government in Gujarat and the installation of the Vaghela government, was published
in *The Statesman*, 18 November 1996.

were suitably modified to claim restitution to office. The high court referred the issues to the Supreme Court which ruled, 3–1, in favour of the former prime minister. The governor had acted on a letter from 66 members of the house of 124.

In a judgment of compelling logic, Chief Justice Ademola observed:

The conclusion is inescapable that the framers of the constitution wanted the house to be responsible at every level for the ultimate fate of government and the premier. The horizon must be larger than leaving it to one man. The governor might eventually be the instrument used to effect this, but his position as final arbiter must be dictated by events in the House or events emanating from the house, and not by a letter, however well meaning, signed by a body of members of the house ... I believe that the constitution contemplated proceedings in the house as being the touchstone of whether the premier (with his government) commands the support of a majority of the members or no longer commands such support. I think that the House of Assembly cannot be relieved of its responsibilities and duties as the house by a letter to the governor signed by members of the house. It will be an unduly narrow and restrictive interpretation of the powers of the house—and a correspondingly unduly wide interpretation of the powers of the governor—if, in the circumstance, Section 33(10) is interpreted in any other way except in a way which makes it clear that the evidence emanates from proceedings of the house.

These observations, made in 1962, are very relevant to our situation.

Justices Taylor and Bairamian concurred. Dissenting, Justice Bratt said that 'the clearest way in which it can possibly appear' that a prime minister is no longer in a majority 'is by an adverse vote', but that is not 'the only source'. He proceeded to cite a laboured, hypothetical case. He did however 'agree that the greatest caution is necessary in assessing the weight to be given to reports of anything said or done outside the house'. It was severely limited dissent.[2]

Adegbenro appealed to the privy council which reversed the ruling in a judgment delivered by Lord Radcliffe whose reputation has received a deserved knock lately. It was in the worst traditions of the privy council in the narrowness of its approach and its double

---

[2]D.O. Aihe and P.A. Olugede, *Cases and Materials on Constitutional Law in Nigeria*, (Oxford University Press, 1979, pp. 2–11, Judgments of the Supreme Court of Nigeria.

standards when former colonies, especially those in Asia and Africa, were concerned.[3]

Radcliffe accepted that Section 33(10) was 'derived from the constitutional understandings' in Britain, but argued disingenuously that 'the practical application of these principles to a given situation, if it arose in the United Kingdom, would depend upon the actual facts of that situation.' Can you believe that in any such situation the queen would dire act on such evidence and sack the prime minister?

In this context it is absurd to say that in democratic politics speeches or writings outside the house, party meetings, speeches or activities inside the house short of actual voting are all capable of contributing evidence to indicate what action this or that member has decided to take when and if he is called upon to vote in the house, and it appears to their Lordships somewhat unreal to try to draw a firm dividing line between votes and other demonstrations where the issue of 'support' is concerned.

Having accepted that the letter of the constitution was based on British conventions, he ruled the opposite to assert that in the text the 'governor's power of removal is not limited in precise terms'—the plea advanced by some politicians in India and rejected by the Supreme Court in 1974 in Samsher Singh's case. Radcliffe went so far as to suggest that British precedents provided no clue. He did recognize, though,

the dangers of governor arriving at any conclusion as to his premier's support in the house except upon the incontrovertible evidence of votes recorded there on some crucial issue. There are indeed such dangers. Expressions of opinion, attitude or intention upon such a delicate matter may well prove to be delusive. He may judge the situation wrongly and so find himself to have taken a critical step in a direction which is proved to be contrary to the wishes of the majority of the house or of the electorate.

Nigeria amended the constitution to nullify this ruling and abolished appeals to the privy council. It is unthinkable that such a judgment would have been delivered had a British prime minister been dismissed. It was a wanton obiter by the privy council in 1964 which so angered the people as to set off a chain of events leading to the repeal of the 1948 Constitution of Ceylon.[4] Professing great 'respect' for it, Jinnah, nonetheless, had 'no hesitation in saying that

[3] *Adegbenro* vs *Akintola* (1963), AC 614.
[4] *The Bribery Commissioner* vs *Pedrick Ranasinghe* (1962), 2 AC 172 at pp. 193–4.

the privy council have on several occasions absolutely murdered Hindu law and slaughtered Mohammedan law'. Its homicidal passions did not spare constitutional law, either.[5]

One would have thought that the ruling was eventually buried not only by our Supreme Court but also in the pronouncement of P. Govinda Menon, Union Law Minister, who said on 11 November 1967 that 'the relative strength of the government in the legislature can only be tested on the floor of the house through a relevant vote and then the governor cannot take any cognizance of any changes in party or personal loyalties—on the basis of public parade of its strength by the opposition'.

The 33rd Emergent Conference of the Presiding Officers of the Legislatures, held on 6 April 1968, agreed: 'In no circumstances' should the governor decide on loss of support 'even if the members make their opinion known to the governor in writing'. He has necessarily to form a tentative opinion at the time of the chief ministers initial appointment. The rules on this are clear enough.

On 18 August 1996 the Governor of Gujarat, Mr Krishanpal Singh, received a memo signed by 46 MLAs expressing want of confidence in the Suresh Mehta ministry. The party position was: BJP 120; Congress 44; Independents 16; and 2 vacancies in a house of 182. Dissidents had to be at least 48 strong to pull down the ministry with Congress support. The very next day the governor flew to Delhi and met, *inter alia*, Mr P.V. Narasimha Rao and Mrs Sonia Gandhi besides government leaders.

On 20 August Mr Vaghela floated his Rashtriya Janata Party in which former minister, Mr Dilip Parekh's Gujarat Janata Party was eventually to merge as the Mahagujarat Janata Party. On 24 August the governor sent the memo to the assembly secretariat for verification of the signatures. Eighteen of them had allegedly signed under duress. This was crucial. A split to be valid under the defection law required one-third of the 120 BJP members. That was for the Speaker, Mr Harishchandra Patel, to rule on, not the governor. In a letter to the governor on 30 August he said that there was no split since 13 MLAs had informed him of their dissociation from the 46. Each side issued whips to its flock. 92 MLAs pledged loyalty to Mr Suresh Mehta on 2 September. The

[5]Syed Sharifuddin Pirzada (ed.), *The Collected Works of Quaid-e-Azam Mohammad Ali Jinnah*, vol. ii (1921–6) (Karachi: East & West Publishing Co., 1986), p. 309.

signatures of 94 faithfuls were verified personally by the secretary of the assembly on 3 September. That day, the deputy speaker, Chandubhai Dabi, simply recognized the MJP and adjourned the assembly. Reconvened by the ailing speaker hours later, it was adjourned again by Mr Dabi. 92 BJP members and 5 Independents appeared before the governor but he declined to identify or count them.

Another event however took place on 3 September which has been overlooked. It is of decisive significance. The note that was circulated to the press when the Union Home Minister, Mr Indrajit Gupta, held his press conference on 19 September records that event:

The chief minister writes to the governor on 3 September requesting the latter to send a message under Article 175(2) convening the house to take up the business of vote of confidence motion. However, before the governor could reply, he sends another letter on September 7, 1996, requesting the governor to now send a message under Article 175(2) of the Constitution to convene the house to take up the no-confidence motion against the deputy speaker (saying that he had already proved his majority before the governor on 3rd evening). Governor replies on 9th September clarifying that no message under Article 175(2) to take up no-confidence motion against the deputy speaker could be given since the governor cannot make a presumption of the illegality of the deputy speaker's ruling till it is set aside by a competent authority.

The advice was repeated on 10 September and rejected.

This was utterly unconstitutional. The chief minister's advice was binding on the governor. Even had the adjournment been valid or challenged in a court, it did not debar the governor from summoning the house. His is an independent power as the Supreme Court and Madras high court have pointed out in cases concerning Punjab (1968) and Tamil Nadu (1972), respectively. In the Punjab case (1968) an ordinance was enacted to force the partisan speaker to conduct pressing financial business without adjourning the house.

The Supreme Court did not consider the validity of the governor's message since, evidently, no one contested it. Article 175(2) reads: '(2) The governor may send messages to the house or houses of the legislature of the state, whether with respect to the Bill then pending in the legislature or otherwise, and a house to which any message is so sent shall with all convenient despatch consider any matter required by the message to be taken into consideration.' Madras high court ruled explicitly on this. It is 'a direc.ive to all concerned, is at once a mandate and a mandate pregnant with details as to the subjects to be discussed in the assembly session'.

In both cases the speaker was out to obstruct while the governor acted on the chief minister's advice and foiled the attempt. In Gujarat the governor was in cahoots with the deputy speaker and twice refused to act on the chief minister's advice. This was constitutional outrage. A similar message was sent by governor Motilal Vora to the UP assembly on 17 June 1995. It was unconstitutionally foiled by the speaker, Mr Dhani Ram Varma.

In this situation Mr Vaghela had no difficulty in mustering support. The speaker summoned the assembly on 18 September. He died on 16 September. Dabi was 'ill' when the house met. A desperate Suresh Mehta went on to make his own assaults on the Constitution: a chairperson, Mr Daulat Desai of the BJP, was appointed in breach of the rules; a motion of confidence moved though it was not on the agenda; and plainclothesmen, evidently assembled for action, entered the house and beat up the Opposition. This alone justified imposition of president's rule.

If on 3 and 12 September, when they appeared before the president, the BJP's MLAs were in a majority, a month later they were not. The governor changed his mind on parades. On 20 October he went so far as to write to both sides to assemble their men before him by 4 p.m. on 22 October. The BJP refused. Mr Vaghela displayed his 40 men plus nine Independents on 21 October. Two days later president's rule was lifted and he became chief minister. Even affidavits were sworn, the governor warning the dependants, in obvious ignorance, that they would not be permitted to change their minds, apparently not even in the assembly.

Mr Vaghela won a vote of confidence on 29 October, thanks to Congress support (46); 13 Independents, and his own 44. The speaker, Mr Gumansingh Waghela, expunged from the record the proceedings of 18 September; as had the UP speaker on 19 June 1995. Madras high court had ruled that the speaker's attempt 'to expunge certain proceedings from the debates' was 'without power'.

The BJP's two-thirds majority (120), won in elections on 13 March 1995, eroded. Twelve were expelled between 17 and 27 August. On 18 September only 91 voted for the chief minister's motion; 17 defied the whip. Fifteen changed loyalties thereafter.

The 17 and 15 acted in violation of anti-defection law. At no time did one-third leave the party together to qualify for a split.

There is another aspect which even the Supreme Court glossed over when it pronounced on this law. A split is not a matter of mere numbers. Paragraph 3 of the Tenth Schedule clearly speaks of a split in the legislature party 'which has arisen as a result of a split in ... original political party', the organizational wing, as happened to the CPI in 1964 and the Congress in 1969. An open split on issues; not a sudden revolt by conspirators in the assembly. The organization must split first and the legislature party as 'a result' of the split.

We owe to the genius of the Sarkaria commission the bright suggestion on verification of signatures. When the house is not in session 'a governor may receive reliable evidence (e.g. one or more letters signed by, or a no-confidence motion proposed by, a majority of members with their signatures authenticated by the secretary of the assembly) that the ministry has lost its majority'. This suggestion is of a piece with its three authors' lack of expertise, in this field.[6]

Bar Justice R.S. Sarkaria, one was a bureaucrat the other an economist. They were asked to probe centre–state relations, not conventions of parliamentary democracy which, as Dr. B.R. Ambedkar said on 30 December 1948, are 'exactly the same' in the centre and in the states. No one bars a legislator from approaching the president or the governor. That does not mean they should put up letter boxes outside their gates to receive memoranda and even motions of no-confidence from mid-session topplers, especially given the context of toppling in India. A good test: Would the commission have made this suggestion apropos the President?

The results have been as absurd as the commission's views. On 25 August 1995 Mr A.N. Tiwari, the principal secretary to the governor of Andhra Pradesh, Mr Krishan Kant, asked the secretary of the assembly 'to certify the genuineness of the signatures of the legislators appearing on the memoranda' submitted to him. The speaker submitted a report to the governor verifying the signatures as genuine.

A motion of no-confidence must be sent to the assembly secretariat, not the governor, and it is none of its business to verify signatures for the governor. It is impertinent of him to cast such a

[6]Report of the Commission on Centre–State Relations, pt I, p. 128, para 4.11.10.

duty on the assembly. Such an arrangement impairs the integrity and dignity of both the governor and the assembly. If the governor receives a memo from legislators, nothing prevents him from sounding the chief minister and signatories. If he feels that the challenge is a serious one, the obvious course is to insist on the summoning of the assembly.

When the anti-defection law was being discussed with the Opposition, Rajiv Gandhi promised to provide later that the assembly alone would decide the fate of the government. (Such a provision exists in the Pakistani Constitution. Articles 91(5) for the prime minister and 130(5) for the provinces 'require the chief minister to obtain a vote of confidence from the assembly'). As Speaker of the Lok Sabha, N. Sanjiva Reddy suggested a constitutional amendment to the same effect.

Two other reforms can help. One is the constructive vote of confidence as provided in Article 67 of the Basic Law of Germany: 'The Bundestag may express its lack of confidence in the federal chancellor only by electing a successor with the majority of its members ...' The motion must also name a successor.

The other is to ask the legislature to elect the prime minister or chief minister. It could be asked, to the exclusion of any other business after the election of the speaker, to proceed to elect, without debate, one of its members to be the prime minister by a majority of the entire house, and failing that, on a second ballot, by a majority of those present and voting. A variant is Article 63 of the Basic Law. It says that 'the federal chancellor shall be elected by the Bundestag without debate upon the proposal of the federal president'. He selects, the house endorses. The selection should be done away with. Let the house alone decide.

54
The States and Foreign Relations[1]

Mr Jyoti Basu's visit to Dhaka was probably the first instance of its kind in which the chief minister of a state of the Indian union parleyed with the head of a foreign government. Involved were important issues of foreign policy directly affecting the interests of his own state. Protests at his trip, partisan as ever, died down in the wake of the successful conclusion of the India–Bangladesh agreement on sharing the waters of the Ganga.

That is however no reason why the constitutional aspects of this unprecedented action should not be discussed. Chief ministers have, in the past, negotiated deals with foreign governments and organizations on investments, trade, and specific projects. Dr B.C. Roy was said to have written out a 30-odd page agreement on one such deal with France. Negotiating an accord on the Ganga waters however belongs to a different class altogether.

Little do the critics realize that not only does the constitution not preclude such negotiations, if conducted with the centre's approval, but Mr Basu's effort was in the best spirit of genuine federalism. The Minister for External Affairs, Mr Inder Kumar Gujral's deservedly high praise of Mr Basu suggests more than central approval. The political reality is that, without Mr Basu's active participation, West Bengal would not have accepted the accord and, without the state's acceptance, no government of India could have

[1]This of a two-part article, written in the context of Mr Jyoti Basu's visit to Dhaka in 1996, was published in the *Statesman*, 31 October and 1 November 1996.

concluded the agreement. The centre invited his participation, wisely and constitutionally.

Therein lies a lesson for all who read the text of the constitution literally divorced from the realities. It proves the truth of Justice Felix Frankfurter's aphorism: 'constitutional law ... is not at all a science, but applied politics, using the word in its noble sense.'

Article 253 gives a carte blanche to the centre: 'Notwithstanding anything in the foregoing provisions of this chapter (on centre–state relations in the legislative sphere), parliament has power to make any law for the whole or any part of the territory of India for implementing any treaty, agreement or convention with any other country/countries *or any decision made at any international conference, association or other body.*' The italicized words were added on 14 October 1949 without debate in the constituent assembly just as the text was on 13 June 1949. No one perceived its wide sweep.[2] If the government of India concludes an international convention on, say, health, parliament will have the power to make any law to implement it despite the fact that the subject falls in the State list. More, it applies not only to a treaty but covers any 'decision' made at any international 'conference', association or 'other body'.

Sir Ivor Jennings threw up his arms in alarm as he read this and said:

It does not specifically refer to conferences, associations and other bodies representing governments, and, on its face, it would seem to apply to any international organization representing, let us say, universities or trade unions. Nor would it seem to matter that the organization had merely advisory powers. The word 'decision' cannot mean a binding decision, for the assumption is that legislation is needed to implement it. If this is the correct interpretation, the union parliament can acquire jurisdiction over university education by the simple process of a decision of the Inter-University Board of India, which is an international body, because it contains representatives of universities in Burma and Ceylon. One notes, too, that the Comintern and the Fourth International are international bodies. This is such a startling invasion of states' rights, thrown in casually by a few words at the end of an Article, that one doubts its correctness. Possibly, a court would hold that 'international' implied a governmental organization, that it applied to 'association' and 'body' as well as 'conference' and that 'body' had to be read *ejusdem generis* [in the same sense as the preceding words].[3]

[2]See CAD, vol. x, p. 277 and vol. viii. p. 813 respectively.
[3]Ivor Jennings, *The Indian Constitution.*

Entry 13 in the Union list reads: 'Participation in international conferences, associations and other bodies and implementing [sic] of decisions made thereat'. Entry 14 concerns 'entering into treaties and agreements with foreign countries ...', Entry 12 concerns the UN. They are all encapsulated in Entry 10: 'foreign affairs; all matters which bring the union into relation with any foreign country'.

Article 73 (1) says that 'subject to the other provisions of this constitution, the executive power of the union shall extend (a) to the matters with respect to which parliament has power to make laws'. The government's executive power extends to all matters in the Union list.

But even a rigid, centralist constitution like ours allows for play at the joints. Article 258 (1) does just that. It says: 'Notwithstanding anything in this constitution, the president may, with the consent of the government of a state, entrust either conditionally or unconditionally to that government or to its officers functions in relation to any matter to which the executive power of the union extends.'

This provision empowers the government of India to delegate to a state government 'functions in relation to any matter' that falls within the purview of the centre's executive power, foreign affairs included. The only proviso is the state's 'consent' to such delegation. Concretely, the union could have asked the state of West Bengal, as such, to conduct formal negotiations with Bangladesh on sharing the Ganga waters and the state government could have entrusted the task to its chief minister.

Of course, Mr Basu is much more than the chief minister of an important state. His services have often been sought by the centre in the past on issues of national policy. In this case, in truth, though not in form or in law, he acted as the union's envoy to Bangladesh, not unmindful of the interests of his state and of the union, all in the good spirit of Article 258. The fact remains that the realities of today mock at Article 253 which was drafted in the climate prevalent in 1949. In the USA the requirement of ratification of treaties by the Senate takes care of the states' rights. Our Rajya Sabha (council of states) has long ceased to perform its function as a guardian of states' rights, thanks to the fraudulent entry of persons who do not reside in the state but are elected by its legislature in breach of the law and the members' solemn affirmations.

Australia provides an instructive lesson. Section 51 (xxix) of the

Commonwealth of Australia Constitution Act, 1900 makes external affairs a subject on which parliament alone can make laws. The high court construed it over the years to imply power to legislate even on state matters in order to implement a treaty.

One such decision in 1983, in the Franklin Dam case between the Commonwealth and Tasmania, created a furore. A majority (4–3) ruled that it empowered legislation legislation on state matters to implement a treaty. The subject came up before the Australian Constitutional convention at Adelaide. On 29 April 1983, it resolved:

That this convention, expressing its concern that the traditional balance of legislative, executive and judicial powers between the Commonwealth and the States may be destroyed by an expansionary interpretation of Section 51 (xxix) of the constitution, directs that a subcommittee be established to—(a) examine the scope of powers arguably possessed by the Commonwealth parliament under Section 51 (xxix); (b) consider the possible effect of these powers on the division of legislative, executive and judicial powers which had traditionally existed in the Australian federation; (c) suggest mechanisms involving both the Commonwealth and the States whereby Australia's international obligations may be met whilst, at the same time, preserving the traditional distribution of legislative, executive and judicial powers under the constitution; and (d) formulate such mechanisms into proposals to be submitted to the next session of this convention.

The subcommittee reported in September 1984. The constitutional convention simply approved its report on 1 August 1985, when it met at Brisbane and passed the buck to the states premiers' conference. The subcommittee's report provide a wealth of information.

In June 1982 the state's premiers' conference adopted 'Principles and Procedures for Commonwealth–State Consultation on Treaties'. It fell into three parts: consultation, treaty negotiation process, and federal–state aspects. 'The states are informed in all cases and at an early stage of any treaty discussions in which Australia is considering participation'. A detailed procedure was laid down. 'Where State interest is apparent, the Commonwealth should—wherever practicable, seek and take into account the views of the States in formulating Australian policy and keep the States informed of the determined policy.'

The document noted that 'in particular cases', States' representatives are included in delegations to 'international conferences which deal with State subject matters'. It observes, 'The purpose is not to share in the making of policy decisions or to speak for Australia' but to ensure that the States know what is afoot and are in a position 'to put a viewpoint to the Commonwealth. However, State representatives are involved as far as possible in the work of the delegation.'

Some countries try to insert the 'federal clause' in treaties making ratification contingent on their States' approval. Australia has demurred to this but under the 1982 document the Commonwealth would have agreed to consider the clause on a case by case basis in treaties 'involving matters governed by State law, but not in matters traditionally governed by Commonwealth laws'. Here again, an elaborate procedure was provided.

On 3 November 1993, the Prime Minister, Mr Bob Hawke, wrote to the premier of Tasmania to convey the government's decision 'to endorse the principles and procedures' so long as they did not entail 'unreasonable delays'. While rejecting federal clauses, it was prepared to make a 'federal statement' when signing a treaty, the draft of which he enclosed. It would draw the attention of the signatories to Australia's federal system and the fact that implementation would be effected by exercise of the respective powers of the centre and the states 'and arrangements concerning their exercise'.

Mr Hawke refused to abandon central power but promised to 'consider relying on State legislation where the treaty affects an area of particular concern to the States and this course is consistent with the national interest ...'. Sir Humphrey Appleby would have approved of this anodyne formulation. Even so in 1984 the subcommittee set up by the constitutional convention in 1983 recommended establishment by the premiers' conference of an advisory Australian treaties council.[4]

Unlike the Australian constitution, the Indian constitution contains an explicit provision (Article 253) enabling parliament to override the federal distribution of power in the implementation of a treaty or decision at an international conference. That is no reason however why some procedures should not be devised to ensure better consultation with the States and greater latitude in negotiating trade agreements with foreign governments.

In June 1948 the government of India offered the Nizam of

[4] *Proceeding of the Australian Constitutional Convention 1984*, vol. ii, External Affairs Sub-Committee Report p. 8. Much has happened since as the statement by Alexander Downer, Minister for Foreign Affairs on 2 May 1996 shows. The states have a greater voice than the Rare.

Hyderabad a draft 'Heads of Agreement' on defence, foreign affairs, and communications. They were reserved for the government of India. Paragraph 7 added a qualification: 'Hyderabad will, however, have freedom to establish trade agencies in order to build up commercial, fiscal, and economic relations with other countries; but these agencies will work under the general supervision of, and in the closest cooperation with, the government of India. Hyderabad will not have any political relations with any country.' Do the states of the Union of India deserve less?[5]

It will not violate the federal principle one bit. On the contrary it will fulfil it. Witness Australia. It has moved miles since the Brisbane convention in 1985. In 1995 the Senate's legal and constitutional references committee held hearings on treaty-making and submitted a report entitled: 'Trick or Treaty? Commonwealth Power to make and Implement Treaties.' The word 'trick' reflected fears that the power to negotiate treaties could be abused to undermine federalism. Almost all its 11 recommendations were accepted by the Australian government.

On 2 May 1996, its foreign minister, Mr Alexander Downer, announced the government's decision in a detailed statement to parliament. It will ginger up both processes: parliamentary scrutiny of treaties and consultation with the States. Treaties will, as a rule, be tabled in parliament 'at least 15 sitting days before the government takes binding action'. Simultaneously a 'National Interest Analysis' will also be tabled setting out reasons for ratifying the treaty. Two new bodies will be set up: a Joint parliamentary committee on treaties and 'a Treaties Council' which had been rejected a decade ago. Far from weakening the federation consultation with the states only strengthens it.

---

[5]White Paper on Hyderabad, GOI, 1948, p. 49, para 7 of the Heads of Agreement offered to the Nizam in June 1948 permitted him 'freedom to establish trade agencies' and virtually to develop trade as well as 'fiscal and economic relations'.

55
States and Education[1]

If the West Bengal government were to prescribe a textbook on civics which had a chapter on corruption in public life, richly illustrated with references to Bofors, HDW, and the like, it is unlikely that the centre would acquiesce. It is unthinkable that it would have kept quiet if any government of Kashmir were, likewise, to prescribe textbooks citing the UN resolutions and advocating a plebiscite.

That the centre should fumble about its powers under the constitution when some state governments encourage the spread of hate against minorities or deny them their rights under the constitution to education in their mother tongue reflects much worse than constitutional illiteracy. It reveals a lack of will, not unmixed in some quarters in New Delhi with sympathy for such state governments. Attacks on the country's secular creed are as dangerous as those on its unity.

One wonders why the centre had to wait till the BJP governments' dismissal to take a close look at the kind of textbooks they had prescribed. Will it plead helplessness if they are returned to power and proceed with their hate campaign from where they left off last December?

Sources in the ministry of human resource development have told the press that the centre plans to acquire powers to prevent the states from distorting textbooks. This will be done by giving teeth to the National Steering Committee on School Curriculum

[1]This article was written in the context of the doctoring of textbooks by the BJP state governments in Madhya Pradesh, Uttar Pradesh and Rajasthan prior to their dismissal following the demolition of the Babri Masjid in 1992. It was published in *The Statesman*, 5 July 1993.

which is now an advisory body. The sources profess to be haunted in this instance by 'the spirit of federalism'. The phantom will be amused.

The constitutional position is now hardly in doubt. After the 42nd Amendment, education has ceased to be a matter for the states exclusively. It was deleted from the State list of topics for legislation Entry 11 which reads: 'Education, including universities, subject to the provisions of entries 63, 64, 65 and 66 of List I (the Union list) and entry 25 of List III (the Concurrent list)'. The first group of entries (63–6) excluded from the State domain institutions of national importance existing (BHU and AMU) or to be established by parliament; ones for scientific or technical education declared by parliament by law to be of national importance; and union bodies for professional training or promotion of research. Also saved for the union (Entry 66) was the power for 'coordination and determination of standards in institutions for higher education or research and scientific and technical institutions'.

Entry 25 in the Concurrent list, as it originally existed, innocuously reads: 'Vocational and technical training of labour.' The 42nd Amendment gave it a power and potency all its own. As mentioned earlier, it simply deleted Entry 11 of the State list. In place of the original Entry 25 in the Concurrent list it substituted one that reads: 'Education, including technical education, medical education and universities, subject to the provisions of entries 63, 64, 65 and 66 of List I; vocational and technical training of labour'.

The Concurrent list contains entries of legislative topics on which both the union and the states may legislate. In the event of conflict, the union law prevails. The executive power of each is co-extensive with the scope of its legislative power. No statutory authority is needed for a government to publish its own textbooks.

What the 42nd Amendment (1976) did, in plain words, was to remove education completely from the exclusive domain of the states. It has made it, instead, a matter on which exclusive powers are vested in the centre relating to matters mentioned in entries 63 to 66 of the union list. The power to legislate in relation to primary and secondary education as also in relation to universities is no longer for the states to exercise exclusively. The union has an overriding power and, what goes with such power, an overriding duty. The power to legislate on education includes within its purview 'the power to legislate in respect of medium of instruction', the Supreme Court ruled in 1962. It includes also 'the power to prescribe the syllabi and courses of study'. These powers can now be exercised by the centre.

The 42nd Amendment was rightly condemned as a measure designed to institutionalize the dictatorship which Indira Gandhi had installed during the emergency. The condemnation, however, cannot extend to features that were independent of the repressive provisions of the amendment. The 44th Amendment (1978) removed almost all of them, including some, but not all, those concerning the states' powers in relation to law and order. It wisely did not touch the changes concerning powers in relation to education which the 42nd Amendment had made.

Truth to tell, the 42nd Amendment corrected a grave error perpetrated by the framers of the constitution. They had mindlessly taken over from the corresponding provisions of the government of India Act, 1935. In doing so, they sinned against the light for already by the time the constituent assembly came to debate, on 2 September 1949, the draft provision which became Entry 11 in the State list (giving the states exclusive power in relation to education), the states had given ample warning that those powers would be abused. The centre's check was, therefore, necessary even in 1949.

That warning was delivered in one of the most prescient and impassioned speeches ever delivered in the constituent assembly. The speaker was Maulana Hasrat Mohani, one of the greatest Urdu poets of the century and a freedom-fighter whose sacrifices were second to none. It was a moment of anguish for him for reasons more than one. The Maulana was a staunch advocate of the states' autonomy. 'It would be astonishing to you all why I, a protagonist of provincial autonomy and an opponent of making a strong centre, am trying to make this particular item [education] a central subject. Education should be included in the Concurrent list and not be made a provincial subject.'

Maulana Hasrat Mohani spelt out his reasons cogently, citing the experience in his own State, Uttar Pradesh:

I have proposed this because provinces have adopted an autocratic and quite unreasonable attitude in regard to the question of the medium of instruction in education, regarding which provinces have been given power to take any decision they like, irrespective of the wishes of the centre or of the people. This has been possible because it is a provincial subject and provinces can take any decision they like and they can have any medium of instruction.

This is how Uttar Pradesh had begun 'to misbehave' as early as in 1949. The Maulana said:

The UP government has adopted a strange procedure. They say that Hindi is the provincial language, and their regional language is Sanskritized Hindi, and that Urdu has no place in the province. I am not saying this to you at random. You will be simply surprised, if I tell you what is happening there, Mr Purshottamdas Tandon. The agenda is also framed in Sanskritized Hindi and the list of questions is also prepared in Sanskritized Hindi. And if anybody happens to send his questions in Urdu, they are thrown away. This is not all. They have issued instructions in districts that anyone who wants registration of documents concerning immovable property, must produce the document in Hindi. And if the document is brought in Urdu, registration is refused. Please tell us what to do in these circumstances. Urdu is not the language of Muslims only, it is the language of Hindus also.[2]

The framers of the constitution and the leaders of the government of India chose wilfully to shut their eyes to what was afoot in Uttar Pradesh. What has been perpetrated over these past four decades is nothing short of a linguistic genocide of Urdu in large parts of the Hindi belt and particularly in UP.

In the constituent assembly, Maulana Hasrat Mohani pleaded simply that education be imparted in the mother tongue in the primary and secondary stages, but his basic right was being violated in UP under the very nose of the Centre. He cited concrete cases, quoted the Radhakrishnan report, the conclusions of the education ministers' conference and the remarks by Rajaji, then governor-general.

He rightly said:

The three provinces, namely, Delhi, UP, Bihar, and Mahakoshal or CP should be made bilingual provinces. And those whose mother-tongue is Urdu should be given instruction in the same language. The assertion of UP government that its state language is Hindi and its regional language is also Hindi and that Urdu has no place there and that Urdu should be wiped off the face of the earth, is high-handedness. You know very well that the birthplace of Urdu is UP.

He was however against making education an exclusively Union

[2]CAD, vol. ix, pp. 882–3, see also pp. 1452–9 for Maulana Azad's historic speech on his resignation from the Committee on the national language.

subject. He urged only that 'the centre should have the power of setting them [the States] right in case they do anything unjust'.

Despite the president, Dr Rajendra Prasad's prodding, Dr B.R. Ambedkar did not reply to the debate as chairman of the drafting committee. Instead, Mr T.T. Krishnamachari replied on its behalf. On this occasion he became an ardent champion of provincial autonomy. He cited two safeguards. The centre's powers of coordination (under Entry 66 of the Union list) and the fundamental rights of the minorities to preservation of their language (now Articles 29 and 30 of the Constitution). These have proved to be a frail reed in the face of the anti-Urdu campaign in the Hindi belt. Krishnamachari's was an altogether slipshod performance; experience has proved Maulana Hasrat Mohani right.

The Sarkaria commission on centre–state relations pointed out that the 42nd Amendment only gave effect to the recommendation of the Sapru committee in 1964 that education be made a concurrent subject.[3] The Sarkaria commission noted that while the centre had acquired the powers under the Amendment it had not exercised them. 'There has been no follow-up legislation by the union under this head' (education). The minister of human resource development, Mr Arjun Singh, has his work cut out for him: draft a central statute that undoes the wrongs done to the minorities by the states. They betrayed the trust reposed in them by the founding fathers of the constitution.

The centre has ample power in both respects: opposing textbooks that distort history and spread communal hate and ensuring full respect for the right of parents to educate their children in the mother-tongue.

[3]Report of the Commission on Centre–State Relations, p. 56.